CW00645894

In the beginning,

there was the Big Bang,

the molten masses cooled

and the galaxies formed,

life emerged from the seas,

humans developed . . .

La felicità va in **Lambretta**

THE ULTIMATE HISTORY AND ENCYCLOPEDIA

THE
SCOOTER

ERIC DREGNI

BIBLE

© 2022 Quarto Publishing Group USA Inc.
Text © 2022 Eric Dregni

First Published in 2022 by Motorbooks, an imprint of The Quarto Group,
100 Cummings Center, Suite 265-D, Beverly, MA 01915, USA.
T (978) 282-9590 F (978) 283-2742 Quarto.com

Motorbooks titles are also available at discount for retail, wholesale, promotional, and bulk purchase. For details, contact the Special Sales Manager by email at specialsales@quarto.com or by mail at The Quarto Group, Attn: Special Sales Manager, 100 Cummings Center, Suite 265-D, Beverly, MA 01915, USA.

26 25 24 23 22   1 2 3 4 5

ISBN: 978-0-7603-7556-3

Digital edition published in 2022
eISBN: 978-0-7603-7557-0

Originally found under the following Library of Congress Control Number:
2006281037

Cover Design: Cindy Samargia Laun
Cover Image: Kailey Flynn/Alamy Stock Photo
Page 2 Image: akg-images/UIG
Design: Cindy Samargia Laun
Page Layout: Cindy Samargia Laun

Printed in Singapore

Table of Contents

Foreword 7

Introduction:
Mondo Scooter 9

1 The Pioneer Motorscooters
1902–1930 13

2 The Great American Scooter Craze
1935–1940 23

3 Military Motorscooters
1939–1945 45

4 The Golden Age of the Motorscooter
1946–1954 51

5 Mass Mobilization
1955–1960 93

6 The Mod Years
1960–1975 129

7 The DIY Years
1976–2000 147

8 A New Millennium
2001–On 161

Scooter Encyclopedia
A–Z 176

Acknowledgments 316

About the Author 316

Index 317

THE MAKERS
of
Moto Scoot

present the
CHALLENGER

● STURDY
● ECONOMICAL
● SMART

Foreword

BY ROBERT H. AMMON, CUSHMAN PRESIDENT

The circumstances that led to building the prototype of the first Cushman motorscooter were interesting to say the least.

Aviator Colonel Roscoe Turner endorsed the Motor Glide scooter that E. Foster Salsbury had created in early 1936 in Los Angeles. Sometime in that same year, Roscoe Turner brought his air show to Lincoln, Nebraska, just down the road from the Cushman headquarters in Omaha. Turner toted along with him this little Evinrude-powered Salsbury, and a neighborhood kid saw this scooter and decided that it would be fun to have one of his own. He found some angle iron and wheelbarrow wheels, and built himself a motorscooter. And he used a Cushman "Husky" engine from a lawn mower to power it.

We at Cushman found out about this scooter by chance. One day my dad, Charles Ammon—known affectionately to Cushman employees as "Uncle Charlie"—was at our spare parts depot in Lincoln and he looked out the window and saw the kid on his scooter buying parts. We were in the business of building and selling engines, and this scooter inspired my dad with the idea of making motorscooters to build and sell more engines. He charged me, with the help of our engineering department, to this task.

We built that first Cushman scooter when I was 19 years old. The frame was made from 1-1/4-inch angle iron but we soon learned that it wasn't strong enough. We then used 2-inch channel iron, which did the job. We learned early on that a rigid frame was essential, and that channel-iron design lasted a long time for Cushman. We used wheels from a wheelbarrow mounted with 4.00 × 8-inch tires, and had an engine in it and running in about 30 days.

I had read an article from the Engineering School at the University of Nebraska about the correct geometry for a bicycle or motorcycle. I developed the first scooter's steering head angle so that the tail end of the steering head was at a point behind where the wheel touches the ground. When I got the scooter stable enough so I could drive it with no hands, I knew it was ready.

Our goal was to build just a good, sturdy, two-wheel scooter. It was a very crude-looking thing, of course. But from those couple of prototypes came the first Cushman Auto-Glide, which went into production in late 1936. With the success of our first scooter, we continued to build motorscooters until Cushman was the largest scooter maker in the United States.

I first talked with Michael Dregni and Eric Dregni about fifteen years ago when they were compiling information for their first book, *Illustrated MotorScooter Buyer's Guide,* which included a detailed history of Cushman and the Cushman motorscooters. Their first book also told the story of the development of American scooters and their influence on the scooters that were produced throughout the rest of the world following World War II, particularly the famous Vespa and Lambretta.

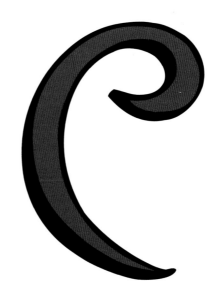

**Looking Good
on a Lambretta TV175**
High heels, white sunglasses,
and blood-red lipstick were the
perfect accessories when riding a
Lambretta to get groceries at the
neighborhood Food Fair.

Introduction: Mondo Scooter

In the beginning, there was the Big Bang, the molten masses cooled and the galaxies formed, life emerged from the seas, humans developed, and in 1902 the first motorscooter was created. By now, more than 25 million scooters have seen the light of day. It began with a Big Bang. It continues with a putt-putt.

Scooters are funny. They are mechanical marvels on two wheels. Streamlined spuds. Mutant oddballs of Jet Age styling gone berserk. Innovative inventions shoehorned like sardines into miniaturized monocoque bodies. Engineering and styling enigmas, the stranger the better. They are two-wheeled pogo sticks, Italian hairdryers, Pushmans, dustbins on wheels, motorized lemons. Their names can be swear words, or their names can be uttered in worship by the faithful. They are the weird and the wonderful. They are the cute, the quaint, and the curious.

Throughout the ages, motorscooters have meant different things to different folk. Scoots have been cheap transportation for people without enough pennies for a car. They have been rebellious hot rods for misunderstood Wild Ones. They have carried lovers and warriors, priests and poets.

Even today, when motorscooters inspire collectors to search of their mythology and memorabilia, its different strokes for different putt-puttniks. To some, it's nostalgia for the classic Cushman "Turtlebacks" and Eagles and a remembrance of

"Scooters were only a fashion even though it lasted for several years. Plenty of scooters had been made with little or no sales success until the Lambretta appeared and just why a device so ugly and awkward looking became a rage almost overnight, is something of a mystery."

—Vincent motorcycle designer and scooter curmudgeon Philip Irving, *Black Smoke*, 1978

Putt-Putt Dreamer
A genealogy of human beings and wheels, starting with a baby carriage. Graduating from the pram, the wee tot moves on to terrorize town with a push scooter. Just add an engine, and the push scooter becomes a motorscooter, the next object of desire in many a childhood dream.

Motorscooter Precursors
The pioneering motorized two-wheelers—the 1868 Sylvester Roper steamer and 1885 Gottlieb Daimler Einspur—set the style for later-day motorcycles and motorscooters. Scooters developed based on four principles: smaller wheels, step-through chassis, engine-covering bodywork, and overall ease of use.

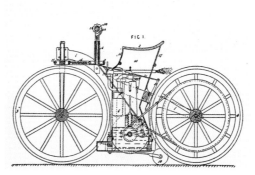

9

Scooter Cool
The Mods and Mod Revivalists personify scooter cool. Steed of choice is often a Lambretta—here a curvaceous two-tone TV175 Series II retrofitted with a too-funky Series III front disc brake. Tim Gartman's at the controls, Jessika Madison riding pillion.
Courtesy of Tony Nelson

"The history of technology is part and parcel of social history in general."

—John Ellis,
The Social History of the Machine Gun

things past, those long-ago golden buzz-cut days of the American summer. To others, it's the full-bore two-stroke roar of a Vespa or Lambretta in anger, crowned by enough headlamps to light the night.

Explaining what inspires the scooter faithful ain't easy either. Tell a pal you like scoots and some hoot, some holler, most all smirk. Others nod, and immediately launch into a dialectical discussion of the brake swept area on the first generation of 98cc Vespas. Explanation is not needed. If you have to ask, you just ain't gonna understand—and most Harley-Davidson folk don't have a clue what we're talking here.

Explaining what motorscooters have meant to society in the past 100 years is also something most people could care a hounddog's flea about. To them it's all a tale told by an idiot full of sound and fury—although sound and worry may be closer to the truth.

Still, that truth is as weird and wonderful as a scooter itself.

PRODUCT LIABILITY LAWSUITS ON WHEELS

Scooters have played a profound role in the world. Not only did they inspire the development of product liability laws, but they were also a missing link in the development of both riding lawn mowers and golf carts. And that's not all.

Scooters were born of bad times, economic depressions, and down-on-our-luck decades. The first scooter that truly made its mark was the Salsbury Motor Glide, created in the United States during the Great Depression by scooter visionary E. Foster Salsbury as cheap transportation for the depression-weary masses.

The second great scooter, Enrico Piaggio's Vespa, bowed onto the Italian scene in the days after the dust cleared from World War II. The Vespa had the same mission as Salsbury's Motor Glide, but the Vespa eventually traveled further. Alongside Ferdinando Innocenti's Lambretta and numerous other scooters, the Vespa and its kin provided the wheels beneath Europe and Japan's reconstruction.

Even today, scooters continue to provide cheap and cheerful transportation to much of the world, including India, the planet's largest scooterized society, still riding decades-old Lambrettas and Vespas and continuing to build new versions of the venerated elders.

> *"The scooter is a device that we refuse to grace with the description of motorcycle."*
>
> —Richard Hough, *A History of the World's Motorcycles,* 1973

ON THE ROAD TO
A BETTER WORLD

Along the way and just by happenstance, scooters transformed society. For a window of just a few years following World War II, scooters played their part in reviving the European and Japanese economies before new cars and trucks were being mass produced. And along with hauling wares to market, scooters carried Romeo in search of Juliet, transported the whole family to the beach on the weekend, brought the city to the country and the country to the city. All along its route, the scooter helped disseminate ideas and culture far and wide.

Scooters also allowed women a newfound freedom of mobility, which, no matter how hard people tried, also gave women a newfound freedom of expression, exposures to new ideas, and a vision of broader horizons. We've come a long way, and scooters carried us part of the way.

Ironically, the motorscooter's history in the US of A was very different from that on the rest of the planet. Born in the USA, the motorscooter movement was some of the earliest of American-made popular culture to spread throughout the world, dating back to the first license-built version of the 1915 Motopeds built in Germany. But in the land of land yachts, scooters never truly caught on, always being considered putt-putt toys or hobbyist vehicles.

THE POPE, THE WHO,
AND THE ICE CAPADES

Throughout history, it's easy to dismiss the scooter's role as being as small as the scooter's own elfin wheels, but motorscooters moved mountains one rock at a time.

Scooters have driven around the world. Broken land speed records. Sailed the high seas and crossed the English Channel fitted with pontoons and propeller. Danced the tarantella. Fought in bullfights. Been blessed by the Pope. Parachuted behind enemy lines. Fitted with bazookas. Packed with plastic explosives and used as terrorist bombs. Carried Gregory Peck and Audrey Hepburn on a Roman holiday. Fought alongside the Mods in the Brighton Beach wars against the Rockers and their brutish BSAs. Inspired Pete Townshend to hurl his Rickenbacker through his Marshall stack. Given Bo Diddley wheels to travel with his gee-tar. Run road races, endurance races, and off-road races. Brought the family on vacation to Norway. Wowed Fourth of July parade-goers across America with the Shriner Motor Corps' daredevil antics. Fought Communism. Fought Democracy. Carried the Good Word. Transported the rebel, the priest, and the Queen of England. Even starred in the Ice Capades.

So without further ado, here's the humble tale of the motorscooter.

**All For One
and One For All!**
Three of the greatest motorscooters to ever ride Planet Earth. Scooters are a blend of styling, speed, and eccentricity. If they have to be explained, you just won't understand. These three are owned and were restored by scooter impresario straordinario Vittoro Tessera of Milan, Italy. From left—with drum roll and applause, please: Styled like a two-tone primped poodle, the fabulous French-built Terrot; center, the scooter that saved the world, a 1950s 125cc Piaggio Vespa; right, the putt-putt to make Buck Rogers green with envy, America's Salsbury Super-Scooter Model 85.
Courtesy of the owner: Vittorio Tessera

AUTOPEDING

— SOMETHING NEW IN TRANSPORTATION

"Something New in Transportation…" Autopeding was indeed a new way to see the world, as this early brochure promised. The single-cylinder four-stroke 1.5 hp engine saved your weary gams the woes of walking—all for just the $100 price of the Autoped. Surely, a revolution in personal transportation was on the way!

The Pioneer Motorscooters 1902–1930

The first motorscooters were gee-whiz gizmos arriving in a cloud of exhaust in a time of horses and bicycles. They were so far out, so amazing, so unbelievable, that someone somewhere probably quickly decried them as a portent of the coming of the apocalypse.

Scooters debuted at the dawn of the Age of Speed, and suddenly everyone was in search of a vehicle to propel them forward at velocity. Before the turn of the century, speed to most meant a horse or to the lucky few, an iron horse. A bicycle craze in the 1890s had given folk a taste and now, tipsy with the promise, they were ready for more.

Who could imagine what kinds of speeds were even possible with the advent of Nikolas Otto's internal-combustion engine? But these were the days of the true hot rodders, decades before the term was coined in southern California in the 1940s for the hopped-up versions of something that already existed. These hot rodders—men like Frank Duryea, Henry Ford, Oscar Hedstrom—took horse-drawn carriages and bicycles and injected them with one of those newfangled gasoline engines and created a new monster.

Everyone who was anyone had to have one of these powered vehicles, and the race was on. Ordinary citizens, who didn't truly know the meaning of the word fast, suddenly couldn't get enough speed. In the coming years in the Age of Speed, velocity would change the world, inspire architecture and industrial design in the form of Streamline Moderne that shaped everything from roadside diners to coffeepots, and even create a new philosophy in the form of Futurism. Italian Futurist Filippo Marinetti was infatuated with speed, as he wrote in his manifesto in 1909: "We say that the world's magnificence has been enriched by a new beauty: the beauty of speed. A racing car whose hood is adorned with great pipes, like serpents of explosive breath—a roaring car that seems to ride on grapeshot—is more beautiful than the Victory of Samothrace. . . . Time and Space died yesterday. We already live in the absolute, because we have created eternal, omnipresent speed."

Ennobled by musings akin to these, inventors in garages throughout Europe and across America begat their own automobiles, "motocycles," and motorscooters. Building a scooter was relatively—perhaps, too—easy. Add the essential ingredient of motorized motive power to junior's abducted push scooter, and presto, the motorscooter was born. Some makers went whole hog, adding extras like a battery-powered lighting system, a full sit-down chair, or even bolting on something that could be labeled a brake.

Problem was, these first motorscooters never went far. The pioneering scooters were crude and clumsy, and often made it from point A to point B, but not back again. Alas, while development of the automobile and motorcycle sped ahead, the lowly scooter was left in the dust. Since these pioneering scooters were born from the child's scooter, it was an image the refined motorscooter was never able to outrun.

Monet-Goyen Vélautos
French firm Monet-Goyen married the bicycle (le vélo) with an automobile to create the Vélauto. Inspiration likely came from the pioneering Auto-Fauteuil—or may simply have been the result of some other crazed inventor's vision. The 1921 Vélauto (right) boasted a 117cc engine while the 1922 Super Vélauto (left) upped the ante with a 270cc engine. The wicker seats were très civilized.
Courtesy of François-Marie Dumas

"If Madame has to meet a friend at 11 o'clock in the Bois de Boulogne, at noon be at home for lunch, then shop at the big stores downtown, and later in the evening dine with friends in the suburbs, she would never be able to do all this by taking outrageously priced taxis that are impossible to flag down. Knowing this, Madame bought a Skootamota, the woman's machine 'par excellence' that is easy to drive, doesn't demand any mechanical knowledge, and doesn't need a garage."

—Early French ABC Skootamota advertisement

The Creation of the Motorscooter

MANKIND'S FALL FROM GRACE

"Invention breeds invention," prophesized Ralph Waldo Emerson, likely dreaming of the future debut of the motorscooter. The horse-drawn carriage—when fitted with a gas-, electric-, or even steam-powered engine—begat the automobile. The bicycle—when bolted to one of those cantankerous, oil-spewing "infernal"-combustion motors—begat the "motocycle," as it was termed by the Indian firm in its early days. And the children's push scooter—when hijacked and mounted with a smoke-coughing engine of some dubious repute to power the wheels in place of junior's hard-working gam—became the motorscooter.

The early motorscooters must have appeared as otherworldly contrivances to most civilians. While brochures may have boasted that soon everyone would save their soles by hopping on a motorscooter, that future was still far off.

Auto-Fauteuil

Upon its debut in 1902, Frenchman George Gauthier's Auto-Fauteuil must have seemed like a Jules Verne spaceship come to land on the cobblestoned streets. It was certainly a far-out vision of the future in the pioneering days of motorized vehicles, and won the dubious honorary title of first motorscooter. With its dwarf wheels, step-through frame, and even a small cowling to shield riders from the messy engine, the Auto-Fauteuil established the basic precepts of the scooter as distinguished from a motorcycle. Born in the city of Blois, Gauthier's machine was first powered by a four-stroke single-cylinder De Dion motor displacing 269cc; later engines included a 500cc Peugeot and a big-bore 545cc. By 1914, a gearbox was available to handle all the power.
Courtesy of François-Marie Dumas Archives

Auto-Fauteuil Carrying Priest

Jesus may have relied solely on donkeys, but his followers jumped onto motorscooters as soon as they were invented; here, a French abbé carries the good word into the future on an early Auto-Fauteuil. Inventor Georges Gauthier was also the first of many scooter creators to give their machine an oddball name: Auto-Fauteuil translated as "automotive armchair," which was nothing if not honest in its description. Perhaps amazingly, the Auto-Fauteuil remained in production until 1922.
Courtesy of François-Marie Dumas Archives

1902–1930

1916 Autoped

The Autoped Company of Long Island, New York, hailed its 1914–1915 creation as "The Wonder of the Motor Vehicle World," which could only begin to describe the scooter! The idea was simple: Appropriate Junior's push scooter, bolt an elfin engine to the front wheel with direct drive, and you're ready to ride off into the future. The Autoped was also license-built by Germany's Krupp with a 155cc four-stroke motor and by Czechoslovakia's CAS. Autoped production halted in 1921.
Courtesy of the owner: Jim Kilau

Autoped and Doughboy

The U.S. Army considered drafting the Autoped for patriotic service. With this secret weapon to lead the bayonet charge out of the trenches, who knows what the outcome of World War I might have been— the allies might even have lost! Alas, the scooter would have to wait for World War II to see action.

The Motorscooter Craze

GOING WILD FOR PUTT-PUTTS

The first of many subsequent scooter crazes burst into being in the United States, England, and the European continent in the 1910s and 1920s. The American-made Motoped and Autoped were quaint and cute, and became the wheels beneath the fad.

The first motorscooters featured a small, raspy, oil-spewing engine mounted above the front or rear wheel, usually with chain drive to a wheel sprocket or direct roller drive onto the tire. Some had gearboxes. Some had clutches. Many were single-speed and boasted of such weak power they did not even need a clutch. A tall steering rod ran from the front forks ending in handlebars often equipped with a throttle and brake lever. These early scooters had a central floorboard to stand on, usually just inches from earth, so the driver could put a foot down to the safety of solid ground should anything untoward happen.

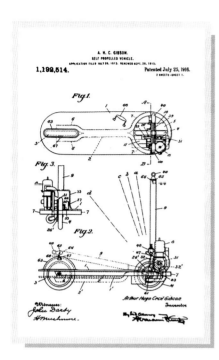

Autoped Patent
The simple design of the Autoped was unveiled in this U.S. patent drawing filed in 1913 and awarded in 1916 to far-sighted inventor Arthur Hugo Cecil Gibson.

"There was a sudden scooter boom. The idea of an inexpensive runabout for one caused a miniature furore, and a dozen or more firms got busy. Here, it seemed, was easy money."
—The Motor Cycle, 1935

Autopeding Golfer
Presaging the golf cart, the Autoped was the ideal thing for those men in kelly green to ride around the links.

Motoped at Dizzying Speed
Brave souls out for a ride on their Motoped—although the look on the woman's face suggests less than glee. With the bulk of the 1.5 hp engine mounted aside the front wheel, which was controlled by that near-vertical steering-rod spindle, more than one intrepid Motoped pilot likely visited terra firma gluteus maximus first. Fortunately, the fall from grace was not a long one, as the floorboard was only inches above ground so the driver could easily reach earth—a wise feature since the Motoped boasted no brakes. Riding such a scooter was not for the faint of heart.

1902–1930

Those Daring Young Folk on Their Motorscooters

READY TO RIDE OFF INTO THE FUTURE

There was no set mold to motorized transportation at the dawn of the movement. Inventors, engineers, and various crackpots all created their own vision of a vehicle and touted its gee-whiz qualities before an unsure world. Auto-bicycles, motor-tricycles, arm-chairs-on-wheels—who knew who would hit the jackpot?

One thing was certain, though: They were exciting times, and the future appeared bright—although many a horse must have counted its blessings as it chewed some well-earned hay, looking on with bemused befuddlement.

1920s Unibus and Bowler-Hatted Rider
A very British gent in his bowler rides off into the bright future aboard his Unibus.

Sweet Lass on Her Unibus
"The Car on Two Wheels" concept was tried even back in the 1920s! Built by England's Gloucestershire Aircraft Co. of Cheltenham, the Unibus disappeared as quickly as it arrived, debuting in 1920 and lasting until just 1923. This may have disproved the Unibus' advertising slogan, "To see the Unibus is to want one." Unfortunately, not enough people did the later. The world could have been a much better—or at least more interesting—place if they had.

1912 Militaire
The American Militaire was part motorscooter, part spaceship, a far-out vision of the future in the pioneering days of motorized vehicles. The humble ad copy stated: "It is radical, we admit, but so was Fulton's steamboat, and Marconi's wireless, and Westinghouse's brake." All of which leads one to believe that even way back in the past, the future often arrived one day too soon.

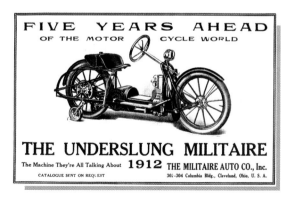

"They vibrated to an extent that was almost unbelievable and their reliability was far from high, and they were not exactly comfortable with their small diameter wheels and small-section tyres. The scooter was killed—by the scooter."
—The Motor Cycle, 1935

1902–1930

1919 ABC Skootamota
This daring young lady on her ABC Skootamota fords a raging river on her way to afternoon tea. Her trusty steed, the Skootamota, was at the forefront of a scooter revolution that swept Great Britain in 1919. The early motorscooter was just the thing for Milady to ride to tea. Social hour talk no doubt centered on neighborhood gossip, new crumpet recipes, and the bore and stroke of the latest Skootamota.

A Putt-Putt for Pithy Ladies

JUST THE THING TO RIDE TO TEA

The first motorscooters were quaint vehicles at best, and they were not taken too seriously even at the time. Created for pithy womenfolk to putt-putt to town for shopping or afternoon tea, the scooter allowed Milady to stand upright so her neatly ironed dress did not suffer a wrinkle. Thus was born the motorscooter's first sales pitch.

The scooter was just a passing fancy in the Roaring Twenties, going the way of the Charleston and steam-powered automobiles. The first wave of scooters died by the side of the road as quickly as it was born.

"Had the scooter lived, and not died stillborn as a result of makers rushing into production with untried and crude machines, we should probably have seen it develop into a most useful type of vehicle."

—The Motor Cycle, 1935

1919 Autoglider De Luxe

Returning from the horrors of World War I, many British soldiers were seized by poetic wanderlust and took to the road in search of the meaning of life. One result was a scooter craze that lasted for a full summer, that of 1919, when everyone everywhere was talking scooters. The Autoglider was crafted by Charles Ralph Townsend's Townsend Engineering Co. of Birmingham. This scoot was an ideal wandering companion to ride to the end of the earth at Land's End and gaze at the sea and ask, Why?

Tank-Treaded Roadless

Explain this, if you will... Yes, Victoria, it's a motorscooter with tank treads. The British Roadless rode on a single narrow rubber track that allowed it to traverse most any terrain. Those handlebars turned the forward end of the track assembly, and the 2.75 hp Douglas flat-twin powered the Roadless to a 20 mph top speed. It was a scary thought.

1919 ABC Skootamota

The Skootamota was ideal for ladies with its step-through frame making way for petticoats and frilly frocks. British engineer Granville Bradshaw crafted the scooter in 1919 powered by a 147cc intake-over-exhaust engine and later supplanted by a 110cc OHV motor. But the big advance heralded by the Skootamota over the Autoped was the applauded addition of a seat. Couthness had come to the motorscooter, and pioneering machines such as the Skootamota set the style for scooters to come.
Courtesy of
François-Marie Dumas

The Great American Scooter Craze 1935–1940

The true ancestor of the modern motorscooter was assembled like Frankenstein's monster from odds and ends, bits and pieces, something borrowed, something blue. The creators were two young Californians, "financier" E. Foster Salsbury and inventor Austin Elmore. In this case, the mad creators' castle was the backroom of Salsbury's brother's heating and plumbing shop in Oakland. The year was 1935.

America was sunk in the midst of the Great Depression, but Salsbury had a vision of a cheap and cheerful vehicle that would propel the country forward to prosperous times. He witnessed the great aviator and feminist Amelia Earhart putt-putting about the Lockheed airport at Burbank on one of the rare Motopeds that was still alive and running. The vision was an inspiration: "It got me started thinking about building a real scooter," Salsbury remembered in 1992.

Salsbury's Motor Glide sparked a second scooter craze starting in the mid-1930s. The first craze that began with the Autoped and Motoped in 1915 had died away, and Salsbury's timing was perfect. Not only had twenty years passed and many people had forgiven—or at least, forgotten—the sins of past scooter builders, but now people actually had a need for what the motorscooter offered.

Where Salsbury led, others followed. After Salsbury spurned a bid for the Husky motors built by the Cushman firm in Lincoln, Nebraska, Cushman kickstarted its own Auto-Glide scooter into life in 1936—and created a scooter empire that eventually endured far beyond that of Salsbury. In Chicago, the Moto-Scoot and Mead Ranger scooters coughed to life in 1936; they were joined soon after by the Powell, Rock-Ola, Crocker Scootabout, Keen Power Cycle, the aptly named Puddlejumper, and many others.

This second generation of scooter makers took up where the earlier scooters had left off—and paid heed to several important lessons that the pioneers had learned along the way. The internal-combustion engine was now much better developed, and these new scooters were more reliable machines

"The Salsbury Motor Glide is the greatest woman catcher I have ever seen."

—Air racer and barnstormer
Colonel Roscoe Turner

with hardy engines. They boasted real gearboxes, brakes that actually braked, and after 1937, many had a radical torque converter transmission, again following Salsbury's lead. But most importantly for the scooter's future acceptance, the new models were dressed in bodywork that covered the engine and other dirty mechanical bits so drivers never had to soil their hands. The motorscooter had been civilized.

OPPOSITE:
Lovely Lass and Crocker Scootabout
While innocent jazz rhythms wafted forth from the Smalltown, USA park gazebo, a revolution was hatching in back-alley garages. The motorscooter was here to stay. E. Foster Salsbury's Motor Glide and Robert Ammon's Cushman Auto-Glide were born, followed by a whole wave of others, including Albert G. Crocker's stylish Scootabout. There was no escaping the future.

1935–1940

Colonel Roscoe Turner and Motor Gliding Kids
To promote the opening of Salsbury's first dealership, in San Diego in 1936, Roscoe Turner led a gang of scooting youth in terrorizing the unsuspecting neighborhood.

Salsbury Motor Glide

THE MOTORSCOOTER THAT STARTED IT ALL

E. Foster Salsbury had a vision. Inspired by the sight of aviator Amelia Earhart dashing around the Lockheed airport at Burbank, California, on an ancient Motoped, he decided to create his own scooter for the masses. Salsbury enlisted the aid of inventor Austin Elmore, and together the dynamic duo created the first Motor Glide.

The Motor Glide made its debut at the February 1936 Airplane and Boating Show in Los Angeles' Pan-Pacific Auditorium. Salsbury showed off his scooter to barnstorming aviator Colonel Roscoe Turner who was thrilled by the Motor Glide and became a Salsbury spokesman, helping the fledgling firm find a market.

1937 Salsbury Aero Model Motor Glide
Salsbury did not rest on its laurels, as the fledgling firm wasted no time updating its scooters. In late 1936, the arrival of the new 1937 model was announced—less than a year after the Motor Glide's debut! It was now powered by a Johnson four-stroke. The operating instruction boasted just two steps: "First—Give the Motor Glide a push and step on. Second—Give it gas by opening the throttle with your right hand and away you go."
Courtesy of the owner: Herb Singe

Colonel Roscoe Turner and 1936 Salsbury Motor Glide Number I

A portrait of firsts: Here is the first Salsbury ad, printed in February 1936 magazines, showing the first Motor Glide with the firm's first endorser, barnstormer Colonel Roscoe Turner. Touted in ads as "America's best-known flying ace," Turner was actually more of a showman, but he got attention. The engine on this first model ran via direct roller friction onto the rear tire. Power came from an Evinrude Speedibyke single-cylinder two-cycle engine of 5.1ci (82.5cc) creating a puny .75 hp. As Foster Salsbury noted in retrospect, "It worked fine on dry pavement." Not exactly a glowing endorsement, but in a few months, engine rotation was reversed and chain drive added as a remedy. The scoot was now able to venture forth after a rain. Salsbury estimated that only 25–30 of the roller-drive Motor Glides were built.

Ride a MOTOR GLIDE!

COLONEL ROSCOE TURNER arriving home on his new Motor Glide after completing one of his recent airplane trips.

THE NEW MOTOR GLIDE was designed and built for Colonel Roscoe Turner to carry in his airplane for transportation to and from the many airports on which he lands.

Colonel Turner's MOTOR GLIDE has been so enthusiastically received by the Aviation World that it has become necessary to go into production on this model to supply the demand for this new sensational mode of transportation.

The public is beginning to realize that the MOTOR GLIDE is practical for many purposes in addition to that for which it is used by Colonel Turner. Ride a MOTOR GLIDE for a new Thrill! Glide along effortlessly mile after mile. Ride it to work; visit friends and interesting places. Use it for deliveries, collections

and other business purposes. It costs so little. Ride the MOTOR GLIDE five miles for one cent. The lowest cost transportation available.

The MOTOR GLIDE is sturdy, safe, economical, comfortable and dependable. Built with the best standard parts and materials obtainable. Weighs 65 pounds and fully equipped with lights, horn, airwheels, etc. The handle bars are built to fold down so that it can be carried in your car, plane or boat.

Place your order now for early delivery. For further information call or write

THE MOTOR GLIDE COMPANY

OAKLAND—1450 Harrison St., HIgate 2480 • LOS ANGELES—1041 N. Sycamore Ave., HEmpstead 8131

February 1936

> *"I had no idea what the market for a scooter would be. It was pure invention—very far out for those days."*
>
> —E. Foster Salsbury, 1992 Interview

1937 Salsbury Aero Model Motor Glide

The features of the Motor Glide were legion and legend. "Dash hither and yon in gay abandon . . . glide out to the country club or to the beach," tantalized the superlative-loving copywriter. The scoot parks on a dime, turns in a 3ft circle, "eases through traffic like an eel," and gets 150 miles to a gallon of gas. In addition, "it's as safe as an armchair and as dependable as time."

1937 Aero Model

Here it is!

YOUR PERSONAL RUNABOUT

FEATURES OF THE AERO MODEL MOTOR GLIDE

MOTOR GLIDE WILL TAKE YOU PLACES AT LOWEST COST

1935–1940

**1937 Cushman
Auto-Glide Model 1**
*Cushman's first production model,
the aptly named Model 1, made
its soul-stirring debut in 1937.
At the heart of the Auto-Glide was
the Husky engine with a whopping
1.5 hp worth of motive power.
Although it was advertised as the
"Newest Riding Thrill," all that
dizzying power added up to only
a 30 mph top speed. Cushman,
ever the clever marketeers,
promoted the slow speed in its ads:
"Low speed ensures safety.
Auto-Glide is not a 'speed wagon.'"*
Courtesy of the owner:
Jim Kilau

Cushman Auto-Glide

BIRTH OF A MOTORSCOOTER EMPIRE

The Cushman Motor Works of Lincoln, Nebraska, followed Salsbury's lead into the novel motorscooter market. In mid-1936, Salsbury requested—and then rejected—a bid for 1,000 of Cushman's famous Husky engines that he planned to use in his scooter. Cushman chief "Uncle Charlie" Ammon saw the writing on the wall, and assigned his son, Robert, to create what became the Cushman Auto-Glide.

With the success of its first scooter, Cushman continued to construct the most long-lived American motorscooter in a dazzling variety of unique models. And as Vespa became synonymous for scooter in the rest of the world, Cushman stands for scooter to most Americans even today.

**1939 Cushman
Auto-Glide Deluxe**
*The superlatives flowed fast
and furious in describing
the virtues of the new
Auto-Glide Model 2 with its
2 hp Husky. Cushman also
introduced its three-wheeled
Model 9 Package-Kar, the
economy Model 21,
and Deluxe Model with
two-speed gearbox. As this
brochure brayed, the
Auto-Glide was "ideal
for work, school,
deliveries—any place
you'd use a car!"*

Proud Auto-Glide Rider

The Auto-Glide boasted state-of-the-art scooter engineering. Operation was easy: the "smooth-as-velvet" clutch for the single-speed gearbox was operated by the left foot, the rear-wheel drum brake was controlled by the right foot, and the handlebar throttle by the right hand. For accessories, Cushman offered a bolt-on bicycle light.

"We were in the business of building and selling engines. The idea of making a motorscooter was to build and sell more engines."

—Cushman chief Robert H. Ammon, 1992 Interview

WARD TRACTOR PLOW

A Sturdy, Simple, Light Weight Tractor and ONE MAN PLOWING OUTFIT. The first successful Plow Hang to carry the plows directly under the Tractor Frame. CUSHMAN—the most powerful engine, per weight, ever put on a Tractor—CUSHMAN.

Simple
Powerful
Durable

No Useless Dead Weight

Efficient Transmission

Large Wheels in Proportion to Weight Carried

Automobile Type Front Axle and Steering Gear

Turns Easy and Short

Plows
Easily
Detached

Plows are Close Coupled

Plow Bottoms and Beams Only

Plows Pulled from Front Ride Free Behind

Plows Easily Raised, and Machine Backs into Fence Corners

Only One Man to Operate

Ward Tractor Plow with Cushman Engine

Cushman's roots stretched back to 1901 when Everett and Clinton Cushman began building engines in their basement. Cushman engines eventually powered everything from racing boats to farm tractors. In 1922, Cushman created its famed Husky engine that powered the Bob-A-Lawn mower—and soon, legions of scooters.

1937 Cushman Auto-Glide Model 1

Despite the halo surrounding the Auto-Glide, the 1937 Cushman was a crude affair. Salsbury approached Cushman in 1936 requesting 1,000 Husky engines to power his Motor Glide, but then bought elsewhere. With a copy of Salsbury's blueprints in hand and inspired by a neighborhood kid's homebuilt scooter, Cushman welded up a prototype of its own—why let a good idea go to waste? Cushman's frame was made of channel steel that amounted to a heavy-duty, heavy-weighing affair. "Suspension"—not a word that appeared in many scooter ads of the day—came from the 3.50 × 12-inch balloon tires, the padded seat, and the rider's gluteus maximus.

1935–1940

Relax with a *Moto-Scoot*

SAFE!
DEPENDABLE!
ECONOMICAL!

Thrilling — yet you relax. Astounding high mileage at an amazingly low cost — 120 miles to the gallon. Easy to operate

"The World's Greatest Economy in Transportation"

Sturdily Constructed

The Moto-Scoot is made under exacting specifications to give it a long life. It can be safely operated by any man or woman, boy or girl . . . the ideal conveyance for trips . . . or just to run around in the city. The cost is surprisingly low — $99.75 f.o.b. factory at Chicago, fully equipped with lights.

Manufactured by MOTO-SCOOT MANUFACTURING CO., Chicago, Illinois

Ideal for Deliveries

1937 Moto-Scoot
Norman A. Siegal had a golden vision of the future riding on two diminutive wheels powered by an elfin engine. In 1936, the 27-year-old hired three workmen, withdrew his savings, and rolled up his sleeves to begin building his Moto-Scoot. Siegal had obviously studied Salsbury's Motor Glide and done his homework—right down to naming his creation. The only thing preventing a patent infringement lawsuit was that Salsbury forgot to patent his creation back then. If you didn't look closely, you might have missed the engine and taken the Moto-Scoot for a child's push scooter, but it's there— a .5 hp Lauson.

Moto-Scoot And Mead Ranger

THE MOTORSCOOTER CRAZE MOVES EAST

At about the same time as Cushman rolled out its Auto-Glide, the Moto-Scoot Company in Chicago was launching its new motorscooter as well. The prototype Moto-Scoot scooter was created by visionary Chicagoan Norman Siegal.

Nearby, the venerable Mead Company had been building bicycles since 1889, and had created a vast marketing network for its famous Ranger pedal cycle. By 1936, Mead was ready to follow the trend to motorized two-wheelers, and signed on the dotted line to have Siegal build badge-engineered Moto-Scoots as the new and novel Mead Ranger scooter. With its established sales avenues, the Mead became one of the best-selling early scooters and the Mead–Moto-Scoot deal continued through the 1950s.

1938 Moto-Scoot
Styling came to Moto-Scoot in 1938 with a wicker-pattern engine cover that was years ahead—in fact no one ever followed this look. Power from the new Lauson engine was a whopping 1.5 hp via direct drive without any of the tiresome hassles of a clutch. Rear suspension was all in the bicycle seat springs, probably pilfered from a Mead Ranger bicycle; front suspension came from the inherent flex and compression of solid metal. The cylindrical tube on the steering post held batteries for the feeble headlamp and taillamp. Braking was at the rear only—no one trusted front braking much in those days, and rightly so as the cheap lining materials were prone to lock up if the brakes were actually applied. Top speed was now a breathtaking 30 mph.
Courtesy of the owner: Herb Singe

MOTO-SCOOT

America's Most Popular Motor Scooter

FOR SPORT, UTILITY AND TRANSPORTATIO

1939 Moto-Scoot

By 1939, Moto-Scoot—with the aid of its Mead Ranger sales—was indeed "America's Most Popular Motor Scooter," as this brochure boasted. Time magazine profiled Norman Siegal as the scooter king of 1939. Siegal built 186 Moto-Scoots in his firm's first year, 1936, and was churning out 4,500 in 1938 with dreams of building—and hopefully, selling—10,000 of the midget machines in 1939. It was not for naught that Time crowned Siegal "the Henry Ford of the scooter business."

> "Moto-Skoot [sic] inventor Norman Siegal is the Henry Ford of the scooter business."
>
> —Time magazine, April 3, 1939

Mead Ranger

Mead Co. of Chicago was so taken with Siegal's creation that it hired the motorscooter mogul to craft badge-engineered versions of the Moto-Scoot as Mead Rangers. Mead had established outlets every-where for its bicycle line, and so became the first large-scale scooter retailer. In the 1930s, nationwide advertising for small firms like Salsbury was near impossible, relegating the Motor Glide to being a West Coast phenom. Larger companies like Cushman and Mead ran ads in national magazines such as Popular Mechanics where the techno-minded could write away to order the gee-whiz scoots.

The Sensational NEW *Ranger* SCOOTER

Motor Marvel of the Age!

for
CHEAP · SAFE
TRANSPORTATION
HEALTH *and* PLEASURE
PROFIT *and* BUSINESS
OUTING *and* TRAVEL

Ranger

1935–1940

CUSTER SCOOTER IS TOPS

1941 Custer
Why do Americans love to name motorized vehicles in honor of fallen despots and maniacs? From the DeSoto to the Dodge Coronado, conquistadores have been faves. The 2.5 hp Custer scooter from Dayton, Ohio, brought to mind General George Armstrong Custer and Little Bighorn. Perhaps these names were indicative of the vehicles' integrity as well. Still, no one ever built a Wyatt Earp-mobile, Mother Theresa skateboard, or Martin Luther King golf cart. It's one of those academic questions that scholars love to endlessly debate, and we'll leave it in their hands.
Courtesy of the owner: Jim Kilau

*"Dash hither and yon
in gay abandon . . . "*
—1936 Salsbury Motor Glide Ad

Puddlejumpers And More

FOLLOWING THE LEADERS ALL THE WAY TO THE BANK

The design of Salsbury and Elmore's 1936 Motor Glide spread like wildfire. By the end of 1936, every other back-alley garage in America seemed to be a scooter factory and the back pages of mass-circulation magazines like *Popular Mechanics* were chock full of ads for potboiler scooters. Jukebox maker Rock-Ola had its motorscooter offering that battled for buyers alongside the Powell, Minneapolis, aptly named Puddlejumper, and many more. It was a motorscooter craze sweeping the nation.

The Salsbury Motor Glide had defined the Five Commandments of a motorscooter that set the style for all scooters that were to follow: A small motor placed next to or just in front of the rear wheel; a step-through chassis; bodywork to protect the rider from road spray and engine grime; small wheels; and an automatic transmission/clutch package (which Salsbury would introduce in 1937). All other scooters that came after the Salsbury had at least three of the five tenets.

1938 Rock-Ola
Canadian David C. Rockola made his name famous emblazoning it across the belighted bellies of his jukeboxes built in Chicago after Prohibition's repeal. Rockola went for the gold when the timing was right, and so next entered the scoot biz. Just as jukeboxes were dressed in chrome frou-frou and Buck Rogers class, Rock-Ola scooters were stylish little two-wheelers—at least they had compound curves in their rear bodywork, more than you could say for the Cushmans. In 1938, you could choose between the Deluxe with 1 hp Johnson "Iron Horse" or Tourist with .75 hp. The most exciting feature was the "revolutionary new Floating Ride" suspension— yup, those screen-door springs on the forks.
Courtesy of the owner: Herb Singe

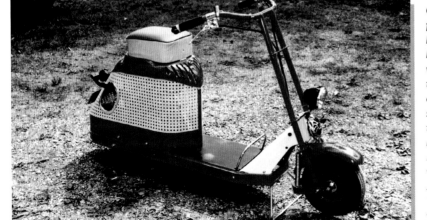

1938 Puddlejumper

When Midget Motors of Kearny, Nebraska, announced its Puddlejumper in 1938, boyish hearts must have done somersaults. Here was Buck Rogers' spaceship come to earth, or at least a scoot that could blast off. The styling was far beyond what neighboring Cushman was creating, and must have inspired many a scooter stylist (if there was such a thing) to rush back to their drawing boards. The Puddlejumper was truly streamlined, leaving other scootmakers to cry tears in their beers. Three models were offered—the Standard, DeLuxe, and three-wheeler ("self-balancing"!) Powertrike—with either gas or electric power. But never mind all that. The Puddlejumper had something no other scootmaker promoted: "Plenty of Leg Room."

1939 Powell Streamliner 40

Channing and Hayward Powell built vehicles to the tune of a different plumber. Based in Los Angeles, the dynamic duo created a scooter line from their first 1939 Streamliner through a gaggle of 1950s miniature motorcycles, when they switched over to plywood-bodied pickup trucks. This Streamliner was powered by a 2.3 hp Lauson engine with "forced blast cooling" (a glorified flywheel fan). But the key here was the streamlining, which in the 1930s was becoming a term of adulation for anything with curves. The Powell's streamlining was a key to decreased aerodynamic coefficient of drag and optimum handling prowess as it huffed and puffed to reach its top speed of 30 mph.
Courtesy of the owner: Herb Singe

1935–1940

Auto-Glide

THE HEART OF THE
Auto-Glide
CUSHMAN HUSKY ENGINE

Here's the powerful, dependable 4-cycle "CUSHMAN HUSKY air-cooled Engine, known for years as one of the very finest built. Light in weight, but. Oh! Spectacular sensational performance it is! Complete with kick-starter, muffler, auto-type carburetor. Two sizes: 1 H. P. and 1½ H. P.

DISC CLUTCH

The AUTO-GLIDE picks up speed quickly and smoothly from a standing start, because of its special Disc Clutch. Operation with a slight pressure of the left foot on the clutch lever. It has a spring-steel disc with double facing of finest velvet finish clutch material. Accurately machined. Easy to install. AUTO-GLIDE is a step at intersections without killing the engine.

Over 120 Miles To The Gallon
More Than 30 Miles Per Hour

Operates Like An Auto .. Has Starter,
Clutch, Throttle, Brake, Balloon Tires.

Comfortable and Convenient .. Fills the Gap
Between the Bicycle and the Automobile.

Here, at last, is Sensationally LOW-COST Transportation . . . and Delivery Service! Operates for actually ONE TENTH the cost of an auto! Only about ⅛¢ per mile! Light weight . . . only 170 to 190 pounds, yet is built extra rugged throughout and powered with Cushman Engine.

Wheelbase, 49 inches. Built close to the ground, and is unusually easy to balance. It is the safest vehicle on the road—no center bar—just step off on either side. Seat only 25 inches from ground. Operates perfectly on dirt, gravel or paved road.

AUTO-GLIDE has almost every feature you expect in a good automobile—and controls much like one. You start the Engine with a slight push on the handy kick-starter . . . Roll the machine with a little shove of your foot on the ground! . . . throw in the smooth-as-velvet disc clutch—and You're Under Way! Convenient hand-throttle controls your speed up to 30 miles an hour, as the powerful Cushman Husky engine whisks you quickly to office, factory, school or a pleasure spin. Kari-Pac model is ideal for light deliveries.

The CUSHMAN MOTOR WORKS, LINCOLN, NEBR.

"Cheaper Than Shoe Leather"
SCOOTERS SAVE SOLES IN THE GREAT DEPRESSION

All scooter ads of the late 1930s hailed the go-forever-on-a-teaspoon-of-gas fuel consumption and inexpensive operating costs. This second coming of the motorscooter arrived at the right place in the right time: America during the Great Depression. E. Foster Salsbury had envisioned his scooter being an ideal substitute for an automobile for people who didn't have the money in those bad times. And a Motor Glide was a perfect second car for people who were a little better off. Cushman and others followed this thinking—to the point where Cushman even boasted that operation of its scooters was "Cheaper than shoe leather."

Bad times were the mother of invention for motorscooters. The first scooters of 1915–1920 failed because they were frivolous toys; the Salsbury, Cushman, and Mead Moto-Scoot scooters were born from economic necessity and succeeded. The mass mobilization to motorscooters in Europe and Japan after World War II would follow this same pattern. And still today, the scooter makers that survive and thrive sell primarily to a market that needs economic transportation.

AN OUTSTANDING ACHIEVEMENT!

The "CHALLENGER"
Designed and Built by the Makers of "MOTO-SCOOT," to meet the definite demand of an exceptionally low priced vehicle with an exceedingly low maintenance cost. The "CHALLENGER" has been tested and approved . . . you will be amazed at its outstanding performance.

"The Magic Carpet of Bagdad"
Just imagine owning this remarkable little vehicle that gives you a new motion, rivaled only by the mythical "MAGIC CARPET OF BAGDAD."
Imagine possessing the power to step on the platform and almost at the expression of a wish to be able to GO . . . through the heavy mazes of traffic into the open spaces and into the countryside . . . Relax with the MOTO-SCOOT "CHALLENGER."
Thrill with the MOTO-SCOOT "CHALLENGER." Get out into the open road . . . open your throttle wide . . . and away you go . . . ahead of the line of traffic . . . Thrill to the instantaneous response of your throttle . . . the steady purr of the engine . . . as it sweeps you to your destination.

DELIVERED PRICE
$69.50
Federal Tax Paid
Subject To Local Sales Taxes

120 MILES PER GALLON!

The Moto-Scoot "CHALLENGER" has everything. This sturdy motor scooter embodies many of the features that made the Standard and De Luxe Moto-Scoot, the Hit of the World. The "CHALLENGER" features *Moto-Clutch*, enabling the rider to keep the "CHALLENGER'S" motor idling when the vehicle is motionless.

The added feature of a built-in carrier, makes this vehicle ideal for carrying packages, parcels, books, etc. The astoundingly low price, comes within the means of everyone.
See your closest Dealer for an actual demonstration and you will be convinced that the Moto-Scoot "CHALLENGER" is the new modern method for economical transportation.

**1939 Cushman Auto-Glide
and Glide-Kar**

*"Cheaper than shoe leather,"
was the promise from on high
for the economy the Auto-Glide
provided, and it was just the
thing for those trying to save
money following the Great
Depression. It was also the
raison d'être of the
motorscooter in the minds of
visionaries like E. Foster
Salsbury and Norman Siegal,
so why not tout the economy?
Cushman sure did: "Why walk
or use an auto when you can
Glide for 1/3¢ per mile!" But
the question for academics
persists: Was it truly cheaper
than shoe leather?*

*"If you want to conserve Gasoline
and Tires . . . and save money
to invest in War Bonds,
you should consider our Motor
Scooters. . . . Remember
a 'D' Ration book is good
for 1-1/2 Gallons a week . . .
at 100 miles per gallon
that's better than a 'B' Book."*

—Floyd Clymer's sales pitch
for the Victory Clipper scooter

1938 Rock-Ola

*The riches awaiting the
daring entrepreneur who
signed on as a dealer for
a scoot line must have
been fabulous given the
enthusiasm with which
builders such as Rock-Ola
promoted the possibilities.
The motorscooter must
have been a miniaturized
smoke-spewing gold mine
on two wheels—and if
you're reading this now
you're probably too late to
get in on the ground floor.*

Build your own JET ENGINE!

Order these plans today

1. JET PROPELLED BICYCLE, Assemble your own. Photo and instructions, $1.00.
2. HOW TO MAKE EXPERIMENTAL JET ENGINES. Seven sheets drawings with information and instructions $2.95.
3. BOTH OF ABOVE in one order $3.75. SEND NO MONEY. Order both at once $3.75 C.O.D. in USA plus c.o.d. postage. Send check or Money Order and we pay postage. Get other information too. Rush Order.

J. HOUSTON MAUPIN, Dept. 55, Tipp City, Ohio

SAY YOU SAW IT IN POPULAR MECHANICS

SEND NO MONEY

Build-It-Yourself Scooters

"FIRST FIND AN OLD WASHING MACHINE MOTOR . . . ."

Too much free time in the garages of suburbia has led to the invention of everything from early scooters to Apple computers. All you needed was a jig saw, some plywood, a couple of baby carriage wheels, and an old washing machine motor, and you too could be the neighborhood Wild One.

In the late 1930s, handymen across the country mailed their 25 cents in for dubious kits or putt-putt plans advertised in *Popular Mechanics* to be the first on the block to troll down the street in what to the untrained eye appeared to be nothing more than junk on wheels. One person's junk is always another's treasure.

The Latest... Greatest...
ZIPSCOOT

POSITIVE DURABLE BRAKE   NATURAL PEDAL CONTROLS

GENUINE GOODYEAR TIRES   FREE ENGINE CLUTCH

AIRFLOW DESIGN   FINGER TIP THROTTLE

Amazing Speed

1949 Zipscoot
Curiously reminiscent of Cushman's Auto-Glide, America's Outstanding Scooter Value could be had for a fraction of the real thing's cost— assuming you were skilled with a wrench. The boasted top speed of 30 mph is unlikely, unless on a treacherous downward slope.

"This Speedy Scooter Will Assure You Plenty of Fun"

Back when anything could be built with a little bit of old-fashioned American ingenuity, build-your-own scoot blueprints were a staple of Popular Mechanics magazine. Although they were a poor cousin of factory-made scoots, most folk viewed the scooters as the same sort of recycled-washing-machine-motor death traps.

1939 Renmor Constructa-Scoot

Proof positive that scoots indeed came from children's push scooters! Renmor offered this petite putt-putt with or without the $30 motor. After all, if the customer bought the cheap version, dad's lawn mower engine or mom's sewing machine motor could be bolted on and achieve the same break-neck speeds.

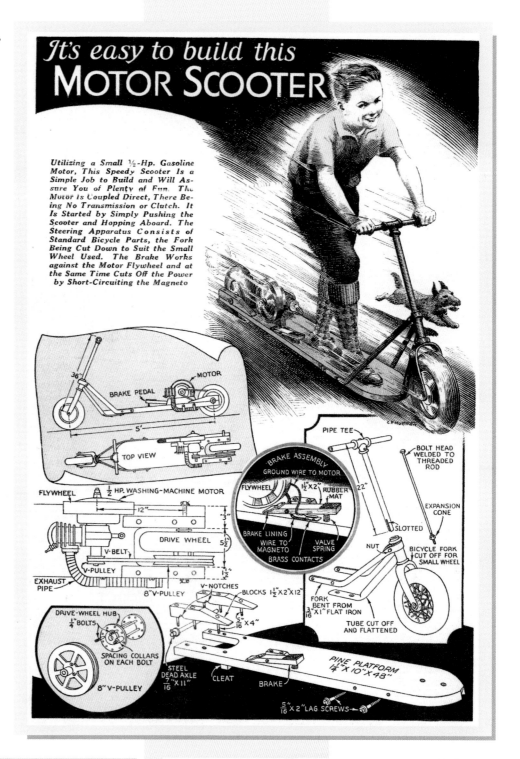

It's easy to build this **MOTOR SCOOTER**

Utilizing a Small ½-Hp. Gasoline Motor, This Speedy Scooter Is a Simple Job to Build and Will Assure You of Plenty of Fun. The Motor Is Coupled Direct, There Being No Transmission or Clutch. It Is Started by Simply Pushing the Scooter and Hopping Aboard. The Steering Apparatus Consists of Standard Bicycle Parts, the Fork Being Cut Down to Suit the Small Wheel Used. The Brake Works against the Motor Flywheel and at the Same Time Cuts Off the Power by Short-Circuiting the Magneto

1935–1940

The Fully Automatic Scooter

SALSBURY'S TORQUE CONVERTER SETS THE PACE

The earliest motorscooters were hardly mechanical marvels. The engineering was crude, heavy, and only slightly more reliable than a donkey. All that changed in late 1937 when Salsbury announced its new 1938 Motor Glide Models 50 and 60 with Self-Shifting Transmission. The future was here today.

Suddenly the motorscooter ante had been raised to new, dizzying heights, and Cushman, Moto-Scoot, and others who wanted to stay in business rushed to create their own versions of Salsbury's automatic clutch and torque converter. Even today, the son of Salsbury's self-shifter lives on in scooters from Vespa to Honda, and E. Foster Salsbury still receives his royalty check.

**Acrobat and 1939 Salsbury
Motor Glide Model 72**
*Look, no hands! Riding the
Salsbury with its Self-Shifting
Transmission was so simple,
actress Mildred Coles could
scoot along with her feet doing
the driving. Salsbury ads and
stunts showing women on
Motor Glides were more
than just cheesecake, as the
scooters were aimed at a
market looking for an
economical vehicle that was
easy to use. This was the future
in scooters, and it was definitely
as new as tomorrow.*

1939 Salsbury Self-Shifting Transmission

It was the shot heard 'round the scootering world heralding a revolution. In late 1937, Salsbury introduced on the new 1938 Motor Glide its most radical feature: the Self-Shifting Transmission, as the firm termed its new automatic clutch and torque converter. The primary drive was via a V-shaped rubber belt running between spring-loaded pulleys; as speed increased, the pulleys compressed together, creating a larger circumference for the belt to ride. Thus, the "gear ratio" could alternate between an "infinite number of ratios," as Salsbury ads boasted. This technology was startlingly innovative in 1937, and every scootmaker that wished to survive created its own version—regardless of patents.

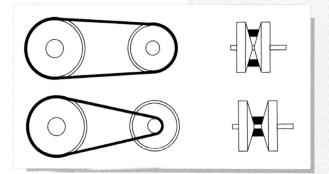

"The 1938 Motor Glide is the last word in personal transportation and far exceeds my fondest expectation for performance."

—Air racer and barnstormer Colonel Roscoe Turner

1942 Salsbury Super-Cycle

The new Super-Cycle featured "almost" 3 hp and Salsbury's patented Dynamic Drive. Sidecars, front fairings, and extra seats were all offered; the scooter was moving uptown.

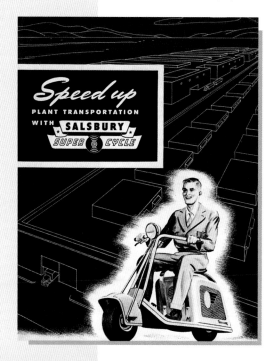

Motorscooter Polo

Riding their 1939 Salsbury Motor Glide Model 72 scoots, these lovely lasses battle it out in a game of scooter polo. As this 1939 newspaper clipping states, "Leave it to Hollywood to do something different. The perfect ingredients for sure-fire publicity shots are bathing beauty starlets—in their customary costumes—doing something dizzy." (Fear not: no one was really getting dizzy, as the kickstands are all safely touching Earth.)

1935–1940

Bathing Beauty and 1939 Crocker Scootabout

Beauty came to the scootering beast in 1939 when Albert G. Crocker created his Scootabout. The mechanicals of the Crocker were typical of the time, but not so its flowing bodywork. The Motor Glides and Auto-Glides initially did not venture beyond single-plane folds in their bodywork—after all, scooters were built on a budget and sold as a utilitarian device.

The Crocker was formed of sinuous bodywork with two-tone paint that added a further dimension to the curvaceous lines. The tail section covered the wheels with fender skirts, the design coming together at the rear in a teardrop. With its Streamline Moderne shape and flashy Art Deco paint scheme, the Scootabout foreshadowed the spirit of the Jet Age scooter styling that was to come.

The Chic Motorscooter

STYLING COMES TO THE PUTT-PUTT

And then in the late 1930s, motorcycle tuner, racer, and builder Albert G. Crocker created his Scootabout scooter, also in California. The Scootabout's engine and solid front suspension were typical of the time, but not so its flowing bodywork. Crocker followed the tenets of Salsbury's mechanical design but added the Sixth Commandment of a scooter: styling.

1941 Crocker Scootabout

This 1941 flyer signified a meeting of two great minds: Crocker and salesman, promoter, and all-around motorcycle kingpin Floyd Clymer. Crocker was a former colleague of Harley-Davidson's famed engineer William Ottaway when the duo worked for Thor motorcycles; Crocker was later an Indian dealer and racer, so he was well placed to be a thorn in everyone's side. Crocker also built the great 1930s Crocker V-Twin motorcycles that singlehandedly caused Harley and Indian more grief than any event up to the 1950s British motorcycle invasion. Clymer, meanwhile, was a motorcycling ambassador with his hands in more aspects of cycling than anyone could count, including Clymer Motors of Los Angeles and his later cycle magazines. When Clymer decided he needed a scooter to sell during the craze, he called up Crocker, who created this machine. But the Scootabout never scooted about much: production probably numbered less than 100—as did production of Crocker's infamous motorcycle.

1939 Crocker Scootabout

A study in styling contrasts. Underneath the flowing bodywork, the Crocker had advanced little from the Motor Glide: It featured a rigid chassis without suspension (springs were added in 1941), an automatic clutch, and a brake on the rear wheel. But the streamlined engine cover inspired scooters of the future by adding complex curves to the metalwork, and suddenly that little scooter was cute—a great sales point! As a Crocker flyer shouted, the Scootabout offered "New Luxury in motor scooters." Courtesy of the owner: Herb Singe

1935–1940

When smokers find out the good things Chesterfields give them .. nothing else will do

The Modern Woman and 1936 Moto-Scoot

By the late 1930s, scootering was all the rage, and Chester-field cigarettes promoted an image of the modern woman dashing about on her own two-wheeler and daring openly to smoke a cigarette. Think of this 1937 magazine ad as a precursor of the 1970s Virginia Slims ads with their slogan, "You've come a long way, baby!" In 1937, this ad signified an even longer journey as smoking had been a feminine taboo for centuries. The Moto-Scoot also promoted the image of the freewheeling woman freed from earthly chains and duties, which had indeed been one of the first sales pitches for scooters. The look of astonishment on the male hitchhiker's face undoubtedly turned to disappointment as the woman, her two-wheeler, and her pack of cigs disappeared over the next hill, leaving him with lipstick traces, dust, and cigarette and exhaust smoke.

The Quaint Sport Of Scootering

OVER HILL, OVER DALE, THE SCOOTER GOES EVERYWHERE

Like wildfire, the scooter became a craze, and people took to doing daffy things aboard their newfound friend. Those Hollywood types took to tearing up the town on their Salsbury scoots, while across the country scooter rental shops allowed anyone with a couple pennies to terrorize traffic on a putt-putt.

It was the birth of the quaint sport of scootering.

Moto-Scoot
Goes Uptown

In the glory days of Pierce Arrows and Duesenbergs, what could have induced more side-splitting hoots of laughter than even the notion of someone dashing to the opera on a Moto-Scoot? (They must be nouveau riche!) This 1939 Collier's magazine cover was probably created half in jest at the blossoming scooter craze and half in fear that such a sighting could actually occur. But what a way to go: Leave the chauffeur at home to raid the fridge and save pennies on gas all at the same time. Note that Milady is not sitting side-saddle but instead showing a bit of racy leg as the dynamic duo arrive at the theater, wave off the valet, and find the best parking spot nestled betwixt two Packards. (Definitely nouveau riche.)

October 7, 1939

Collier's

THE NATIONAL WEEKLY

5¢ A COPY

JAMES WILLIG

CORONADO FEVER

"Enjoy Life While You Live."

—Philosophy espoused in 1937 Cushman ad

1930s Regal Model 200
"Take to the open road ... the long, smooth road before you," taunted this Regal brochure. With its Clinton 1.5 hp engine and 30 mph top speed, the Regal was all about getting away from it all.

1935–1940

41

Everyone Is Motor Scooting

There's Nothing Like the NEW ORIGINAL *Moto-Scoot*

NET WEIGHT, 300 LBS.
89½" OVERALL LENGTH

Spare tire wheel, tire and tube available that fits either front or rear. Change your Scoot tire the same as you would your car tire.

MODEL 945 SUPER STREAMLINER
Specifications

2 Speed Transmission	7 to 1 } Gear Ratio	2-Tone Paint
Briggs and Stratton Engine	4⅞ to 1	1¼ Gallon Capacity Fuel
5.1 H.P. at 3200 R.P.M.	Extra Silent Muffler	Tank
Welded Tubular Steel	4:00 x 8 Tires	Ignition Lock and Key
Frame	Internal Expansion Brake	Timken Roller Bearings
59" Wheelbase	89½" Overall Length	Throughout

Fully Enclosed Weather Protected Package Compartment

ASK FOR FULL DETAILS TODAY

Styling and the 1930s Moto-Scoot Model 945 Super Streamliner

"Style" was a relative term when it came to scoots, as the arguably svelte and slinky Super Streamliner proved. The back compartment held a spare tire, and this brochure promised you could "change your Scoot tire the same as you would your car"—surely a magical sales pitch!

Streamlining and the 1938 Moto-Scoot

The concept of speed grasped the world through the heroic feats of pioneering aviators, and streamlining was a result of a new hybrid of science and engineering—aerodynamics. Needless to say, aerodynamics were of utmost importance at scoot top speeds of a breathtaking 30 mph. The Moto-Scoot's wicker engine cover was half Streamline Moderne, half wastebasket on wheels. Nevertheless, the aerodynamic efficiency must have been fabulous—witness the speed streaks captured on film on the cover of this rare brochure. Look closely, and you may agree that this woman's cape was being held aloft by a helping hand later airbrushed out.

High Tech Scooters, Circa 1930s

THE SOUND AND THE FURY

Tomorrow and tomorrow and tomorrow did not always arrive when you rode a motorscooter in the 1930s. Marvel at their motors, but mechanical marvels they weren't.

Still, scooters were a fun fad, a quaint little vision of the future, and all around, their mechanical features were probably on par with the cars of the time.

1939 LeJay Electric Rocket

The gas-fueled internal-combustion engine was not the only motive power to propel motorscooters. By mailing in your hard-earned 25¢ to the LeJay Manufacturing Co. in Minneapolis, you could get "complete simplified plans" to build your own Rocket. As this 1939 mail-order ad boasted, the Rocket was suitable for sidewalk use, which was a less-than-inspiring sales pitch. As far as has been uncovered by scooter archaeologists, no one was ever inspired by the Stanley Steamer automobile in trying to construct a steam-powered scooter pot-boiler.

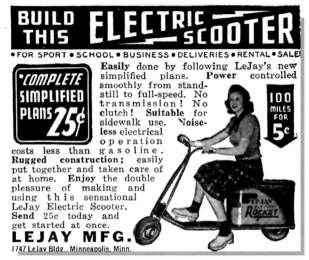

BUILD THIS ELECTRIC SCOOTER

• FOR SPORT • SCHOOL • BUSINESS • DELIVERIES • RENTAL • SALE

COMPLETE SIMPLIFIED PLANS 25¢

Easily done by following LeJay's new simplified plans. Power controlled smoothly from standstill to full-speed. No transmission! No clutch! Suitable for sidewalk use. Noiseless electrical operation costs less than gasoline. Rugged construction; easily put together and taken care of at home. Enjoy the double pleasure of making and using this sensational LeJay Electric Scooter. Send 25c today and get started at once.

LEJAY MFG.
1747 LeJay Bldg., Minneapolis, Minn.

100 MILES FOR 5¢

SKOOT-MOBILE, America's finest skooter, is designed and built like an automobile. Note to the right the photograph of the two speed transmission and clutch, which provides low gear for power and hill climbing and high gear for speed and economy. Note also the large size auto-mobile-type brake which provides plenty of stopping power for any emergency. The knee-action front end smooths out the roughest roads, assuring comfortable riding, and the compact, air-cooled engine delivers up to 120 miles per gallon of fuel.

SKOOT-MOBILE'S main frame is of welded tubular steel construction and assures ample rigidity and freedom from warping and weaving.

The Economy Car, shown below, has a capacity up to a quarter of a ton and makes an ideal delivery service for retail merchants who demand speed and bed-rock economy. Every SKOOT-MOBILE is guaranteed for one year against defective parts and workmanship.

SEND FOR DESCRIPTIVE LITERATURE ... FREE

USE THIS COUPON NOW

SKOOT-MOBILE, INC.
5835 Ravenswood Ave., Dept. 384, Chicago, Ill.
Please send me full details and descriptive literature on SKOOT-MOBILE. I am interested, as the check mark will indicate.

☐ For personal transportation   ☐ For Delivery
☐ Dealer

NAME_____

ADDRESS_____

CITY_____STATE_____

1930s Skoot-Mobile with sidecar

With the addition of what looked like a miniature coffin on wheels, the Skoot-Mobile became a family troop carrier capable of hauling Pop, Mom, and little Suzy. Salsbury, Cushman, and Moto-Scoot all offered a sidecar to transform their scoots into precursors of the minivan, yet the Skoot-Mobile promised it was "America's finest."

1939 Star Put-Put

Techno gee-whiz magazines like Popular Science were the national sales tool for upstart scootmakers everywhere. Before the dawn of the Information Age, the United States was far from an information superhighway—more like a country backroads of gab, gossip, and cookie recipes shared over the backyard fence. For the fledgling scooter builder, the means to reaching a large audience was limited, and Popular Science ads were the savior in newsprint. Here, scooters from potboiler makers such as the Star Put-Put Co. did battle for earthbound Buck Rogers wannabes.

Waxing Poetic On Scooter Woes

The true unsung heroes in the scooter engineering epic were the ad writers. Creativity, exaggeration, and exclamation points coursed through their veins like gasoline through their scooter's engines. They waxed poetic to accentuate the positive and hide the many flaws, creating putt-putt poems in what to the uninitiated was mere ad copy. It was a Herculean task if ever there was one. Herewith, consider some of their finest phrases:

- **"Streamlining"** was the perfect description for refrigerator-like styling from Salsbury to Crocker to today

- **"Floating Ride"** was Rock-Ola's term for suspension made up of two screen-door hardware-store-variety springs

- **"Sane Speed"** was Cushman's way of promoting lack of speed: "FAST enough to get there quickly and SLOW enough to be absolutely safe."

- **"Forced Blast Cooling"** was the Powell Streamliner's inflated promotion for its flywheel fan, which appeared on most every scooter on the market

- **"Self-Balancing"** ballyhooed anything with more than two wheels, as with the three-wheeled Puddlejumper Powertrike or Cushman's Side Kar

- **"Iron Horse"** was Rock-Ola's name for its Johnson 1 hp engine, likening it to a steam locomotive

"Suspension" and the 1937 Auto-Glide Model 1

Suspension—or the lack thereof—was one of the major arenas of battle on the scooter technology front. Protecting the rider's gluteus maximus paid dividends in scooter sales, so makers rushed to add "suspension" to their hitherto rigid-framed wares. Still, despite all the advances, American scoots—even into the 1960s—were never renowned for their ride quality.

1935–1940

Cushman MOTOR SCOOTER **Airborne Scooter**

MODEL 53 A

NOW Available for Civilian Use

AT LAST a closely guarded war secret can be told. During the preparation of the American Forces for the invasion of Germany, we were called upon to design a special Cushman Motor Scooter for the United States Army Paratroopers and since our victory in Germany, this very important piece of war transportation is available for civilian use.

We are proud to present this Model "53A" Airborne Motor Scooter to the American public for their use in safe, economical and enjoyable transportation.

This Airborne Scooter was designed and built to withstand the rigors of war. To this sturdiness has been added all the features of our regular scooter to assure you of an easy, comfortable ride.

The picture above illustrates how the Cushman Airborne Scooters are dropped by parachute from planes in the sky to give the paratroopers extra maneuverability on the ground.

The "Airborne" scooter was designed and built sturdy enough to withstand the severe shock and jolt in landing. Powered by the famous "Husky" engine, this machine travels over all kinds of terrain, through mud, sand, up steep inclines and even through underbrush. It has met the rigorous tests of war and earned an enviable record for speedy, dependable transportation at an amazingly low cost.

IN THE CITY

ON THE FARM

CUSHMAN MOTOR WORKS

LINCOLN 1, NEBRASKA

Military Motorscooters
1939–1945

Secret weapons win wars. Vikings had their long ships. Trojans had their horse. Hannibal had his elephants. Conquistadors had their galleons. And in World War II, the Allies had paratrooper scooters.

Dropping scooters out of the sky began as a European pastime. It's rumored that the Nazis created a miniature motorscooter to accompany the *fallschirmjäger* on invasions, but no photos or descriptions of such a scooter have surfaced. Near the start of the war, meanwhile, the Italians crafted the Aeromoto, a micro-sized four-wheeled paratrooper putt-putt built by Società Volugrafo of Turin.

It was the British and Americans, however, that perfected the paratrooper scooter: the British built their Welbike while the Americans had the Cushman and Cooper. Development of the paratrooper scoots was top secret during the war, but spies were actually more interested in the big bang of the Manhattan Project.

During World War II, scooters were shanghaied into service on other fronts as well, fighting for peace, dignity, and the American way with all the nationalistic fervor the elfin engines could muster. Scoots were drafted into the military to serve as base and airfield go-fers.

On the home front, scooters fought in civvies; most US car makers were converted solely to military contracting, so the government granted special dispensations to some US scooter builders to build scooters as civilian wartime transportation. Riding a scooter became a wartime duty, as patriotic as flying the flag or planting a victory garden.

Motorscooters may not have won the war, but they were certainly the mice that roared.

"All's fair in love and war."

—Shakespeare

OPPOSITE:
Paratrooper Scooter
Motorscooters valiantly served their various countries during war with vigor and valor. On the homefront, prewar scooters were ideal transportation due to gas rationing. On the battlefield, they made decent shields to hide behind from bullets. The Cushman Model 53 Airborne scooter was based on the desire to have instantly mobile paratroops dropped behind enemy lines. Concealing the scooterized troops' location, on the other hand, could be a difficult matter with a puttering two-stroke and a trail of blue smoke.

1939–1945

Paratrooper Putt-Putts

SCOOTERS FROM HEAVEN

The strategy was simple. Paratroopers would drop in the dead of night deep behind enemy lines, unpack their elfin scooters, and lead a true charge of the motorized light brigade on putt-putts. Nothing would stand in their way.

The logic was sound, but the means left something to be desired. These scooters never went into wide-scale use, and ended their service to be sold off as war surplus, finding a welcome home with today's scooter collectors.

World War II could have ended differently if scooters had been allowed to fight for their country—the Allies could have lost.

RESTRICTED

A1609A 4-23-44 | ABERDEEN PROVING GROUND | ORDNANCE DEPT.
Proj.11-2-1. Cooper Airborne Motor Scooter. Right front.

*1944 Cooper War
Combat Motor Scooter*
*While Hitler was shooting V1 rockets at
Britain, American mad scientists were testing a
new secret weapon, the Cooper paratrooper
scooter. In the midst of World War II, the US
government scoured the country for the best
scoot maker and came across Cushman and
Cooper. Cooper's scoot was a Powell A-V-8 that
Frank Cooper decorated with his own decals and
reinforcing bars so it could withstand being
dropped from planes. Although the US Army
preferred it, the contract eventually went to
Cushman since the Army wasn't impressed with
Cooper's "factory." This photo was taken from
the official US Army test of the Cooper.*

Volugrafo Aermoto Paratrooper Scooter

The Volugrafo was certain to do damage if dropped 5,000 feet onto the enemy. Soldiers could lug the Volugrafo around like a 50lb suitcase or drive the 125cc two-stroke over nearly any terrain thanks to the two-speed gearbox. Società Volugrafo of Turin manufactured the Aermoto, possibly the first paratrooper scooter anywhere. The Aeromoto subsequently inspired an arms race as the Allies rushed to create their own paratrooper scooters.

> *"World War II is responsible. Sprawling war plants and the mobility-conscious armed services found a myriad of uses for the powered runabouts, which previously had been notable chiefly as a special headache to traffic safety planners."*
>
> —Business Week, 1946

Cushman Auto-Glide 34

"This was a tremendous thing. We were making scooters when Ford couldn't get tires to make cars," Robert H. Ammon recounted about his wartime scooter production. The War Department decided that scooters were economical civilian transportation so Cushman was able to pump out up to 300 putt-putts daily during the war. The Auto-Glide 34 was not used in combat, but rather to wheel servicemen around bases. Nevertheless, drab military green was a must, as opposed to the earlier bright colors to lure the public to reach for their pocketbooks. This was the last model to carry the name "Auto-Glide."

1952 Bernardet with Gun Trailer

The French joined the scooter arms race with the Bernardet, ideal for toting artillery to the front. Courtesy of the François-Marie Dumas Archives

1939–1945

Putt-Putt Attack!!

TOP SECRET SCOOTERS

The military motorscooter was conceived to make Hitler's Blitzkrieg look positively sluggish. Scooters were to give individual mobility for all troops as they revved their miniature motors in bloodthirsty patriotism. Despite numerous attempts to create military motorscooters, however, the patriotic putt-putts remained pacifists.

Perhaps the idea was wrong. Perhaps scooters could have been used as instant foxholes when dropped from 1,000 feet. Or simply just dropped on the enemy. Or perhaps their true story has never been told; perhaps they served their country as the ultimate counter-espionage decoy, allowing the plans to fall into enemy hands and divert attention from the Manhattan Project.

The truth may never be known.

1950s Brockhouse Corgi
Post-World War II, the Welbike was honorably discharged, domesticated, and renamed as the Corgi. The name wasn't a demotion in stature, though, and Corgi scooters were manufactured by Brockhouse of Southport for years following the hostilities.
Courtesy of the owner:
Jim Kilau

"The scooters were drafted into our war plants to deliver small parts between buildings. Sidecars were added to convert them into mobile soda fountains for carrying refreshments to production-line workers. Other sidecar combinations were equipped for ambulance duty and fire-fighting."

—Popular Mechanics, 1947

ACMA Vespa
Military Scooter

This French-made stealth machine was never put into combat; the mere threat of its existence probably detered many a war. If the bazooka were fired on this Vespa, the enemy would probably be more stunned by the number of back flips the scooter made rather than the earth-shaking firepower. Even in 1993, scooters were used as weapons in guerrilla warfare with a series of "scooter bombs" in Calcutta, India.

Iwo Jima and the Sacred Moto-Scoot Clutch

When Moto-Scoot visionary Norm Siegal set off with the US Marines to serve his country, he still had scooters on the mind. His time in the trenches was spent envisioning a new automatic clutch—even while bullets were flying over his head. He pieced together his brainstorm with scrounged parts and carried the clutch everywhere, worried that someone might steal his idea before he could patent it. Storming the beaches of Iwo Jima, Siegal manned a foxhole on the waterfront and decided to bury his clutch in the sand for safety. Soon after, Japanese soldiers attacked from the rear flank, wounding Siegal.

He regained consciousness on an ambulance boat leaving Iwo Jima. Remembering his sacred clutch, he leapt to his feet, stole a skiff, and paddled back to shore. As he was digging up the clutch, his commanding officer told him, "If you can dig, you can fight," and handed him a gun. Wounded a second time, Siegal got off the island, this time with his beloved clutch.

Lambretta Fold-Up
Paratrooper Scooter

Inspired by the Volugrafo Aeromoto, Innocenti created this prototype paratrooper scooter. The engine was based on the Model C 125cc engine, without all the frills of fancy bodywork. After all, this was war.
Courtesy of the
Collezione Vittorio Tessera

1939–1945

The Golden Age of the Motorscooter 1946–1954

Bad times begat motorscooters. As the dust cleared away in the days following the end of World War II, scooter makers blossomed throughout Europe and Japan. Just as in the dark years of the Great Depression in the United States, scooters were suddenly seen as the Platonic ideal in cheap transportation to mobilize the masses. If German philosopher Immanuel Kant had written a treatise on motorscooters, and scooter scholars do not believe he did, his categorical imperative would have been the perfect scooting sales pitch: The greatest good for the greatest number.

In the early postwar years, the world rebuilt itself, and "The New" burst on the scene from all fronts. No idea was too outrageous, no invention too far flung, and science would save us all, as many believed it had done in creating the atomic bomb and ending the war.

"The New" was everywhere. The bikini bathing suit, created by French couturier Louis Reard, was first modeled by a stripper at a Paris fashion show in 1946. In California in 1950, Fender introduced its first mass-produced solid-body electric guitar, the Esquire, dubbed by many as "an electric canoe paddle." In Japan in 1952, Sony launched the first pocket-sized transistor radio. In the US of A in 1954, Swanson Frozen Foods debuted the TV Dinner.

In both Italy and Japan, the first scooters hit the road in 1946; France, Germany, England, and others had their own makers within several years, most often licensed versions of the Italian makes, from Lambretta to Parilla.

This third wave of scootermania shaped a further clause in the definition of a scooter: Motorscooters were born from economic necessity. The first scooters of the 1910s and 1920s had been gadabout toys, and failed. The second wave of scooters, sparked in the United States, was a by-product of the Great Depression.

"Just like Henry Ford put the workers on wheels in America, we put automotive transport within the reach of people who never expected to travel that way."

—Enrico Piaggio, *Newsweek*, 1956

Postwar, the European and Japanese economic recovery rode atop the midget wheels of motorscooters, as well as other mopeds, commuter motorcycles, and micro cars. Cushman even helped establish the Belgian Cushman firm under the auspices of the US Recovery Act.

It was the dawn of the Golden Age of the Motorscooter.

OPPOSITE:

Bella Donna *and* **1955 Vespa**
Following World War II, motorscooters appeared everywhere like flowers in the spring. Italy and Japan developed and released new scooters almost simultaneously in 1946, and the rest of Europe was quick to follow. The American makers meanwhile merely pushed prewar designs back into business. The Golden Age of the motorscooter was at hand.

4

1946–1954

MP5 Paperino
Piaggio designers Vittorio Casini and Renzo Spolti noticed Vittorio Belmondo's funny-looking SIMAT scooter and knew that Italy needed postwar transport. By merely adding a legshield to Belmondo's basic design, Piaggio dubbed its creation the MP5, then nicknamed it Paperino, or Donald Duck—although its doubtful Piaggio ever applied for a trademark license from Walt Disney. The scooter featured a Sachs motor positioned centrally rather than on the side as in later Piaggio scooters giving them the classic Vespa lean. "Admittedly," Enrico Piaggio later said, "the first motor scooter was a horrible looking thing, and people ridiculed us to our faces." Estimates of production numbers of the handmade Duck range from 10 to 100, and only two are known to exist: one missing many parts at the Piaggio factory in Pontedera, and this complete Paperino discovered recently still running in a small Sicilian town.
Courtesy of the owner: Roberto Donati

Italian Motorscooter Pioneers
FROM MICKEY MOUSE TO DONALD DUCK

Mussolini banged his bare chest atop a FIAT tractor to prove the superiority of all things Italian. So when Disney characters infiltrated Italy, Il Duce outlawed their foreign names; instead, Mickey Mouse was Italianized to *Topolino* and Donald Duck became *Paperino*. FIAT took this as a cue to name its people's car the Topolino.

FIAT's scooting ambitions were eclipsed by the war, but SIMAT succeeded in building one of the first Italian scooters in 1940. Across town in Turin, Aermoto built the little Volugrafo parachuting putt-putt to help the Fascists annex Albania and conquer King Zog without a shot fired.

Ferdinando Innocenti witnessed the British paratroopers putsing around on Corgi Welbikes and called up Colonel Corradino d'Ascanio to pen the first Lambretta. D'Ascanio declined.

Meanwhile, Enrico Piaggio put designers Vittorio Casini and Renzo Spolti to work on a scooter based on the SIMAT. Perhaps as a result of accidentally killing Mussolini's son when a Piaggio P108B plane crashed, Piaggio got the go-ahead from the Allies postwar to build the MP5, nick-named Paperino. Only later would Corradino d'Ascanio develop the Vespa.

FIAT Prototipo
As early as 1938, Italy's largest automaker began investigating building a scooter. This FIAT sadly never went past the prototype stage, but the likeness to America's Cushman was more than obvious.
Courtesy of the Collezione Vittorio Tessera

1946 V.98 Prototipo

Legends abound concerning early Vespa prototypes. The wheels and their stub-axle mounts are rumored to come from leftover World War II bomber landing gear. The engine is believed to have been a starter engine for Piaggio wartime airplanes. Enrico Piaggio was in such a hurry to get the Vespa to market that there was no time for full testing of the prototypes, so they were driven on dirt roads without air filters to facilitate wear and tear on the internal organs. D'Ascanio led Piaggio's aeronautics division prior to World War II and was an authority on aeronautics, aircraft engines, and stressed-skin bodywork where the body did double duty as the frame in a monocoque unitized design. The adaption of the monocoque body to the Vespa placed it at the far cutting edge of automotive technology in 1946; today this design is used on cars throughout the world. The Paperino had a central tunnel housing to channel cooling air to the engine; the Vespa prototype did away with this, instead having cooling vents in the 98cc engine's side cover and a step-through design ideal for women in skirts. The V.98 prototype was first shown to the public at the 1946 Turin Show, and 100 pre-production prototypes were built before the assembly lines started rolling.

1946 Gianca Nibbio

The Nibbio was the first Italian scooter to hit the market following World War II, just months ahead of the Vespa. Built in Monza, it used a standard tube frame covered by sheet-steel bodywork. Suspension was advanced for a scooter: telescopic front forks and a rear swing arm with an avant garde monoshock mounted beneath the engine. That engine was a 98cc two-stroke creating 2 hp. In 1949, Nibbio construction was transferred to the San Cristoforo firm of Milan. Having a company named for San Cristoforo, the protector of travelers (who was later impeached by the Vatican after having done centuries of good work), must have been good advertising for a scooter.

1940s SIMAT

While Piaggio's 1945 Paperino scooter was thought to be the dawn of the second Italian Renaissance, the idea actually stemmed from designer Vittorio Belmondo's SIMAT scooter and later the 1941 Velta VB model. A scaled-down version was licensed to Volugrafo, which dropped scooters from the skies as Italian lightning-brigade paratrooper putt-putts.
Courtesy of the owner: Vittorio Tessera

"The Vespa will always look like this, even when it's driven by a nuclear engine and goes on the moon"

—Corradino d'Ascanio, Vespa designer

1946–1954

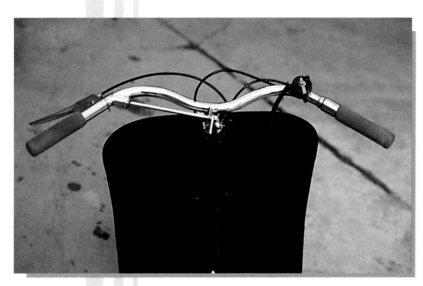

The first production Vespas were crude but charming machines. Shift linkages were all by mechanical rods and any sort of rear suspension was but a dream in a rider's eye. This is the 48th Vespa built.
Courtesy of the owner: Roberto Donati

The Birth of the Vespa
THE SCOOTER THAT SAVED THE WORLD

Società Anonima Piaggio was founded in 1884 by Rinaldo Piaggio in Genoa, Italy, to make woodworking machinery and later, railroad cars. In 1915, Piaggio delved into aviation, inventing such innovations as cabin pressurization. In the waning years of the war, the Piaggio factory at Pontedera was subjected to urban renewal courtesy of B-17s; the surviving machine tools were confiscated by the Nazis. The factory was rebuilt after the end of hostilities, and Piaggio began looking for a new product to sell.

Development of the Piaggio Vespa began in autumn 1945, just months after the liberation of northern Italy; the first Vespa was for sale in April 1946. From its beginning, the Vespa revolutionized the motorscooter, and from that day forward it became the standard—even the Platonic ideal—by which all other scooters the world over were judged.

1946 Vespa Sales Flyer

Piaggio named its scooter the Vespa not for the ancient Roman emperor Titus Flavius Sabinis Vespasianus, but rather for the buzzing of its two-stroke engine that sounds like a wasp, or *vespa* in Italian. The styling of the scooter's tail also bore an odd metallic resemblance to a wasp's abdomen. But Piaggio's Vespa was not the only Vespa around: Rival makers MV Agusta and Moto Rumi also offered motorcycles named Vespa, although as soon as Piaggio's scooter caught on they were lost in the shadows of the Vespa's limelight. Throughout the world, scooter became synonymous with Vespa and the words are almost interchangeable: in Paris, parking signs refer to all scooters as Vespas; in Italian, there is even a verb meaning "to ride a Vespa," *vespizzare*, which was surely born by the early Piaggio sales slogan that called on the hordes to Vespizzatari, literally to Vespize yourself. In 1946, the first year of production, 2,484 Vespas were built; in 1947, production skyrocketed to 10,535. By 1994, Piaggio had built more than 10 million Vespas. It all began with this advertizing brochure, the first Vespa sales flyers.

The Salsbury Connection?

In 1938, E. Foster Salsbury sent a sales agent to Europe armed with top-secret blueprints and photos to discuss licensing Salsbury scooter production to potential scooter makers. The agent met with many firms throughout England and the continent; E. Foster Salsbury said in a 1992 interview that, while he himself was not on the licensing trip, he believed that Piaggio was one of the firms approached. No records remain of the trip in Salsbury's archives, so the scootering world may never know for sure the provenance of a Salsbury-Vespa lineage. The one thing known for certain is that in those days with a second world war looming on the horizon, no European firms actually signed on the dotted line to build a licensed version of the Salsbury.

> *"Our over 10,000 employees were thrown out of work by the bombings and by the fact that, as soon as the war was over, our production fell to zero. In fact, we were prohibited from making airplanes by the peace treaty. So you see it was essential that we find a new peacetime product for the sake of the Piaggio Company and our employees."*
>
> —Enrico Piaggio, *American Mercury*, 1957

1948 Vespa 125

Your ticket to la dolce vita, the original 1946 Vespa was a bare-bones, no-frills scooter: It had a single saddle seat and was powered by a 98cc engine that created a puny 3.3 hp and propelled the scooter to only 35 mph. With the introduction of Innocenti's 1947 Lambretta, Piaggio was forced to refine its model. The Lambretta came with two seats, marking it in people's minds as a more "social" scooter in the best Italian sense of the word and was powered by a 125cc engine from birth. By 1948, Piaggio matched the Lambretta by adding a second seat for side-saddle riders and creating a 125cc engine by increasing the bore, which pumped up power to 5.5 hp and top speed to 44 mph. In addition, the front and rear suspension was redesigned to give a smoother ride and combat the old problem of braking squat.
Courtesy of the Collezione Vittorio Tessera

1946–1954

Looking Fine in 1955
The Vespa was refined annually, both mechanically and physically. The early Vespas boasted a rounded voluptuousness in keeping with the robust Marilyn Monroe image of the early 1950s. By the late 1950s, the styling was facelifted, resulting in a sleeker, more bare-bones scooter that matched the Twiggy lines that were the coming rage.

1951 "Vespone"
By 1951, the Vespa was the pre-eminent scooter the world over, already a legend beyond its miniscule size. This Vespone, or giant Vespa, model was a masterpiece of understatement for the 1951 Fiera di Milano. It towered some 15ft in the air, complete with monster kickstarter and massive whitewall Pirelli tires. It was only the beginning for the motorscooter as icon.

"Piaggio & Compagnia Spa presents a lightweight utilitarian motorbike, the Vespa, with a two-stroke 98cc engine, three gears and a maximum speed of 60 km/h. Fuel consumption 50 km per liter. Maximum feasible gradient 20 percent. Deliveries will begin in April."

—First notice of the Vespa, in the Italian newspaper
Corriere dell'Informazione, March 29, 1946

Early Development of the Vespa
THE BEST SCOOTER MONEY COULD BUY

Vespa quickly became synonymous with scooter, and to many people the words are still interchangeable. Since its design was a watershed in scooter technology, many people believe it to be the first scooter ever built. Not so. In fact, the Vespa was not even the first Italian postwar scooter; the Gianca Nibbio wears that crown, and there were also early scooter prototypes built by FIAT. Instead, the Vespa was more important than being simply the first; the Vespa was the best.

Piaggio's Vespa was a scooter a grown person could ride with dignity to work or on vacation, and so the Vespa spread the good word about scooters throughout the world. The Vespa was reliable. It was economical. It protected its rider from road spray and motor oil. Its superior engineering demanded the respect of even motorcyclists. As a Calabrian scooterist told *American Mercury* magazine in 1957, "Wherever donkeys go the Vespa goes too."

In the end, the Vespa went miles further than the donkey.

Vespa Creator
Corradino d'Ascanio Speaks

D'Ascanio's Vespa was truly revolutionary, incorporating features of motorcycles (two wheels, easy-to-use handlebar-mounted controls, and saddle seats), airplanes (monocoque unit design and single-sided stub axles), and automobiles (protective bodywork, covered motor, and floorboards). In an interview with Italian RAI television, d'Ascanio told of his inspiration in creating the Vespa:

"Naturally at the beginning of the project I was terribly enthusiastic about the idea of designing something new. I did everything I could to make a critical assessment of all existing vehicles and spent sleepless nights trying to understand the project in the clearest, simplest terms.

"Then one day some ideas came to me and I sat down at the drawing board and tried to define the problem like this: I began by drawing a person sitting comfortably on a chair. I drew two wheels symmetrically in front of and behind the person, a mudguard running down from the seat and covering the wheels, and handlebars above the front wheels. Automatically, the Vespa took shape."

D'Ascanio also outlined his parameters in creating the scooter to an Italian magazine: "Having seen motorcyclists stuck at the side of the road many times with a punctured tire, I decided that one of the most important things to solve was that a flat should no longer be a large problem just like it wasn't for automobiles.

"Another problem to resolve was that of simplifying the steering, especially in city driving. To help this, the control of the gear shifting was placed on the handlebars for easy shifting without abandoning maneuverability, making its use intuitive for the novice.

"Another large inconvenience with traditional motorcycles was oil spraying on clothes, so I thought of moving the engine far from the 'pilot,' covering it with a fairing, and abolishing the open chain with a cover placing the wheel right next to the gearchange.

"Some solutions came from aeronautical technology, with which Piaggio was obviously familiar, such as the rear tubular wheel holder borrowed directly from the undercarriage of airplanes. The single shell frame surpassed even the most modern automobile design since the stamped bodywork of strengthened steel was a rarity."

Papal Blessing for the Millionth Vespa
In April 1956, the millionth Vespa rolled of the assembly line, and the occasion was marked by (surely spontaneous) celebrations throughout Europe. The million-mark was tallied from combining worldwide Vespa production; the Piaggio factory in Italy now manufactured 500 scooters a day, and factories in France, England, Germany, and elsewhere were building Vespas under license. A celebration was held in Pontedera and the Pope was there to give his beatific blessing on the scooter that had provided the wheels for Italy's reconstruction. Vespa Day was declared throughout Italy with festivities held in fifteen Italian cities, including a convoy of 2,000 Vespas traveling en masse through Rome and halting all traffic. It was all a public relations coup for Piaggio, seconded certainly only by the upcoming millionth Lambretta, which would roll off the Lambrate line in the late 1950s.

Lambretta

*"Let the wife use the family car.
Go to work on the
amazing Lambretta."*

—1950s Innocenti ad

Innocenti's Lambretta is Born

TO THE TUNE OF A DIFFERENT PLUMBER

Just months on the treads of the Vespa came Innocenti's Lambretta. The first Lambretta was as different from the Vespa as you would expect of a scooter created by a plumber versus an aviation engineer. Whereas Piaggio's d'Ascanio used a sheet-metal monocoque frame-body unit, Innocenti went with what its designers knew best—and had factories filled with—pipes.

Ferdinando Innocenti was a plumber before starting his company in 1931 to produce steel plumbing pipes and tubing. During World War II,

Innocenti produced artillery shells and pontoon bridges, but following the Fascists' defeat, Innocenti and his general director, Giuseppe Lauro, looked for a way to turn swords into plowshares. They came upon the idea of building a scooter that all of Italy could afford to own and operate.

In 1945–1946, the duo assigned engineer Pierluigi Torre to create a scooter, which they named the Lambretta after the factory's site in the Lambrate quarter of Milan.

1948 Lambretta Model A

Innocenti's Lambretta Model A was as revolutionary as Piaggio's Vespa. The Vespa was technologically advanced whereas the Lambretta was spot-on in its utilitarian design. The Lambretta was more traditional with motorcycle-like features: The chassis was a traditional tube frame, not suprising coming from Ferdinando Innocenti, a former plumber-turned-pipe manufacturer. The Model A lacked protective bodywork and had only scanty legshields compared to its chief rival, but what it fell short of in covering, it made up for with a larger 125cc engine compared to its 98cc Vespa counterpart. The two-stroke, single-cylinder measured 52 × 58 mm with its upright cylinder inclined slightly forward. Power was 4.3 hp with a top speed of 40–44 mph. Drive to the rear wheel was via an enclosed shaft with bevel gears turning the axle. The first Vespa went on sale in April 1946; by October 1947, the first Model A Lambretta rolled off the assembly lines and the race was on. Within a year, Innocenti would manufacture 9,669 of its Model A.

Courtesy of the owner: Vittorio Tessera

1949 Lambretta Model B and Happy Lass

This lass was happy to have an updated Model B. Innocenti's A was not as grand a hit as the firm had hoped for, partly because buyers lacked confidence in the elfin 7-inch tires. Thus, in December 1948, Innocenti created a revised version, called naturally enough, the B. This new model rode on larger, 8-inch wheels, featured a left-hand twist-grip gearchange using a push-pull cable system rather than a foot lever, and in an effort to keep up with Vespa, rear suspension. With the B, Innocenti had a hit.

The New Lambretta Poster

A "new" Lambretta arrived almost every other year—as did a "new" Vespa. It was tit for tat in an ongoing war between Innocenti and Piaggio in the time-honored tradition of the Romans and Visigoths, Montagues and Capulets, and everyone within the Italian government.

1946–1954

Early Development Of The Lambretta

WIN FRIENDS AND INFLUENCE PEOPLE

The Lambretta was ultimately no less influential or important than the Vespa, yet it remains even today in the shadow of its rival—except among most Mod cognoscenti and the masses of India, the latter being no small crowd.

Consider its (ongoing) history: The Lambretta spawned more numerous imitators than the Vespa (the tube frame with sheet-metal bodywork being easier to copycat), several long-lived license-built versions such as the German wünderkind NSU and the Spanish Serveta, and is still being prolifically built today in India despite being decades out of date.

**Courting Couple
and Lambretta C**
Love blossomed on two wheels
nearly everywhere around the
world, making one wonder if
Cupid was a Vespa or
Lambretta fan?

*"Americans export
Coca-Cola. Japanese
export Sonys. Russians
export Kalishnikovs.
Italians export Vespas
and Lambrettas."*

—Proverb

**1959 Lambretta
LD125 Series IV**
The D replaced the C in
1951 with a redesigned
frame, front fork tubes
enclosing the front
suspension springs, larger,
8-inch tires, and a new rear
suspension setup with the
engine hung by pivoting
links and suspended at the
rear by a single damper.
In 1954, Innocenti built its
most powerful scooter to
date, a 148cc that created
6 hp—and of course
Piaggio quickly responded
with its own 150cc model.
The LD was refined and
perfected, and with the
full bodywork, provided
everything the Vespa had
from its start. The LD
debuted in December 1951,
and the LD150 followed in
November 1954. Also in
1954, a high-class electric
start model was available.
In late 1956, the LD125/57
and LD150/57 were
launched as two-tone
luxury models.
Courtesy of the owner:
Michael Dregni

**1953 Lambretta Model
LD125 Brochure**
The new C was based on a
completely redesigned chassis
fitted with the tried-and-true
4.3 hp shaft-drive engine.
The A/B chassis with its
twin-tube construction was
replaced by a single
large-diameter main tube.
Trailing-link front suspension
eased the ride, and would
become characteristic of almost
all subsequent Lambrettas.

1946–1954

LO SCOOTER 4 MARCE 150 CC. "59"

Iso s. p. a. AUTOMOTOVEICOLI - BRESSO (Milano)

1950 Iso Diva

Iso's history followed the ups and downs of the Italian postwar economy in textbook fashion. Iso of Bresso entered the scoot market in 1948 with a resumé of building refrigerators. Like Piaggio and Innocenti, Iso owner Renzo Rivolta saw the need for economical transportation. Iso's Diva was the Ferrari of scooters, and indeed Rivolta soon turned to building his own gran turismo automobiles.

"The adventure of scooters is surprising. These tricky motors were born in Italy. Supplied with very small diameter wheels and, as a result, prone to 'gyroscopic moments' without which these machines would have literally invaded the territory of the automobile. Huge factories, populated by technicians who should know better, construct thousands of these homicidal scooters."

—Famous aviation constructor Gabriel Voisin,
Mes mille et une voitures

The Second Italian Renaissance

FATTA IN ITALIA

The Vespa and Lambretta were not the first motorscooters after World War II—they were simply the best. Other Italian firms followed suit and produced legions of scooters that swarmed over the roads of Italy in the postwar days.

The late 1940s and early 1950s were boom years for motorscooter makers. Amongst the most proaglific were the firms Iso, which debuted its first scooter in 1948 after years of having built refrigerators, and Moto Parilla, which launched its scooter in 1952. Guzzi, MV Agusta, FB Mondial, Benelli, and others all followed the leaders to the marketplace.

1953 Parilla Levriere 150

Moto Parilla was created in the back of a truck diesel-injector repair shop on the outskirts of Milan in 1946. Parilla's Levriere, or "Greyhound," debuted in 1952 as a refined scooter with a powerful 125cc engine, telescopic forks, 12-inch wheels on alloy rims, and stylish bodywork. In 1953, a 150cc version was added. The Levriere created a whole family tree of copies: Sweden's Husqvarna bought Parilla chassis in 1955 and mounted HVA engines; Germany's Victoria Peggy was a Levriere in disguise; and the Levriere was the major influence behind Zündapp's first Bella.

Courtesy of the owner: Bruno Baccari

1954–1960 Moto Rumi Formichino

There's a certain exquisite poetry in moving from manufacturing miniature submarines to building motorscooters. Like Piaggio, Donnino Rumi turned his swords into plowshares, creating Moto Rumi in Bergamo in 1949 to build eccentric motorcycles and scoots. Rumi's first scooter was the Scoiattolo, or Squirrel, followed by the Formichino, or Little Ant, of 1954–1960, which was without doubt a motorscooter masterpiece. The chassis and bodywork were of an innovative unit design cast from aluminum alloy in three structural sections that were assembled with studs. Both Rumi scooters were powered by the firm's unique 125cc horizontal two-cylinder two-stroke engine, which pushed the Ant to a top speed of 105 km/h. Normale, Lusso, Economico, Sport, and racing Bol d'Or versions were available.

RUMI 1960

"FORMICHINO" motor-scooter 125 c.c. Standard

ENGINE: twin cylinder, two-stroke, two side-by-side horizontal cylinders with ignition at 180° - bore 42 mm. - stroke 45 mm. - cylinder 124,68 c.c. 6 h.p. at 6,000 r. p. m. - compression ratio 6,5 to 1 - lubrication: the pistons, barrels and crankshaft big ends are lubricated by the petroil mixture - the crankshaft main bearings are lubricated by the oil in the gearbox crankcase - gear box in unit with engine at 4 speed shifted by foot - clutch: multiple discs in oil - primary transmission by toothed gearing, the secondary one by chain - Speed 53 miles per hour - normal consumption 113 miles per gal.

BODY: bearing body in die cast special light alloy at high resistance - petroil tank with a capacity of 1,1 gals. incorporated - front suspension is by spring forks and leading links; rear suspension by swinging arm on rubber blocks - wheels are interchangeable - tyres 3,50 x 10" - central and internal shoe brakes - electrical equipment fed by alternator flywheel - switch on the handle bar.

ENGINE: twin cylinder, two-stroke, two side-by-side horizontal cylinders with ignition at 180° - bore 42 mm. - stroke 45 mm. - cylinder 124,68 c.c. 8 h.p. at 7,200 r.p.m. - compression ratio 7 to 1 - Carburetor dell'Orto MB 22A - lubrication: the pistons, barrels and crankshaft big ends are lubricated by the petroil mixture - the crankshaft main bearings are lubricated by the oil in the gearbox crankcase - gearbox in unit with engine at 4 speed shifted by foot - clutch by multiple disks in oil - primary transmission by toothed gearing, the secondary one by chain - speed 62 miles per hour - normal consumption 81 miles per gal.

"FORMICHINO" motor-scooter 125 c.c. Sport

RUMI FOND. OFFICINE - BERGAMO - Via G. B. Moroni, 255 - Tel. 36-888

1946–1954

1952 Bernardet 250 BM
Once free of German shackles, the Bernardet Frères set to work after the war producing some of the most chic putt-putts to be seen on in front of the neighborhood Bistro. The long wheelbase offered stability rarely seen on imports, and the split-single 250cc Violet engine on most Bernardets made them win any drag race with a Vespa. In the mid-Fifties, French fascination with cowboys hit the Salon de Paris as a Texan version of a Bernardet complete with saddlehorn on the pillion pad, leather fringe hanging from the handlebars, and simulated rhinestone saddlebags. Unfortunately for the rest of the world, Bernardets were seldom seen outside France.

Scooters *à la Française*

ZUT ALORS! SCOOTERING IS FRENCH

While France can boast some of the earliest scooters—the Auto-Fauteuil and the Monet-Goyon—the 1950s were boom years for French scooters, many of which never were sold beyond its borders.

The Bernardet brothers designed outlandish two-tone styling and never-copied bodywork that gave the illusion of speed. What's the point of going fast if people can't see you? The long wheelbase offered a sturdy ride in all models, unfortunately for scooter aficionados everywhere, Bernardets never crossed the Rhine, English Channel, or Pyrenées for the rest of the world to gawk at pure speed standing still.

While most scooter manufacturers were looking for a quick buck in what they thought was a scooter gold mine, Peugeot entered the scooter world for keeps. To prove the longevity of their two-strokes, two French Air Force marshalls braved a ride from Saigon to Paris in 1956 arriving on the Champs-Elysées to almost as much fanfare as Lindbergh's transatlantic flight from New York.

1950s Peugeot S55 and S57
"La Petite Auto à 2 Roues et à 2 Places" was Peugeot's promise. These two beautiful Peugeot scooters broadened this French carmaker's base into the world of two-strokes while other car builders were stuck in the four-wheel rut. The red Peugeot S55 dates from 1955, two years after its smashing debut in 1953, and the other Peugeot S57 from 1958, showed the world that the front fender of the scooter could be more than wasted space and put a glovebox, in the spirit of the rear-engine VW Beetle.
Courtesy of François-Marie Dumas

1952 Scootavia
The Scootavia was a brutishly beautiful scooter as only the French could build. With its four-speed gearbox and 175cc AMC engine, it had power to match.

1949 Paul Vallée
In keeping with the liberal mentality that made France great, SICRAF borrowed liberally from early Italian design of the Lambretta masking the imitation with a slightly darker paint job. This stylish S.149 model with a peppy 125cc Ydral motor was all the rage to cruise through the Arc de Triomphe on a moonlit night. Paul Vallée lost its touch, however, when it veered into the abyss of three-wheeled vehicles with a doozie called "The Singing Cleric."
Courtesy of François-Marie Dumas

LE SCOOTER 54 125 cm³

MOTOCONFORT
Ets Robert PIEL s. a.
29, avenue de la Grande-Armée, PARIS (16e). PASsy 86-45
Équipement   Accessoires
LIVRAISON RAPIDE - VENTE A CRÉDIT

162, rue Édouard-Vaillant, BEZONS (S.-et-O.). ARC. 70-58
LIVRAISON RAPIDE - VENTE A CRÉDIT
Accessoires   Équipement
MOTOBÉCANE
Ets Robert PIEL s. a.

1954 Motobécane 125 SC
Monsieur Ham debuted a Motobécane/Motoconfort scooter at the Salon de Paris in 1951 equipped with a four-stroke, 5 hp engine and style that could only come from Parisian showrooms. Lovingly dubbed the "Mobyscoot," the SC added reverse hand levers and sleek but rotund lines to Ham's original design.

La Belle and the Terrot
"La vie est belle" with a Terrot 54, proclaimed the French maker. The Terrot was one of the most unique-looking scooters of all time, resembling a primped and coiffed French poodle on wheels— beautiful, in other words. It was, indubitably, "Une Splendide Réalisation 100% Française." Bien sûr, it goes without saying: Who else could build such a motorscooter?

1946–1954

1951–1958 Maico Mobil

On the cover of Das Motorrad, *Maico called its Mobil, "Das Auto auf 2 Rädern." Dirigible on two wheels may have been more like it, but the enveloping bodywork was Maico's attempt to convince Germans that two wheels were better than four. Maico debuted the Mobil in 1950 with a herculean frame to support the armor-plated paneling. Underneath the bodywork, the Maico Mobil was more a motorcycle than scooter due to its 14-inch wheels, heavy-duty duplex-tube frame with a crossbar between the rider's legs, telescopic front forks, and its sheer bulk. Maico's own brochures said it best: "With its latest product, the Maico-Mobil, Maico have introduced a completely novel type of machine which lies mid-way between the conventional motor cycle and the scooter; it may be that this will prove to be the true touring machine of the future." The future didn't last long for the Maico Mobil, but today the car on two wheels remains one of the most amazing scooters of all time.*

German Scooter Engineering
VOLKSROLLERS: THE TINY WONDERS

Germany jumped onto the motorscooter boom at the end of the 1940s with Teutonic vigor. As German industry was wracked by the ruin caused by extensive Allied bombing, few factories had any capacity to produce their own scooters from scratch. Instead, firms licensed to assemble Italian scooters with their own nameplates: Hoffmann began assembling Vespas in 1949, NSU created Lambrettas starting in 1950, and Zündapp created its version of the Parilla Levriere starting in 1953.

By the early 1950s, the German makers had forsaken the Italian engineering for not living up to their standards and created their own scooters from the wheels up. Started by the push of an electric switch, propelled by powerful engines, and riding on supple suspension, the new breed of German scooters were among the most luxurious *volksrollers* in the world.

"In the shadow of the Wurmling Chapel, made famous by the well known song by Ludwig Unland, lies an extensive factory, animated by the spirit of progress, and staffed by men who take an intense pride in their work. This is the birthplace of Maico."

—1955 Maico Information Bulletin

1955–1957
TWN Countessa
With great fanfare, the German Triumph TWN launched its deluxe Countessa as "the whispering motorscooter" due to its smooth and quiet 200cc engine.

Goggo-Roller
The Goggo-Roller looked like a scooter that needed to lay off the sauerkraut and würst. Available with your choice of 125cc, 150cc, or 200cc engine, it needed the extra displacement simply to haul itself around.

*"Live joyfully with wings—
drive an Adler."*
—1955 Adler Junior ad

1952–1956 Bastert Einspurauto
Bastert's luxurious Einspurato, or "One-Track Automobile," was pure style on two wheels. The bodywork was designed by Frenchman M. Lepoix and beaten into German aluminum. Its 13-inch wheels and lowdown seat made for a low center of gravity and smooth ride with your choice of either a 175 or 197cc engine. Only 1,200 were made.

1946–1954

prima

Above all, the NSU-PRIMA is recognised by most people as the most beautiful motor scooter

Turquoise blue - Umber white

Better riding - PRIMA riding!

Drive better -

Drive Prima

Machines with a World-Famous Name -

Prima V · Prima III + III K   Prima II

NSU Prima Brochure
"Drive Better—Drive Prima" was the slogan for NSU's flagship scooter.

1958–1960 NSU Prima III
By 1957, the Prima was refined as the high-class Prima 175cc Fünfstern, joined by the 150cc Prima III, a simplified, democratic version of the V, of 1958–1960. The Prima was equipped with everything from electric starter to an electric fuel gauge, foglight, and radio. The Prima III was available as a K (kickstart) model from 1958–1960 and the KL ("Luxus" with electric start) for 1959–1960, The Prima V was exported worldwide and imported into the United States by Butler & Smith of New York City. Butler & Smith even got a Prima V on the Price is Right TV game show in June 1959. The correct, winning price was $555.

NSU's Five-Star Motorscooters
WITH HELP FROM LAMBRETTA AND VOLKSWAGEN

In war-torn Germany, the quickest route to scooter production was licensing with an established maker; in 1950, NSU began fabricating Lambrettas in Neckarsulm under a five-year contract using Innocenti C/LC engines shipped from the Lambrate works and bodywork stamped out at the nearby Volkswagen factory.

But the Germans had no patience for certain features of the Lambretta, which they found lacking in good Teutonic over-engineering. Soon, NSU was building the majority of components for its scooters. In 1955, the NSU-Innocenti contract expired and was not renewed. Instead, in 1956, NSU introduced a Lambretta that was not a Lambretta; this was NSU's version of what a Lambretta should be, the Prima, Italian for First.

1950s NSU Prima Production

The NSU-Innocenti contract expired in 1955 and was not renewed. Instead, in 1956, NSU introduced a Lambretta that was not a Lambretta; this was NSU's version of what a Lambretta should be.

Always competitive and class-conscious, NSU chose to call its new scooter the Prima, Italian for First. The engine was NSU's version of the shaft-drive Lambretta LC, still producing 6.2 hp.

The Prima D was only ever planned as a stopgap scooter to serve NSU's faithful during the year when the contract with Lambretta was scrapped and a new NSU scooter could be made ready.

prima

Cooling fan
Dynastarter
Crankshaft
Clutch
Gearbox
Final drive
Rear wheel brake

1957–1960
NSU Prima V Engine

German engineering at its best: NSU's amazing Prima engine. The one-cylinder two-stroke boasted a cylinder that was horizontal and transverse to the chassis. The flywheel magneto was at the front of the engine with the new four-speed gearbox to the rear of the crankshaft with a single-plate clutch mediating between the two. Final drive was via bevel gears. The complete engine unit was suspended from the frame by a front pivot mount and damped at the rear by a shock absorber with well-cushioned preload to handle the best German beer drinker. The 175cc electric-start Prima V engine had an oversquare design of 62 × 57.6 mm and a four-speed gearbox. Power was now 9.5 hp, all electrics were 12 volts, and top speed was 56 mph.

1946–1954

"It would be difficult to speak too highly of the Zündapp's navigational properties."

—Motor Cycling, December 1953

Zündapp's Beautiful Bella

THE MERCEDES-BENZ OF MOTORSCOOTERS

In 1951, Zündapp strived to jump on the scooter bandwagon. The firm developed a scooter prototype itself, but decided to go the easy route that NSU had gone in licensing to build Lambrettas. Seeing that Vespa and Lambretta were already being sufficiently copied, Zündapp built its Bella scooter based on the 1952 125cc Parilla Levriere.

Throughout the 1950s, Zündapp continued to refine its scooter into one of the best machines on the autobahn.

1964–1984
Zündapp R50

Basking in the Greek sun, this 50cc model replaced the grand old Bella in 1964 as the times were a changing. And in creating this new model, Zündapp turned away from the now-defunct Parilla model back to Lambretta and its new Slimline design with easily removable side panels, headlamp on the handlebars, 10-inch wheels, and handlebar gear change. The 49cc engine was based on the Zündapp Falconette moped. Unfortunately, the company fell on hard economic times in 1985 after producing a total of 130,680 scooters; the entire Zündapp stock and machinery were sold to China. Approximately 1,500 Chinese workers went overland to Munich by train to pack up all the equipment to ship to the People's Republic. During the two weeks of loading, the Chinese workers slept in the packing crates to save money.

Een scooter van aanzien . . . . om mee gezien te worden

Bella R203 Brochure
The first Bella of 1953–1955 was the R150, soon followed by the R200 of 1954–1955. For 1953 only, Zündapp created the Suburbanette, designed and named for the great American suburbs; sold only in the USA, it was never a success story, and today remains the rarest Zündapp scooter. The Bella was upgraded for 1955–1956 as the R151 and R201, now with restyled bodywork and electric start from 12 volt electrics. In 1956 came the R153 and R203, followed by the Bella R154 of 1956–1958 and R204 of 1957–1959. The rare Bella R175S was built from 1961–1964 alongside the last of the 200cc models, the 200 Type 551-026 and 200 Type 560-025 of 1959–1962. By the early 1960s, sales had plummeted and only about 2,000 of each of these models were made. The Bella's beautiful life was over.

The Family Bella
In postwar Germany, a Bella was indeed a beautiful thing, providing transportation for the whole family as the country rebuilt.

1946–1954

**1946 Fuji Rabbit
and Happy Woman**
In 1946, Fuji Heavy Industries
of Tokyo created Japan's first
motorscooter, the Rabbit, the same
year as the first Vespas went into
production on the other side of the
world. In that year, only eight
Rabbits were built but in the
following years the assembly lines
multiplied production to make the
scoot's namesake proud. The Rabbit
was a rustic little scooter, similar in
style to prewar American models;
Fuji had done its homework.
A padded cushion provided seating
and suspension; a luggage rack was
mounted behind. The Rabbit was
based on a 135cc four-stroke single
producing 2 hp. Top speed was an
ambitious 55 km/h.

Mobilizing Japan

THE AMERICAN SCOOTER'S RISING SUN

Italy's Vespa and Lambretta have always overshadowed the development of other motorscooters, but following World War II Japanese companies responded as quickly as the Italians to their country's need for cheap transportation by building scooters. The first Japanese scooter was offered in 1946, the same year as the Vespa. The premier scooter, named the Rabbit, was built by Fuji of Tokyo. Mitsubishi, a builder of the famed Zero-San fighter for the Japanese Air Force, followed in 1948 with its Pigeon scooter.

Not surprisingly considering the proximity to the US and their lightning-fast inception, these first Japanese scooters copied the style of prewar US scooters. Fuji scooter engineers had done their homework well, and the early Rabbits followed the tenets of scooter design laid down by the Salsbury way back in 1936–1937.

While these first scooters were clear copies of postwar US designs and were rustic at best, Japan soon developed efficient luxury scooters as good as any ever built by the Germans. The Japanese appetite for scooters was as strong as the Italians. In 1946, just eight scooters were built in Japan, all by Fuji; by 1954, more than 450,000 scooters were on the road with the country's total production at 50,000 annually. By 1958, total annual production was 113,218.

1950 Mitsubishi Pigeon C-21
During World War II, Mitsubishi was one of several builders of the Zero-San for the Japanese air force. Like Piaggio, the postwar Mitsubishi turned its talents in aircraft engineering to the field of scooters. In 1948, Mitsubishi introduced its first Pigeon, the C-11 with a 1.5hp 115cc two-stroke engine and pure Salsbury Motor-Glide styling. In the 1950s, the Pigeons began breeding offspring models. The C-21 was introduced in 1950 with a 150cc two-stroke engine of 3hp. From the late 1940s and into the 1960s, Fuji and Mitsubishi would control the Japanese scoot market as a Far Eastern Piaggio–Innocenti zaibatsu duo.

1954 Fuji Rabbit S-61 III
It was still too soon to forget the war—especially when the Japanese were building better scooters than the American models—so when Mitsubishi's fabulous Silver Pigeon line was imported into the United States by the Rockford Scooter Co. of Rockford, Illinois, no mention was made that these scooters were built by the Japanese firm that also built the infamous Zero-San fighter. In fact, with anti-Japanese sentiment still running high in the late 1950s, no mention was made that these were even Japanese scooters—invoking memories of Pearl Harbor would not have sold scooters. Rockford also wholesaled Silver Pigeons to Montgomery Ward, which sold them through its vast mail-order catalog as Riversides. This 1954 C-57 was powered by a side-valve 192cc engine producing 4.3 hp.

1955 Honda KB
Soichiro Honda's story is a classic Horatio Alger rags to riches tale—translated into Japanese. Born the son of a village blacksmith, he got his start producing a radical new piston ring pre-World War II. During the war, his fledgling company built wooden propellers for the Japanese air force. After the war, Honda turned his hand to designing economical motorbikes and scooters. Honda first created a motorized bicycle, the Model A, in 1947 and built it in a shed. In 1953, the motorbike gave way to the first Cub clip-on motor, which developed into the Cub moped line that continued all the way into the 1980s as the Passport. Honda built its first scooter in 1954, the Juno KA, based on a 189cc OHV engine. In 1955, the KB replaced the KA with a 220cc OHV engine of 9hp. The styling of these first Honda scooters was either bizarre or futuristic, depending on your point of view. It continued the Japanese scooter design philosophy of more is better, and was dressed up with miles of molding.

1946–1954

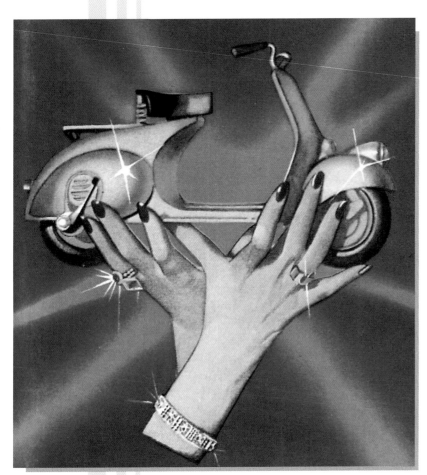

Scootering English Style

A VACATION INSPIRATION

While on vacation to sunny Italy in 1948, Englishman Claude McCormack, chief of the venerable Douglas motorcycle firm, got religion. While other tourists were swatting at the menace of the Italian scooters buzzing like insects around the Trevi fountain, McCormack saw a gold mine on wheels. Douglas began importing Vespas, showing its first "Douglas" Vespa at the 1949 Earls Court Show in London, and plans were announced to build 10,000 Vespas in England. It was the beginning of a long, prosperous history of English-built scooters.

Other English motorcycle makers such as Triumph, BSA, Velocette, Excelsior, and even the high-and-mighty Vincent with its Piatti tie-in launched scooters in the coming years. And a host of upstart makers also hawked their wares, including the infamous Lawrence Bond, whose various two-and three-wheeled scooter and micro-car creations are recalled by the British today with much the same fondness the country feels for the V-1 rocket.

"These are to Certify that by direction of His Royal Highness The Prince Philip, Duke of Edinburgh, I have appointed Douglas (Kingswood) Ltd. into the place and quality of Suppliers of Vespa Scooters to His Royal Highness . . . ."

—1967 Royal Warrant for the supply of Vespa to HRH Prince Philip

1959–1965 Triumph Tigress

Hailing from the beloved Triumph motorcycle company, the Tigress bore a name that was the feminine version of the famed Tiger motorcycle. Underneath the bulbous bodywork was an engine heads above any other scooter of the era: a four-stroke 250cc vertical twin with overhead valves! Performance of the 250cc engine was all a scooterist could have wished for—in fact, the 250cc prototype was so fast it had to be detuned for production. But the Tigress was not a success, arriving in the market with too much too late. Everyone within Triumph seemed to understand this except management. Don J. Brown, sales manager for the US West Coast importer, wrote a confidential letter in 1958 prophesying the scooter's failure. Brown stated that "My own view has been from the beginning that we are facing a 'market drift' from what . . . this country needs in the way of scooters." In fact it was a market drift from what any country needed. Just close your eyes and think of England.

1959 Excelsior Monarch

Excelsior of Birmingham arrived on the scooter market in 1959 with its stately, plump Monarch scooter powered by a 147cc two-stroke.

Piatti

In a realm of bizarre scooters, the Piatti was a king among kings. Vicenzo Piatti built the elfin scoot in England in the early 1950s around a dwarf 125cc engine. Its styling was quaint, curious, and downright silly—all winning it a crown among equals.

Courtesy of the owner: Vittio Tessera

1946–1954

The Social Appliance

REBUILDING THE WORLD IN THEIR OWN LIKENESS

Innocenti called its scooter a "social appliance" in what was probably an off-target Italian-to-English translation. Nevertheless, the term carried a much larger truth.

Bad times begat motorscooters, and spawned by the thousands in struggling, diehard factories throughout Europe, scooters provided the wheels on which Europe's immediate postwar reconstruction rode. Scooters were inexpensive social appliances in many senses of the word—inexpensive to purchase, repair, and operate—and soon became a necessity. Scooters carried food to market, brought the country to the city and the city to the country, spread ideas and culture, transported Romeo in search of Juliet, and almost overnight carried Italy and much of the rest of Europe into the modern world; it was the dawn of a second European renaissance.

By the time people had more money in their pockets—due in part to their trusty steed, the scooter—those same scooterists turned their backs on their Vespas and made a down payment on a FIAT 500, Volkswagen, or Citroën 2CV. Many people turned their scooters over to their children, or junked them by the thousands to scrap metal yards, remembering their faithful scooter with all the fondness of a carpet bombing.

The road to recovery had been steep, but the two-stroke, exhaust-burping, oil-burning scooter had climbed the hill.

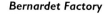

Bernardet Factory
*Not only were motorscooters easy to use
and technologically advanced, but there
were also thousands of them rolling off the
assembly lines and so they were inexpensive
to purchase and own. More scooters than
cars were built in the immediate postwar
years as scooter design was simpler and
production required less capital on the part
of a startup or recovering company. And
many firms of all types in postwar Europe
offered their employees time payment plans
to purchase scooters.*

Cruising Main Street on the Grocery Getter

The ideal grocery getter—with an air of elegance. In the post-World War II years, Mrs. Mary R. Spoor, 71, tooled around Danville, Illinois, on her Cushman Glide-Kar three-wheeler to do her shopping and visiting.

1952 Norwegian Homebuilt Scooter

After the dark days of World War II, commodities such as food and motorscooters were not easy to come by. In Norway, taxi-driver Kristoffer Gjevre spotted a newspaper picture of an Italian scooter, but such a social appliance was not available in the frozen north. So, in his spare time, he built this "Bigge" in his garage using wheelbarrow wheels, DKW motorcycle brakes, sawn-off 1920s Harley-Davidson front forks, and a DKW 98cc engine. The front fender, legshield, and floorboards were made of homebent sheet metal whereas the engine cover was crafted from plywood. All in all, it was a modern scooter that balanced so well it could be driven hands off. Painted a brilliant green, it was a confirmation present for his son, Ole, who drove it every summer day—and still proudly pilots it today. Courtesy of Ole Birger Gjevre

"The best way to fight Communism in this country [Italy] is to give each worker a scooter, so he will have his own transportation, have something valuable of his own, and have a stake in the principle of private property."

—Enrico Piaggio, Time magazine, 1952

NSU Prima V as a Second Car

The NSU Prima Fünfstern of 1957–1960 was the ideal second car for the German plutocrat. With engineering to inspire envy in Mercedes-Benz owners of the time, the Prima was perhaps the foremost luxury scooter of all time—and it boasted almost as many chrome doodads, extraneous lights, and jet-styled airscoops as the best cars of the late 1950s. The suspension was even tuned for heavy-duty doppelbock consumption.

1948 Lowther Lightnin'
Lowther modestly hailed its wares as "The 'Park Avenue' Scooter with the 'Main Street' Price." The weird styling was enough to make any scooterist green with envy. Lowther built scooters for several years, even badge-engineering putt-putts for the great Indian motorcycle firm, but when's the last time you've seen one? Those Park Avenue types probably have them all hoarded away.

"Advice to Teenagers: When it comes to combs and scooters, never a borrower or a lender be. Instead, start dropping hints to Mom and Dad about the new Topper."

—Harley-Davidson Topper ad

Scooters Made in America

A SEPARATE AND DISTINCT SPECIES

The United States was the Galápagos Islands of motorscooters. American scooters were a species that evolved on its own separate from the other continents—and without the benefit of "inspiration" from other scooter makers. While American scooters—especially the prewar Salsbury—were influential to many Japanese and a handful of European scooter makers, US makers largely ignored the styling and engineering advances made in Europe and the Far East—until it was too late.

Salsbury's scooters were so successful prewar that they were bought up by AVION, Inc., which soon came under control of the fledgling Northrop Aviation Corporation; by 1949, Northrop had given up on scooters.

Other makers were more successful. Moto-Scoot and Mead continued to prosper, as did newcomers such as Mustang. In fact, scooters were on such a boom that mail-order merchandisers like Sears Roebuck and Co., Montgomery Ward, and Gambles began selling massive quantities of scooters by mail. It was the dawn of a new scooter golden age in the USA.

1964 Mustang Stallion

The Mustang was certainly a different breed of steed. The story began with a budding young Californian engineer named Howard Forrest who loved to race anything with an engine. In the 1930s, he ran midget sprint cars, which formed the source of two mainstays of Mustang design: powerful small-bore engines and small wheels. He toyed with motorcycles before joining forces with entrepreneur John Gladden to produce the first Mustang Colt of 1945–1947. Half motorcycle, half scooter, it ran on 12-inch wheels, was powered by a prewar English Villiers single, and was named in honor of the P-51 Mustang fighter of World War II. Mustang continued to roll out new models, including the revived Colt of 1956–1958, Pony of 1959–1965, Bronco of 1959–1965, Stallion of 1959–1965, Thoroughbred of 1960–1965, and Trail Machine of 1962–1965. Mustang's demise came with the arrival of Honda; the year 1965 was a sad one for American motorscooters as Cushman curtailed production of its Silver Eagle line and Mustang production was grinding to a halt.

Courtesy of the owner: Jim Kilau

1960–1965 Harley-Davidson Topper

The Harley-Davidson Topper was a Hell's Angels starter scooter, complete with the coveted pull-start engine that would wow them on main street Sturgis. The first Topper was released in 1960 to fanfare promoting it as "Tops in beauty and tops in performance." The Topper boasted a two-cycle 10ci (165cc) engine laying on its side with the single cylinder facing to the front, which was supposed to eliminate the need for a cooling fan. The Scootaway automatic transmission used a centrifugal clutch and V-belt with final drive by chain; ratios were "infinitely variable." As this 1960 ad puffed, "Mom's a Topper fan, too! She likes its good looks: sharp, clean lines molded in tough beautiful fiberglass." That's perhaps because mom recognized the Topper's styling influence: her new Frigidaire. By the end of 1965, the Topper was but a memory. Harley-Davidson chose to follow the road traveled by Cushman in cancelling its scooter and shifting to golf carts. Harley-Davidson is probably still kicking its corporate self for building this one.

1940s American Moto-Scoot

Moto-Scoot was back after World War II as the American Moto-Scoot, yet little else had changed but the name. In 1946, Salsbury would debut its radically innovative Super-Scooter Model 85 and even Cushman's new 50 Series "Turtlebacks" had developed since prewar days. Moto-Scoot, however, was a holdover to the past. The styling had changed to look like a humpbacked wedding cake on wheels, but even this facelift when meshed with the old-fashioned motor dated the Moto-Scoot. Still, the company kept churning out scooters in a vast array of models. But the honeymoon was over, and Moto-Scoot was gone by the mid-1950s.

**1947 Salsbury
Super-Scooter Model 85**
Northrop produced the
Model 85 for two years
during which time Foster
Salsbury estimated that a
mere 700–1,000 units
were built and sold,
including exports to
Germany. But as Salsbury
remembered of the Model
85's demise, "Demand fell
off when cars started
becoming available again
and Northrop halted
production." It was a sad
finale for a great scooter.
Courtesy of the owner:
Vittorio Tessera

Salsbury's Super-Scooter Spaceship

BUCK ROGERS' WILDEST DREAM COME TRUE

It was the motorscooter to make Buck Rogers green with envy, an unblinking vision of a bountiful future for the scooterist, as new as tomorrow and twice as flashy. It was the Salsbury Super-Scooter Model 85, in Standard and Deluxe versions.

From stem to stern it was chock full of technical wonders, innovative inventions, and the truly bizarre. It was the motorscooter that made Cushman's "Turtleback" look like a Model T, the Vespa look like it was designed by Rip Van Winkle, and the Lambretta as if it had crawled out from under a prehistoric rock.

It was also too much of a good thing, didn't sell, and was gone from the market within three years.

> *"Even the fast-flying airplane has to rely on the lowly
> scooter when taxiing into a parking area at the airport."*
>
> —Popular Mechanics, 1947

1947 Salsbury Super-Scooter Model 85 Brochure

The new Super-Scooter was hailed by Northrop as the "Most Completely Automatic Vehicle Ever Built." The engine was a Salsbury-built 6 hp four-stroke single-cylinder set at an angle toward the rear of the scooter. It featured the exclusive Straight-Shot carburetion system with a short, but admittedly angled intake manifold. Nevertheless, the 1946 brochure promised the power "will take you up steep hills at car speed." The torque converter was standard on both models, and for further ease of operation, the 1946 brochure didn't even use the words throttle or brake when describing the two control pedals: they were simply the Stop and Go pedals. The 85 DeLuxe, however, could be ordered with an auxiliary hand throttle. Perhaps the most interesting feature of the new 85 was the one-sided front forks with a stub axle inspired by airplane strut design. But the suspension was provided by two, different-rate coil springs housed within an elongated steering head. At the rear, a single coil spring did the damping. Within the tail body-work was a spare tire and luggage compartment "ample for most shopping trips." The 85 had come a long way from the Motor Glide.

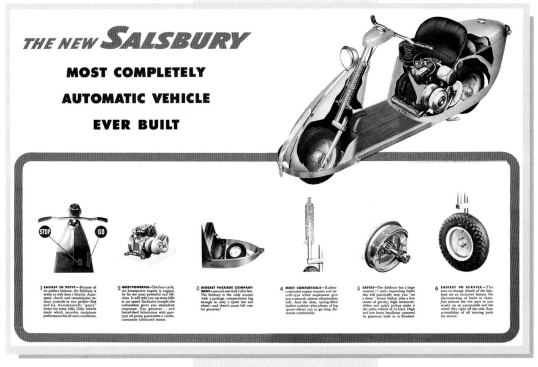

THE NEW **SALSBURY**

MOST COMPLETELY
AUTOMATIC VEHICLE
EVER BUILT

Martha Vickers and 1947 Salsbury Super-Scooter

It was outrageous. It was radical. It was the motorscooter of the future—and destined to be the most desirable motorscooter of all time.

1946–1954

The Classic Cushman "Turtleback"

THE ALL-AMERICAN MOTORSCOOTER

World War II was good to the Cushman Motor Works. Cushman came out of the dark war days on top of the US scooter world after years of building military motorscooters.

In 1948, Cushman launched its new line, the 50 Series, which won the hearts of American scooterists and was bestowed with the affectionate nickname of the "Turtleback" due to its streamlined rear engine cover design. Cushman kept the look through the 60 Series.

But the end was in sight for the good old Cushman. In 1949, Cushman debuted its new miniature motorcycle, the Eagle, which soon took over the sales lead from the venerable "Turtleback."

In 1957, two important events took place for Cushman. On May 10, 1957, the Ammons family sold Cushman to Outboard Marine Corp. (OMC), the long-time maker of Johnson and Evinrude outboard motors. Also in 1957, the step-through scooter was redesigned as the 720 Series with "modern" looks that resembled a refrigerator on two wheels. The classic Cushman "Turtleback" was gone—but never forgotten.

> *"Cushman is ready for the boom in business. Its president, Robert H. Ammon, has had the company working on 'Detroit' principles for several years. Under its former job-shop setup, Cushman couldn't begin to turn out its present volume—over 10,000 scooters a year. But by scaling assembly line techniques down to small-plant operation, Ammon has pushed dollar volume up to $35 million a year—90 percent of it from scooter sales—and steered the company into first place among U.S. scooter manufacturers."*
>
> —Business Week, August 19, 1950

1949 Cushman Model 62 Flyer
Lilliputians everywhere rejoiced at the arrival of the new Model 62. "It's Twice the Scooter!" proclaimed Cushman, ushering in a new era of gigantic scooter sales numbers.

Cushman Serves the World!
Cushman's 52 was the all-American scooter. In late 1948, it was replaced by the 62 Pacemaker. The new 60 Series were powered by a variety of engines: the 4 hp Husky was the staple; a 5 hp version was optional.

1957 Cushman 720 Series Step Thru
In 1957, Cushman debuted its radical new 720 Series of scooters to replace the classic "Turtleback" 60 Series. The new 722 Pacemaker and 725 RoadKing models carried over the 60 Series names but little else. Almost everything had been redesigned and modernized—especially the new bodywork, which was either as "modern-as-tomorrow" or just boxy, depending on how you looked at it. Cushman said the new design had "eye-catching beauty" and termed the styling "streamlined." Whether you agreed or not, the value of any streamlining was dubious anyway at a 40 mph top speed.

"Second Car" Out of the Picture?
Following the war, Cushman continued to promote the economy of the scooter as a second car, but the market in America was shifting. The Cushman may have been the land yacht of motorscooters, but in the boom years of the 1950s, most people could afford a second car, and scooters became a novelty item for hobbyists and teens.

1946–1954

1949 Vespa Record-Setter
By the late 1940s, the war between Piaggio and Innocenti moved to the racetracks, where full-bore road-race and record-setting Vespas and Lambrettas outdid each other at record paces. One week, Vespa owned the world scooter speed record, only to be beaten by Lambretta the next. Throughout the 1940s and 1950s, both firms built a long line of works racers; this record-setter was thinly based on a production Vespa, and Piaggio even built a special prototype for a Sport scooter backed by a belief that as the economy recovered, there would be demand for a high-performance sporting model. The timing of the Sport prototype was too early, but the idea was sound; Piaggio's great Gran Sport model would use features of the racing and record-setters.

"I could have been riding it hands off at 100 mph."

—Mustang record-setter Walt Fulton on his 100.0 mph average in four runs at Rosamond dry lake, California in April 1952

Timekeeper and 1954 Vespa
Keeping time for Scuderia Ferrari's Formula 1 racing team, was this bella donna *with her Vespa.*

The World's Fastest Motorscooters

LAND SPEED RECORDS ON 10-INCH WHEELS

Innocenti started it all. In October 1950, scooter pilots Masetti, Romolo Ferri, and Dario Ambrosini ran a Lambretta Model B 1,592 km at an average speed of 132.6 km/h. Lambretta held the world's scooter speed record, and naturally this galled Piaggio. Early in 1951, Vespa struck back and beat the Lambretta record, upping the ante to 170 km/h. In August 1951, Ferri set a score of world records—one of which was not broken for more than 20 years—on a super-streamlined Lambretta. His top speed with the 125cc torpedo was an astonishing 121 mph. In 1965, Englishwoman Marlene Parker topped 130 mph with a 200cc Lambretta but the FIM ruled it unofficial.

Throughout the 1950s, Piaggio and Innocenti battled it out for top-speed supremacy in a never ending attempt to best the other. Surprisingly, this war for speed and endurance was largely ignored by other European scooter makers who left Innocenti and Piaggio to their own devices. On the other side of the pond, however, American makers Mustang and Powell dueled with each other for the speed title on the dry lakes of California and the Bonneville Salt Flats.

1949 Lambretta Road Racer and Model B

"33 World Records conquered by the motor scooter Lambretta" shouted this display. Motor scooter was used loosely here; compare the stock Model B in the foreground with the factory-built road racer—yes, the nuts and bolts were interchangeable between the stock and race versions, but little else. Road racing and record-setting were just two further arenas for the Vespa and Lambretta gladiators to do battle throughout the 1940s, 1950s, and 1960s.
Courtesy of the Collezione Vittorio Tessera

1959 Vespa GS Racers in the Giro di Tre Mare

Wherever there was a street that could be closed off on Sunday, scooter, motorcycle, and bicycle races were held in Italy. Production-racer scooters such as the 150 Grand Sport ruled the races, beating all comers—especially the Lambrettas before the TV found speed and reliability—in the early 1960s.

1951 Lambretta Recordsetter

Scooter speed records might appear to be an oxymoron, but that's just the point! This Lambretta hit 190kmh in 1951—a truly impressive and terrifying thought. Any relationship to your street Lambretta is purely coincidental.

100 mph Grocery Getters

In the 1990s, scooter racing continues in Italy, England, and the United States as well as other countries. The American Scooter Racing Association was formed in 1989 by Vince Mross of West Coast Lambretta Works in San Diego. ASRA holds several races annually in southern California with hot-rodded Vespas and Lambrettas in a range of stock and modified classes. Custom-framed Lambrettas with Jet 200 or 200 SX engines are at the top of the class.

We've taken something designed to go to the grocery store and made them go 100 mph."

—Scooter racer Chito Cajayon, *Cycle World,* 1991

A souped-up Lambretta leads two Vespas through a twisty in American Scooter Racing Association action. Any relation to a 500cc Grand Prix Honda—or a stock scooter—is purely accidental. ASRA

Motorscooter Racers

HANGING OFF AND RUBBING KNEES

Put a human being on two wheels, add motive power, and you just have to see how fast you can go. And if you meet another similarly equipped human, you have a race.

Scooterists started racing each other the first day two of them met on a road. The first organized races took place in postwar Italy when a scooter offered the ideal entry into road racing on a budget that could not afford the latest FB Mondial motorcycle or even a resurrected prewar Guzzi racer. Naturally, it was Piaggio and Innocenti who went for each other's jugulars in the scooter class, with occasional challenges from Rumi.

The year 1955 saw the birth of true scooter racing when the French 24-hour Bol d'Or endurance race was staged at the Montlhéry circuit with scooters competing in classes for standard, sport, and racing models. In that first year, a 150cc Lambretta ran in the 175cc motorcycle class finishing 25th overall and first in class. In 1956, despite legshield-to-legshield competition from Rumi, Lambretta continued to rule.

Off the English coast, the Isle of Man Scooter Rally attracted hundreds of scooter racers in a competition that mimicked the famous motorcycle Tourist Trophy, or TT, race that circled the island. In the United States, NASCAR, the stock car racing association, sanctioned oval dirt-track scooter racing with the premiere held in July 1959 at the New York City Polo Grounds baseball stadium. In typical dirt-tracking stance, the driver would slide the scooter through turns with one foot out.

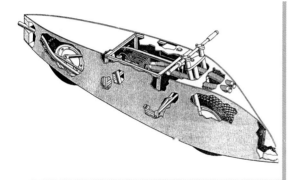

1950 Powell Streamliner
In 1950, war was declared between American scooter makers Powell and Mustang. A land speed record Mustang hit 86.12 mph; Powell vowed to fight back. In its Experimental Department, Powell's Tony Capanna built a hot-rod P-81 that he believed would top 100 mph. He reworked a P-81 engine to 28ci (458cc) run on 10 percent nitro-methane fuel. Capanna then lowered the frame stance for better aerodynamics and built a streamlined body of 1/8-inch plywood that looked a capsized dinghy; he rode on top like a shipwrecked sailor trying to stay afloat. Cycle magazine reported in January 1951 that Capanna set a new class record at El Mirage dry lake: 83.83 mph average.

> *"The sport of racing merits special consideration whether in and of itself or whether for its singular values. This sport that you cultivate requires a certain force of character, a harmonious force of the whole body whose energy manifests itself above all in the loyalty and in the disciplines of life. But more efficacious and more exalted is the reality of your symbolic race toward the glory of eternal life. Since you are loyal to the Christian life and you want to conquer not just a trophy that can be passed on to other hands, but a holy, indestructible crown."*
>
> —Pope Pius XII to the Vespisti racers of Italy in the 1950s

Lambretta V-Twin Racing Motorcycle

In 1950–1951, Innocenti created a motorcycle—and it was a masterpiece, a 250cc double-overhead-cam V-Twin racer. Designed by Ing. Pierluigi Torre, who was responsible for the Lambretta scooter, and Ing. Salmaggi, responsible for the Gilera Saturno and Parilla dohc motorcycles, it was first shown to an awed public at the 1950 Salone di Milano.

1951 Lambretta 250cc Bialbero
Innocenti's secret weapon, the 250cc double-overhead-cam V-Twin racing motorcycle created in 1950–1951. The V of the engine ran transverse to the chassis in the style of Moto Guzzi's V-Twins. Each cylinder measured square at 54 × 54 mm. Originally beginning life with a single overhead cam on each cylinder, it was modified to dohc to produce 29 hp at 9500 rpm. Drive to the rear wheel was via a shaft as used on the Lambretta scooters of the time. Earl Workman Collection

Innocenti had aspirations of contesting the 250cc Grand Prix class, but in the end, the 250cc V-Twin was run at only a handful of races. Its best showing came in August 1952 at Locarno, where Romolo Ferri was running second to Fergus Anderson's Guzzi Gambalunghino before retiring.

So the Lambretta retreated without ever winning a race. Or did it? Perhaps it had won the most important race it could have competed in, that of showing the rest of the Italian industry that Innocenti could build a motorcycle to be reckoned with should any other major maker think of building a scooter.

1954 Vespa and New York Calendar Girl
The 1954 Piaggio calendar took Vespisti on a tour of the world, from Rome to Egypt to New York, showing the "natives" and the uses they put to their Vespas. Christmas shopping in Gotham was made easy by the Vespa 125cc, but the ride must have been a bit chilly in such a short skirt. The mink stole no doubt saved the day.

La Bella Donna And Lo Scooter

SEX APPEAL FOR BOTH SEXES

Sex sold scooters just as well as sex sells most everything from laundry detergent to beer. But with motorscooters in the 1950s, advertising the putt-putts by draping a member of the female persuasion over the flowing bodywork served as a twisted double entendre.

Sure, a calendar pinup of Gina Lollobrigida straddling a Vespa inspired many an Italian boy with dreams of that 1954 150cc with its new 57 × 57mm square engine. But the scooter companies' advertising was sex appeal in another sense of the word as well.

The calendars and ads also promoted the idea of owning a Vespa to women. The scooter was easy to operate, didn't spray road grime or engine oil on you due to its stylish all-encompassing bodywork, and you could wear a dress while driving it, versus a motorcycle or even a car, which made you hitch up your skirt on entry and exit. The scooter was a fashion accessory along with lipstick, painted fingernails, and high heels—and you could operate it while wearing lipstick, painted fingernails, and high heels.

Lambretta
INNOCENTI

Jayne Mansfield

What's Your Astrological Sign?
Brigitte Bardot sang that nothing came between her and her Harley-Davidson, which was supposed to make you wonder what she wasn't wearing when she rode her cycle. Piaggio of course could not be upstaged by that, and in this 1960s calendar pinup offered the ideal riding outfit for your Vespa: a fur coat. And nothing more.

Jayne Mansfield and Lambretta Li125
Gentlemen prefer Lambrettas.

Eve, the Apple, and a Dürkopp Diana
Tempting indeed was the Diana, with its 194cc 12 hp engine that was good for an alluring 100 km/h top speed. German maker Dürkopp called on the gods to assure its scooter's fortune; in honor of the goddess of forests, it named its two-wheeled temple the Diana. The Diana's introduction in 1954 was splashed across Dürkopp ads when Miss Germany "won" a Diana and posed on her beloved scooter for a photo op. Three different Diana models were offered: the basic Diana of 1954–1959, and the Diana TS 175 and Diana TS 200 Sport of 1959–1960.

1946–1954

89

Shake, Rattle, and Roll

THE SOMETIMES FINE ART OF MOTORSCOOTER ENGINEERING

In the beginning, there was the Big Bang, then followed the putt-putt. Motorscooters missed out on some of the finesse afforded by evolution, however.

In the marketplace it was always survival of the fittest, of course, but no one ever blamed motorscooters for being mechanically advanced. Sure, scooters were innovative in their packaging, shoehorning motorcycle components into a dwarf chassis. And yes, they were inexpensive to buy, meaning they had to also be inexpensive to build and thus used inexpensive components. In sum, many a scooter could take you from point A to point B—but not all of them could bring you back again.

Consider the engineering history of America's pride, Cushman, the name that has become synonymous with motorscooters in the United States. Founded by cousins Everett and Clinton Cushman, the two had to continually repeat basic engineering courses at the University of Nebraska. Everett soon dropped out. The valiant Clinton sweated for seven years to be awarded a bachelor's degree in electrical engineering. Meanwhile, the dynamic duo were creating their first Cushman engine in their basement in 1901, an engine that became the foundation of their empire of boat, farming, lawn mower, and scooter motors.

Not to pick solely on Cushman, of course, consider the wise and wonderful Piaggio Vespa as well. Academics look back at the Vespa as a marvel of scooter engineering. In truth it was a marvel of economy. Launched in 1946 by a firm emerging from World War II with its factory reduced to rubble by a B-17's concept of urban renewal, the Vespa was crafted from leftover, war-surplus parts. Legend has it that the engine was a rehabilitated version of a Piaggio bomber's starter engine and the novel single-sided front strut was war-surplus aircraft landing gear.

The Vespa's most renowned innovation, its steel monocoque chassis-body, was also a brilliant cost-saving invention. In the war-torn economy of the late-1940s, metal for fabrication was at a premium; Ferrari, the grand gran turismo car builder, even sent workers out in the dark of night to dismantle metal advertising signs to be reused as bodywork. For Piaggio, what was more creative in terms of both engineering and the bottom line than building a single chassis-body unit instead of doubling the raw material needed to build a separate frame and body?

Piaggio was also in such a holy rush to bring its scooter to market ahead of Ferdinand Innocenti that the firm accordioned years of prototype testing into weeks. Test drivers roared along dirt backroads sans air filters on the carburetors; the dust ingested sped up the engine's destruction and Piaggio engineers did their best to factor in the effects of age. Lo and behold, the Vespa went from prototype to production in a blink of the eye—or should that be, wink.

Back at the ranch at Cushman, product testing was reduced to the level of an art. The military-spec Model 51 Airborne scooter was "perfected" by hoisting it with a rope strung over a stiff branch on a tall tree behind the factory and then unceremoniously dropped. Broken bits were fixed, and once the scooter reached the point where it didn't bust anymore, the design was ready.

Even then, few scooter makers in the early years had such a thing as quality control. Long-time Cushman worker Donald R. Yates remembered, "We never got all the boo-boos out of them." Others tell of a safety inspector in the Cushman factory who had to jump for his life from a runaway scooter.

Engines were the weak link as they did the most work. The full bodywork hid the motor—and told the hidden story: Scooters were created for people who didn't want road spray on their clothes or dirt under their fingernails. Thus the 1,000-mile checkup was usually but a wistful dream. Engines worked overtime and got no vacation; they wore out, burned oil, backfired, wouldn't start, seized, and blew up like hand grenades. All of this meant full-time jobs for budding youths in the newly created scooter service profession. Whether they were cheap side-valve four-strokes or bare-bones two-strokes, scooter engines were built to be rebuilt.

And then there was the suspension—or lack thereof. Few early scooters had suspension, and most

Lambretta Service School

Study hard: There's a lot to keep up with if you're going to try to own and operate a scooter.

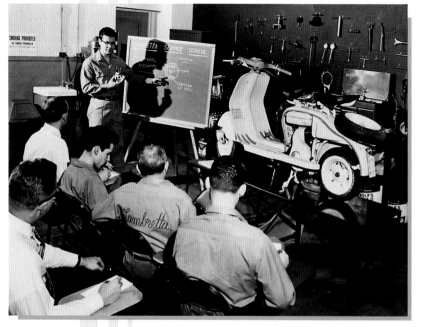

putt-putts rode like vibrators on wheels. Suspension was taken care of by the horsehair padding in the scooter's seat and the rider's derriere—whichever was plusher. When the pioneering Salsbury firm mounted two hardware-store variety screen-door springs to the front of its fabulous Motor Glide, it boasted of a technical marvel as new as tomorrow. And when its major rival, the Chicago-built Moto-Scoot bolted on barrel springs, suddenly the scooter world had dual-rate damping.

The Vespa's novel one-sided front suspension, meanwhile, was seen as more of a novelty. It worked fine and dandy as long as you didn't actually hit a bump or apply the brakes. When you did, it was like riding a high-speed pogo stick gone crazy.

Even with "suspension," many scooters at speed were notorious for shedding parts like a dog sheds fur. Recollected Cushman connoisseur Darrell Ward, "I'll never forget that special feeling of the wind in your hair when you're going good on a Cushman and then—poof. You just lost a bearing and you look back, hoping to see where it landed."

And then there was the transmission—or, again, the lack thereof. Pioneer putt-putts eschewed the complication and cost of gearboxes, opting for direct drive to the rear wheel, which also saved the tiresome hassles of a clutch. Salsbury introduced its regally named Self-Shifting Transmission in 1937. It was actually a glorified rubber band running on spring-loaded pulleys that contracted with centrifugal motion, thus increasing the pulley-to-pulley size ratio. It worked well, except that when you put a load on the scooter—such as a rider—the transmission tended to slip. Nevertheless, any American scooter that was anything had its own "automatic transmission" in no time, patents be damned.

Other makers went the more traditional route, offering gearboxes with two—and more!—speeds. Usually they worked; other times they jammed, sheared teeth, clutches were sanded down to velvet, or they kicked back like an angry mule.

As for brakes, some early scooters didn't bother. The pioneering American Autoped looked like junior's hijacked push scooter fitted with one of those cantankerous, oil-spewing "infernal"-combustion motors. The Autoped had no brakes, and riders were left to use their feet on the pavement to halt their progress, Fred Flintstone-style.

In 1961, however, the Innocenti Lambretta Turismo Veloce 175 dropped anchor with a radically new mechanical front disc brake. Yet the high-tech chic didn't come without woes of its own: These brakes were notorious for warping when they got hot, such as by the friction of braking.

All of these technical marvels added up to one big product liability lawsuit—except there was no such thing way back when. From the late 1940s through the 1960s, mail-order catalogers Gambles, Sears, Roebuck, and "Monkey" Ward sold Doodle Bug,

Stranded on the Roadside mit Zündapp R204
Waiting for help was a hobby many scooterists were forced to take up.

Cushman, Vespa, and Lambretta scooters by the thousands; when—not if—they broke, most folk just parked them in the barn and went on with their lives.

The true, unsung heroes in the scooter engineering story were the ad writers. Superlatives, exaggeration, and exclamation points coursed through their veins like gasoline through the scooters' engines. They waxed poetic to accentuate the positive and hide the many flaws, creating putt-putt poems in what to the uninitiated was mere ad copy.

The ad writers labor of love was a Herculean task if ever there was one. Their finest phrases rivaled Shakespeare: "Streamlining" was the perfect description for refrigerator-like styling on every scooter ever built. "Floating Ride" was what the Rock-Ola scooter builder termed its suspension made of two hardware-store screen-door springs. "Sane Speed" was Cushman's way of promoting lack of speed—"FAST enough to get there quickly and SLOW enough to be absolutely safe." "Forced Blast Cooling" was the Powell Streamliner's inflated promotion for its flywheel fan, which appeared on most every scooter on the market. "Self-Balancing" ballyhooed anything with more than two wheels, as with Cushman's Side Kar. "Iron Horse" was Rock-Ola's name for its wee Johnson 1 hp engine, likening it to a steam locomotive. "Plenty of Leg Room"—only the Puddlejumper scooter had it!

Today, the world's a different place, and product liability lawsuits have muffled many a scooter engine's cry. Cushman, Inc. still receives letters calling for a scooter revival, according to the *Wall Street Journal*: "They ask why we ever stopped making them," says Cushman spokesman Jerry Ogren. "Today, the product liability lawyers would probably just follow our customers around."

No wonder Piaggio, Innocenti, and many others sold off their old scooter tooling to fledgling firms in India, China, and other Third World countries.

1946–1954

Mass Mobilization 1955–1960

Motorscooters were true democratic machines. Any family could afford one, anyone could drive one, and no class was above them. Even HRH Prince Philip, the Duke of Edinburgh, purchased a fleet of Vespas to putt around the grounds of Buckingham Castle. And to further cement their democratic role, Enrico Piaggio boasted that his machine was the perfect tool to fight Communism.

Scooters mobilized the masses. Horses and donkeys were made obsolete as motorscooters used their puny horsepower to pull farm carts, market wagons, and micro-sized mobile homes. Mere automobiles had never ventured into the cobbled streets of some rural Italian hill towns perched on mountain sides; scooters broke trail by winding their way through the narrow streets, spreading the news of the 20th Century.

Scooters were a social appliance. With no fear of getting oil on your trousers or burning your silk-stockinged leg on the exhaust due to the side panels, passengers hopped on the pillion seat for a ride. Isolde found Tristan and Romeo eloped with Juliet. Clubs formed to meet others of the same motorized ilk, plan weekend putt-putt getaways, and lament over scooter woes. International rallies were organized where proud scooterists broadcast their fervent nationalism with native customs, folk dances, games, and anything else that could be done on a scooter. Scooters mobilized people like never before.

As a *New Yorker* reporter reported in 1957, "This is more than a fad, it's a revolution and I don't see how anything can stop it." There was more than just a touch of fear in his voice.

"Priests in Italy, according to a Vatican report, currently own 30,850 motorscooters, and in terms of sacraments and good works, the average priest's efficiency has climbed to about 3,000 percent over that of his road-trudging 19th century predecessor. Another straw in this high wind is the decline of the more introverted Benedictines and foot-slogging Franciscans in favor of the fast-moving Jesuits, whose high-octane practicality thrives on the motor-scooter age. Pope Pius XII has been a longtime friend of automation; last fall he called for 'greater and greater speed to the glory of God.'"

—*Time* magazine, 1952

OPPOSITE:

On the Road to a Better Future
Life was definitely good in the late 1950s. Prosperity was at hand—or at least visible from your Vespa. The two elfin wheels and hard-beating engine of the motorscooter had helped carry the world to prosperity's door. Now, the future looked so bright you had better be wearing shades.

Buon Anno, Amici!
And of course there were the annual putt-putt pin-ups.

Model and New Models
The front line in the Vespa-Lambretta War was the showroom. When the latest Lambretta bowed with a new, neater, or larger gizmo, a brand-spanking-new Vespa was soon out with a bigger and better version of said gizmo. Here was the new Spanish Serveta Slimline 150 Silver Special for 1965. You can bet your spare tire that a new and improved Vespa was on its way.

The Vespa–Lambretta War

ABSALOM! ABSALOM!

The Vespa-Lambretta War erupted in the time-honored tradition of the Romans and Visigoths, the Montagues and Capulets, and everyone within the Italian government. It started that day in 1947 when Innocenti introduced its Lambretta to battle the dominance of Piaggio's Vespa for the newly created motorscooter market.

The war was fought on every conceivable front—and even a few inconceivable ones. Model specifications, seating setups, paint schemes, road racing and record-setting, owner's club membership, millionth-scooter-built celebrations, and even endorsements from the latest stars and starlets of the day. A Vespista would not be seen dead on a Lambretta, and for the Lambrettista there was no doubt that the Milanese soccer teams Milan and Inter could beat Genoa. And if your Vespa sputtered to a halt in Milan's piazza del duomo, abandon all hope and run for your life.

Those Amazing Young Men on the Scooters!
Stunts proved scooter superiority, at least to the faithful.
Vespa stunt drivers display their scootering prowess.
Not to be outdone, Lambrettisti pile even more on.
The one who won, won.

Scooterists and Vespa in Traditional Costumes
Organizing the faithful into owner's clubs was one way to inspire loyalty to the cause, whether the cause be Vespa or Lambretta. Vespa clubs around Europe gathered annually for the annual Eurovespa hoopla, of course sponsored by Piaggio. At Eurovespa 1962, the Vespa Club de España dressed its members and its Spanish-made Vespas in folk garb to celebrate age-old traditions.

1955–1960

A Cushman and Thou
Nothing could be finer than riding sidesaddle on a Cushman 720 with the one you love.

Scooting With the One You Love

ROMANCE AMID THE TWO-STROKE EXHAUST

Scooters often lead you down the road to love. Whether it's Romeo buffed up by his scooter-inspired virility or Juliet swooning over his Lambretta's chic class, motorscooters are a one-way ticket to that many-splendored thing.

Blame it on Gregory Peck and Audrey Hepburn. Ever since the dynamic duo fell in love while touring the Eternal City on a Vespa in the 1953 William Wyler fairy-tale film *Roman Holiday*, scooters and l'amore have never been the same. Scooters, once blamed by tourists for raising a ruckus in Rome, were suddenly the vehicle of romance, on the same level with the gondolas of Venice.

Several generations fell in love via motorscooters. While American teens were borrowing the keys to dad's DeSoto, European youths were kickstarting their family's Zündapp to life. Vespas provided the wheels for many a courtship and romance blossomed on a weekend Motoconfort cruise to the country. Cupid rode a Rumi Formichino, and love was in the air surrounding scooterists—if you could breath through the two-stroke exhaust, of course.

"Young couples, she riding side-saddle prettily and revealingly and he, heading deliberately for every bump to jounce her into holding him tighter."

—American Mercury, February 1957

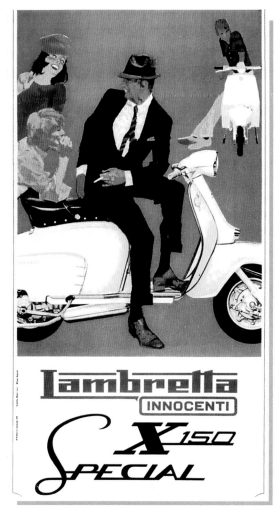

> *"Sports riders in this country
> are mostly either single or newly
> marrieds (scooters are so conducive
> to romance that there is a fast turnover
> between these categories)."*
>
> —Popular Science, 1957

Lambretta Inspires Virility
*Frank Sinatra, look out!
Nothing wins women like
a Lambretta X150 Special,
a fedora, and a coolly toted
coffin-nail. The bobby-soxers
were agog at the well-dressed
man with a Lambretta.
Presumably the lonely joe in
the background has the latest
Vespa for wheels and it
probably won't start either.*

**Want to Go For a Ride
in the Country?**
*Is she wowed by his
Hoffmann Vespa, or is
she laughing at it?*

1950s CZ Czeta
*It was big, it was bold, it was . . . ugly.
With too much chrome trim,
two-tone paint, and bloated
bodywork, the Czech Czeta proudly
boasted more styling faux pas than
any other scooter anywhere.
That's what makes it so cool!*
Courtesy of the owner: Per Arne Imbseu

Scooters Across Europe

THE RISING TIDE OF SCOOTERISTS

Patriotic and capitalistic firms across Europe rushed to put their citizens on two wheels following World War II. Alongside Italy, Germany, and England, France was the most prolific builder of scooters. The first Vespa under license was constructed in France by ACMA in 1950, soon to be followed by scooter creations from Peugeot, Terrot, Motobecane-Motoconfort, and many more.

The Spanish scooter world was typical of many European countries, from Czechoslovakia to Sweden. The firm Lambretta Locomociones SA (later renamed Messrs Serveta Industrial) began building Lambrettas under license in 1952 and Vespa SA was

building Vespas in 1962. Montesa created its own bizarre scooter in 1959 that looked like a park bench on wheels and later built the Italian Laverda Mini Scooter under license.

Another route to building scooters was epitomized by the Belgian Cushman firm, created in 1950 to build US Cushman scooters for the Belgians under license. As part of the European Recovery Act, Cushman supplied components including Husky engines, transmissions, wheels, and more to the firm; the Belgian firm made its own frame, forks, bodywork, and other parts.

1958 Montesa Scooter

"Agricultural" would be a compliment to the looks of Spain's Montesa. Perhaps it was a scoot designed to a fascist esthetic, debuting during the long "reign" of Fascist Generalissimo Francisco Franco. Whatever, the Montesa scooter was an oddity in a scooter market full of oddities. Laugh if you will, the Montesa was avant garde in construction: Instead of a standard step-through design, Montesa opted to mount two seats atop its fiberglass bodywork, surely some of the earliest use of fiberglass in scooter lore. The hottest features were the seats and luggage rack mounted on rails so they could be adjusted fore and aft.

1959 BFC Libelle

The Danish BFC firm launched its Libelle with obvious nod to the styling of the Lambretta in front and the Vespa in back.
Courtesy of Ole Birger

1955–1960

*"It's an unwritten code for
scooterists to greet each other."*

—Scooterist quoted in
New York Times Magazine, 1958

Putt-Puttniks Of The World Unite!

SCOOTERISTI SUPPORT GROUPS

Sure, torque, brake swept area and coefficients of drag are always good for a few laughs, but scooter clubs were more than just an excuse for questionable behavior. They became a cultural phenomena and their meets were social occasions and an acceptable excuse for questionable behavior.

Usually these events were sponsored by the parent company, most often Piaggio and Innocenti, to increase sales and encourage acceptability of their wares. During the late 1950s, however, scooter meets became an international event with various nationalities flaunting their native culture and competing for the most impressive getups, always with a scooter, of course. Displays would range from synchronized scooting to dancing the tarantella on Vespas to largest number of people on a single scooter. These events often lasted for days and eventually reached such a large number that they became a wholesome Sturgis rally.

Piaggio Pride
At the 1954 Motoraduno Nazionale in Turin, Vespisti accidently and spontaneously park their 485 scoots to form the Piaggio logo as visible only from the air!

C'mon Join the Fun!
It's Hawaii Day in balmy Kent, England, as The Innocents parade about town—which was sure to convince non-members to join up.

1955–1960

Factories As Icons

EPIPHANY IN STEEL

In the 1930s and 1940s, recovery from the Great Depression was epitomized by factories spewing out smoke from their chimneys. In the 1950s and 1960s, scooter ads heralded the factory as an icon of progress, cleanliness, and efficient mass-market technology. The production line reigned supreme as photos showed line-ups of row upon row of scooters to prove that quantity equals quality.

The number of factories that produced scooters that survived in Europe past the 1960s can be counted on two hands. While some factories were able to sell off their tool and dies to Third World countries, others successfully shifted with the market and produced miniature cars or anything else that was selling. The Piaggio factory outside Genoa was able to hold on and keep producing Vespas, while their arch-rival Innocenti moved to producing Innocenti (Austin) Minis. Meanwhile the other European motorcycle manufacturers that had dabbled in scooters stuck with what they knew best and covered up the scooter skeletons in the closet, claiming it to have been but a passing fad.

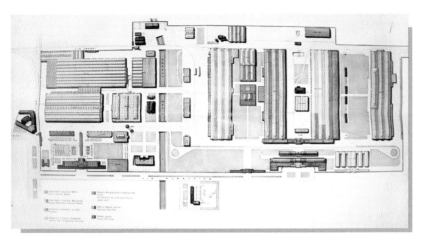

Workers of the World, Unite!

After a hard day's work in a faceless Bauhaus factory, every worker can go home with a smile as long as they're on a Bastert. Although the Einspurauto (meaning "Single-Track Car") may have been curvaceous with an elegant dashboard and styling, the factory from whence they came lacked the sumptuous lines that made this scooter a gem.

Lambretta Heaven

Enough to make any Lambretta aficionado drool in lust. Every 60 seconds a brand new Slimline rolled off the assembly line to a happy new owner. "There's a color or color combination just for you! Match your personality from the wide range of available colors," exclaimed the ads. As if the 6.6 hp of the Li125 wasn't enough.

BASTERT

elegant + schnell

SLIMSTYLE

"The electro-magnetic test bed is the altar of destruction on which will be sacrificed the body of a Lambretta."

—1966 Innocenti publicity film, *We Carry On*, describing the mechanized production of the Lambretta factory

1955–1960

Scooter Raids!

AROUND THE WORLD ON A PUTT-PUTT

Once on a scooter, one gets bold—often too bold. No mountain is too high, no desert too hot, no distance too great, thus raids. Thinking their shiny new scooter capable of anything, crazy youngsters would travel ridiculous distances driving straight through the night just to show that nothing could stop them.

The final destination of raids was often a scooter rally or club meet, some of the only people who would truly appreciate that someone just drove hundreds of miles on a vibrating two-stroke. Tales of raids range from circling the globe to conquering the jungle to ping-ponging across the U.S. any number of times.

*Running Away Forever–
or at Least For a Day*
Armed with only a Cushman,
these two 14-year-olds planned
their trip through Texas and
Louisiana with not a fear in the
world. In 1947, all one needed
was a map, napsack, and
confidence that the scooter's
engine would not seize on the
road to the sunset.

*"No hill too steep,
No road too rough,
Nowhere too far . . . "*

—Heinkel Tourist advertisement

No hill too steep,
No road too rough,
Nowhere too far...

**Only Kryptonite
Can Stop You Now**
*In ad prose worthy of
Superman, there was
nowhere too far for the
intrepid Heinkel Tourist.*

The World's Your Backyard
*E. Foster Salsbury, right, checks
the gas level on Vancouver
dealer H. C. Hemenway's scoot
before the brave Canadian
leaves the California factory for
the 1,358-mile dash home.*
Courtesy of the E. Foster
Salsbury Archives

**Postcard for the
Folks Back Home**
*Never forget to drop
a line to Ma!*

SURE IS FINE FARMING COUNTRY HERE!

1955–1960

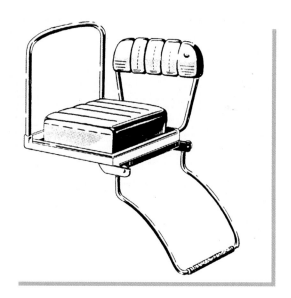

**Riding Side-Saddle
on a Vespa 160 GS**
Side-saddle was of course
the original way those of
the female persuasion
should ride a motorscooter.
But all of that was about to
change, due in a large part
to the scooter. Suddenly,
women had mobility, which
brought freedom, which
brought wider horizons,
which eventually brought
change to women's status.

Scooters and Women's Emancipation

RIDING SIDE-SADDLE NO MORE

Motorscooters played a starring role in the emancipation of the modern Italian woman. The British magazine, *Picture Post*, documented "A New Race of Girls" in 1954, stating that "the motor scooter gave her new horizons," as quoted from Dick Hebdige's semiotical analysis of the scooter in *Hiding in the Light*. A 1954 Innocenti promotional film for England, entitled *Travel Far, Travel Wide*, showed an airplane stewardess (in itself an image of the modern woman) on her Lambretta. The narrator announced that "The air hostess can become the pilot herself—and there's plenty of room on that pillion for a friend!" And who should climb on to the pillion but the airplane's male pilot.

Along with freedom of mobility, scooters were a catalyst in changing female fashion, symbolic of changes in status. *Picture Post* even went so far as to say that the scooter—along with beauty competitions and films—"consummated" the Italian woman's emancipation. As proof it pictured film stars Anna Magnani and Sophia Loren and talked about a new breed of "untamed, unmanicured, proud, passionate, bitter Italian beauties"—all riding scooters. Italian women had come a long way from sitting side-saddle on the pillion.

"The narrowing of the new look skirt was dictated in order to prevent it getting tangled up with the wheels. The slipper shoe was created for footplate comfort. The turtleneck sweater and the neckerchief were designed against draughts down the neck."

—*Picture Post*, 1950

Diana

KRAFTVOLL, ELEGANT UND FAHRSICHER

Looking Good on a 1947 Lambretta Model A

Buttoning up her leather jacket before blasting off on her brand-spanking-new Lambretta, this woman had come a long way on two wheels. As many 1950s style magazines proclaimed, even hair-dos changed in response to women's access to scooters: Headscarfs protecting long locks gave way to short hair as the ideal style for wind-in-the-hair riding. But all of this did not come as easily as simply kicking over a scooter engine: Innocenti's prudish Lambretta Notiziario *owners' magazine lamented that "one is all-too-frequently tormented by the sight of badly trousered women on motor scooters."*

"I bought a brand new Lambretta 150 for $300 and put on thousands of miles driving around Manhattan on weekdays and out to Fire Island on weekends. En route, I discovered that the scooter provided a reliable litmus test of male character. Those who were threatened by it didn't last long in my affections."

—Letty Cottin Pogrebin, Ms. magazine, 1987

Putt-Putt Fashion

French and Italian scooter magazines lead the way in sketching women's fashion designed for scootering.

De bon matin...
En janvier...

Classy Lady and Dürkopp Diana 200

Scooters were designed with women in mind, from the 1919 ABC Skootamota to the premier Vespa. The enclosed bodywork protected clothes from roadspray and inclement weather, and the open step-through design facilitated dresses and ever-shorter skirts. The engine was reliable and mechanicals were covered, meaning you wouldn't get dirt under your fingernails. Controls were simple to use even if you had never driven a motorized vehicle before. And floorboards were de rigeur instead of motorcycle pegs, which were hell in high heels.

1955–1960

1952–1954 Ducati Cruiser
The luxury scooter was born when Ducati launched its fabulous Cruiser at the 1952 Milan Fiera Campionaria boasting features far beyond any scooter of the day. The Cruiser was a zoot suit on wheels; it was draped in elegant two-tone bodywork produced by the celebrated carrozzeria Ghia. The long right side cover swung open effortlessly on a front hinge to reveal the 7.5 hp 175cc OHV engine, 12-volt electrics, electric start, and an automatic hydraulic torque converter transmission. The Cruiser actually had to be detuned to meet the Italian government's maximum scooter speed limit of 80 km/h. Ducati was partly funded by Opus Dei, the Vatican's investment arm, but even with Papal blessing, the Cruiser was only produced for two years.
Courtesy of the owner:
Vittorio Tessera

The Luxurious Motorscooter

CRUISING THE PIAZZA IN STYLE

In 1952, Moto Ducati launched a new concept in scooters with its Cruiser. Here was utilitarian transportation but with stylish luxury, the first *gran turismo* scooter, in the style of Enzo Ferrari's new GT automobiles. Ducati designers reasoned that the economy was improving and people would want to move upscale, but still could not afford a car. But the Cruiser was too much too soon, and it was gone by 1954.

But the *gran turismo* idea behind the Cruiser did not fade away. Inspired by the luxury scooter concept, other scooter makers would launch their own luxury models within the coming decade.

1957 Cosmo Scooter

Cosmopolitan Motors of Pennsylvania offered its badge-engineered Cosmo in the mid-1950s. Built by Puch, the Cosmo was the Cadillac of scoots, bedecked with a vicious red paint, quaint two-tone saddle, windscreen, spare wheel, front and rear luggage racks, and miles of chrome doodads. The only thing it lacked was tailfins. Never mind. This was high scooter style circa 1957,

1950s NSU Prima Dashboard

The array of gauges, buttons, and knobs would make a jet pilot feel at home. While the NSU Prima may not have reached mach speeds, the dashboard was the coolest of the cool. Here you had a clock, speedometer, odometer, choke, key to the electric ignition, battery warning light, grocery bag holder, and glovebox.
The Cadillac of the time didn't even have a grocery bag holder!

Sun Goddesses on 1950s Maico Mobils

Scooters were by definition enigmas, but the Maico Mobil was an enigma among scooters. These sun goddesses cum housewives were on their way to market with their grocery getters when they stopped to exchange gossip, cookie recipes, and mileage comparisons. Their Maico Mobils were among the coolest scooters ever built—and probably ever to be built. These women knew it.

1955–1960

Vespa paradiso per due

Le proverbiali doti di arrampicatrice della Vespa diventano insuperabili nella G.S.

Velocità, ripresa, stabilità, comfort, eleganza, economia, sono le qualità della Vespa G.S. che emergono in ogni condizione d'impiego.

Paradiso Per Due

"Paradise for two," this early 1960s Vespa GS brochure promised, made this the grand touring motorscooter for swingers. In 1957, Innocenti had responded to the Vespa Gran Sport by offering its Lambretta TV 175. With a 175cc competitor threatening to steal its two-stroke thunder, Piaggio created its 160 GS of 1962–1964 by enlarging both the bore and stroke of the 150 GS engine to 58 × 60 mm, making it capable of 8.2 hp at 6500 rpm via a Dell'Orto SI 27/23 carburetor for a top speed of 65 mph. As this brochure stated, "Speed, acceleration, stability, comfort, elegance, economy, these are the qualities of the Vespa GS that emerge in every condition of employment." Couldn't have said it better ourselves.

The Vespa Gran Sport

THE SCOOTER THAT TRANSCENDETH ALL KNOWING

Piaggio and Innocenti also took heed of Ducati's *gran turismo* Cruiser scooter. By the mid-1950s, the time was right for a luxury scooter. Italians had extra money in their pockets: That extra money could buy a more stylish scooter with extra power and luxurious accessories that could be driven to work during the week and be loaded up for a trip to the sea or a picnic in the country on weekends.

In 1954, Piaggio beat Innocenti to the punch, launching its Vespa 150 Gran Sport, a refined and perfected high-performance touring and sporting model. Innocenti responded in April 1957 with its Lambretta Turismo Veloce 175. Again the two scooter giants were locked horn to horn in competition.

1955–1961 Vespa 150 GS Racer

When Piaggio debuted the Gran Sport at the Salone di Milano in late 1954, they must have known they had created something special. The GS stunned everyone. It featured a new engine with a square 57 × 57 mm and 6.7:1 compression ratio, pumping out 8 hp at 7500 rpm via a UB 23 S 3 Dell'Orto carburetor. Backed by a four-speed gearbox, the GS reached 62 mph (100 km/h) on new 3.50 × 10-inch wheels. The GS pictured here in Milan alongside a Team Vespa racing team VW Transporter, was modified for racing with aerodynamic wheel covers and the early-model spare tire stored on top of the central tunnel as the left sidecover now housed a luggage trunk. The 150 GS came with a bench seat for two people and was available exclusively in metallic grey. With the GS, Piaggio had refined and perfected its scooter into a high-performance touring and sporting model that is still today considered as perhaps the best scooter ever.

1960s Vespa GS Brochure
Speed and style ruled with the GS.

"Paradiso per due."

—Vespa Gran Sport flyer, 1960s

Tough Scooter Chick and 1964 Vespa 160 GS
The cool scooter and typical leather-jacketed scooter hoodlum of the 1960s. By the middle of the decade, Piaggio sensed that the market for scooters had shifted: Sales of utilitarian scooters were being displaced by mini- and full-sized cars, and scooters were becoming a cult symbol of the growing youth market, winning an image as a mode of transportation primarily for teenagers before they could afford a motorcycle or four-wheeler. Piaggio responded in 1964 by enlarging the 160 GS engine to create the 180 Super Sport, which replaced the GS as the top-of-the-line Vespa until 1966. The 181cc engine was based on 62× 60 mm, creating 10.3 hp at 6250 rpm. The 180 Super Sport obtained a new body-chassis, straying from the classical rounded styling of the GS to the angular look of the mid–1960s. The SS was superceded by the 180 Rally of 1968, which was in turn followed by the Rally 200 and Rally 200 Electronic of 1972–1977.

1955–1960

1957–1958 Lambretta TV 175 Series 1 and LD125
TV stood for Turismo Veloce, or "Touring Speed," a scaled-down translation of gran turismo into scooter-speak. Innocenti's TV1 was a completely new design from the wheels up when it debuted in 1957. The 170cc two-stroke engine measured a square 60 × 60 mm and delivered a powerful 9 hp, significantly more than any earlier Lambretta or Vespa. A fourth gear was shoehorned into the transmission and the shaft-drive of all earlier Lambrettas was shelved in place of a modern enclosed duplex chain drive that required no adjustment, lubrication, or cleaning. Wheels were now 10-inch with 3.50 × 10-inch Pirelli tires. The TV1's bodywork enveloped the scooter like fluid metal; the curves followed the scooter's function with rich expanses of flowing steel that made the new Lambretta look more modern than Piaggio's GS, which only a trained eye could differentiate from the first Vespa of 1946. But there were problems looming. The TV concept was right, the timing was right, but Innocenti's execution was wrong. Whereas Piaggio's GS became its best scooter of the 1950s and 1960s, the first series TV 175 was a dismal failure. It was underdeveloped and won a reputation for poor reliability that haunted Innocenti into the 1960s. Never mind: In January 1959, the redesigned TV2 would be a worldbeater.

Lambretta Turismo Veloce

HORSEPOWER CORRUPTS ABSOLUTELY

The Piaggio-Innocenti Wars flared in the mid-1950s on the luxury scooter front when the Vespa GS was released in 1955. Suddenly Vespa ruled the roads. But it couldn't last, and it didn't. In 1957, the Lambretta Turismo Veloce was launched as a 175cc high-powered rocketship—25cc and 1 hp more than the GS could muster.

The first TV, however, was a failure. Rushed into production, it won Innocenti a reputation for unreliability that the firm fought throughout the 1960s and 1970s to live down (it was probably the Vespisti who spread the rumor).

But never fear. In 1959, the TV Series 2 bowed with a new engine based not on the old TV1 but on the highly successful Li125. With the TV2 and the subsequent TV3 of 1962, Innocenti was crowned king of scooterdom. If power corrupts, then horsepower corrupts absolutely.

Lambretta TV 175 Series 2 and Li125
By 1960, the TV was indeed "prettier, faster, and better," as Lambretta brochures brayed. It was an ideal touring machine, living up to its name Turismo Veloce. Fitted with either the standard twin saddle seats or the optional two-person bench seat, the Series 2 Lambrettas provided motive power for many a vacation or just a romantic outing in the 1960s. These two Series 2 Lambrettas stand tall in Trondheim, Norway. Courtesy of the owners: Steinar Nesje and Ralph Henriksen

1960 Lambretta TV Series 2

Funky cool brochure graphics as only the Italians could dream of promoted the key identifying feature of the Series 2: The headlamp moved to the handlebars to cuddle beneath a streamlined cowling that also incorporated the speedometer unit. But there were many more changes under that exquisite bodywork. After just sixteen months of production, the TV1 was junked to be replaced by the TV2, which was a new scooter based not on the TV1 but on the phenomenal new Lambretta Li125 of 1958. The only items carried over from the TV1 were the name and the body style, but that too was updated. The new 175cc engine was a larger-bore version of the Li125 engine at 62 × 58 mm, creating 8.6 hp. With the TV2, Innocenti had its flagship sporting scooter that it should have had in the TV1. The TV2 would receive a facelift in 1962 with the introduction of the new Lambretta Slimline styling, and carry on to 1965.

Courtesy of the Collezione Vittorio Tessera

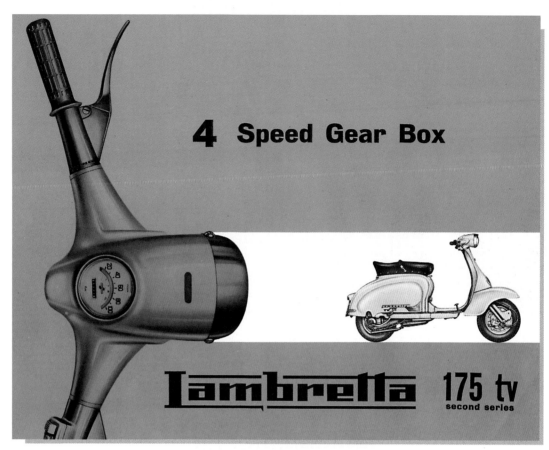

1962–1965 Lambretta TV 175 Series 3 Slimline

Forget the Ferrari, the new Slimline Lambretta was pure modern, angular cool. In 1961–1962, the bodywork of the Li and TV was redrawn. The Slimline styling was sleek and angular with flash replacing the fleshy look of the earlier Lambrettas. The Slimline looked like a Lambretta on a diet; the curvaceous Marilyn Monroe styling that characterized the 1950s Lambrettas was shed in favor of the thinner Twiggy look of the 1960s. The TV3 wore the new go-fast Slimline styling over a high-perfomance 8.7 hp engine and front hydraulic dampers for a smoother ride. With the TV3, a 20 mm Dell'Orto replaced the late TV2's 21 mm. The TV3 dropped anchor with a mechanical disc front brake that pressed a full-circle pad against the rotor. It was not the first use of a disc brake on a motorcycle but it was the most influential, leading the way for motorcycle and automakers in the mid-1960s. Under the old hot-rodder's dictum that there's no replacement for displacement, the 175cc engine was increased to 200cc for a TV 200 model, aka GT 200, which lasted until 1965.

1955–1960

Scooter Stunts And Putt-Putt Promotions

MANIFEST DESTINY, SCOOTER-STYLE

As an alternative to the automobile, scooters hit the market with such force that nearly every motorcycle company considered going into the lucrative scooter biz. Producing one, however, was never enough; publicity and outrageous promotion was the key to assure success. Shameless gimmicks promoted everything from scooter sports, like polo and bullfighting, to drivers' education schools and scooter service stations.

Apart from posters and advertisements, publicists presented photo ops showing a new class of young people interested in cheap transportation, meeting fellow scooterists and being on the cutting edge of style. You too could join this hip avant-garde club—if you could afford a scooter. You could use their special mechanic shops, participate in their rallies, and try any range of dangerous or goofy stunt on your scooter that would be written about in their next newsletter. If you owned a scooter, you belonged.

Scooter Alien Invasion
Lunaires—"moon men"— invade Paris in 1956 aboard space-styling Vespas.

Scooter Joust

Bold knights in shining armor aboard their equally shiny Bernardet scooters set off into battle—presumably against rival knights on a rival scooter make.

A Driver's Ed Horror Film in the Making

The driving instructor's nightmare—driver's ed behind the handlebars of a scoot. At least with this Lambretta Li125 Series II, the handlebars could be controlled by the backseat driver.

"The scooter is a daring and noisy announcement that its passengers are individualists with a continental flair but without the purchase price of a Continental Mark III."

—New York Times Magazine, 1958

Teeter-Totter Thrills

Stunts proved scooter superiority, at least to the faithful followers of each marque. At its annual get-together, Vespa Club of Lisbon members displayed their scootering prowess in time trials and teeter-totter tricks before an awed crowd of fellow riders.

1955–1960

Weekend Warriors on Two Wheels

PUTT-PUTTS ESCAPE PACKAGE TOURS

The idea of getting away for the weekend was finally made a reality to anyone who could afford a scooter. Finally a way to get out of the crowded cities to the crowded beaches. But now, vacationers were no longer boxed in by specific destinations of trains, but rather they could find the exclusive cabin to get away from it all. Nevertheless, beaches and mountain getaways were swarmed with tourists on buzzing Vespas in search of the perfect tan. Or at least if you could get to a vacationing hot spot, the ambitious tourist could simply rent a scooter for the weekend and zip away from the crowds.

Herculean Task
Packing up for a secret weekend getaway was never more fun than with a Hercules 200cc scoot.

Vespa Double Duty
As this 1955 brochure proved, your friendly Vespa could do double duty, taking you to work on weekdays and into the country on weekends to get away from it all.

Every Day's a Holiday
The Lambretta LD125 made every day a holiday—until it broke down when you were trying to return home.

Les Belles Weekends
Les dimanches *and* les vacances *were certainly belle with a Vespa.*

The Evil Scooter Menace

BEWARE THE UNWARY TOURIST . . .

By 1956, 600,000 scooters were buzzing along Italian roads. Tourists to golden Italy, however, had little respect for the scooter's role in mobilizing the reconstructed country; instead, the camera-toting hordes despised the un-picturesque sight of the Vespas swarming like insects around the Trevi Fountain, blurring their snapshots for the folks back home and filling the air with the choking scent of two-stroke exhaust.

This stupidity continues to the present day in such trendy snobola "style" books as *Italian Country* by Catherine Sabino (Potter, 1988), which describes a quaint tourist's view of Umbria: "Passageways an arm's length in width will never hear the rumble of an automobile, or with any luck, the irritating buzz of the Vespa."

"Among Italy's contributions to civilization, the motor scooter cannot be counted as an unmixed blessing. A visitor to Florence, for example, may be lulled to sleep by the strains of La Tosca *emanating from the municipal opera house but he is in for a rude awakening when the opera lets out. Indeed, the noise made by a thousand homeward-bound Florentines, most of them riding motor scooters that sound like riveting guns, is enough to drive a tourist back to New York for a little peace and quiet. Now it appears that Americans won't be able to escape motor scooters even by staying home. Not content with making the Italian night hideous, Piaggio & Co. has launched a determined assault on the American market. The prospect is in a literal sense disquieting."*

—Fortune, August 1956

Heinkel Tourist on Tour

Not content to rattle all the windows on the strasse in their hometown, this Dutch couple even brought their three-wheeled scooter menace to America! All part of a 14-month around-the-world honeymoon trip via scooter, according to Jan and Leny Hoe, who arrived in New York with their aptly named Heinkel Tourist mit seitenwagen. After crossing America, the duo were on their way to Australia, Ceylon, India, Pakistan, Iran, Turkey, and home via European byways. If their marriage could survive that, it could survive anything.

Roman Holiday—Ruined!

You just aimed your Kodak Brownie for an out-of-focus shot of St. Peter's when one of those pesky little Vespas zipped in front and ruined your photo for the folks back home. No wonder they're named after insects!

Polizei mit *Vespas*

It's a conspiracy! You went to the Old Country to see the quaint sights, and those darn scooters are everywhere—why even the police ride them! These two Düsseldorfer troopers should be justifiably proud of their Hoffman Vespas with the spiffy searchlight mounted on the handlebars. As those Blues Brothers said, cop lights, cop tires, cop two-stroke 125cc engine....

1955–1960

Motorscooters By US Mail

"SOME ASSEMBLY REQUIRED"

Down on the farm or in small-town America far from the centers of commerce, the concept of mail-order shopping blossomed after the turn of the century. Led by catalog retailers such as Montgomery Ward and Sears, Roebuck, you could mail or telephone in your order for everything from a new frock for mom or a suit for pa to a full-size upright piano for junior—farm tractors and pre-fabricated houses and barns were even offered!

Motorscooters were available by mail before World War II through *Popular Mechanics* ads, but when the Gambles Stores began selling Doodle Bug scooters in 1946, mail-order motorscooters took on a whole new meaning. Suddenly, thousands of putt-putts were being sold through catalogs by Gambles, Sears, Roebuck, and "Monkey" Ward. Large profits were reaped from the little scooters, and the Doodle Bug, Cushman-Allstate, and Ward's Riverside motorscooters became household names.

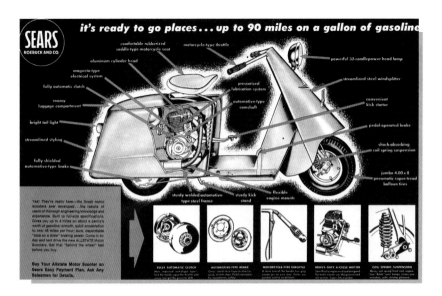

"All-new fresh-as-a-breeze styling!
All-new distinctive colors!
Shipped partially assembled
in wooden crate."

—1959 Sears, Roebuck catalog ad
for Allstate Jetsweep

1946 Beam Doodle Bug

Roy Rogers had Trigger, Dale Evans saddled up Buttermilk, Gene Autry hotspurred Champion, the Lone Ranger and Tonto rode Silver and Scout respectively, but the elfin Doodle Bug became the dream of many a young American buckaroo in the 1940s. In 1946, Gambles signed the Beam Manufacturing Company of Webster City, Iowa, to build the Doodle Bug. Beam chose the tried-and-true 1.5 hp Briggs & Stratton engine to power the Doodle Bug via a belt drive, although for a short period, the B&S engine was out of stock and Beam filled in with a Clinton 1.5 hp, making the Clinton-powered Doodle Bugs rare insects. The chassis was a simple tube frame covered by scant rear bodywork and a cylindrical gas tank cantilevered off the tail in the best Ford Pinto manner. A simple cushion seat sat atop the engine; buckhorn handlebars were welded to the steering rod. In place of front forks, the sheet-steel fender cradled the wheel. The Webster City factory hatched Doodle Bugs in four build lots of 10,000 scooters each for a total of 40,000. To many Americans, the Doodle Bug became synonomous with scooter.

Courtesy of the owner: Jim Kilau

1961 Riverside Lambretta Li125

"Monkey" Ward carried Lambrettas, badge-engineered as Riversides. This 1961 Slimline Li125 was recast as a Riverside with an identity crisis by riveting a chrome emblem to the legshield and slapping on an instruction sticker in English. Ward also sold Mitsubishi Silver Pigeons, which had been based on the Lambretta LD125.

1965 Cushman Super Silver Eagle Series II

In early 1961, Cushman debuted an all-new, all-aluminum OMC Super Husky engine for the new Silver Eagle. But the new engine came about as a cost-saving effort by OMC; the first Silver Eagles literally shook themselves apart as they were held taut in the rigid Eagle frame. By 1962, the new Floating Power Chassis was developed with Power Frame rubber engine and transmission mounts to cope with a new Super Husky that included counterweights to balance vibrations. This 1965 Super Silver Eagle boasts most of the options available at the time: electric-starter, speedometer/odometer, full dresser kit, and white sidewalls. The Super Silver Eagle was truly "the big name in little wheels." But in early 1965, the Eagle became extinct when production ceased. It was not the end of Cushman, however. The firm quit scooters to build the three- and four-wheeled industrial Trucksters, Mailsters for the US Post Office, and a new Golfster for the grown-up kids in kelly green who had once buzzed Main Street on an Auto-Glide and could now tour the links in a Cushman golf cart. It was the dawn of a new Golden Age for Cushman.
Courtesy of the owner: Jim Kilau

The Cushman Eagle

A SCOOTER FOR REAL MEN

In 1949, Cushman unveiled its new motorcycle in miniature, the Eagle. It was a radical departure from the step-through design to a scooter reminiscent of the big-twin motorcycles of the time that ruled the American roads—the Harley-Davidson Knuckle-head and Indian Chief.

The Eagle laughed at the scooter design set in stone by Salsbury nearly two decades earlier. In creating the Eagle, Ammon and Herb Jesperson looked back to the Powell P-81 and the Mustang lines: the workings of the engine were proudly on display without engine covers and owners were not afraid to get their hands dirty working on these "real" machines. And these were machines for real men, riders who weren't afraid to swing their legs over the gas tank.

All in all, historical hindsight has crowned the Eagle as the right scooter at the right time for the United States. The Eagle became the best-selling Cushman scooter ever.

Cushmans on the Go

While the rest of America was busy building bomb shelters, the smart set was out riding Cushman's great Eagle. The new Eagles combined "soaring ride with rugged roadability," according to a 1960 brochure. As always, Cushman ads were chock full of buzzwords to back the solid sales the Eagle line was turning in. "Just to look at the brand new Super Eagle and Eagle is to feel an urge to take to the road. Why not yield to that urge? Swing into the saddle, ease open the throttle, and learn a new definition of fun." Why not indeed? In those long-ago buzz-cut days of American summers past, there was nothing cooler than cruising on a Cushman Road King and Super Eagle. The Super Eagle was an updated model with a "streamlined" rear body section, including the Super Eagle 765-88 of 1959–1964 with 7.95 hp engine and 765-89 of 1959–1963 with 4.8 hp engine.

Cushman Comics

Reading like a religious tract to tempt the faithful to scootering, this Cushman advertising comicbook extolled the virtues of the Cushman Eagle.

1951 Cushman Eagle Brochure

The Eagle took the mechanicals of the 60 Series step-through scooter and shoehorned them into a novel miniature Harley-Davidson chassis with a rigid rear—hardtail in Harley parlance. Bodywork was at a minimum to show off the Husky's muscle, as this was a scooter for real men. Debuting in December 1949, the Eagle was powered by the round-barrel 5 hp Husky engine with a chrome-plated exhaust pipe swooping down to the right. The two-speed transmission was operated by a "suicide" handshift on the left side of the gas tank in the best Harley tradition. Drive on the first 765 Eagles was shifted from the left side to the right, the opposite of all preceding Cushman scooters. The first Model 765 Eagle Series I was built 1949–1954; in April 1952, the new square-barrel 5 hp and the new 7.3 hp engines were optional. From 1952–1954, the Model 762 Eagle was offered as a stripper economy model Eagle without the dreary hassles of a transmission.

"Somebody in our sales department wanted a scooter that looked like a motorcycle with gas tank between your legs. It turned out to be a hell of a good idea."

—Robert H. Ammon, 1992 interview

1955–1960

Land Ho!
Sure, Magellan traversed the globe by sea, but would he have been so brave as to traverse the English Channel by scooter? George Monneret boldly sailed from Calais to Dover on his 125cc Vespa outfitted with pontoons and paddles hooked up to the scooter engine. When he reached the white cliffs, he zipped up to London in record speed, making today's Chunnel seem positively sluggish.

Aqua-Scoots And Sno-Scoots

NO WATER TOO ROUGH, NO SNOW TOO DEEP

Once upon a time, Britannia ruled the seas. In the 1950s and 1960s, English entrepreneurs hoped to regain past glory by applying their seafaring knowledge to the ever-versatile scooter. These aqua scoots, however bulky, inefficient, and unpopular, were the direct precursors of the Jet Ski, and equally as deafening to relaxing beach goers.

In 1956, the Amanda Water Scooter lead the armada with the help of a Vincent engine, but its fiberglass hull melted down, drowning one test driver. Believing this mishap forgotten, a Lambretta conversion kit (applying ideas made famous in old *Popular Mechanics* magazines) used paddle blades attached to the rear wheels, which hopefully didn't spray too much water on the back of the first mate. This $25 kit appeared at the 1965 Brighton motorcycle show. As part of the ongoing Vespa-Lambretta rivalry, a Vespa was equipped with pontoons and crossed the English Channel in a historic publicity stunt.

Finnish Ski Patrol
To defend Suomi from the Reds next door, the Finns doffed their wooden skis for two-stroke power in 1950. Camouflaged white with white wheel covers made the Vespa invisible—except for the piercing engine noise through the frigid air.

"I'm now working on a couple of collapsible pontoons and a propeller drive. So this summer, when I ride the scooter up to the lakeshore, I'll just keep on going. And maybe—souped up a little and equipped with rotor blades— it'll lift off the ground."

—A Do-It-Yourselfer quoted in
Popular Science, 1961

Scooter Party Barge
Even more proof that scooters can do anything, possibly even pull waterskiers. This 1939 aqua-scoot makes any tropical island a two-stroke paradise, at least until the tidal waves hit. Once upon a time these motorized wonders posed competition for speed boats, but with hindsight appear to be a bizarre mix of pedal boats, catamarans, and jet skis.

*"Snow, however, is navigable
if you know your stuff."*
—Popular Science, 1957

Snowmobile on Two Wheels
With ad copy yelling the "Slimstyle by Lambretta is the absolute ultimate in motor scooters," these youngsters just couldn't resist hitting the slopes in their new Li. In true exclamatory duplicity, Innocenti bragged that the Slimstyle "handles like a bike, rides like a car." Some early pioneer motorscooters were even armed with treads on the bottom for maximum traction. And rumor has it that mad (garage) scientists in the frozen North even decked later scooters with skis and chains on their tires. Why they didn't just purchase a snowmobile is anyone's guess.

1955–1960

Scooters And Sidecars

BRING THE WHOLE FAMILY!

Once pa married ma courtesy of their scooter-inspired courtship, they need space for little junior on the putt-putt. Enter the sidecar, a one-wheeled, single-seat, bolt-on addition that allowed you to tote the whole family about like sardines in a motorized tin.

Sidecars were the rage in the 1950s and 1960s, a stepping stone on the way to a mini- or full-sized car for the growing family. Sidecars were built by makers around the world, and were attached to everything from Cushmans to Nortons.

But by the mid-1960s, sidecars were out of fashion as quickly as they had arrived. Mini-cars such as the Mini, FIAT 500, Volkswagen, and Citroën 2CV provided weather protection beyond simple legshields.

Call them a scooter with a bolt-on coffin or the precursor of the family safari wagon, that Heinkel mit Steib seitenwagen was once the rage of the roads.

Motorroller mit Steib Roller-seitenwagen
Steib of Nürnberg are famous the world over for their stylish sidecars. Steib built sidecars in a range of models from this scooter sidecar through sidecars sized for 250cc and 500cc motorcycles.

Relief Wagon
Fitted with a sidecar, this Harley-Davidson Topper was the perfect wagon to deliver relief pitchers to the mound at Milwaukee Braves games. Walter Davidson himself pilots the craft with ace hurler Warren Spahn ready to throw.

The Death of a Salesman . . .
JoeBe stood for Joe Berliner, who was standing on the left in this photo showing off his Ventruck model. Joe Berliner was one of the stalwarts of American motorcycling, importing Glas Goggo-Isaria and Zündapps for years to the United States. The Ventruck combined one of JoeBe's Goggo-Isaria scooters with an ice cream refrigerator on a two-wheel axle. What will they think of next?

Golden Vespa Duo
Hoffman Vespa crowned it Die Königin—the Queen— and it was certainly a scooter fit for royalty. Gowned in gold with red paint and chrome trim set off by whitewalled tires and faux wire wheels, this 1953 sidecar outfit was a throne on three wheels for the regal scootering set.
Courtesy of the owner: Hans Kruger

1955–1960

The Mod Years
1960–1975

One of the most enduring styles that sprang from the back streets of London is that of the Moderns. In the early 1960s, the standard of living was on the rise. While mum and pop picked up an auto, the new teenager market demanded a high performance steed for their friends to ogle while they zip by the coffee shop. These scooters, however, came as an afterthought to the Mod agenda: another piece of jewelry to match the slick Italian clothes and the moptop dos.

The Mods were preceded by the Teds and rivaled by the Rockers. The dapper Teddy Boys outdid each other in their slick outfits and patent leather shoes as they bopped to the music of American rock 'n' roll. The Rockers, on the other hand, slicked their hair, wore leather jackets, and weren't afraid to bop a passing Mod. In general, however, Rockers didn't pay the Mods much attention since they were busy popping coins in the Ace Bar jukebox, kick starting their Café Racer, and blasting around the block before the song ended. Mods viewed Rockers as greasy and smelly, while the working class Rockers viewed their antithesis as prissy and sissy. Unfazed by the competition, Mods sat proudly on their Lambrettas, or Italian Hairdryers as the Rockers called them.

Mods' scooters went through many phases as they constantly tried to outdo each other. In the late 1950s, the early post-Teddy Boy phase caught everyone listening to cats like Monk and Mingus, and driving their stock scooters fresh from the crates. Two-tone paint jobs soon became the rage. The mid 1960s saw decked-out Lambrettas with every bell, light, and horn they could get their hands on and blasting The Who and Otis Redding. Since then, revivalist scooter clubs have stripped down their scooters to the bare-bones one week, then coated their side-panels with air-brushed band photos the next week, and finally returned their scooters to stock.

In 1964, the Mod-Rocker wars climaxed with a violent melee on the beaches of Brighton. In a promotional frenzy, Innocenti sponsored a scooter meet to the delight of Mods from all over Britain. The event fell on a Bank Holiday, so numerous Rockers had road tripped to the sea to stroll the boardwalks and blast some four-stroke exhaust in the face of their two-stroke rivals. Soon, scooters were tipped, beach umbrellas thrown, and haircuts ruffled. The land of tabloids was willingly shocked as the exaggerated rumble was splashed on the front page of every newspaper.

> *"The Mod way of life consisted of total devotion to looking and being 'cool.' Spending practically all your money on clothes and all your after hours in clubs and dance halls."*
>
> —Richard Barnes from *Mods*

Mods began as mostly well-off West-Enders who hung out on Carnaby Street in search of some fun. They weren't afraid of ruffling a few feathers with greasy rockers on their BSA Gold Stars and Triumph Bonnies just as long as their Lammie would get them to the club in time for the Skatalites' show.

OPPOSITE:
Going Modern
Sandra Dee gets enthusiastic with her new Vespa 50.

Mod Revival
Cruising a back alley on a glorious two-tone Lambretta TV175 Series II twenty years after and an ocean away—the Mod revival hit the USA and Europe in the 1990s and is still going strong. Tim Gartman steers, Jessika Madison holds on tight.
Courtesy of Tony Nelson

It's a Mod, Mod World

THEIR GOD WORE SHADES

The world was indifferent to Mod scooters—referring to them mockingly as "Italian hairdryers"—until they decked them out with every headlight, mirror, horn, and any other chromed piece of equipment they could put their hands on. Now, they couldn't be ignored as their scooter jewelry on their weighted-down steeds blinded other drivers and pedestrians shielded their eyes to the reflecting sun from their chrome trinkets. The Mods, however, merely accentuated a trend to gussy up their scooters that began in the 1950s and later continued with customized Harley hogs. Anybody who was anybody had a scooter, but who was willing to spend more than the actual cost of the vehicle on chrome trinkets?

To this day, scooters have been unable to doff their connection with Mods. To many this is reason enough to fix up an old Lambretta; to others, this is why they won't go near them and stick to rebuilding a BSA Gold Star.

"You've got to be either a Mod or Rocker to mean anything. Mods are neat and clean. Rockers look like Elvis Presley, only worse."

—Mod Teresa Gordon quoted in the *Daily Mirror*, 1964

Safety Conscious Mod

"All me horns, lights, and rearview mirrors are here for safety, officer," pleaded the Mod. Style takes strange detours down odd roads in different eras. This Mod-ified Lambretta was pure cool in 1960s Britain.

"I don't wanna be the same as everybody else. That's why I'm a Mod, see?"

—Jimmy, *Quadrophenia*

"Rumble in Brighton Tonight!"

So sang Brian Setzer of the Stray Cats more than a decade after the infamous Mod-Rocker battles on Brighton Beach. This still from Quadrophenia shows the evil rockers on their Triumphs and BSAs taunting lone Mod Chalky on his scoot. Even though The Who's movie came after most of the rivalry between the Mods and Rockers had calmed down, Quadrophenia still remains the fictional documentation of the era inspiring many new Mods to fix up abandoned Lammies.

1960–1975

Jim and John
THE TWIN-TONES

45 EP ECONOMY PACKAGE

RCA VICTOR
EPA-4107

A "NEW ORTHOPHONIC" HIGH FIDELITY RECORDING

JO-ANN
BEFORE YOU GO
MY DANCING LADY
ONE MAIL A DAY

The Twin-Tones with Twin Lambrettas
It just didn't get any swinging-er than Jim and John and their twin Lambretta LDs. The Twin-Tones rocked your socks off with this EP in 1960.

Rock On The Roll

HYMNS TO THE MOTORSCOOTER

"Get on your bad motor scooter and ride/ When the sun comes up, everything gonna be all right."

—Montrose,
"Bad Motor Scooter"

Scooters have probably inspired more innovative swear words than heavenly hymns. But there have been several songs sung to the scooter.

In 1947, Innocenti announced the arrival of its first Lambretta scooter with a catchy advertising tune played night and day over RAI radio. The ditty was one of those "shave-and-a-haircut-two-bits" opuses that you could not get out of your mind no matter how hard you tried—and is still whistled to this day by Milanesi caught off guard.

Then in the 1960s came the Italian hit, "Lambretta Twist," and on dance floors everywhere the crowd was twisting—everyone, that is, except Vespisti.

The most eloquent testimonial to the scooter was surely The Who's *Quadrophenia*, a rock 'n' roll opera telling the tale of the Mod-Rocker clashes in 1960s England. A Vespa graced the album cover as well as

the movie poster, and the sinking of a scooter ended the film with symbolic eloquence. Throughout, The Who were turned to 11 with Pete Townshend smashing Rickenbackers through Hiwatt stacks and Roger Daltry yodeling in "The Punk Meets the Godfather." "I ride a GS with my hair so neat/Wear a war-torn parka in the wind and sleet."

The 1970s brought us glam rock, afros, platform boots, and quintessential seventies band Montrose with its hard-rocking hit, "Bad Motor Scooter." Complete with revving-engine guitar sounds (probably made by the rare and coveted Hemi stomp box), this was the scooter's Easy Rider anthem destined to set putt-puttniks' hearts aflutter: "Get on your bad motor scooter and ride/When the sun comes up, everything gonna be all right."

Amen.

> *"I ride a GS with my hair so neat/*
> *Wear a war-torn parka*
> *in the wind and sleet."*
>
> —The Who, "The Punk Meets the Godfather"

Rock 'n' Roll Anthem to Scooters

The rockingest scooter album ever has to be the Who's *Quadrophenia,* a rock 'n' roll ode to the Mod-Rocker Wars of the 1960s as well as to the Vespas and Lammies the Mods rode. In the flick, Sting makes his appearance as the quintessential Modern, complete with scoot. This album should be played loud and proud.

Travelling Far on an Allstate

Bo Diddley had guitar and traveled on his Allstate Jetsweep. This 1960s Bo album did not feature any references to his motorized friend, but Bo's signature riff may have been inspired by the beat of his scooter's heart. With the brilliant red-and-white color scheme, this was high scooting fashion stateside in the 1960s.

Count Basie Rides Again

The Count went cruising in 1960 on his whitewalled Vespa, playing Kansas City jazz for the faithful.

1960–1975

Movie Stars And Motorscooters
THE PUTT-PUTT ON TV AND FILM

While General Motors had Pat Boone as their mascot, scooter makers couldn't afford the big guns, so they settled for paparazzi photos of stars on their putt-putts. Perhaps the most famous scooter photo of all time is Amelia Earhart on a Motoped which did more for promoting motorscooters than any number of clever ad men. In a major coup for Innocenti, Paul Newman appeared on the cover of *Scooter* magazine piloting his Lambretta through heavy traffic. And guitar hero Bo Diddley featured an Allstate Jetsweep scooter on the cover of his album complete with a square-body Gretsch guitar.

Burl Ives Goes Scottish
Burl Ives shares a laugh with a pint-sized admirer on a Lambretta LD. The singer was usually spotted with his guitar and legions of fans, so this snapshot was definitely an Innocenti publicity coup to inspire folkies everywhere to go two-stroke. One of the original design features of scooters was the open area between the driver's legs to allow dresses, or kilts, to be worn.

Cyd Charisse and Vespa SS
Cyd shows off her gams—which may have come in handy walking her Vespa home after if failed to start while out for a night on the town.

Spanky's Safety Patrol
The Little Rascal becomes a little copper as he zooms these youngsters to safety in his Powell Streamliner scooter with sidecar. Although the scowling youth was premature to drive a scooter, Powell's ads boasted anyway, "Everyone who can ride a bicycle can ride a Powell Motor Scooter!"

1960–1975

135

> *"Everyone knows that damage is done to the soul by bad motion pictures."*
>
> —Pope Pius XI

Putt-Putts Go Hollywood

THE SILVER SCREEN'S SEAL OF COOL

Audrey Hepburn and Gregory Peck did more for the cause of scootering in one short jaunt through Rome's piazzas than possibly any other single event. *Roman Holiday* imbued scoots with instant hipness, and to this day, tourists to the Eternal City still pay huge fees to rent Vespas to relive their fairy-tale ride.

In other films scooters starred as both heroes and villains. Federico Fellini's *La Dolce Vita* featured newsman Marcello Mastroianni in his Lancia spyder while whirring Vespas encircle his car in hopes of getting the scoop first. Mastroianni always had an angle on news stories, but could never quite escape from the flock of scooters that constantly swarm wherever he goes. The most famous of these muckrakers was the photographer, Paparazzo, whose scooter transported him to remote hideaways of the stars, so he could snap scandalous photos.

Quadrophenia showed primped mods on Lambrettas battling the naughty rockers on BSAs and Triumphs to the blasting sound of Pete Townshend's wailing Rickenbacker.

Come September
Not to be outdone by Audrey and Gregory, Rock Hudson and Gina Lollobrigida went on a Roman holiday of their own in 1961. Scoot of choice? A choice two-tone Lambretta Li Series II.

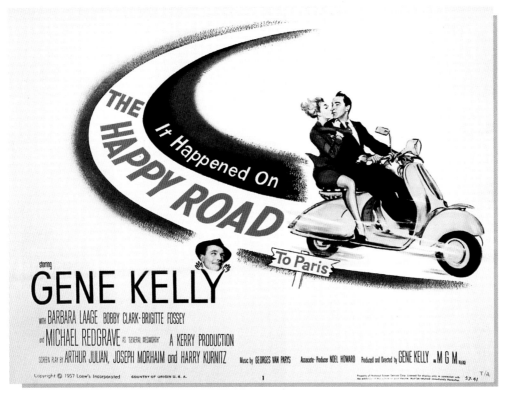

The Happy Road
Gene Kelly and Barbara Laage found love on the road to Paris thanks to their Vespa in 1957's The Happy Road.

1960–1975

Drive fast, drive loud is the motto for scooterists in fair Italy where every stoplight is the starting line of a grand prix and every ride is a race. Scooters were not made to stroll; they were built to zoom. In the Stoplight Grand Prix, the power-to-weight ratio of a Vespa allows you to beat out a Ferrari for the first 10ft, so always take advantage of this to blow some two-stroke smog in the gran turismo snob's snout. Every Ferrari and FIAT will then pass you up on the strada—until the next stoplight, when the scooters sift back through the traffic to the front, and puff off at the starting line once again to repeat the whole process. If you must drive slowly, be certain you're in low gear so the engine roars at high rpm. The sound will ricochet off the walls of the houses lining the streets, waking everyone from their siesta. Don't forget to saw off a good 6 inches of your exhaust pipe for maximum volume and speed. Just remember, loud fast rules!

How to Drive Like an Italian
RIDE LOUD, RIDE FAST

There's only one true rule to driving in Italy that all must follow: It is illegal to allow someone to be in front of you. All traffic tricks, go-fast fantasies, two-wheeled cornering maneuvers, and one-wheeled braking dance steps derive from this basic maxim.

So whether you are driving a Lamborghini Miura or a Lambretta LD 125, the rules of the road are the same—except with a motorscooter you have more to prove. Here's some trick tips on how to drive like a Italian.

La Bella Figura

The object of riding a scooter is maximum visibility to create una bella figura, or "a beautiful figure"—better known in American slang as simply "being cool." The trick, however, is to never, ever act as if you realize you're making a scene—that would be creating una bruta figura, "an ugly figure." There are several tricks to the trade here. First, if your Lambretta is coughing out vast billowing clouds of exhaust, remedy this tuning oversight by wearing Ray-Bans. Second, if your engine seizes at speed, simply broadside the scooter to a stop and pretend you were going to park or had planned on ditching the thing right there anyway. Among the worst moves you could make is having your scooter break where the coffeeshop crowd can see you. The rule here is to never repair a broken-down Vespa on the side of the road: Not only will you be visible to the passersby, but you also stand a chance of getting oil on your Versace clothes. A scooter breakdown can only happen while riding with a member of the opposite sex and can only be intentional, usually occurring in a secluded, wooded spot.

Roman Holiday *Revisited*

Gregory Peck and Audrey Hepburn did more for the cause of scootering in one short jaunt through Rome's piazzas than any other single event. Scooting through modern Rome, however, is like going to war. Revisiting Rome recently, a few unwritten rules of riding came to light:

- **Always drive as fast as possible**. If you don't have your scooter floored, folks will wonder what's wrong with your ride.

- **Street signs are mere suggestions.** "One-way signs are intended for cars," scooterists will tell you. Follow them into an onslaught of traffic. If you're worried about getting a ticket, just follow the pack of Vespas, Velociferos, and Scarabeos and there's no way the police will be able to pull over all the insubordinate scooterists. Besides, the police go the wrong way too.

- **Obstacles are to be overcome.** American City Magazine wrote in 1966 that "Scooters evade barriers, jump over traffic islands, cut through parks, bump down hills or steps, and slice through narrow openings." The same applies for modern Rome. Asking any native for directions will yield helpful hints like "Just go right up on the sidewalk, through the public garden." If you protest saying it's illegal to drive there, the inevitable response is, "Oh no, with a Vespa you can go there." Just don't get caught.

- **Ignore other drivers**. If motorists see you notice them, they know that you will stop and avoid hitting them. This is the scooterist's blind leap of faith. Just go, the sea of traffic will part.

- **The world is your parking lot.** The same applies for modern Rome as applied to the Big Apple in a New Yorker article from 1957, "You can park scooters almost anywhere without getting a ticket. In a metered area, the usual thing is to park them sidewise, between two parked cars. In theory, a scooter hasn't any right to be there, but the police seem to overlook it. Truth is, nobody seems to mind what scooters do." Take advantage of it. If by some bizarre happenstance you do get a ticket, or multa, ignore it.

- **Traffic lights are for decoration.** If you have a red, it's merely a warning that you may have to dodge cars coming from the side. Or as a Roman cabbie said, "Scooterists are all color blind."

- **No cop, no stop.** "In Rome there are many laws, so you can pick and choose which ones to follow," any Roman will quickly tell you. Polizia in Campo de' Fiori simply wag their index finger to warn off scooters from the pedestrian-only square, only to see the same scooter zip through the piazza from a different entrance.

- **Small is beautiful.** Use your size. A scooter may not be able to pass a Lamborghini Diablo on the Monza racetrack, but in Roman traffic, just sneak right between the legions of creeping cars passing through the triumphal arches. Nothing gets the goat of a Ferrari driver like a Lambretta leaving him in the dust. Even Popular Science back in 1957 agreed, "In heavy traffic you can retaliate by nuzzling in along stalled cars and chugging ahead . . . the scooter, a deft and agile machine, can pick its way through vacation-time traffic tangles like a chipmunk through a wood pile."

- **Chatting on your telefonino.** Driving a scooter usually requires two hands to control the gears, clutch, and gas, making talking on your telefonino an art that requires the skill of a gymnast. If you've no one to call, light a cigarette using your third hand.

- **Making una bella figura.** Always act as if someone is watching, but never pay them mind. If no one really notices you, try this old trick: whip out a hacksaw and cut off the last few inches of your tailpipe for some further volume. To avoid ruining your bella figura when your damn two-stroke engine kills again, pretend that this spot was exactly where you meant to stop. Remember, the only time your scooter can break down is in a secluded spot with someone you love.

Accessorize for Speed
As in the fashion world, accessorizing your look is the key to dressing for success. With scooters and their puny top speeds, you can't always drive fast, thus you must at least look like you're driving at maximum velocity. This 1950s Vespa is decked out for piazza cruising with so many aftermarket accessories that it attracts carabinieri to write up a speeding ticket even while it's parked: chrome trinkets, shiny but nonfunctional engine trim, big-lipped bumper overriders, wire headlamp stoneguards, whitewall Pirelli tires, spare wheel with leatherette cover, metallic cable covers, and a St. Christopher's medal are almost essential as a starting point. In the land of bolt-on chrome exhaust extenders, you can never accessorize too much.
Courtesy of the
Andrea Franca Collection

1960–1975

Microscopic-Sized Mini-Scooters

VOODOO PUTT-PUTT (SLIGHT RETURN)

The next step in the mobilization of the masses lay in mini-scoots. Just pop them in the trunk of your car and where the road stops, the fun begins. No more of that tiresome walking to get from point A to point B with these petite putt-putts; you can drive right to the door, fold up the scoot and carry it with you—all 50 lb.

Although they may appear to be condensed versions of larger scooters, these mini powerhouses often contained potent little engines with a good power-to-weight ratio on rare aluminum frames that zipped the rider along with no protection whatsoever. Luckily, the speeds made getting hurt almost impossible.

The target markets for mini fold-up scooters was boaters, pilots, and especially folks in starter homes at trailer parks. In raving over the Centaur scooter, an ad copy writer crowed, it's "a perfect blessing around the trailer-park or campsite and folds away so neatly when we're on the go."

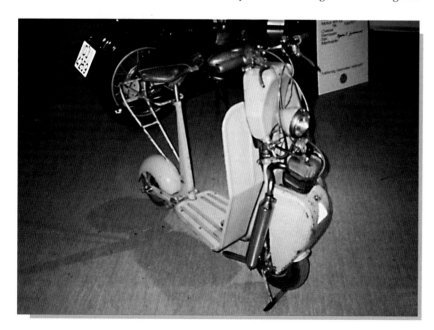

**Collapsible Argyle
Scooter Cub**

*In a mere 15 seconds, the
elfin Argyle could be folded
up like a briefcase—albeit,
a 50lb. briefcase!*
Courtesy of the owner:
Jim Kilau

Mohs Electric Scooter

*The Mohs was so far ahead
of its time that years past
before anyone could see
the idea of electric scoots
as anything more than a
liability. The selling gimmick
of this particular scoot was
its ability to carry heavy
people, since its other
qualities—a maximum
speed of 15 mph and a
range of 16 miles per
trip—left something
to be desired.*

**1950 Argyle Scooter
Cub and Happy
Scooterist**

*Amidst motorboats and
Winnebagos, lovely Rita
Barry shows off an Argyle
at the 1950 Chicago
Outdoors Show. The Scooter
Cub "will carry two heavy
people," Argyle said.
At shows like this, Argyle
attempted to conquer an
untapped market, the
mobile home bunch; as the
ad copy proclaimed,
"Trailer enthusiasts
particularly like the
convenience of the
Scooter Cub."*

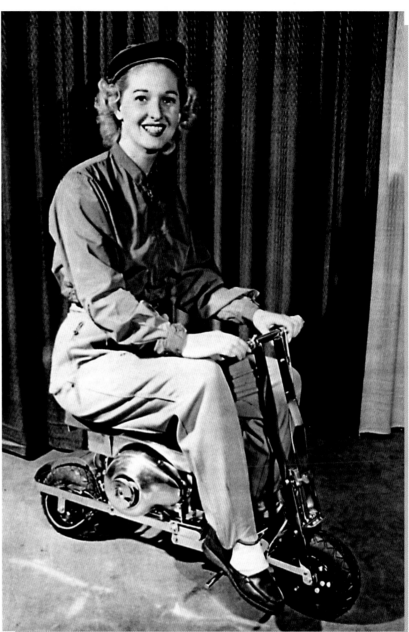

Carries this 210 lb., 6' Man, 15 M.P.H., with ease.

MOHS ELECTRIC SCOOTER
For Industrial, Institutional and Pleasure Use

*"The all-portable, fold-away Centaur
was simply made for trailer and
camper folk. It's so sturdy—yet
it folds up so small it fits under
the dining-room table. And the
Centaur is wonderful, practical
'instant-transportation'!"*

—Centaur sales flyer

1960–1975

Four-Cylinder Mustang
Yes, Victoria, it's true: There was indeed a four-cylinder scooter, Mustang impresario Howard Forrest's own custom. A fan of four-cylinder engines from his days racing midget sprint cars, Forrest first acquired a 1931 597cc Ariel Square Four engine and shoehorned it into a slightly modified Mustang chassis. This Mustang-Ariel became Forrest's own favorite commuter for several years. With a little surgery to his Mustang frame, he later built this machine shown with a custom four-banger. Bored on another day, Forrest replaced the Bumble Bee engine in a further Mustang with a BSA 350cc Gold Star engine.

Motorscooter Believe It Or Not!

THIS REALLY HAPPENED—REALLY!

Not only is truth stranger than fiction, it also tends to be more outrageous. This ages-old maxim is especially true when it comes to motorscooters.

Believe it or not, the scenes you are about to see actually did happen. The proof is in the pictures.

Motorscooter Toreadors
Bullfighting on motorscooters was like playing Bizet's Carmen on a kazoo. These mechanized toreadors straddle a Parilla Levriere scooter as they prepare to lance a bull before the corrida crowd in Lisbon, Portugal, in 1956. No doubt the scooter was painted bright Ferrari red to lure the bull as the riders crossed their collective fingers that the engine did not die at an inopportune moment. This, too, really did happen.

Scooters on Ice

The 1955 Ice Capades show toured the United States
featuring such spectacles as a re-enactment of Peter
Pan on skates as well as the Fantasy in Pink grand finale
of Ravel's Bolero. The true spectacle, however, was
Autorama: America's fascination with the motorscooter
came alive in song and dance, choreographed on ice
with no less than 19 Lambretta LD 125 Series 1
scooters. The traffic police rode their putt-putts on ice
without augering in, rivalling even the Shriners in
scootering prowess. Meanwhile, the Ice "Cop" Ades, Ice
Ca"Pets," and the El-Dorables pirouetted around the
buzzing scoots wearing gas pumps on their heads as
well as skating outfits with car grilles on the front and
hood ornaments on their tiaras—all while trying not
to choke on two-stroke fumes. This really did happen.
Courtesy of Hymie's Vintage Record City

*"In Spain, there has emerged
a new style comic art. A garishly
costumed toreador 'fights' the
bull on a Vespa between acts
of an orthodox bull-fight."*

—American Mercury, 1957

1960–1975

Shriner Motor Corps

THE RIGHT STUFF

Shriners are to motorscooters what Chuck Yeager and his band of test pilots are to super-mach jet fighters. When it comes to scooters, the fez-capped Shriners have The Right Stuff.

Who hasn't been stunned by a Shriner Motor Corps' dazzling riding skills, intricate death-defying figure-eight maneuvers, and devil-may-care round-abouts at a Fourth of July Main Street parade—too stunned to even move your hand to catch the taffy the Shriner jocks deftly toss you at the finale. Liken them to the US Navy's Blue Angels or the Air Force's Thunderbirds if you will, Shriners and motorscooters were made for each other.

The Shriner fad for scooters started with Bob Ammon, Cushman's chief. Ammon was a long-standing Shriner, and offered Cushmans bedecked with accessories and chrome trinkets to his brethren at bargain prices.

It's fitting that these "Turtles"—to appropriate a jet test pilot slang term for the best of the best—first rode Cushman Turtlebacks. Just as a Harley is the motorcycle of choice for the Hell's Angels, the Cushman is the preferred ride for most Shriners. Sure, you may have witnessed their prowess on a Vespa, Honda, or Harley-Davidson Topper, but Shriners and Cushmans go together like Shriners and fezzes.

Shriner Cushman Eagle
Looking natty, this Cushman Eagle is decked out in options from Cushman's special Shriner Option Package, including saddlebags, oompah air horn, and chrome on most everything that can be chromed. Cushman alone offered these accessories to Shriners on its scooters as well as the Vespas Cushman began importing in 1961; only later did other scooter and motorcycle makers such as Harley-Davidson or the American importers of BMW and Japanese machines jump on the bandwagon with Shriner accessories.

Shriners with the Right Stuff
Sponsored by the Yazoo Lawn Mower Center, a Cushman authorized dealer, the Hejaz Temple Motor Corps was ready to wow the crowd at a Fourth of July parade in their hometown of Greenville, South Carolina. Thirty riders strong, their figure-eight maneuvers must have been a sight to see back in the 1960s.
Courtesy of the Shriner Sam Nelson Archives

1960–1975

The DIY Years
1976–2000

The United States, Europe, and Japan gave birth to motorscooters, but in many places, the economic climate progressed so dramatically that the days of scooters buzzing down Main Street was going the way of the horse and buggy. Nostalgia ran rampant for better days when Vespas, Fujis, and Cushmans reigned supreme in the town piazzas and pedestrians complained of scooters' pollution, noise, and dangerous speeds rather than the much larger scourge: automobiles.

When Innocenti ceased production of its Lambretta in 1972 and Piaggio yanked the Vespa from the American market in the '80s, the end seemed nigh. This forced die-hard scooterists to pull out the pliers and Haynes manual to restore the classics.

The good ol' days lived on in the form of retro scooter clubs idolizing the past and digging old Allstate Vespas and Riverside Lambrettas out of barns and fixing them up better than new. Driving a restored scooter down the road now turned heads like never before, and old-timers weren't afraid to tell tall tales of bygone days of Cushman splendor and the Italian invasion of slicker scooters.

> *"I disagree with them about cycle maintenance, but not because I am out of sympathy with their feelings about technology. I just think that their flight from and hatred of technology is self-defeating. The Buddha, the Godhead, resides quite as comfortably in the circuits of a digital computer or the gears of a cycle transmission as he does at the top of a mountain or in the petals of a flower. To think otherwise is to demean the Buddha— which is to demean oneself."*
>
> —*Robert Pirsig,* Zen and the Art of Motorcycle Maintenance

Snake Oil Scooter Repairs
IT CAME FROM WITHIN THE GARAGE . . .

The sound and the fury—or is that the sound and the worry? Sad but true, motorscooters do break down despite the promise of the maker that miles would continue to unroll beneath your dwarf wheels, trouble-free mile after trouble-free mile, forever and ever, until death do you part.

When a scooter broke, it was often "repaired" by a ham-handed mechanic—usually its owner—who had never had the side cover off until that sad, fateful day. Naturally, quick-and-easy remedies were developed by scooterists around the world to keep their beloved machines on the road. Here are some of the best of the worst— with a caveat to perform these miracle cures at your own risk, as none of them are recommended by these authors, who have nary a rounded bolt head on their Lambrettas.

OPPOSITE:

Michelangelo's Motors
Overlooking Florence, a bronze copy of Michelangelo's David and a modern Italian David get fewer looks than the two beautifully restored Slimline Lambrettas. The fine Italian hand that launched the Renaissance in this city in the 1500s influenced modern design 400 years later. Alas, the market tanked for these classic scooters. Art restorers, a.k.a. mechanics, had to bring these masterpieces back to their former glory before newer versions were launched in the next millennium.

7

1976–2000

Waiting for Help on the Side of the Road

Repair Tips #2 and #3: Always dress your best for success when riding off over hill and dale on your scooter. This way, you won't scare off anyone who may stop to help you when you find yourself on the side of the road. On the other hand, when the clutch in your Lambretta 75 finally sands itself smooth after a couple weeks of use, the repair is as simple as a can of Coca-Cola. Merely dump the contents onto the clutch and let sit for 15 minutes. The super-sugarized soda pop will have your clutch working again as soon as it dries. This will not work for more permanent repairs, of course. To truly fix a clutch, you must let the Coca-Cola dry overnight.

If All Else Fails, Paint It

Repair Tip #6: One of the best tuning tricks for scooters is paint. If your brakes wheeze with asthma, your engine farts black smoke, and rust blossoms like cancer on the rest of the scooter, simply buy a can of spray paint and shoot. The results will wow your friends, making them ask, "When did you get the new scoot?" The trick's on them of course, just as many people would swear this Agrati Capri scooter on the island of Naxos, Greece, is brand spankin' new—especially with its tuned exhaust. Other repair tips include this one from a reader in Dubuque: Instead of painting, get some wood-grained contact paper and paste it to the side panels for that chic Country Squire station wagon look.

Fun and Carefree Days Ahead

Repair Tip #1: When those fun and carefree days on your Vespa suddenly come to end as you fly over the handlebars due to a seized engine—which is usually just a matter of time with a two-stroke scooter—let the overcooked engine cool down for a good 15 minutes. Then put the scooter into second gear, tie a clothesline to your friend's Plymouth Volare, and tow the scooter behind the car until the engine frees up. It usually only takes a block or two. If this age-old cure does not work, let the scooter cool its heels overnight and try again. There are two other routes to repair seized engines: 1. Rebuild the thing, or 2. Make an offer on the Volare.

And If New Paint Fails, Take the Train

Repair Tip #7: It would be just your luck, of course, to have your freshly painted Lambretta's engine eat itself for lunch outside this train station in Lambrate, the Milan suburb that was once home and namesake to the Innocenti factory that created your marvelous scooter. Quietly park your sizzling putt-putt behind a bush, buy a ticket home, and hope no Vespisti are watching.

Hey, Wanna Buy a Scooter?

Repair Tip #5: Would you buy a used scooter from this man? "This Vespa is the one so-and-so raced across the Sahara Desert, breaking the world record in 1955, but for you, my friend, a special price reflecting its special value." Sure, but make sure you check the depth of the tire tread so you won't have to buy new rubber any time soon. Always think before buying that special scooter— even from your special friend.

Full-Race Lambretta LC 125

Repair Tip #4: There's nothing like the tinny roar of a two-stroke engine about to detonate after a loud downshift in front of the local coffee shop watering hole. But to keep your scooter riding that razor's edge of high performance, you must now and then perform what's called a tune-up. A "tune-up" in motorscooter vernacular is needed when the scooter isn't running loud enough. The traditional cure is simple, effective, and cheap. Get a saw and cut off a good 6 inches (15 cm) of the exhaust pipe. This trick two-stroke tuning tip has been perfected over the decades by scooteristi everywhere, making for a scooter that not only sounds louder but is of course faster. The other route to full-race glory is to bolt on a motorcycle megaphone exhaust, as shown on this (believed-to-be ex-works racer) Lambretta LC 125 spotted in Salta, Argentina. Megaphones create a blunderbuss of orgasmic aural ecstasy for the rider and endear scooters to passersby. Get one today!

1976–2000

Classic Redux
JUMPING ON VESPA'S TRAIN

"The future of the future is the present," pronounced cultural historian Marshall McLuhan, and modern scooter manufacturers took note. In the past, groundbreakers like the original Autoped, E. Foster Salsbury's Motor Glide, and d'Ascanio's Vespa ignored what the market supposedly wanted and went with a dream of the future. Now, designers know that rehashing old styles with a modern twist gets the scooters off the showroom floors.

Aficionados tend to forget the hours spent with grease up to their elbows fixing their old Lambretta before their hot Friday night date. With modern technology on their side and the benefit of hindsight into what designs stood the test of time, nostalgic scooter creators invented the Scarabeo, Vino, Velocifero, and the Honda Shadow, with the best of both worlds: classic styling and reliable, powerful engines.

RIGHT AND BELOW:

Bella Stella
Judging that the market wanted nostalgia more than some fancy new scooter, the Genuine Scooter Company from Chicago improved on the almost-classic P series Vespas with modern updates like disc brakes and gas shocks.

Chianti Red Vino
Using the Italian mystique earned through years of films such as Roman Holiday, *Yamaha followed suit with smooth lines dating back to d'Ascanio's original 1946 Vespa. Yamaha assumes its clientele is constantly checking the mirror: "Fashion counts, so this one gets a chromed speedometer, headlight shell, mirrors and trim pieces." Then the copy adds, "Function's important too." Ignoring Mothers Against Drunk Drivers, Yamaha named its newest four-stroke Vino to connote all those tipsy trips through the piazza after a four-course supper with wine pairings.*

Velocifero

LEFT:

Velocifero
Made from the original Vespa molds that were sold to India and bought back by Italjet, the 49cc Velocifero hit the market by storm with Piaggio unable to sue for copyright to put up a fight since they had sold the rights years prior. Italjet then beat Piaggio to the punch again by fearlessly attacking the US market, being the sole new Italian scooter on American roads. It was proclaimed one of Vogue's "10 Most Wanted," with text saying it's the "wheels of choice for hip Brits like the band Oasis," ignoring the fact that Oasis singer Liam Gallagher brags about his metal Zündapp Bella. Regardless of what scooter purists claim is the pinnacle of scooterdom, styling's return to the putt-putt heydays of yore in the form of the Velocifero, the Scarabeo, and the Nuova Vespa is a promise of good scooters to come.

RIGHT:

Monument to Love
This Indian Bajaj Chetak is pampered in front of the Taj Mahal as a symbol of India's love for its homemade scooter from Vespa molds. Buyer beware! This photo from a Bajaj promotional booklet opens the possibility that either the Vespa clone is being revered for its unmatched beauty or the damn thing broke down again and we had to take the boat to work.

RIGHT:

Mirrored Mod Stella
British Mods will forever be associated with oodles of mirrors and lights jutting from the legshield like rays from the sun. Owner Kent Aldrich opted for a Stella, a newer Vespa clone of the PX series, rather than fixing up an older Vespa, to use as a daily driver. Affixing the mirrors to the legshield and handlebars required near genius mechanical prowess. Often the mirrors extended more than a foot past the edge of the side panel. The untold secret is most scooters jitter so much when riding that the long-stemmed mirrors are pure decoration.

1976–2000

Majority World Motorscooters

MASS MOBILIZATION ALL OVER AGAIN

With often similar economic circumstances to the US during the Great Depression and postwar Europe, countries from India to Taiwan needed cheap transportation, and European manufacturers could unload their antiquated scooter tools and dies.

In 1972, Scooters India bought Innocenti's scooter tooling and has continued manufacturing late 1960 Lambretta models, all the while increasing horsepower, speed, and efficiency. Following its lead, Zündapp sold off its stock and tools in 1985 to China.

Not to be outdone by rival Lambrettas and other makes, PGO of Taiwan makes scooters that resemble Vespas, and for a time, Bajaj of India pumped out more Vespas than Piaggio in Italy.

LEFT: **Argentinian Repair Manual**
One of the main reasons that the developing world has remained scooter country is that the mechanical beasts are never laid to rest. They are continually repaired through any means possible, and if they are totaled, every part can be reused to revive another aching scooter. This manual was printed in 1965–ten years after the debut of the Lambretta TV 175—but still failed to put a true TV on the cover, opting instead for an LD.

RIGHT: **Move Over, Dumbo**
Never mind that its abbreviation stands for a powerful firecracker in English, Bajaj pushed its M80—a Honda Cub clone— as better than the faithful pachyderm as its "rugged all-terrain performer." No wonder street demonstrations across India led to loyal scooters owners who "expressed in spontaneous emotion of 'Hamara Bajaj' Hindi for 'our Bajaj.'"

"Taiwan is the motorscooter capital of the world."

—Popular Science, May 1994

"In a car you're always in a compartment, and because you're used to it you don't realize that through that car window everything you see is just more TV. You're a passive observer and it is all moving by you boringly in a frame. On a cycle the frame is gone. You're completely in contact with it all. You're in the scene, not just watching it anymore . . ."

—Robert Pirsig, Zen and the Art of Motorcycle Maintenance

Siambrettas and Iso Divas Galore!
Pedestrians walk by these scooters as Americans would walk by another Ford Taurus, uninterested. In the foreground, a Siambretta LD missing its spare tire and chrome side panel piece is accompanied by a pair of Iso Divas and a string of other mopeds, motorcycles, and other scooter wannabes.

Proof of East Bloc Collusion!
Jawa and ČZ were merged under state control in 1945, and the Communist board ordered them to make a scooter, which appeared in 1946 at the Prague Fair. The result was the pug-nosed wonder, the Čezeta, which carried such highfaluting nom de guerre such as the Bohème, the Manet, and the Tatran. Even if the design couldn't live up to the artistic names, it sure would be fun to drive this missile-looking putt-putt around Cuba waiting for the next invasion of the Bay of Pigs. Courtesy of Sasha Wellborn

Classic Remnants
Two classic Italian scooters, which are now seldom seen out on the streets of Rome, are parked unceremoniously on a sidewalk in Salta, Argentina. The first, a chromed Lambretta D sans paneling, which would have been the LD, or Lusso, model. The second, a Rumi Formichino, or "little ant," with a two-cylinder 125cc engine that could leave many 250cc motorcycles of its era in the dust to breathe its two-stroke exhaust.

1976–2000

The Scooters That Never Were

THE WORLD COULD HAVE BEEN A BETTER PLACE

It's true, the world could have been a better place if these scooters had seen the light of day. Alas, they may not have brought peace, love, and understanding, and made the world more interesting by their mere existence.

1935 Gyroscope-on-Wheels

Los Angeles inventor Walter Nilsson created his Uniscooter in 1935 that was part motorcycle (due to its large wheels), part scooter (due to its small wheels), and part motorized gyroscope (due to everything else). Nilsson's one-wheeler actually operated like a wheel within a wheel—except that it incorporated four wheels in all. The outer wheel was driven by the one-cylinder engine, which propelled the wheel by gear cogs; the three small wheels worked like runners. The driver sat upright inside the contraption and steered with the auto-like steering wheel. According to notes on the flipside of this newspaper photo, the Uniscooter was steered "by a secret device that causes the wheel to lean and thereby turn while allowing the rider to keep upright." Nilsson drove his machine to a top speed of 18 mph (29 km/h) in second gear; he reported that higher speeds were feasible if he only had a custom pneumatic tire, which would set him back $800. Total cost of this invention was $5,000—in 1935! Buck Rogers must have been green with envy. Herb Singe Collection

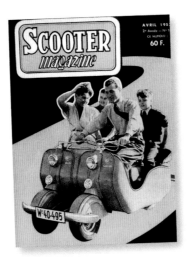

NSU Double-Scooter Car

NSU was always a creative company. In 1952, the far-seeing NSU inventors took out their welding torches and fabricated this three-wheeled NSU-Lambretta designed for "those persons who like to keep three wheels on the ground." In 1953, those NSU visionaries were back with their recharged welding torches to cobble up a prototype car made from two NSU-Lambretta 125 scooters welded together side by side. Bathtub-like rear bodywork was added on to allow for four saddle seats. The handlebars on the left-side scooter had a bar running across to the steering rod of the right-side scooter so the two front wheels could be controlled by the one set of handlebars. This really happened. Herb Singe Collection

The Four-Wheeled Scooter

NSU dabbled in three-wheelers—as seen on this page—but Messerschmitt, Piaggio, and Innocenti all made similar little vehicles. Instead, the double scooter was invented for the whole family. While Maico and other scooter brands boasted "Das Auto auf 2 Rädern" (the auto on two wheels), NSU could brag about its "Roller auf 4 Rädern" (scooter with four wheels). With a windshield, a top, and a steering wheel, NSU would have simply invented the scooter car.

Slick Magazines and Scooter Zines

FROM DOODLEBUGGING TO DO-IT-YOURSELF

The dawn of scooter writing began as advertising copy, such as a 1937 Autoglide ad, which takes a prestigious position in the scooter annals of dubious claims: "NO COST AT ALL. Why, it's actually cheaper than walking." Even *Time* magazine extolled the virtues of "doodlebugging" in a pre-Doodlebug article in 1939: "Postman Smith . . . stands at the back of his doodlebug, putt-putting along at four to twelve miles an hour. For a delivery, he leaves his scooter contentedly burbling at the curb, manages to save not only foot-power but some 23% of the time formerly needed to cover his route."

To promote their products, both Innocenti and Piaggio put out newsletters, such as the *Lambretta Notizario*, to their clubs as forum for discussion, but mostly to hawk their wares. Slick magazines such as *Motorcycling*, *Classic Cycle Magazine*, *Svet Motoru*, and many others offered only reviews of the latest models.

Occasionally journalists focused on scooter culture, but mostly as a surreptitious positive product placement to encourage planned obsolescence and conspicuous consumption. Even as late as 1981, *Cycle* magazine reinforced tired stereotypes: "Motor scooters have always been Warm Puppy Good Things, symbols of happiness and frivolity in days when motorcycles were symbols of malevolence, darkness and perversity."

This all changed when two British journalists interviewed a gaggle of Mods for the 1964 book *Generation X* (not to be confused with Douglas Coupland's book of the same title two decades later). The *X* referred to another nameless Lost Generation that had been too long ignored. "I think old people are ridiculous. So phoney, everything they do is false. I'm rude to my mum and ignore my dad, and that's how it should be," said nineteen-year-old David from London.

The die was cast, the scooterists took over the narrative from the profit-seeking companies, and soon zines and slick magazines focused as much on the people as the product.

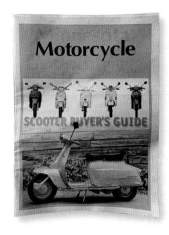

"You want to hit back at all the old geezers who tell us what to do."

—a Mod quoted in Generation X

Breath of Exhaust: Scooter Detuning Works
A zine from the St. Paul scooter scene circa 1989 depicted "Boltstrippers Anonymous" and the makeshift mechanics who haphazardly repaired (and pushed) their old Vespas and Lambrettas through the capital city. "Ne'er too tight is a bolt!"

ABOVE: **Scooters Invade Motorcycle Mag**
Vespa enthusiast Jeremy Wilker convinced Minnesota Motorcycle Monthly to feature his regular column on much cooler scooters, despite the editors' strange obsession with motorcycles. He helped them see the light and even landed a cover story with a sleek Lambretta. Courtesy of Jeremy Wilker

LEFT: **Slick** *Scootering*
Not to be confused with Scooter, Scooters, or Scoot magazines, Scootering has had the longest run of them all, with a distinct British take on the bikes. It's not just for the purists who want stock scooters, but also for custom paint jobs that look more like a kandy-kolored tangerine-flake streamline dune buggy than a two-tone Lambretta. Still, these are the go-to pages to keep connected in the UK scooter scene. Courtesy of Dan Clare at Scootering

San Fran Scoot!

The slickest scooter magazine yet sported a decidedly artistic bent, borrowing the Vespa font for its logo and the Lambretta font for the "Quarterly." Scoot Quarterly came by way of the Bay Area and hit the stands in August 1997 thanks to Casey Cole and Barry Synoground, who ran it until November 2003. After twenty-six issues, a new crew took over, making it Scoot Magazine and allowing some new scooters into the mix. Courtesy of Casey Cole

Scooter Fan Clubs' Calendar

The busty babes on Italian Vespa cheesecake calendars were mere mythological paintings, so one scooter racing team idolized the '90s icon Winona Ryder as the mascot for its calendar to ensure speed and win more races against the rockers.

"He's one of those do-gooders from Minneapolis who recycles."

—Steve Jacobs, Mod from St. Paul circa 1989, denigrating rival scooterists across the river

Shoe Sidecar and Other Oddities

Scooterworks' catalogues proved a must-read, and the $5 price tag was nothing for enthusiasts to drool over all the cool accessories and possible upgrades to their classic Vespas. If Scooterworks didn't have the parts, finding them was virtually impossible and required a trip to Italy or England, or scouring old barns for abandoned Vespas. Courtesy of Jim Kolbe

Scooter City, Milan

A REPORT FROM THE TRENCHES OF THE VESPA-LAMBRETTA WAR

To complete my indoctrination into the scooter world, I learned Italian and moved to Milan in the Lambrate area, named for the dirty Lambro River flowing by an enormous factory. My friends who live in Lambrate point to an abandoned old building: "That's where they made Lambretta scooters." What was supposed to be paradise was slated to become a shopping mall.

Before arriving, my dream of Italy consisted of hopping on an old Vespa like Gregory Peck (preferably with Audrey Hepburn on the pillion seat) and zipping through the back streets of Rome. I just needed one old Vespa, and I'd heard that the Vespa factory outside of Pisa has produced many millions of Vespas to roam the roads of the world. Italian scooter collectors in Milan insisted that their Lambretta was the best scooter in the world. Longer, sleeker, and more mechanically innovative, Lambrettas fell victim to the Vespa's lower price and soon became mostly relegated to collector showrooms.

"Milan is an occupied city," an Italian Lambretta rider lamented. No, it's not taken over by the Germans from the north or the Spanish scourge, who have long since left. Even the Veneziani and the Austro-Hungarian empire have lost their claims. No, no, it's much worse, they told me: "Milan is occupied by *Vespisti*."

Vespisti, the Italian word for Vespa aficionados, buzz through the streets on their two-wheeled "wasp" scooters, defying traffic lights and weaving through stalled traffic. They block the sidewalks, parking their Pisa-made scooters to annoy pedestrians as the police surprisingly ignore their audacity. Perhaps the fuzz were unable to combat the swarm of buzzing wasps. This lawlessness was nothing new to Milan. In the old days, however, the blatant scooter violations were committed by the home team, the *Lambrettisti*, and therefore largely tolerated.

One weekend, I ventured over to motorcycle exhibition in Segrate in the outskirts of Milan not far from the old Lambretta factory to assess the damage of the supposed Vespa attack on Lambretta's home turf. Most everyone was drooling over classic motorcycles, but I wasn't interested in these grease buckets. When I asked a couple of men gazing at a Moto Guzzi if they could tell me where the scooter area was, they laughed, "I thought that Vespas weren't allowed here!"

Ignoring their jovial ignorance, I wandered through the exhibition past the makeshift espresso bar, where lines of men dosed up on the steaming brown liquid to increase their excitement about their beloved vehicles.

There, raised on a velvet-covered pedestal, sat a shining Lambretta, part icon, part defiance against Vespas, but mostly a symbol of inspiration to go fix up those old Innocenti scooters and recall past Milanese glory.

A huge group gathered around the scooter, arguing furiously with arms gesticulating madly. As I approached, the crowd became silent and every head turned to check me out. My scooter contact was a man named Vittorio, who came out from the crowd and assured them, "It's OK, he's one of us. He translated my book."

They nodded toward me and resumed their discussion. Today's topic/argument was the perennial discussion of the supposed superiority of the older uncovered Lambrettas with an exposed engine compared to the later "sheathed" scooters with metal side panels and legshields. While lines were being drawn in the carpet, a few Lambrettisti approached me, introducing themselves under their breath.

Giorgio, the editor of *Scooter* magazine, gave me a copy of his publication, in which there was a curious shortage of Vespas. When I asked about it, he told me, "Nobody is *really* interested in Vespas. People put up with them since there are more Vespas made than any other Italian scooter."

Meanwhile, Vittorio, who had set up the impressive Lambretta display, joined us. He glared at the grandiose Vespa Club di Milano display occupying the center of the largest tent and asked rhetorically, "Why should they get the prime spot with all that space? And look, there's no one even there!"

When I told them that I was going to take some photos of the Vespas because I'd like to write a book on scooters, Giorgio instructed me to ask them how they got the best spot in the tent. Suddenly, I was a scooter spy checking out the competition. When I asked if anyone wanted to join me over at the Vespa display, they just shrugged as though they'd seen all that stuff before. They bid me well as I crossed enemy lines.

More than a dozen scooters lined the large, red-carpeted aisle to the center area, where a couple of well-dressed Vespa bureaucrats stood in front of a huge banner declaring their simple mantra, "Vespa!!!" Suddenly an old German Vespa advertisement had new meaning: *Über alle ist Vespaland* ("Vespaland is above all"). Obvious scooter propaganda.

As I approached the empty walkway lined with ribbons, banners, and trophies, one of the prim, name-tagged Vespisti greeted me, immediately grabbing my hand and shaking it profusely, exclaiming, "*Buon giorno.* I'm Marco." He was obviously thrilled to have someone pay attention to the impressive assortment of classic Vespas. He encouraged me to take photos and spoke ad nauseam about the history of each scooter and its honorable owner.

Just then, an Armani-clad man strutted up the aisle to his position at the head of the display, and a couple other Vespisti fawned over him. Marco became noticeably nervous and whispered that this was the president of the Vespa Club Milano. Marco interrupted and exaggerated that I had come all the way from the United States to admire the display and meet the esteemed leader. The president was not impressed and told me, "Of course. People visit us from all over the world. Af-

ter all, we are one of the largest and most important Vespa clubs in the world." He insisted I attend one of the weekly Vespa meetings where they discuss the merits and marvels of Vespa scooters.

I told him I would like that but worried I would be construed as a Lambretta spy. It was time to pose the treasonous question: "How come the Vespa Club Milano was given the largest and most prestigious area, when the Lambretta club was given an area just a quarter the size?"

He stared at me in disbelief and said, "Well, as you can see, we have the largest display and the most scooters; therefore, the Vespa is the most important scooter. Is it not true?" I shrugged noncommittally, not willing to argue with his circular logic. Instead I assured him I'd be at their next meeting.

Instead of returning to my compatriots at the Lambretta display and further fanning the flames of scooter rivalry, I headed for the coffee bar. All the Lambrettisti were getting more wired on shots of espresso, so I couldn't avoid being a double agent and revealing what the Vespa club president said. I didn't know whether their faces grew red out of anger or the caffeine flowing through their veins had taken effect. Regardless, I didn't wait around to find out and escaped before a scooter rumble erupted.

Rallies, Races, and Runs

FASTER! LOUDER!

Patches, T-shirts, and posters proved to be the canvases for artists to express their scooter-inspired passions during the lean years of the '90s, when Italian manufacturers had abandoned the US market. The specter of *Quadrophenia*, *Roman Holiday*, and other scooter flicks had embedded images into our collective brains, and we sought to recreate a new movement.

In an era before cell phones, scooterists had to rely on their own mechanical prowess to get out of a bind when that damn Lambretta broke down again. Suddenly a three-hour tour could seem like being shipwrecked on the side of the road. Never fear! Be one with your vehicle. Clean off the spark plugs, shoot a bit of ether into the cylinder, and bump start the scooter down a hill.

Making it to a rally, ride, or raid with a revamped classic scooter proved to be nothing short of heroic, and only fellow scooterists could really understand.

Scooter Dü Two
In homage to Hüsker Dü, the seminal Twin Cities punk band, Jeremy Wilker designed the artwork for the annual scooter rally in the Twin Cities, envisioning that their album Land Speed Record *was actually referring to Vespas— never mind that the actual "land speed record" on two wheels was 100 mph (160 km/h) made by a Mustang scooter in 1952. In the Twin Cities, Mods mixed in with the early punk rock scene as Chris Osgood from the Suicide Commandos rode along with Hüsker Dü's drummer, Grant Hart.* Courtesy of Jeremy Wilker

RIGHT: **Raves and Rages**
Casting off its hippy past in favor of a Modernist future, San Francisco became a hub of scooter hubbub in the late 1990s with rallies and stylish magazines. Loud bands were required for any decent scooter rally, as seen in this 1998 Scooter Rage poster. Courtesy of Casey Cole

FAR RIGHT: **Go to Groningen!**
Before Piaggio opened its museum in Pontedera, Vespa clubs across the world carried the torch and kept the classic old scooters running and raiding at rallies. While most in Italy were regional raduni, or gatherings, some lured Vespisti from across the continent, such as this 1998 EuroVespa in the northern Dutch city of Groningen.

Lost Again!
Before GPS ensured we'd never lose our way, scooterists relied on maps and their wits, as seen in this poster by Katy Smith. The "No Direction Home" rally paid homage to homeboy Bob Dylan from Hibbing, Minnesota, who never quite found his way back to living on the frigid Iron Range or in his birthplace in Duluth. Courtesy of Katy Smith

Flyers, Patches, and Postcards
Scooter rallies from the '90s and 2000s had to have patches, posters, and other cool artwork to get out the word and so attendees could show fellow scooterists all the places they'd been. Some paid homage to bands, anime, Lego, or other pop culture icons who would have been so much cooler if they'd been on two wheels, followed by a trail of two-stroke smoke. Courtesy of Matt DeVries

A New Millennium 2001–On

By the end of the last millennium, the worldwide scooter boom seemed destined to disappear, but it has just switched theaters and shows no sign of subsiding.

More significant than clubs restoring the classics is the developing world scooter boom showing the rest of the world how it's done—even if the designs were mostly based on Italian classics. Today, more scooters zip around cities than ever before. Honda has produced millions of Cub scooters that carry drivers from Mexico to Sri Lanka, and Yamaha and Suzuki are close competition.

China, Taiwan, and India's entrance into the world market changed everything. No longer could European and American manufacturers compete with the cheap labor and mechanical know-how. Most notably, Piaggio reentered the American market with its sleek new Vespa, which now attracts a high-class clientele rather than merely mobilizing the masses.

Scooter Shops and Boutiques
VESPA BATH SALTS FOR WEARY SCOOTERISTS

During the lean years before the new scooter millennium, few shops supplied necessary spare parts to keep their rides on the road. Cushman stores continued to service their four-wheeled vehicles, but owners of two-wheelers were left in the lurch and forced to scavenge at swap meets. In the age before the Internet connected the world, West Coast Lambretta Works in California and Scooterworks in Chicago mail-ordered new-old parts and rebuilt engines.

It was the dawning of a new era of upscale scootering, and suddenly the Vespa was a status symbol. "If you don't care about quality or image, buy a plastic Yamaha scooter. If you want to buy into the Vespa lifestyle, we're the place," said Jim D'Aquila, the co-owner of the Vespa Boutique in downtown Minneapolis in 2002.

What's that? Did you say "boutique"? The unfortunate moniker did little to dispel the "Italian hairdryer" slur but seemed to fit the new digs. Where else could you find Vespa watches, Vespa silver cufflinks, Vespa perfume, Vespa bath foams, Vespa herbal cream, Vespa bath oil, and Vespa bath salts (in strawberry, mint, musk, and rose scents)?

The ET4 and ET2 were released in 1996, and six years later, the new Vespas invaded America. To open a new Vespa store, entrepreneurs reportedly need to plunk down a hefty chunk of change: $350,000. *Minnesota Motorcycle Monthly*'s scooter columnist Jeremy Wilker referred to the Vespa store as "the Gap approach" when fifty-one such boutiques opened around the United States.

Motorcycle riders once again had to share the road with their smaller cousins. Gary Kiese, co-owner of a Vespa Boutique, was stumped by scooter talk, however: "I can answer any questions you have on Ducatis and other Italian motorcycles." Could it be that the Rockers have won after all?

"Vespa is the Gucci bag of scooters."

—Bob Hedstrom, talking about the new Vespa compared to its competition

8

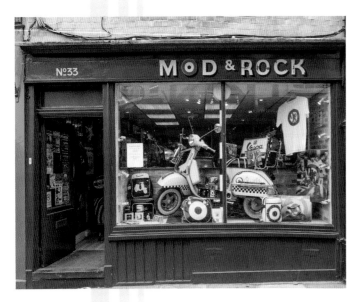

Roman Mod Holiday

Not far from the Spanish Steps lies this Mod & Rock shop in the heart of Rome, where Audrey Hepburn once risked Gregory Peck's life on a Vespa. The irony of this Italian shop glorifying English Mods, who glorified Italian style, seemed lost on the storekeeper. Never mind, he still had the coolest stock of scooter memorabilia, as only the Italians can do it.

Scooterville, USA

Begun in the '90s near Dinkytown, USA, Scooterville soon moved its digs in Minneapolis. The Vespa Boutiques went bust, and Piaggio realized that downhome scooter shops had kept Vespa's dream alive all these years. Scooterville survived the Great Recession of 2008 and the Minneapolis Uprising of 2020 while buildings burned around it. The city smoldered, but scooters boomed.

Running Like Clockwork?

Anyone who has ever owned a Lambretta knows they don't work like a Swiss watch, and you need to constantly tinker with them. Lambretta watches sought to cash in on the nostalgia of the iconic scooters. Alas, this is the official nail in the coffin to proclaim Lambrettas officially a museum piece and a slice of the rose-colored past that can now be commodified. Wait, does this book do that too?

"We're not Hells Angels, we're hell's dorks!"

—Diane Sawyer, host of Good Morning America, while test driving a new Vespa live on air

The "New" Vespa Comes to America

Just as designers reimagined the Beetle, Mini, Fiat 500, and other iconic automobiles, Piaggio also launched a new Vespa. While all these vehicles originally appealed to a budget-strapped populace in search of wheels, these remakes cashed in on the cachet of these workhorses. Never mind the history of Volkswagen's Third Reich connections, Fiat's fascist roots, or Piaggio's airplane crashing with Mussolini's son aboard. This was a new era!

The classy new Vespas were sleek, modern versions of the classic without all the vibrations and front-brake dipping that made the Vespa infamous, with an expensive price tag to boot. The new Vespas have appeared in any number of TV ads, and Hollywood stars like Jay Leno, Sandra Bullock, Tobey Maguire, Sylvester Stallone, Jerry Seinfeld, Kirsten Dunst, Sarah Jessica Parker, and Robert De Niro have splurged for a new Vespa. Piaggio made the right call, however, by upholding the "Made in Italy" brand of high quality that didn't denigrate the noble Vespa and will make these scooters collector items in the future.

"Every time I'm waiting at a traffic light, there is always at least one pedestrian who, rushing past me, does a double take. 'Whoa, dude, Vespa!' he'll say (or some variation thereof). And he stops, right there in the middle of the street, to admire what's between my legs."

—Bill Buford, author

"La Nuova Vespa"
Piaggio still lived on the edge when the new Vespa cruised into the piazza, like this one parked in Rome. Italians were split. How could Piaggio improve on a classic? The design harks back to the height of scooterdom, when BSA and British Triumph teamed up to produce the Tigress/Sunbeam scooter in 1959, alas at the end of the scooter boom. While Corradino d'Ascanio's muse inspired him to create the first Vespa in 1945, "all the designers were trying to get their name on the new Vespa," said a young Piaggio designer in 1997.

"Women come up and go, 'What's that' . . . then you have to explain that you're married."

—Jay Leno, Tonight Show host talking about riding his new Vespa

Scooterworks Then and Now
In the 1990s, Piaggio and Innocenti had abandoned the US market, so Scooterworks of Chicago was loaded with vintage scooters and the relatively new P-series Vespas. Today, Scooterworks spawned Genuine Scooters, and dozens of modern scooters fill the space—and they generally require less tinkering than the old classics.

The Elite New Wave
As the essential modern scooter in the 1980s, the Elite made the Vespa's line seem suddenly dated. No wonder both Adam and the Ants and Devo stumped for Honda's Elite as the scooter of self-conscious New Wavers with funny hats.

The Evolution of the Scooter
Evoking visions of brutally honest Darwinian theory, Moto Gilera pushed its Runner as the winner of the survival of the scooters. The missing link is downward angular lines of the sport bike to complete the evolution to this 124cc two-stroke. Gilera pushed its scooter as the "Runner," but the name would never go far in the English market due to the pejorative phrase "it's a runner" for a beat-up vehicle that can only run.

Sport Bike Scooters
TWO-STROKE CROTCH ROCKETS

"It is the business of the future to be dangerous," according to historian A. N. Whitehead, but nowadays scooters are fairly safe when compared to the early gadabouts. The look of the new models, however, is pure speed, with angular lines mimicking neon sport bikes.

Now in the design laboratories of Piaggio in Pontedera, a young team of designers from around France, Sweden, and Italy are hashing out the future of scootering with bizarre drawings, most of which will never get beyond the prototype stage. To step into the future, history must be ignored. "We want no part of it, the past," said Marinetti, who knew that to invent anything new, thousands of years of history needs to be put on the shelf.

"To turn a fourteen-year-old child loose on a motor scooter in today's traffic is about as sensible as giving a baby a dynamite cap for a teething ring."

—Gen. George S. Stewart, National Safety Council

Go-Fast Lines
No, this isn't a racing bike itching to tear rubber at Monza. Mimicking not only the crotch rocket sport bikes but also Nike Air Jordan high tops, this Yamaha scoot with three-tone paint job appears to jet into the air even while propped on its kickstand.

The Latest Lambretta

RISEN FROM THE ASHES

The end came in 1972 when Innocenti closed down Lambretta production. Had Piaggio's Vespa won the war? Never say die!

Slimline Lambrettas were produced in vast numbers by Scooters India Limited, with ever-improving technology using the molds from Innocenti's Italian plant. The very last Indian-made Lambretta GP (also known as Vijay Super) came off its production line in 1997.

Old rivalries still smoldered as the Vespa-Lambretta wars lived on in a different part of the world. For a time, Bajaj, the largest producer of scooters in the world, also lay in India, making Vespa clones like never before. Although tough environmental laws made these scooters hard to obtain in the Western world, they were often available as some-assembly-required kits.

Even though Scooters India Limited had bought the Lambretta name and all the molds from Innocenti, somehow other scooters with the familiar Lambretta logo appeared and just dared Scooters India to take them to court.

A new Lambretta prototype was unveiled at the 2005 Motorcycle Dealer Expo in Indianapolis. The never-realized plan was to build the body in North Carolina, thousands of miles from its Milanese birthplace aside the River Lambro and the Indian company that owned the name. Classic Motorcycles and Sidecars (CMSI), which also makes Twist N' Go scooters, followed the Series III lines of Lambrettas for a sleek new scooter with many updates. The 12-inch (30 cm) tires would keep the Lammie from tipping, and the liquid-cooled engine would prevent overheating. The kicker for Lambretta loyalists who spent years under the side panels was the Piaggio automatic engine. Alas, these new models didn't hit the showroom floor in 2005 as planned.

CSMI somehow reasoned that it could use the Lambretta name (it allegedly had licensed the name from Scooters India) and slapped the hallowed name on two embarrassing Taiwanese Adly scooters: Lambretta Uno and Due. These "Lambrettas" didn't make it into the European market and only hit the showrooms of North America; CSMI must have reasoned that Italians and other Europeans would be rightly outraged at this plastic abomination.

Enter Motom of Milan, which had made scooters in the '50s and got back in the game when it deemed the Lambretta name its own. The Lambretta Pato hit the streets as a usurper of the Innocenti throne but basically was just a plastic Chinese scooter with the classic Lambretta logo slapped on the side panels. Motom got it right with its next model, the Lambretta LN, which looks like a slick, updated Lambretta even if the plastic overpowers the metal. Perhaps the switch from Chinese manufacturing to Taiwanese greatly improved the scooter. A tussle over ownership of the marque ensued, and the courts deemed that Motom never owned the rights to the Lambretta name.

That didn't stop others from jumping into the ring. In 2014, Italjet released in Vietnam its Lambretta Lamsport, which is about as close to a Lambretta as a rocket-propelled roller skate.

Then came the Lambretta Consortium, which released the impressive V-Special in 2017 that followed the high standards of the original scooter. Strangely, this new line of sleek Lambrettas hasn't hit the States, but perhaps this has something to do with Scooters India Limited still claiming the rights to the name that Innocenti sold to it. Perhaps SIL will once again pull out the molds to produce the metal classics.

All of this confusion doesn't even mention the Scomadi and Royal Alloy Lambretta clones with models that are perhaps the most true to the original designs.

"Speed is the triumph of effect over cause, the triumph of instantaneity over time as depth, the triumph of the surface and pure objectality over the profundity of desire. Speed creates a space of initiation, which may be lethal; its only rule is to leave no trace behind."

—Jean Baudrillard in America, when he was perhaps praising the merits of a souped-up 1963 Lambretta TV 175

The Martyrdom of Innocenti's Lambretta

In 1966, Innocenti produced a film to commemorate the death of its founder, Ferdinando Innocenti, who died shortly before. The film, We Carry On, idealized the massive Lambrate factory and its mechanized production lines, orchestrated to the sounds of musique concrète and punctuated by blasts of industrial noise. The film was an odd blend of Futurism, Fascism, and Industrialism with the faceless, omnipresent narrator describing scooter construction with orgasmic delight: "The electro-magnetic test bed is the altar of destruction on which will be sacrificed the body of a Lambretta." Both Innocenti and Abraham were willing to sacrifice their son to appease the Almighty (consumer). It was enough to make your senses tingle, and the film won the nonfiction first prize at the Cannes festival.

But Ferdinando Innocenti's death and the late-1960s decline in scooter popularity were hurting Innocenti, along with the constant "blackmail" by unions. By 1970, scooter sales had slackened as buyers were stepping up to automobiles. By 1971, Innocenti halted its exalted scooter assembly lines and sold its equipment for building the DL Series to Scooters India, which was owned by the Indian government.

The plant in Milan shifted from making Minis and Daihatsus to 2,000cc Maserati Biturbos. By March 1993, the final nail was hammered home, laying to rest the Italian Lambretta. Then in 1995, a German businessman, Dieter Höfmayer, announced that he bought the Lambretta name and would begin reassembling the famous scooters in Lugano, Switzerland, with Morini engines from Bologna. Journalists from the Corriere della Sera and other Italian newspapers jumped for joy at the prospect of the Milanese legend once again cruising the piazzas. Alas, the Swiss Lambretta SA never put out a putt-putt.

With the arrival of the Vespa in the United States and other scooters flooding the market, news spread in 2004 that new Lambrettas would soon hit the scooter shops, but the old mythological beast wouldn't rise from the ashes in a less-than-perfect form until 2012.

Meanwhile, the old Lambrate factory was slated to be turned into a shopping mall and then into a large garbage recycling plant. The main office building in Via Pitteri has been transformed into a senior citizen home. All things must pass.

As if Innocenti wouldn't die, in 2021, the city of Milan announced a revitalization project to make the two million square feet of the "crystal palace" section of the factory into a cultural hub with, among other things, an indoor skate park and storage for the classic 1920s-era orange trams that click around town. Most important, the famous Milanese opera house Teatro alla Scala, announced it would use the factory to build sets and as a staging ground. Could an opera to the Lambretta be far behind?

Old Folks' Factory
The main offices of the Innocenti building that produced the Lambretta, De Tomaso Minis, and Ghia Spiders were turned into apartments for senior citizens, who surely drove Lambrettas in their youth. The "Palazzo di Cristallo," or crystal palace, with hundreds of overhead windows to let in natural light, is slated to be a cultural hub of 300,000 square meters, but alas no 24-hour Lambretta endurance races. Courtesy of Giovanni Erba

The Gates of Paradise?
Only a select few can enter Piaggio's portal to discover the magic inside. Just like Willy Wonka's chocolate factory, workers and those with a golden pass can visit the factory floor. Vespisti visitors are kindly guided to the beautiful Museo Piaggio next door.

CLOCKWISE FROM TOP LEFT: **Works of Art**

Sure, Michelangelo may have spent four years on his back painting the Sistine Chapel, but was he ever so lucky to spend time on his knees fixing a classic Lambretta Li125 Slimline? In this square overlooking Florence, Il Divino, or "the Divine" as Michelangelo Buonarroti was nicknamed, turns his head away from this modern classic scooter. Maybe the Master could have gone places, or fare strada, as the Italians say, if he'd had wheels under his feet.

Butcher's Bike

Even the local felines cannot resist this gorgeous Slimline Lambretta that advertises a family-run macelleria, or butcher, specializing in pork jowls and lard. Even here in Florence, just a stone's throw from the Vespa factory in Pontedera, outside of Pisa, some enthusiasts stay loyal to the Lambretta, even if Innocenti stopped making them in Milan decades before this photo was shot. Clearly displaying this Lambretta is a snub toward Pisa, likely in reference to the 1364 Battle of Cascina, in which John Hawkwood (Giovanni L'Acuto) tried to attack the Florentine army as they bathed in the Arno River.

Reviving a Classic

In the search to recreate a stock Lambretta, the Chinese Royal Alloy scooters come closest to reaching this land of Shangri-La. Modern updates were added to prevent the inevitable cursing and cussing about one's "Lambroken." The Royal Alloy is faster and more reliable than the classics, even if some of the plastic around the handlebars—to meet current standards—leaves some purists cold.

Vespas at the Guggenheim; Lambrettas at the Louvre (someday)

PUTT-PUTTS ON A PEDESTAL

"There is a certain residual lawnmower likeness to the exhaust note, I admit, but otherwise the Helix is more motorcycle than scooter."

—David Edwards, Cycle

Perhaps it's a pipe dream to see a Lambretta displayed next to the *Mona Lisa* and Rodin's *Thinker*. Of course scooters belong on the road, but some are so unusual that perhaps it's not sinful to put them on a pedestal for all to see. The Guggenheim Museum in New York paid tribute to the Vespa. Now Corradino d'Ascanio can take his rightful place next to Ghia, Farina of Pininfarina, Ponti, and da Vinci. The work of these visionaries appeared along with the little wasp as a tribute to Italian design in the Frank Lloyd Wright–designed museum, next to a classic Olivetti typewriter and a Bialetti espresso maker.

Scooters are mostly an afterthought—a curiosity—for car and motorcycle buffs who have a little closet with a handful of scooters that rockers can scoff at but secretly admire. Many collectors briefly open their studio to curious onlookers. Roberto Donati from Piacenza had one of the best Vespa collections in the world but recently sold the scooters off—except for his truly rare Paperino, the precursor of the Vespa made in Biella, Italy. Jim Kilau of St. Paul, Minnesota, can rightfully claim one of the best American scooter collections in the world but has only briefly opened his door to scooter aficionados. Here are several of the best; see them while you can!

Sophisticated Scooter
In Stockholm's Old Town, Gamla Stan, a statue of Swedish artist/musician Evert Taube, is challenged by a decked-out, new Mod Vespa. Even if scooters have taken over Stockholm, Sweden's museum to those two-wheeled wonders is four hours away in Källby.

"The sexy, low-slung two-passenger Honda Helix [is] virtually the 'stretch limousine' of the scooter world."

—Consumers Digest

Museo Piaggio
After many other Vespa collectors kept the spirit alive, Piaggio finally made the move to open its fabulous Vespa museum next to its factory in Pontedera in the province of Pisa. The collection of vehicles, advertising, and memorabilia is classy in a way that only the Italians can pull off. Enter next to the Piaggio train and learn how the company survived the lean postwar years thanks to helicopter designer Corradino d'Ascanio, who in February 1945 made a few sketches of a little prototype scooter called MP6. It featured a unique monocoque body, attractive shielding of the engine, and just the small problem of an overheating engine.

Scooter as Canvas
ART ON TWO WHEELS

The stock production-line finish does not suffice for artists intent on making the world their canvas. Henry Ford allegedly proclaimed, "Any customer can have a car painted any color that he wants so long as it is black." Well, that didn't last long, but at least scooter manufacturers grudgingly offered a few different colors.

The factory finish wouldn't suffice as unsatisfied scooterists painted, airbrushed, and affixed any sticker they could find. The wide legshields and side panels offered the perfect medium for a moving art gallery.

Fueled by Folgers
What makes it go? Admirers flock to check out the caffeine-themed decor of Smitty Regula's Percolating Coffee Psycho scooter from Houston, Texas. Courtesy of Ruthann Godollei

TOP: **Soft Machine**
James Buhler covered his scooter in a fantastic array of soft fabrics. His helmet has a fuzzy pastel to match his ride. Courtesy of Ruthann Godollei

CENTER: **Vespa Ecologica**
Livio de Marchi is obsessed with wood and hand carves everyday objects—and entire vehicles—in beautiful wood. His Ferrari F50 floats through the canals of Venice with its inboard engine to prove that at least some cars can drive through the city of water. Here, his perfect wooden Vespa glows and can only be rivaled by his wooden Lambretta—with wooden Mod mirrors. Courtesy of Livio de Marchi

BOTTOM: **Salvador's Side Panels**
The notorious Spanish surrealist Salvador Dalí infamously signed dozens of blank sheets of paper that other artists later filled in to flood the market with fakes. Or were they indeed forgeries since the signature was genuine? Dalí signed the Vespa side panel, but does that make it an authentic piece of his artwork? After all, Marcel Duchamp signed a urinal, which he didn't make, with the name "R. Mutt" and called it art!

Into the 21st Century
TO BOLDLY GO WHERE NO SCOOTER HAS GONE BEFORE

Scooters have inspired many great minds to make brilliant, but often ridiculous, inventions, and the tide shows no sign of subsiding. Honda makes its mini Gold Wing scooter, the Helix. Dozens of companies are producing modern electric scooters. And Piaggio continues to design ever more bizarre-looking Vespa clones. The trend shows no sign of an end.

After the 1960s, scooterists were often looked on with pity as poor folk who couldn't afford a real car, such as a Mini or the Fiat 500. Scooters were viewed as a passing fad that had had its day. The final nails in the coffin were environmental laws putting restrictions and heavy tariffs on dirty two-stroke engines. New, economical engines developed to abide by these laws, and when these new scooters couldn't, they moved to the developing world. The scooter remains undead, however, with renewed interest by new generations who want an economical and convenient form of transportation that will zip them away from the clogged interstate to greener pastures.

The Scooter of the Future?
BMW didn't believe the hype of the 1950s scooter craze, and although it built a prototype scooter in 1954, it didn't throw its hat into the ring and begin production. Then in 1992, BMW showed the C1 scooter at the Cologne Motorcycle Show, which it declared to be a new kind of vehicle: not a car, not a scooter, but somewhere between the two. The C1 boasted all the safety of a car with a roll bar and four-point seatbelt but maintained the easy parking and maneuverability of a scooter. Two different engines were featured at the show, a 125cc and a hefty 250cc.

Brave New Scooter World

ELECTRICS, AUTOMATICS, AND FOUR-STROKES

The bullet-like sound of a two-stroke engine (with the muffler conveniently sawed off) ricocheting off the walls of narrow alleys of Italian hill towns may soon be a simple remembrance of things past. Whew! Finally the Italian after-lunch nap can be taken in peace. Alas, the pep of a potent two-stroke engine and the unforgettable aroma of two-stroke oil burning a trail behind a speeding scooter may leave the air cleaner than ever.

Small four-stroke engines soon met emission standards, even if they were a bit more pricey and trickier to repair. Even electric scooters showed the world a better way and could save the planet one scooter at a time—some governments even offered tax incentives to go all electric.

Not only that, driving new scooters proved easier than ever as gears and clutches went the way of the Autoped. Simply twist the throttle and go. Sure, Motoscoot and others had mastered automatic scooters decades before, but the control of dropping a revving scooter into gear after releasing the clutch is impossible to replicate.

Manual Shift
Once upon a time, Vespisti could rely on their ride to not be stolen because clumsy crooks couldn't figure out how to shift the scooter. Gone are the days of knowing how to use a clutch, as seen on this Genuine Stella that replicates the Vespa hand shifter. Now nefarious thieves can simply twist the throttle and go.

New NIU
While electric scooters have long been possible, only in the 2000s did these battery-powered bikes become truly feasible. Piaggio released an electric Vespa, among other lesser-known makes, and the Chinese NIU is set to dominate the electric scooter market with nearly two million scooters produced annually.

Endurance Vespa
In 1951, Italy hosted the famous Sei Giorni di Regolarità rally, known as the International Six Days Enduro off-road race. The lowly Vespa conquered all through the mountains near Varese on the border with Switzerland. In its honor, Piaggio released the Vespa GTS Sei Giorni, a modern version of the famous scooter to conquer these Alpine passes. This time, a 300cc four-stroke engine powered the Piaggio scooter, with a headlamp lowered from the handlebars to the front mud guard to resemble the earliest Vespas.

A Scooter by Any Other Name . . .

WHEREFORE ART THOU?

The perennial confusion of "what is a scooter?" plagues our humble language. Bob Hedstrom, the owner of Scooterville in Minneapolis, told me, "About half of our calls are looking for push scooters or handicapped ones. I just got off the phone with someone right now looking for an electric wheelchair 'scooter.'" Four-wheeled handicapped scooters somehow got lumped into the bunch, implying that Mods ride slow-moving geriatric lawnmowers.

Then in the 2010s, rental "scooters" littered cities and caused countless accidents. Scooter purists scoff at the electrified children's push scooters plaguing modern metropolises; however, the precursor to the Cushman and Vespa was the Autoped. Sure these motorized push scooters look more like a skateboard with a broom handle than a sleek Zündapp Bella, so the Italians even invented a different word: *monopattino* (or "single roller skate"). The French use the quaint *trottinette*, like a trotting little horse.

With the dawn of two-wheeled mobiles, we must remember that Leonardo da Vinci's famous (and contested) drawing of a two-wheeled vehicle looks curiously like a bicycle—or is it a scooter? Let's just say that the bicycle, monopattino, and motorcycle are all precursors in the stages of evolution to that most perfect form: the scooter.

Guiding Principles for All Future Scooters

Corradino d'Ascanio, the star designer of Piaggio's Vespa, devised six tenets for all future motorscooters. While other brands may have strayed from d'Ascanio's wise words, they were soon brought into the flock when they realized their wayward ways. Here are the commandments of that scooter visionary:

1. *The scooter must be easy to drive.*

2. *Weight must be kept to a minimum.*

3. *Just like a woman's bicycle is easy to mount, so must a scooter be.*

4. *The gearshift shall be mounted on the handlebars for easy handling.*

5. *The driver must be kept clean by the front legshield, floor panels, and covered engine.*

6. *A spare tire must be incorporated into the design of the scooter and shall be easy to change.*

Start 'em Young
A Vespa dad counsels his young one on how to properly shift for maximum speed to outrun the café racers. Courtesy of Ruthann Godollei

Modernizing a Tradition
Even if Vespa designer Corradino d'Ascanio didn't live to see the unveiling of the "new" Vespa, he would have approved. The new design meets all his principles.

Funny Face

THE WORLD IS DECEIVED WITH ORNAMENT

The legshield originally just protected a rider from splashing rain and mud but soon became equivalent to the "face" of the vehicle. Badges, stickers, and emblems adorned the front to give the scooter its personality. The many faces of scooters reveal an attempt to look friendly, fierce, or funny. Does it show what's beneath the body-work, or is the beauty skin deep?

RIGHT: **Ham and Angst**
The two-tone front legshield of a Lambretta Li125 Riverside provides the perfect cachet for ska-inspired band Ham and Angst and harkens back to the fit-as-many-riders-as-possible-on-a-Lambretta game of the early Innocenti raduni (rallies) in Milan.

"Despite modifications in design over the years, the overall conception and placement of the scooter—its project market, its general shape, its public image—remained fixed in the formula: motor cycles as men; scooters as women . . ."

—Dick Hebdige in
Hiding in the Light

CLOCKWISE FROM TOP LEFT:

Mock Malaguti
The front of the Yesterday may harken back to the golden age of automobiles with oversized grilles and chrome. Here, however, the air duct serves no purpose and simply is a trompe l'oeil that isn't really tricking anyone.

Nondescript NIU
The spartan NIU, with its light in the middle of the legshield, looks almost like the protruding muzzle of a big red dog.

Eager Expression
The dual headlamps of the Burgman 400 seem ready for enjoyment. The friendly Suzuki S and the pudgy cheeks make this enormous scooter seem more of a gentle giant than a motorcycle wannabe.

While Rome Burns . . .
Sure, Nero may have fiddled while the Visigoths sacked his city, but he put on a happy face, just as SYM's Fiddle III keeps smiling with a determined yet friendly look.

Wonder Twin Powers Activate!
As a mix between the Transformers and Power Rangers, Kymco could save the universe and get to school on time. The futuristic go-fast lines proved this was not nostalgic for daddy's Vespa.

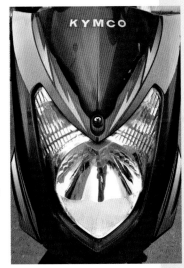

2001–ON

Obey Vespa!

The scooters have a posse and took over Salt Lake City in 2004. Artist Shepard Fairey took a break from his political posters to delve into something far more important: scooters. The Vespa GL SLC (Gran Lusso, Salt Lake City) dominates the frame like Big Brother demanding obedience. Courtesy of Amerivespa and Vespa Club of America

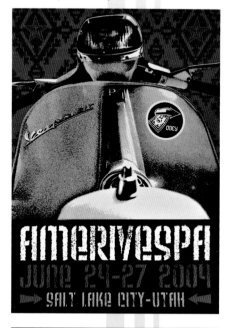

Car versus Scooter

Ah, who wouldn't want to see a Vespa scooter race the Vespa 400 car? Artist Glenn Reid (www.reidstudio.com) catches the moment with this gorgeous poster for the 2003 Amerivespa rally. If only Piaggio had succeeded in mass producing its Vespa car—only 30,000 were made between 1957 and 1961. Courtesy of Amerivespa and Vespa Club of America

Meets in the New Millennium
BIGGER, BETTER, FASTER!

While we can wax nostalgic about the scooter glory days gone, more people are riding than ever before. While European *raduni* may not have a thousand scooters and dangerous stunts, American and UK rallies are better than ever. For example, the Vespa Club of America claims to be the "largest scooter club in the US" since 1992 (perhaps Cushman was bigger?). The US Vespa rallies, Amerivespa (Lambrettas are tolerated), seem to have grown steadily into the 2000s. What's more, the glorious posters, patches, and artwork show that the apex of scooterdom is indeed upon us.

Moulin Rouge Meets New Orleans

Harkening back to the Belle Époque in Paris, Amerivespa descended on the Big Easy in 2014 in this Toulouse-Lautrec-inspired poster. Imagine high kicking the can-can in a Louisiana cabaret from your Vespa saddle. Courtesy of Amerivespa and Vespa Club of America

All-Weather Ride

It's a good thing Vespa engines are covered for all sorts of weather, as seen in this Amerivespa poster for the 2017 rally in Seattle. Neither snow nor rain nor heat nor gloom of night will keep these scooterists from their appointed rounds. Courtesy of Amerivespa and Vespa Club of America

Wear Your Colors

Patches on your Mod anorak proved you'd been around the block and to the latest rallies, so the Bay Area scooter clubs kept up the spirit with these patches to prove who's in the gang. Courtesy of John Curnutt

He's a Demon on Two Wheels

Mach GoGoGo, a.k.a. Speed Racer, introduced the US to manga comics and anime cartoons, and the simple, stop-action frames showed us what speed could be. A Twin Cities scooter rally, Skooter Dü 5, honored the Japanese icon and wondered how great the world would be if only Racer X or Speed Racer had a Lambretta rather than the Mach 5! Courtesy of John Britton

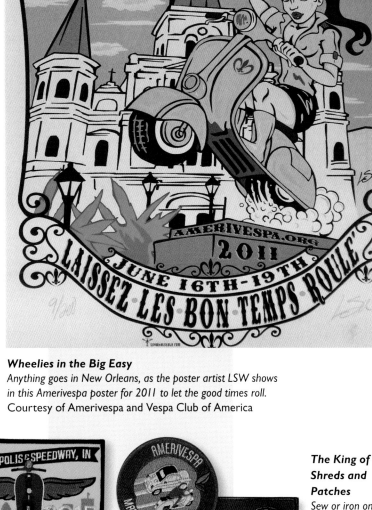

Punk Rock Scooter Rallies

Paying homage to Hüsker Dü and apocalyptic end time prophesies, scooter rallies around the turn of the millennium took a tongue-in-cheek take on pop culture and skewed it to the scooter world. Courtesy of Matt DeVries

Wheelies in the Big Easy

Anything goes in New Orleans, as the poster artist LSW shows in this Amerivespa poster for 2011 to let the good times roll. Courtesy of Amerivespa and Vespa Club of America

The King of Shreds and Patches

Sew or iron on that patch to show that you indeed were there. Some of the patches play off the limited-edition posters, while others harken back to '50s logos. Courtesy of Amerivespa and Vespa Club of America

2001–ON

Scooter Encyclopedia A–Z

Abbottsford UK ★ ★ ★

This early British scooter updated the Autoped with a 2.5hp John engine placed under the seat and double wheels on the front.

ABC Skootamota UK ★ ★ ★ ★ ★

Perhaps one of the most important putt-putts to further the cause was the 1919 ABC Skootamota with a 147cc engine. Built until 1923, the Skootamota later switched to a 110cc overhead valve engine with seat on top of the diminutive 8in wheels. The ABC lacked suspension for the 35kg scooter that could supposedly reach 40km/h. With the idea that the scooter would revolutionize transportation, one model of the Skootamota was a delivery vehicle with a hefty box under the seat behind the driver's feet.

The forward-looking French received the ABC with open arms and became one of the main markets for engineer Granville Branshaw's design. An early French ad proclaimed that:

"If Madame has to meet a friend at 11 o'clock at the Bois de Boulogne, at noon be at home for lunch, then shop at the big stores downtown, and later in the evening dine with friends in the suburbs. She would never be able to do all this by taking outrageously priced taxis that are impossible to flag down. Knowing this, Madame bought a SKOOTAMOTA, the woman's machine 'par excellence' which is easy to drive, doesn't demand any mechanical knowledge, and doesn't need a garage."

Achilles GERMANY ★

Achilles built motorcycles for the Austro–Hungarian empire in the days when Princess Georgiana, the White Rose of Hungary, was to wed his majesty King Zog of Albania.

Achilles offered its Cushman Eagle-like Sport scooter with the choice of a Fichtel & Sachs 147cc or 175cc engine from 1953–1957. The Sport was half scooter—small 10in wheels and floorboard—and half motorcycle with the gas tank between the legs and engine ahead of the rear wheels. The Achilles had power to scale its native mountains, with the smaller Sport at 6.75hp at 4500rpm for a 85km/h top speed, and the larger had 9.5hp at 5250rpm for 90km/h. After Achilles closed shop in 1957, the British Norman motorcycle works bought its machinery.

Accumolli ITALY ★ ★ ★

Built in 1950 and using a Piaggio engine, the Moto-Accumolli looks like a Buck Rogers Space Age two-wheeler that only needs a raygun and a driver in a space suit.

ACMA FRANCE ★ ★ ★

Piaggio's Vespas were license-built around the world. In France in 1950, Ateliers de Construction de Motocycles et d'Accessoires (ACMA) started importing Italian Vespas beginning with 1,200 specimens. In 1951, 8,940 Vespas were manufactured partially

Vespa à la Française
Ateliers de Construction de Motocycles et d'Accesoires (ACMA) produced Vespas for the French market that served any waking need. ACMA is most famous in scooter circles for the audacity of building the much-coveted bazooka scooter. These two-wheeled Vespa tanks with a bazooka that supposedly could shoot four kilometers for the special TAP forces (Troupes AeroPortes). First a parachute was attached to the front forks and gracefully plummeted to the ground from 10,000 feet; then the two-stroke motor started on the first kick to get within range of the bad guys; lastly, the cannon was dismounted from the scooter and BLAMMO!
Courtesy of the Archivo Roberto Dona

If Mrs. (or Miss) Smith

just likes to pop into town to do some shopping or to chat with a friend or to settle those one hundred and one odds and ends that take up so much of our time, - - with the ADLER JUNIOR it will be a pleasure, for she gets everything done in a jiffy!

And here's what Mrs. (or Miss) Smith likes most about the ADLER JUNIOR:-

The electric starter, of course! She just pushes a button . . . and the engine is running. And all the rest of ADLER JUNIOR's controls handle will, the same ease, make riding a mere child's play!

The handy side stand! No need to lift the scooter as when placing it on a centre stand.

The perfect springing! The knowledge of her complete mastery over the vehicle makes her soon feel quite at home on her ADLER JUNIOR.

The elegant, racy appearance!

...And last but not least: the steering lock.

Many admiring glances will follow her, for there's no doubt: She knows how to get the most out of life!

Junior 1955–1957 and Junior Luxus 1957 ★ ★

"Live joyfully with wings—drive an Adler" promised ads for the Junior. Unfortunately, competition raged so fiercely, the Junior practically died in its nest. Upon realizing that the 98cc 3.75hp engine was no match for the larger scooters, Adler designed the 125cc Junior Sport prototype that also never went into production. Instead, it updated the standard Junior to the Luxus with 4hp and other minor changes.

In describing the power of the Junior engine, ads touted "its quick starting, easy hill climbing and steady perseverance on the motor highway can be taken for granted and need hardly be mentioned at all." Was this purple prose a plot to cover up its weak engine?

Fortunately for manufacturers, however, when riding a scooter speed is magnified far beyond reality. In 1957, a New Yorker reporter was taken for a test ride on an Adler and "a moment or so later, hanging on for dear life, we found ourselves breezing down Broadway at what he told us was twenty-five miles an hour, though it felt like ninety." In fact, the top speed of the Junior was 70km/h on its 14in wheels.

Adly TAIWAN ★

These two-stroke scooters come in an electric version or with a Minarelli two-stroke engine also used in the Yamaha Zuma. The parent company, Her Chee, has produced motorcycles since 1978.

Aeon TAIWAN ★

Mostly known for its ATVs and motorcycles, Aeon entered the scooter market in the US and Europe in 1998 with an assortment of scooters big and small—some even on three wheels. Today, most of its big sellers are electric scooters.

Aermacchi ITALY

Like Piaggio, Aermacchi came to motorcycle construction from an aviation background. Aeronautica Macchi, located on Lago Varese, was famous for its racing seaplanes that contested the Schneider Trophy, setting in 1934 the world speed record for piston-engine seaplanes of 440.69mph, a record that still stands today.

MACCHI 125, GHIBLI, AND ZEFFIRO ★ ★

In 1950, the firm introduced its Macchi 125, which, like Moto Guzzi's Galletto, was a motorscooter on large, 3.00x17in tires; Aermacchi's flyer called it "Lo scooter trasformabile"—the transformable scooter. The engine was a horizontal two-stroke single of 52x58mm delivering 5hp at 4300rpm. Several versions were available: the S; the more luxurious N with fuller fenders; the Grand Luxe and the C, both with added, protective bodywork.

on French soil, and the following year they were 100 percent French built. Production skyrocketed in 1952 with 28,280 built and 40,800 the next year. Continuing the stiff competition between Piaggio and Innocenti, in 1952, another French company, Société Industrielle de Troyes (SIT) began production of Lambrettas.

By French law, ACMA had to remove the headlamp from the front fender to the handlebars. In 1962, ACMA ceased production of Vespas and closed its doors due to a recession in France.

Adiva ITALY/TAIWAN ★ ★

Look for the scooters with the little roof and chances are it could be an Adiva. These scooters with relatively large engines – 200 to 400 cc – often come in three-wheeled versions (two wheels in the front rather than back) with a foldable roof. The Adiva was introduced in 2000 at the Salone di Milano as the Benelli Adiva.

Adler GERMANY

At the turn of the century when bicycles moved the masses, Adler led the way with 100,000 bicycles built by 1898. With the development of the internal-combustion engine, Adler shifted from bicycles and typewriters to automobiles, motorcycles, and motorscooters.

This West German make was sold over the border in France, so ad teams copied Terrot's campaign "Le scooter pour TOUS…" (The scooter for everyone) with "Le scooter confortable pour tous" (The comfortable scooter for all).

Aermacchi also released the Macchi 125 U in 1953, named Ghibli after the Saharan wind. The U was a basic, utilitarian version of the standard S model.

In 1956, the Ghibli was soon replaced by another wind name, the Zeffiro, or Zephyr, with 125cc and 150cc version available. Two 150cc models were offered: the base 150 Luxe and the 150/N, a sportster.

CHIMERA 175 AND 250 ★ ★ ★

In 1956, the futuristic Chimera was offered based on Ing. Bianchi's great four-stroke 175cc horizontal pushrod single. Riding on motorcycle wheels, the Chimera was clothed in pressed-steel bodywork that was pure Jet Age. But even when offered in 250cc form, the Chimera failed to find a market; it was years ahead of its time in styling and technology.

BREZZA ★ ★

In the early 1960s, Aermacchi was split in two. The motorcycle division was partnered with Harley–Davidson; the aeronautical side went to Lockheed. In 1963, the motorcycle group released the Brezza, or Breeze, scooter in the style of the Zeffiro with a 150cc two-stroke engine. To fit in with the more popular Lambrettas dominating the market, the wheels were shrunk to 3.00x12in from the more stable 17 inch wheels. The new look was essentially a sleeked-down version of the Lambretta LI Series 2 design.

By 1973, Aermacchi disappeared totally from the motorcycle scene, swallowed up by Harley–Davidson.

Aermoto ITALY ★ ★ ★ ★

Società Aermoto of Turin built the Volugrafo, a stream-lined precursor to the Vespa in the 1930s. The 98cc Sachs engine and the entire frame was covered with a monocoque shell. As with its pre-Vespa contemporaries—Belmondo's Velta, and Piaggio's Paperino, the step-through design was absent.

A later Volugrafo was dropped from the heavens as a lightweight military parachute scooter with dual front and rear wheels and a low-set frame similar in style to the Welbike. The engine on the pokey fold-up scooter was a single-port 125cc two-stroke with a two-speed gearbox.

Aeromere ITALY ★

This company from the mountainous town of Trento produced the prototype Capriolo (meaning small deer) for the Milan Fair in 1962. The sleek scooter with a 150cc engine never made it into full production, perhaps because the feminine version of its name means "somersault" in Italian.

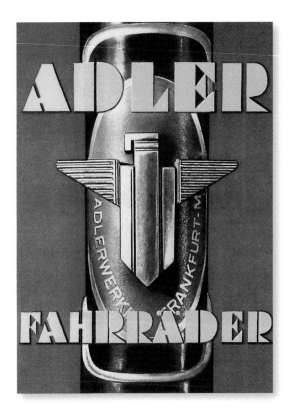

Adler's Eagle
Adler's eagle-like logo harkened back to grimmer days of bold wartime design. Courtesy of the Hans Kruger archives

AGF FRANCE ★

Scooter plans were already in place in 1944 for the AGF, and its claim to fame is the first French scooter to be officially presented to the world. At the 1947 Foire de Paris, the AGF made its grand debut with a 98cc Jonghi three-speed engine and later that year with a 125cc Ydral motor. The design followed the paired-down Lambretta look of the time with an uncovered engine and negligible legshield. Not until 1950 did the definitive version of the AGF appear with a wide choice of an Jlo, a 125cc Ydral, a 100 or 125cc Aubier-Dunne.

In 1952, a sport version hit the market trying to appeal to the market with its "auto à deux roues" (car on two wheels). The 175cc Ydral put out 7hp at 5000rpm and reached 90km/h on the Montlhéry track in the spring of 1953 by a rider from the French Scooter-Magazine.

In 1954, the engine was further souped-up for more speed. The 125cc now put out 6.8hp and the 175cc reached a whopping 10.4hp. AGF missed its market, though, as consumers weren't only interested in power but also the look-at-me aspect of the sleek scooter.

Agrati–Garelli ITALY ★ ★ ★

Agrati introduced its Capri scooter in 1958 based on a brilliant yet simple idea: build a single scooter and equip it with a series of engines and gearboxes to create a complete line to satisfy all markets. Thus, Capris were available with the following powerplants: 3.3hp 50cc with three speeds; 4.3hp 50cc with four speeds; 3.3 hp 70cc with three speeds; 4hp 80cc with three speeds; 5.5hp 125cc with four speeds; and 5.6hp 148cc with four speeds. In 1961, the 50cc Como was released as well with larger 16 inch wheels.

The styling was also simple. Bodywork covered the machine with lift-off side covers in a contrasting color. Two-tone schemes were red and beige, gray and light blue, and light blue and dark blue.

But the Capri had one problem: competition. Piaggio and Innocenti controlled the scooter market and the Capri could not edge its way in; thus, the scooter was doomed to be an exile. The vast majority of Capris were exported throughout Europe from Greece to Great Britain and on into the United States. It was an odd success story for an Italian scooter.

The Agrati–Garelli merger was formed in 1961, made up by Agrati and the Garelli firm that built the ubiquitous Mosquito clip-on bicycle engine post–World War II. In 1961, Agrati continued with a 98cc Capri while Garelli offered a 125cc Capri De Luxe.

Also in 1961, the Como scooter was added to the Capri line. Named not for the Spanish "How?", which surely caused problems in the Iberian market, but for the beautiful northern Lombardy lake. The motor was a smaller 49.7cc two-stroke with a three-speed gearbox. To conform to different European legislation, pedals could be added so this vehicle with 16in wheels was more moped than scooter.

AJS UK/CHINA ★★

Known mostly for the classic AJS and Matchless café racer motorcycles, AJS has recently revived its name and used its technology and classic styling to produce the beautiful 125cc Modena. The tribute to the British Mod past is evident with all the styling cues. The Digita, Firefox, and Insetto may be fine scooters for commuting, but stick with the Modena for eye-catching delight. The AJS Modena is essentially the same as the Lexmoto Milano, a modern reissue of the classic Vespa at an affordable price since it is manufactured in China by Znen. Sure, it may not be a Ferrari, Stanguellini, Maserati, or other race car built in Modena, but it can fool many who just see it as a "Vespa."

Aldimi BELGIUM ★★★

Launched in 1953, Aldimi of Brussels built a scooter named, in all seriousness, the Prince de Liège. It used a 125cc Saroléa engine of 6 hp at 4800 rpm riding atop 3.50x 10-inch tires. In 1954, the Prince de Liège's ego got even larger with a 200cc Saroléa. But even with such a regal endorsement, the scooter did not go far. In 1956, Aldimi switched to building Piatti scooters for Belgium, which had little success either.

Alemanno ITALY ★★

Introduced only a couple years after the Vespa and a year after the first Lambretta, the Alemanno's Alfa followed a similar sporty design with a 50cc Ducati Cucciolo engine. Alemanno followed up the Alfa with a Beta scooter using a Volugrafo 125cc engine.

Allstate USA

Allstate was a fitting brand name for Sears, Roebuck and Co. to sell motorscooters under; after all, Sears saturated the United States with its mail-order catalog and outlet stores.

Sears management must have seen the success the Gambles mail-order company had with its Doodle Bug since 1946, and began shopping for a scooter line in the late 1940s. By 1950, there was

only one reasonable choice: Cushman. Salsbury had gone the way of the nickel Coca-Cola and Piaggio's Vespa, which Sears would begin importing in 1951–1952, was unheard of in the United States at the time.

Cushman was happy to sign on. The Sears deal offered it a new outlet for sales—never mind what Cushman's own dealers said under their collective breath—but it also prevented Sears from offering a competitive line. By 1951, the first Cushman badge-engineered Allstate motorscooters were listed in the famous Sears tome, sent to millions of households across the United States.

As most parts are interchangeable between Cushmans and their Allstate cousins, its important to note that Allstate engine blocks and frames can be distinguished from the Cushmans.

A serial number tag was located on the engine block under the dipstick; Allstate serial numbers all began with the Sears 811. prefix. The engine serial number was also stamped into the block between the manifolds. The scooter serial number was stamped on the left of the steering head.

STANDARD MODEL 3HP 1951–1958 ★★

The basic model was the Standard 3hp, although Sears was inconsistent in calling it either the Standard or the 3hp on and off from 1951–1958; throughout its production run it was given consecutive Sears catalog numbers and the Sears 811.30 model number, all of which were important for locating parts. The 3hp was a thinly disguised Cushman Model 61 Highlander. The 811.30 model name denoted the Cushman Husky 12.3ci engine stamped with 811 for Allstate use; the 30 suffix stood for 3.0hp.

Differences from the 61 were subtle yet all-important. While the 61 was what Cushman called a Sport, meaning it had no rear bodywork, the Allstate was well dressed with bolt-on side covers. Large Allstate decals depicting the outline of the USA with the word Allstate superimposed were placed on the side covers under the seat. The 3hp was only ever available in bright red enamel.

The 3hp could be yours in 1951 for $179.50 cash or at $36 down with monthly payments. The Sears installment plan advantage sold many Allstates through the years when you needed cash in hand at the Cushman dealer.

By 1953, the Cushman tow hitch was offered. In 1957, the rear bodywork of the 3hp was subtly redesigned and catalogued without fanfare; the Allstate decal was now smaller and placed at the rear near the tail lamp. The new 3hp Allstate lasted only one more year; in 1959 it was replaced by the Standard 4.8hp.

DE LUXE MODEL 4HP 1951–1957 ★★★★

Sears called its advanced scooter the De Luxe 4hp but as with the Standard, it was inconsistent in term-

Allstate Ad
Sears Roebuck and Co. flyer for its Allstate "mile-making" scooter line of 1955, including the 3 hp Standard Model and the 4 hp Deluxe Model. Sears introduced its top-of-the-line 4-1/2 hp Vespa in 1953 as the Allstate Cruisaire but did not include it here. In 1955, chief competitor Montgomery Ward was just launching its Riverside line of scooters, which were Japanese-made.

ing it the De Luxe, Deluxe, or 4hp through the scooter's career. The Allstate was based on the Cushman Model 62 Pacemaker with one-speed transmission and automatic centrifugal clutch.

The engine was the famed 14.9ci Husky; Sears ads ballyhooed its "automotive-type camshaft," which was certainly superior to other camshaft types. The rear drum brake was also of the "automotive-type," giving "Dependable 'stop on a dime' braking power," in technical terms. "Runs easily in slow traffic, zooms up to 40 or more for speedy get-away," the catalog stated. The "or more" top speed was 45mph with a tailwind.

The De Luxe 4hp was one of the most stylish scooters of all time, blending a funky "streamlined windsplitter" front fender with avant-garde rear bodywork. The look was set off by chrome trim, swank Allstate decals, and arrow-shaped nameplate. As the Sears catalog pointed out, the styling was "exclusive and advanced!"

The Allstate's look was indeed exclusive compared with the 62. The Cushman had progressed little from the first Auto-Glide—traditional styling was a polite way to say it. The Allstate redesign created a scooter that was a vision of the future on two 4.00x8in wheels at a time when American automobiles were largely still 1940s designs. The windsplitter front fender "quoted" the Salsbury Model 85 design while the tail foreshadowed the chrome and tailfins of the 1955 Chevrolet.

The De Luxe first appeared in the 1951 Sears catalogs available at $219.95 cash. Or you could pay only $44 down and have it shipped in a crate to your front door and offer up monthly payments while you wheeled your way about town.

During its production run, the two chief items that changed on the 4hp were its price, which usually went up, and the color scheme. In 1951–1952, it was offered in bright red or "gay" yellow baked-on enamel; for 1953, only red was available; by 1954, red was supplemented by glass green; in 1955, you could have your 4hp in two-tone only with red highlighted by ivory trim; for 1956–1957, two-tone was out and it was back to red with black trim, although the latex seat cover was now striped.

In 1957, the fabulous Allstate 4hp was retired to be replaced by the equally fantastic Jetsweep.

ALLSTATE VESPA AND ALLSTATE CRUISAIRE 1951–1966 ★ ★ ★ ★

Sears, Roebuck and Co. was famous for selling everything under the sun, so it decided to order 1,000 Vespas in 1951 as an experiment. It offered them throughout the United States via its mail-order catalog as its top-of-the-line Cruisaire scooter accompanying the Cushman-produced Allstates. The $279.95 Vespas sold so fast, that Sears placed a rush order for 5,000 more by September 1951, and planned to buy up to 2,000 more every month thereafter, reported Time magazine in 1952.

Sears always sold the 125cc Vespa with the sole change being the addition of an Allstate emblem to the left legshield, a couple of electrical changes and no front shock. The Allstate model was always priced $10 below the cheapest 5hp Lambretta sold by Montgomery Ward. Sears also offered sidecars and a wide range of accessories.

An easy way to tell the approximate age of the Allstate is by the original paint scheme. Seafoam Green was used until mid-1961 and replaced by blue,

which was used through 1963. From 1964 to 1965, red was used and white was standard in 1966 when both the 150 Sprint and small frame 125 were offered.

As a 1957 Sears ad stated, "The Allstate Cruisaire is the smartest scooter we've ever built [sic]—smart in the advanced brilliance of styling and power—smarter still in the bedrock economy of operation." And as an enthusiastic Sears executive told American Mercury magazine in 1957, "The day may come when a swarm of the minute 6hp Vespas will proudly share the American highways with large 300hp sedans."

That day never came to pass, but Sears did import tens of thousands of Vespas into the United States in the years 1951–1963.

JETSWEEP MODEL 4.8HP 1957–1960 ★ ★

The 4.8hp replaced the 4hp in late 1957 as the Cushman 722 Pacemaker replaced the 62 Pacemaker earlier in the same year. Sears initially called its new scooter the 4.hp in 1957 ads, retitling it the Jet-sweep in 1958 and subtly reworking the name to be the Jetsweep for 1959.

"Look forward to miles of pleasure on this sleek, strong scooter of the future," read the catalog. The Jetsweep "carries you miles in minutes," a claim that certainly could not be challenged.

The Allstate changed during the years along with Cushman's version. Cooling woes had plagued the 722 and cooling louvers were stamped into the rear bodywork to help along the 14.9ci Husky. In 1957, the Allstate was free of louvers; by 1958, cooling louvers appeared on the top deck; by 1959, louvers were on both sections.

From 1957–1959, the Allstate was painted Coronet Red and Dover White two-tone. In 1960, the Allstate reversed Cushman's color scheme with the body painted Mist White and the trim and top deck in Hunter Red.

STANDARD 4.8HP 1959–1961 ★

"All-new fresh-as-a-breeze styling!" the Sears catalog shouted; it should have been a cry of warning. The replacement for the old Standard 3hp was based on the new Cushman 721 Highlander, an ungainly scooter design if there ever was one.

Based on the 12.3ci Husky, the Allstate was painted Hunter Red with reflective silver trim and a black engine and seat. It came to your home "partly assembled," which may have been another warning.

3HP 1960 ★

For one year only, Sears offered a revived 3hp model with an 8.4ci engine based on a 2 15/16×2in bore and stroke. The styling was distinctively slab-sided, set off by a two-tone Temple Gray and Cascade Blue paint job topped by a bare bones cushion seat.

Jetsweep
Allstate's 1957–1960 Jetsweep was a rebadged Cushman 722 Pacemaker, and just as Cushman had numerous problems perfecting its 722, the same changes in engine cooling were made year to year on the Jetsweep. Courtesy of the owners: Keith and Kris Weeks

COMPACT 1961–1962 ★

Sears began selling Austrian-built Puch motorcycles under the Allstate nameplate in 1954; by 1961, it also offered a Puch scooter as its Compact model.

This compact was a beginner's supplement to the Piaggio and Cushman line, as the catalog promised: "Even if you've never driven one you'll soon handle this like a pro." Never mind that the Compact was faster at 42.5mph than the Cushman, had three speeds versus the Cushman's one, as well as front and rear drum brakes.

The engine was an aluminum two-stroke with flywheel magneto ignition. "Listen to its Puch-built engine purr," the catalog copy said by way of seduction. The Puch arrived at your doorstep painted in "lustrous" cream and red two-tone.

SEARS AND CUSHMAN PART WAYS

In 1961, Sears and Cushman went their separate ways. Sears chose to concentrate on its Piaggio and Puch lines, and Cushman made the odd decision to retire its step-through scooters and challenge Sears by also importing Vespas. Sears' decision to sever its relations with Cushman probably helped spell the end of Cushman scooters as much as Cushman's own decision to switch to Piaggio. And in 1963, Sears dropped all scooters from its catalog. It was a sad finale to years of mail-order scootering.

Allwyn INDIA/ITALY ★★

The Allwyn Pushpack was made by Andhra Pradesh Scooters Limited in India under license from Innocenti. Essentially the scooter is a Lambretta Slimline. Incredibly, the company also struck a deal with Piaggio to make Vespas as the PL170.

Alma France ★

The Etablissements Mauriange of Clermont-Ferrand was an old hand at mopeds and ultra-light motorcycles when it entered the scooter business in 1952. The one-seat ST Alma looked like a Moto Guzzi scooter without any thought to esthetics. Riding on 10in wheels, the first Alma was available in grey, beige, or grenadine.

Alma soon produced a second scooter, a Vespa look-alike but without the success that even the first Alma had.

Alpino ITALY ★

To outrun DeSica's bicycle thieves, Alpino produced petite motors to tack on bicycles immediately postwar. Then in 1949, the Marinella prototype debuted with a bulbous space-ship shape but unfortunately probably didn't go into full production. The following year, a 75cc and 125cc Alpino was produced, even though the motor cover made the bike look more like a fan shield than scooter. Alpino kept the large spoked 17 or 18 inch wheels for its 1953 scooter that lost the office fan look and took on the covered-bicycle esthetic. In 1954, the Alpino 48 lost power but gained a total body covering and still didn't sell well. The 1956 Alpino still kept the motorized bike fashion, but by virtue of its extensive bodywork and smaller, 18in wheels, deserves the esteemed mantle of motorscooter. Legshields and a full engine cover protected the rider from unpleasantries.

Not until the Fiera di Milano in 1957 di Alpino present a successful scooter looking like a Honda Cub with a 125cc three-speed, foot shifter. In 1960, Alpino finally understood the game and essentially copied the successful Lambretta Series 2. Alpino's Export scooter came in either 150cc or 175cc versions with electric start on the larger and supposedly capable of more than 100 km/h.

Ambassador UK ★★

Ambassador of Ascot built a healthy number of small-capacity motorcycles for the English market in the 1960s, including a foray into the scooter world. Ambassador's scooter was known simply as the Ambassador.

Based on a fan-cooled two-stroke 173cc Villiers 3L engine of 59x63.5mm, the Ambassador had a four-speed integral gearbox with primary and secondary drive by chain. A heel-and-toe pedal shifted the gears. As Motor Cycle reported in 1960, "acceleration nippy up to maximum speed of about 55 m.p.h."

The Ambassador was of classical scooter construction with a 2¼in diameter main tube frame enclosed by unstressed bodywork. A swing arm at the rear was damped by springs on both sides but a Girling shock absorber on just the right. Tires were 3.50x6in and 12in brakes were fitted front and rear.

The Ambassador was fitted with luxury features over and above its call of duty, including a Siba Dynastart electric starter—which was "silent," according to a flyer—a speedometer and idiot warning lights for ignition, neutral, and low gas level.

In the tantalizing terms of an Ambassador flyer, the bodywork was "styled from stem to stern on graceful modern lines, with an appealing decor." Two-tone paint colors were Raven Black, Sun Valley Cream, or Royal Gold each paired with Grey-stone White, or Carnation Pink and Oyster Grey.

In 1962, Ambassador was sold to the English DMW firm, which ended the scooter's career in the same year.

Ambrosini ITALY ★ ★ ★ ★

In 1952, the Società Aeronautica Italiana Ing. A. Ambrosini & Co. of Milan offered its Freccia Azzurra, or Blue Arrow, scooter. The Ambrosini was a classic scooter mixing style, inventive creativity, and folly—the essence of a motorscooter.

As befitting an aeronautical firm, the scooter's bodywork was perfectly aerodynamic, an essential feature when the Italian government limited scooters to 80km/h. If nothing else, the avant-garde bodywork was pure Jet Age: the headlamp was streamlined into the fender; the horn blended into the legshields; and long, shapely ducts along the side fed air to the engine.

That engine was a Sachs two-stroke 147cc of 57x58mm giving 7.5hp at 5000rpm. A four-speed gearbox was shifted by a foot lever. Tires were 3.00x12in and had, of course, whitewalls.

Essential luxury features of the Ambrosini included a radio with antenna and an automatic engine cut-out gravity switch if the top-heavy scooter turned wheels up.

Ami SWITZERLAND ★

Built in Baden, the Ami scooters were part mini-bike, part scooter and part outboard engine. The prestigious pull-starter rigged up to the side of the engine showed the world that you'd rather be fishing. The Piccolo was born in 1950 with a 48cc four-stroke engine with a two-speed gearbox with a right foot shifter. The tiny 8in wheels somehow managed to hold up when the bike reached 60km/h, perhaps because the whole contraption only weighed 35kg.

The little Piccolo become the little Ami (friend) the following year with an updated 98cc Sachs engine. What looks literally like a knight's shield was added on to the front fork for maximum jousting protection with rival Vespa gangs from south of the border. Available in black, blue, gray and red, the Ami was distributed in France through SCCM of Vichy, always ready to make a deal with its Teutonic neighbors.

Later in 1951, the two-seater Ami 3 was introduced in Geneva with a 150cc Sachs engine. The 7.2hp needed the new 4x10in wheels to stay afloat. In 1953, a new design by the Swiss company for the Ami-Sport AG appeared at the Frankfurt show, but the two-wheeler was built by Achilles in Germany. With a 150cc or 175cc Sachs engine, the Ami-Sport was essentially a covered motorcycle with puny 10in wheels for more maneuverability (some would say lack of imbalance). Achilles teamed up with Ami for the little Ami-Capri as well with a two-speed 50cc Sachs engine in 1955.

AMO GERMANY ★

AMO–Motorengesellschaft GmbH of Berlin sold its fully enclosed scooter with a 48cc two-stroke engine that it designed and Westendarp & Pieper built.

API INDIA/ITALY ★ ★ ★

Automobile Products of India out of Mumbai built Lambretta scooters and mopeds as well as three-wheelers under license. A wide variety of Lambrettas were available, all the way back to the D and LD. Despite the deal ending with Innocenti, API simply changed the name to "Lamby" and "MAC" in 1977 and slightly altered the design.

Apollo SWEDEN ★

In the mid-1950s, M. Berlin & Co. produced the Apollo Biet scooter in Varnamo, Sweden using a Swedish-made JB engine from Malmø in the south.

Aprilia ITALY ★ ★

Although perhaps more of moped, Aprilia's A 4 Scooter was an early dabble in the putt-putt genre for Aprilia in 1963. The 48cc Morini engine was partially covered and the large spoked wheels and pedals made it more bike than not.

The modern firm of Aprilia offered its Amico 50 scooter in the 1980s and 1990s based on a compact 49cc two-stroke of 40x39.2mm. While the frame consisted of steel tube, the formed-plastic bodywork enveloped the metal in dynamic colors.

At the 1992 Bologna show, Aprilia unveiled its animale da città, the Lama scooter. The spaceship styling was created by Frenchman Philippe Starck and topped by a handlebar cover that integrated turn signals to the front and rearview mirrors at the back, the whole affair angled skyward like llama ears.

Soon after followed the wildly successful Scarabeo scooter that harkened back to the Moto Guzzi Galletto with its large diameter wheels. Named for the sacred Egyptian beetle, the Scarabeo soon reproduced into these larger sizes and the swarms filled Italian strade: Scarabeo 50 Street, 50, 100, 125, 250, and 500. The Mojito Custom 50 and 150 strived for more of the old time scooter days with a cross between a Lambretta and a panhead Harley.

Italian teenagers often don't care about any ho-hum nostalgia for the good ol' days, so Italjet released a line of rocket scooters that look more like a Ferrari Modena than a Piaggio Paperino.

In 2004, Piaggio, the parent company of Vespa, bought out Aprilia. That year, the SR 50 Ditech and Sportcity 125 or 200 satisfied this lust for speed and the latest fashion, at least for this year. The Atlantic 125 or 250 even comes in an enormous "maxiscooter" version with a 500cc engine for cross-country touring rather than putsing to the dairy store.

Aprilia scooters soon took up the role as an affordable, reliable scooter, but not as pricey as the Vespa. Still, Aprilia is known more for its record-setting motorcycles, with more victories than any other cycle.

Ardent FRANCE ★

Cannes may be known for its film festival and beautiful beaches, but its scooters have plunged into the abyss of anonymity. In 1951, the petit Baby was displayed, pedals and all, with a VAP-4 engine. The following year hoping to piggyback on the fame of the French Riviera, the Azur was sold with the added incentive of "super ballon" tires and either a 49cc 1.25hp Le Poulain engine for a 45km/h top speed or a 85cc 3hp Le Poulain motor for 70km/h. Finally in 1952, Ardent showed off "le plus beau scooter de Salon [de Paris]" known as the Estérel. Its 65cc Lavalette engine pumped out 2.8 hp moving the scooter to a 65 km/h top speed.

Ardito ITALY ★

Located just south of Milan near Pavia, La Simes was started by a designer Pietro Trespidi who left Alpino. Two versions of his 49cc covered bicycle/scooter saw the light of day, but perhaps the name "Ardito" didn't sit well with the Italian public because it can mean either "bold" or "risky."

Ariel UK ★

Ariel was a once-proud motorcycle manufacturer, renowned for its Square Four models. But by the 1960s, the firm was singing its swan song through the muffler of such creations as the Ariel Pixie scooter-moped.

With a 50cc engine, the Pixie's frame was a pressed-steel spine similar to BSA's Beagle and Ariel's interesting if odd Leader and Arrow motorcycles.

Arosio ITALY ★

The Aros scooter was a spitting image of the recent Iso when it was presented to the public in 1950. Although dual-seat Aros looked sleek with plenty of air slits in the side panels to cool the 125cc engine.

Arqin AUSTRALIA/CHINA ★

These scooters from Jinan Qingqi have been rebranded for the Australian market by Arqin.

Askoll ITALY ★

This company from near Vicenza, Italy, specialized in pumps to drain water from washing machines. In 2015, the company turned its electric engine expertise to electric mopeds (they call them "scooters").

Atala-Rizzato Lygie ITALY ★

Producing bicycles to move the masses, Atala was founded in 1906. After shifting into motorcycles before the war, Atala hooked up with Cesare Rizzato of Padua to jump on the scooter bandwagon in the late 1950s. The 115 A scooter had a small 75cc engine and couldn't shake the bicycle image of Atala. Nearly an identical scooter with a smaller engine was released in 1959 under the French marque Cycles Lygie of Saint Etienne.

Auto-Fauteuil FRANCE ★ ★ ★ ★

Arguably the first scooter in production but arguably not even a scooter, the Auto-Fauteuil boasted that it could mount hills of more than a 22% incline. On medium-sized 16in spoked wheels, this step-through vehicle carried many scooter attributes and probably influenced the ABC Skootamota in the 1920s. George Gauthier unveiled his creation in

1914 Autoped
The idea was simple: take a child's push scooter and get rid of the push by adding power in the form of a gas engine. And folks took to scooters like fish to water. The American-made Motoped, shown here, and Autoped scooters arrived in 1915 – 1916, followed by the British ABC Scootamota in 1919. These early scooters were faddish gimmicks at most, ostensibly designed for ladies to travel downtown for afternoon tea without having to hike up their dresses. It was a fun idea but didn't last long because many of the scooters didn't last long, mechanical reliability being but a dream.

THE AUTOPED

IS THE WONDER OF THE MOTOR VEHICLE WORLD

FIRST MODEL, CIRCA 1914

It's the only motor-driven passenger-carrying vehicle that can be carried into your office or home; so compact that it can be kept anywhere.

For the ladies—shopping, calling, or just "going."

A land tender for autos

So light you can carry with one hand

The Autoped

Folds into small size

The quickest salesmen, solicitors, etc.

For everyman's business and pleasure

1902 and soon postcards of priests putsing around on the little two-strokes were sold to tourists along the Champs-Elysées. Gauthier trumpeted his invention to the skeptical crowd, "The Auto-Fauteil has nothing to do with the motorcycle. It's a car with two special wheels."

With a name meaning "automatic-easy chair," the open-framed Auto-Fauteuil had the right idea of presenting a lazy-boy's option to walking. With a special option of double front wheels, balancing the Auto-Fauteuil was a tiring work-out left to walkers. A side car could be tacked on as well to take a date along. With all these options, the engine size was soon upgraded from a 269cc to 390cc or 427cc in 1914 and finally a 545cc until the end of the Auto-Fauteuil's run in 1922.

Autoglider UK ★★★

Birmingham, England's Townsend & Co. produced the Autoglider during the first scooter boom from 1919 to 1922 usually with a giant 292cc Villiers engine, but don't think that meant a quick scooter. The original models had the rider standing up, whereas by 1920 a seat was standard atop a rounded storage box.

Automoto FRANCE ★★

This French firm released Peugeot scooters a year after the original with its own slick logo and changed the model identification numbers. Peugeot's S.57 was Automoto's SA.3 in 1957 and the S.57B became the SA.3S in 1958.

Autoped USA ★★★★★

The Autoped of New York looking less like a step-through motorcycle than a motorized child's toy, was the first scooter to be built in large numbers and available commercially around the country. In fact, after it was imported in 1916, "Autoped" became synonymous for "child's scooter" in Dutch. The Motoped

set the standard with a 1.5hp engine mounted on the left side of the front wheel giving the scooter a lean, later adopted by Piaggio's Vespa. The Fred-Flintstone brakes relied on the magic of shoe leather, in other words, the Motoped needed some improvements.

The Autoped "Wonder of the Motor Vehicle World" was copied around Europe—some licensed and others not—by companies like Krupp in Germany (with a larger 200cc engine), UK Imperial Motor Industries, and CAS in Czechoslovakia with 155cc (56x63) engine. While bicycles were being banned on many city roads due to residents terrorized by speed, the 1914 Autoped was made for sidewalk use. Even so, ads claimed that the scooter could hit 60km/h (while in reality more like 25km/h).

When Autopeds and Motopeds did drive in the dirt streets, they usually had to navigate around mud puddles and slick cobblestone in the center of cities. Debate raged in city governments as to how to remedy dirt roads. Many city dwellers didn't want better streets because that meant faster bicycles and automobiles and more dangerous accidents for their kids playing in the street, but rich owners of bicycles, motorcycles, scooters, and cars demanded improved surfaces. Proposals ranged from making the streets out of rubber, pine planks, and iron were seriously considered before brick and asphalt were deemed more practical, but not until many trial runs.

Soon copies of the Autoped were popping up across the US and Europe, each with minor improvements to the original. Germany had its DKW Golem & Megola and England had its Wilkinson and Handy-scooter. The English Autoglider De Luxe appeared in 1919 created by Charles Ralph Townsend at Townsend Engineering Co. of Birmingham with a 269cc Villiers engine mounted on front 16in wheel. The Model A was seatless like the Autoped, but the Model D added a cushioned seat which doubled as suspension. Even though ads claimed top speed was 50km/h, bold scooterists claimed to have reached 80km/h, although probably on a steep incline.

Autoscoot UK ★★★

Built in 1919 or 1920, this early English scooter used a Wall engine.

Baccio CHINA ★

In hopes that some of the Italian style will rub off, Baccio uses the Italian flag for its logo and borrowed the name that almost means "kiss" (*bacio* with one *c*"). The engines are based off the Minarelli design and come in three models: DLX 50, VX 50, and VX 150.

Bajaj INDIA ★★

Not many scooter companies can boast that their founder was a disciple and confidant of Mahatma Gandhi, but Bajaj proudly features the non-violent hero in their literature.

In spite of this noble past, India needed transportation, so Bajaj began importing Vespas in 1948. Realizing that Piaggio was getting most of the profits and India had all the cheap labor they could ever need, Bajaj negotiated with Piaggio to begin manufacturing scooters on the subcontinent. Finally, by 1972, Bajaj was independent of Piaggio and two years later the first Bajaj Chetak (essentially a Vespa) appeared. The name "Chetak" came from the horse of the emperor Maharana Pratap; Disney even made a Hindi film called Chetak The Wonder Horse, alas with no scooters on the silver screen!

As the world's largest three-wheel manufacturer, Bajaj was busy making "autorickshaws" but still found time to negotiate a deal to make Kawasakis under license in 1984.

In 1990, the plastic 60cc Sunny scooterette was introduced as "extremely popular with teenagers." In 1996, the Rave and Spirit abandoned the classic Vespa design for the "high-end market." In 1998, the 150cc Legend was released with the dubious claim, "the world's first geared four-stroke scooter."

A Bajaj brochure from the late 1990s skips the modesty when describing itself: "With over 13 million Bajaj vehicles dotting Indian roads, consumer faith in and affection for the Company is overwhelming, and expressed in spontaneous emotion of 'Hamara Bajaj' Hindi for 'our Bajaj.'"

By 2006, the Bajaj Chetak had run its course and was retired, and India mourned this mighty steed. In 2019, Bajaj was back in the scooter sphere with the release of an electric Chetak, but it had shed its classic Vespa look in favor of the bulbous modern look.

Bangor Manufacturing Company USA ★★

Bangor of Bangor, Michigan, sold its Scootmaster in the late 1930s. Powered by a 3hp Clinton and riding atop 4in wheels, the Scootmaster was a no-frills vehicle that bore a suspiciously close resemblance to the Cushman Auto-Glide of the day.

Baotian CHINA ★

These 50cc mini sport scooters come in flashy colors and seek the youth market to buy these inexpensive rides. These scooters are also sent to Germany rebranded as the Rex.

Bashan CHINA ★

The Bashan Peace scooter has a peppy 50cc engine, but as soon as anything breaks, you're on your own. If you want a cheap ride (with no shocks), are handy, and want to get the most miles per cost of the bike, perhaps this is your dream.

Bastert WEST GERMANY ★★★★

Bastert of Bielefeld built its Einspurauto, or Single-Track Car, a monstrous spaceship of a scooter bedazzled by jetpod accents and chrome trim. Although the name rings less than beautifully in English, Bastert's exotic hovercraft with 13in wheels was a rare specimen since only 1,200 Einspurauto's were produced 1952–1956. As of the year 2000, only seven Basterts were known in existence and fetched very high prices.

The Einspurauto had only one easychair seat with a backrest but could easily carry two people due to the powerful engine. The extended fenders added weight making for an 85km/h top speed for the 174cc 7.6hp model and 90km/h for the 197cc 9.5hp model.

Light of India
Once able to sever its ties with Piaggio, Bajaj could pump out as many Chetaks, essentially Vespa copies, as the enormous Indian market could bear. While Piaggio swept under the carpet its past of building planes for the Fascists, Bajaj boasts of its nonviolent ties to Mahatma Gandhi and repelling the English yoke.

7 **X**tra features for **X**tra riding joy!

"Xtra-Super". Those two words describe the NEW Doodle-bug perfectly. Truly, the low priced motor scooter sensation of the nation. More Safety–More Power–More Acceleration–More Fun–More Features to make Doodlebug your best buy–by far. See Doodlebug–Try Doodlebug–You'll Buy Doodlebug!

- **Xtra Safety**—simple handle-bar controls. Be free to watch traffic at all times!
- **Xtra Comfort**—comes from sturdy leatherette seat which is heavily cushioned with springs.
- **Xtra Traction**—heavy treaded 10x3½x4" tires. Doodlebug really holds the road.
- **Xtra Rugged**—sturdy welded steel tube frame. Will take plenty punishment.
- **Xtra Low slung body**—gives Doodlebug a low center of gravity for MORE SAFETY.
- **Xtra Economy**—up to 100 Miles Per Gallon of Gasoline, with a smooth running 4-cycle Briggs-Stratton Engine.

Flexi-Matic CLUTCH

Beam's Doodle Bug
Geared toward the teenage market, the Doodle Bug invented a new scooter lexicon with a "Flexi-Matic" clutch, and "Xtra-Super" everything. The chain of Gambles Five and Ten Stores distributed the Doodle Bug throughout the United States as the first scooter offered in the US in the immediate postwar years, setting the stage for Sears and Montgomery Ward to follow in the '50s. Gambles contracted the Beam Manufacturing Company of Webster City, Iowa, to build its Doodle Bug.

The Einspurauto's main competition was the Maico Mobil, but Bastert's design was "outstanding perfection," according to advertising braggadocio, and included such extravagant luxuries as a fully optioned dashboard. Such high style made for a scooter that was "elegant + schnell"; but it was expensive even in the 1950s when, for the same price, a three-wheeled midget car could be had.

Bastert also produced prototype 120cc, 150cc, and 174cc scooters that unfortunately never saw production.

Beam USA ★★★

In the years after World War II, the Gambles Stores competed with chief rivals Sears Roebuck and Montgomery Ward. Gambles decided it wanted a motorscooter to market; management had seen the sales success of Cushman and Salsbury and believed that with its nationwide outlets, mail-order catalogs, and household name, it could make large profits from the little scooter.

In 1946, Gambles signed the Beam Manufacturing Company of Webster City, Iowa, to build the Doodle Bug, a scooter more elfin than most. The chassis was a simple tube frame covered by scant rear bodywork and a cylindrical gas tank cantilevered off the tail, waiting for a rear end collision to blow up the machine in the best Ford Pinto manner. A simple cushion seat sat atop the engine; buckhorn handlebars were welded to the steering rod. In place of front forks, the sheet-steel fender cradled the wheel.

Beam chose the tried-and-true 1½hp Briggs & Stratton engine to power the Doodle Bug via a belt drive. For a short period, the B & S engine was out of stock and Beam filled in with the Clinton 1½hp. Beam always favored the B & S engine, and the Clinton-powered Doodle Bugs were rarer insects.

The Webster City factory hatched Doodle Bugs in four build lots of 10,000 scooters each for a total of 40,000. Sold through Gambles and Western Hardware stores, these specimens were the dream of many a young American boy.

Beckmann ASB WEST GERMANY

Arbeitsgemeinschaft Schulz-Beckmann scooter debuted at the Frankfurt show in 1953 although only a few ever exited the production line. The firm shortened its name as simply ASB and mounted its winged insignia on the legshield since the full name would encircle the complete scooter.

The 49.9cc Zündapp motor was mounted above the front wheel and fathered 1.5hp for a 45km/h top speed. Simple bicycle fenders covered the wheels, and the only paneling consisted of a half circle covering half of the back wheel behind the floorboard. The large muffler curiously ran the exhaust directly below the floorboard.

Beeline AUSTRIA/CHINA ★

To sell to the German-speaking world, Beeline rebadged Chinese scooters for two markets: the modern mini sport bike crowd with the Pista and the Memory for those nostalgic for the good ol' scooting days.

Belmondo ITALY ★★★★

Vittorio Belmondo built one of the earliest Italian scooters in the 1930s and can claim it influenced Piaggio's Paperino. The Velta sported a similar design as the early Volugrafo with the monocoque body, open handlebars and fork, and a single saddle.

Benelli ITALY/CHINA ★

Benelli of Pesaro was one of the pioneer motorcycle makers of Italy that turned to scooters during the boom years. In 1958, a two-stroke 49cc scooter was put on the market that blended the best of scoots and covered bicycles. Benelli offered its Monaco scooter in the 1960s, which was an awkward blend of moped and scooter powered by a 125cc engine.

The Monaco's lack of success was symbolic of Benelli's troubles, and by 1971 the august firm was bought by Argentine Alejandro de Tomaso, who also would own Innocenti and Guzzi. To meet the ongoing demand for scooters, Benelli offered its S50, S50S, Laser 50, and S125 plastic scooters in the 1990s. At the 1992 Bologna show, Benelli displayed its KB-X50 Race scooter with high-performance components.

In 2005, Qianjiang Motor Group from China bought Benelli and increased its reliance on Chinese manufacturing, keeping its base in Pesaro. In 2021, the company played to its strength of powerful engines for its 150cc Caffenero (black coffee) and 250cc Zafferano (saffron).

Ben Hunt Manufacturing USA ★

Ben Hunt's firm in Walla Walla, Washington, sold the Caper Cycle Road Runner in the 1960s to eager young putt-puttniks. It was based on a two-cycle 2.5hp engine, automatic clutch, and rode on 4.10/3.50×5in wheels. Extra power was an extra-cost item, according to Popular Science magazine.

Benzhou CHINA ★

Benzhou Vehicle Industry Group Company offers an assortment of scooters, mostly available in China. The Zulong comes in various models, one looking suspiciously like the Honda Shadow. The Yiying came in 100cc to 150cc engines. The Retro Star was a two-tone nostalgic ride, whereas most of the others, City Star, Formula One, Formula 2000, and others, aspire to be the mini racers through town.

Bernardet FRANCE

After the liberation of France, the three Bernardet brothers began building automobiles and motorcycle sidecars at their factory in Bourg-la-Reine. Realizing that scooters are little more than motorized sidecars, the frères went to town in 1947.

BERNARDET A.48 AND A.49 1947–1948 ★★★

The Bernardets designed a scooter that went into production in late 1947 as the A.48 model, making them one of the French scooter pioneers. The two-stroke 128cc Ydral engine was backed by a four speeds and situated by the rear wheel without suspension. The totally enclosed scooter had a large front legshield with a Bernardet-Frères coat of arms on the front fender looking like an elf's cap with the headlamp as the tassel. The A.49 updated the A.48 with better cooling among other things, but retained the 4x12in wheels.

B.250 1949–1951 ★★

Presented at the 1949 Salon de Paris, the frères Bernardet's 250cc scooter had a split-single Violet engine designed by the famous engineer Marcel-Violet. The bodywork remained much the same as the earlier models but with rear suspension and a left-side kickstart for the 10hp engine. A shielded spare tire was mounted on the legshield's inside and leather saddlebags hung at rear.

BM AND C.50 1950 ★★

The first series of Bernardets were updated as the BM with a 9hp 250cc engine and the C.50 with a 125cc Ydral engine.

E.51 1951; D.51 AND Y.52 1952–1954 ★★

The second series appeared as the E.51 prototype at the 1951 Salon de Paris with smaller, 8in wheels, lighter in weight, and a 125cc Bernardet motor producing 6hp via four speeds and a right-side kickstart.

The D.51's 250cc Bernardet hit a 90km/h top speed with the kickstart and rear suspension on the left side. The front section was refined with an immovable fender and headlight mounted on the apron. The design differed little from the Y.52 with the half-moon airscoop on the rear sidepanel that gave the impression of the eyelids of an animated scooter. The Y.52 kept the left-kick 125cc Ydral engine with the same 70km/h top speed as the 125cc Bernardet motor.

The French stereotype of the American cowboy came to life in the coveted "Texas" version of the Y.52. The cowhand's scooter came complete with rhinestone saddlebags, fringed handlebars, and studded seats with a saddlehorn on the rear pillion. Displayed at the Salon de Paris on a rug of simulated white cowhide, the only thing missing was cow horns on the front fender.

CABRI L6 AND M60 1954–1959; GUÉPAR 1955–1959 ★★

"Easy to park" was about all that could be said for the Cabri since the classy designs of the early Bernardets were lost. The tall, horizontal 50cc—later 85cc—engine raised the rear section to look like a metal fez, but instead of a tassel, a bicycle seat rose out of the top. In 1955, Bernardet came under the control

Bernardet B-Series
The head-scratching originality of the Bernardet surely made any Parisian gendarme want to pull over the putt-putt for a closer look. Just as the Deux-Chevcaux's odd design stunned the auto world—but ultimately became a French icon, the Bernardet and Terrot scooters melt any scooterist's heart with sympathy and affection.

Bernardet D-51
The Frères Bernardet scooters kept the lefty kickstart into the early 1950s on the D-51 and smaller Y-52. The spiffy new design looked like a sheathed horse suitable for a knight and, in fact, Bernardet scooter clubs sponsored jousting matches with scooterists wearing plate armor.

of Le Poulain, installing its 50x50cc Comet with the Servomatic system. This new model was also sold in Belgium with two-tone paint as the Hirondelle Passe-Partout, or the All-Purpose Swallow.

The Guépar, or Cheetah, first appeard in 1955 as the Jaguar but its name was soon changed due to the litigation threats from the British car maker. The Guépar ws powere by a two-cylinder engine.

In March of 1959, Bernardet-Le Poulain fell on hard times and liquidated the remaining 300 scooters in their stock.

Beta ITALY ★

In the shadow of Brunelleschi's renaissance cathedral, the Florentine company Beta released its 80cc Lince (Lynx) scooter in 1959 to try to keep out the Piaggio scourge from Pisa. In this city of scooters, the Beta's large spoked wheels and semi-covered body didn't offer much new and didn't match up to the high esthetic expectations of its fellow city folk.

Not until four years later did Beta break ground with the 48cc Cicogna (stork) scooter with smaller 10 inch wheels. Although the engine was small, the ground-breaking bodywork kept up with the rapidly-changing Italian scooter designs.

In the 1990s, Beta opted for a sport scooter line that appeals to testosterone-fueled Italian ragazzi. With dashing multi-colored neon bikes—the Ark and Eikon—Michael Schumacher would turn green. Apart from the larger 125 or 150cc Eikon, all the scooters fall into the 50cc category to allow Italian 14 year olds to navigate between the Ferraris on Italian streets. Beta's dabble in the world of scooters soon ended and the company returned to its off-road motocross cycles.

BFC DENMARK ★

One of the rare Scandinavian scooters, Libelle was produced by BFC in the late 1950s.

Bianchi ITALY ★★

Edoardo Bianchi was one of the early motorcycle makers of Italy. All the way back in 1890, Bianchi showcased a motorized three-wheeler. After decades of crafting beautiful racing and road cycles, in 1960 Bianchi built its first scooter, but waited until 1963 to officially release it. The Orsetto, or Bear Cub, was designed by Lino Tonti but took styling cues from the Lambretta. The 4.5hp 48x43mm engine was hung in the center of the scooter below the tube frame with rear drive by a long, enclosed chain. The scoot rode on little 3.50x8in wheels but managed a top speed of 70km/h.

The next year, the Bi-Bi was released as a deluxe version of the Orsetto. The price tag on the Orsetto reached 107,950 Italian Lire, which was relatively cheap by scooter standards of the day. The Orsetto was also sold as the Roma in England by Raleigh of bicycle fame. Production continued through 1964.

Binz WEST GERMANY ★

Binz of Lorchin Würtemberg—not to be confused with Benz of Mercedes-Benz fame—exported its Binz-Roller to such faraway places as Belgium. One of the major selling points was the exotic "Klaxon électrique," the electric horn. The Binz-Roller would be categorized as a mere moped due to its 20 x2.25 in. wheels and bicycle handlebars, but was save by its scooter-like floorboard and body covering.

The choosy scooterist of 1954–1955 could decide between a Fichtel & Sachs 47cc for the S50 model or an Jlo 49cc for the J50. The two scooters had identical bodies as well as speed (40km/h), weight (50kg), gas tank capacity (1.5liters); in fact everything was the same except for the zesty 0.5hp advantage of the J50. In the Netherlands, scooter spotters could chart the Binz under the HDR marque.

Bird Engineering USA ★

An upstart firm based in Cushman's backyard at Omaha, Nebraska, Bird built its Wren scooter in the 1960s with the omnipresent 2.5hp two-cycle Clinton engine. Lights and fenders cost extra.

Bitri THE NETHERLANDS ★

Made by the Nederlandse Scooterfabrik NV in Dokkum, the Bitri was presented in 1954 with a German Jlo 118cc engine delivering 4.5hp at 4500rpm via a two-speed gearbox. Soon, a 150cc Jlo was offered, and in 1957, the Bitri added a 200cc Sachs with four speeds and 10.2hp; electric start was optional.

In 1960, you had four Bitri models to choose from: 150-4 KS Standard and Luxe and the 150-4 ES and 200-4 ES, both with electric start.

Bloom USA ★

BLM couldn't resist calling its Bloom mobile a "scooter moped," as if it couldn't make up its mind. These are definitely scooters, but the battery makes it a bit pokey and more moped like. Still, it has a luxurious "cup holder" to spill coffee in your lap around tight turns.

BM ITALY ★

In the 1960s, BM offered its 75cc two-stroke Minotauro, a big name for a little scooter.

BMW GERMANY ★ ★ ★ ★

BMW never built a production scooter but in 1953 at its early Munich factory, engineers created a prototype for a shaft-driven motorcycle-scooter with bodywork covering its obviously motorcycle-based frame and riding atop 16in wire-laced wheels.

In 1954, BMW created the R10, a prototype for a true scooter, this time based on a 200cc single-cylinder four-stroke engine delivering 8–10hp. Final drive was via a shaft, like the BMW motorcycle and Lambretta scooters of the era. Earles-style triangulated front forks held the front wheel. The bodywork was unadorned, fully enclosing the engine in the Vespa fashion.

Whether the BMW scooter would have been a success is a question for the academics. But amid the market of inexpensive, jangly two-strokes, the scooter would have brought all of BMW's refined engineering to the field, perhaps transforming people's demands.

In 1992, BMW showed its C1 scooter prototype to the Köln Motorcycle Show with a choice of 125cc or 250cc engines. The C1 was a modern plastic scooter with turn signals molded into handlebar covers and topped by a streamlined windshield. The seat was a full sports car-style bucket seat with four-point seatbelt. As a happy medium between the mini Mercedes/Swatch Smart car and a two-stroke putt-putt, the C1 proved a success for European drivers tired of parking problems and the constant drizzle of continental winters.

BMW never fully embraced its "scooters," as evidenced by using the word "urban mobility" and relegating them to the bottom of its list—just as any Harley-Davidson ape hanger blushes when the Topper is broached. Even so, BMW's CE 04, released in 2022, is a remarkable electric scooter with all this esteemed company's technology—even if it looks like you're traveling through town on Darth Vader's helmet.

Bond UK

Bond was the Piaggio of England, one of the firms that provided the wheels beneath Great Britain's postwar recovery. Yet whereas the Vespa was ridden

with dignity and is remembered with respect by the Italians, Bond's various two-and three-wheeled creations are recalled by the British with much the same fondness the country feels for the V-1 rocket.

MINIBIKE 1950–1951 ★ ★

Lawrence Bond started his empire by building the Bond three-wheeled car, moving to the two-wheel Minibike in 1950, an oddity that defies categorization even as a scooter. The engine was simple enough: a ubiquitous Villiers 1F 99cc two-stroke with two-speed gearbox. The frame, however, was pure creativity—or eccentricity, depending upon your point of view.

Made of sheet aluminum, it was rolled and lap-riveted into an oval-section spine with a tube subframe holding the engine. This construction was the main weight savings in the Minibike's mere 45kg.

Cavernous legshields protected the rider from all but a flood while sheet-aluminum fenders showed but a little of the 4.00x8in tires.

Suspension was lacking, unless you counted the two springs on the saddle seat; by 1950, the front forks were telescopic. In 1951, a De Luxe model was added with 125cc JAP engine and three speeds.

BAC GAZELLE 1952–1953 ★ ★

Bond Aircraft and Engineering Company (BAC) created its Gazelle scooter in 1952 based on a Villiers 122cc 10D two-stroke with 4.00x8in tires. The frame was a standard tube affair with front and rear fenders and legshields but only a gawky cage enclosing the engine, much like the German Ferbedo.

By the end of 1952, a second Gazelle based on the 99cc 1F Villiers engine was offered as well as a sidecar with aluminum bodywork. By 1953, rights to the Gazelle were purchased by the Projects and Developments firm. In 1953, Bond two-wheeler production was halted as the firm concentrated on its car.

P1 AND P2 1958–1959 ★ ★ ★

In 1958, Bond created a true scooter in its P1. Powered by a fan-cooled two-stroke 31C Villiers 148cc with a Siba Dynastart electric leg and three-speed gearbox.

BMW Prototype
BMW created this styling mockup in 1954 while considering production of its R10 prototype scooter. Based on a 200cc single-cylinder four-stroke engine delivering 8–10 hp, final drive was via a shaft, like the BMW motorcycle and Lambretta scooters of the era. If BMW had built a high-quality scooter in line with its motorcycles of the time, the world could have been a better place.

The chassis possessed an interesting design—for a scooter and for Bond—with the engine as a stressed member of the frame. Stub axles held the wheels and 4.00x10in tires.

The P1 body was made of fiberglass and the modernistic styling was garnished by two-tone paint scheme, tailfins, and chrome portholes on the sides. In mid-1958, the P2 was added with electric-start 197cc 9E Villiers and four speeds.

P3 AND P4 1960–1962 ★ ★ ★

In 1960, the 147cc 6.3hp P3 and 197cc 8.5hp P4 were released. The new scooters had a different frame that mounted the engines 2.25in lower. The bodywork was also restyled for a curvaceous yet still refreshingly odd look—the styling was "contemporary," according to Scooter Weekly. Options included a windscreen, spare wheel and carrier, and chrome wheel discs.

Bond continued building scooters until 1962 when it returned to producing solely its three-wheeled cars. It was a sad day for the scooter faithful but a joyous occasion for the mini-car fraternity.

B. M. Bonvicini ITALY ★

At the 1956 Salone di Milano, Mario Bonvicini from Bologna presented his 75cc scooter with large, spoked wheels and enclosed engine. Although the peppy scooter could hit 75 km/h, the 3hp scooter had very limited production. In 1959, Bonvicini tried again with the more menacing-sounding Minotauro 75. Perhaps potential scooterists worried that they were the ones to be sacrificed to keep the Cretan monster down as the scooter only survived one more

year. Not until three years later would Bonvicini hit the market again with the more scooter-like 49cc Pokerino with smaller wheels and full body shield.

Boom TAIWAN ★

With a wide variety of engine sizes available in gas-guzzling or electric, Boom mostly sells its scooters in Europe and Russia. Ad copy gushes in broken English about the black plastic floorboards: "The resistant material will allow you rest your foot." You could buy a fleet of these for the price of one new Vespa. One hopes the name doesn't signify the end result of driving on these plastic scooters.

Boudier FRANCE ★ ★

The fiberglass-bodied Super B.58 scooter was designed by M. Pierre Boudier and powered by a Ydral motor with a three-speed gearbox, producing 6.5hp at 6000rpm. The original front apron/fender featured two headlights, coordinated to move with the wheel. By the time of the debut of the Super B.58 in 1957, it was too late to enter an already saturated scooter market.

H. E. Bremer Company USA ★

Bremer of Milwaukee, Wisconsin, offered its Mini-Scoot in the late 1950s with a pull-start 3hp Briggs & Stratton and foldable handlebars.

Breton FRANCE ★

A flashy rubber squeeze horn on the simple Babymoto scooter exhibited the marketing know-how of the Saint-Etienne company Breton in 1952. The 1951 Ducati Cucciolo engine was changed to a 70cc Lavalette in 1953 but was still housed in metal side panels under the luggage rack. Then, in 1954 while Lambrettas were being "dressed," the Babymoto—grown up to be named the Scootomoto—was being "dénudé," but a reinforced cage trapped the petit 3 hp Lavalette engine from escaping.

Briggs & Stratton USA ★ ★ ★ ★ ★

Known mostly for supplying engines to many other makes, Briggs & Stratton made a few of their own scooters in the 1910s. Even so, ads for this early scooter turned up as far away as Japan. One brochure pushed the scooter on the upscale female market, much as the Autoped did: "EVERY woman will find her Briggs & Stratton Motor Scooter the most pleasant way to get there and back—calling, shopping, golfing, tennis, country rides and beach parties all brought nearer, all more enjoyable when she lets her Briggs & Stratton Motor Scooter take her." This Milwaukee make is very rare and used its own engine for this little putt-putt.

Brissonnet/Mors FRANCE ★★

More fond of prototypes than production, Brissonnet created its first scooter design in 1949 with a 50cc Poney engine; a year later, it built a 98cc version. Brissonnet finally went into production in 1951 with its S1C Speed scooter with a 115cc 3.8hp engine that hit 60km/h. The style was based on the early open Lambretta with slight embellishments.

By 1953, Brissonnet gave up making the Sport, and handed over the reins to Mors, which made an even faster scooter. By now a one-piece legshield and front fender unit enclosed the fan-cooled 6hp engine. The Speed Luxe was also presented at the 1953 Salon de Bruxelles with similar styling to the Paris–Nice model. By 1955, Mors also gave up on scooters, and Alcyon took up the Paris–Nice model until 1959.

Britax UK ★

The Britax Scooterette was launched at the 1954 Earl's Court Show powered by a four-stroke 48cc Ducati Cucciolo engine.

Brockhouse Engineering

UK ★★★

The Corgi was based on the Welbike, a lightweight foldable paratrooper scooter built by Excelsior during World War II. Postwar, Brockhouse Engineering of Southport civilized the Welbike as the Corgi, believing that people would need an economical commuter machine and that the Welbike's heroism would serve the Corgi well in the marketplace. In retrospect, Corgi also seemed a better name; the scooter's low-bellied chassis duplicated that of the Queen's favorite dog.

Corgi power was a two-stroke 98cc Excelsior Spryt engine of 50x50mm built by Brockhouse, similar in design to the Villiers Junior de Luxe. The cylinder was on the horizontal, fitting snuggly beneath the steel-tube frame in the center of the wheelbase.

A Wico-Pacy flywheel magneto provided spark. Bodywork was minimal and the Corgi rode atop 2.25x6.25in tires.

Although announced in 1946, two years passed before the first Corgis were available, thereafter selling well to transport-hungry commuters. A bare-bones sidecar was soon marketed as a sort of motorized shopping cart.

In mid-1948, a Corgi Mark II was offered with a dog-clutch that disengaged the drive to provide a neutral gear; the basic Corgi was then named the Mark I. In 1949, a two-speed Albion gearbox and telescopic front forks were options for both models.

Aftermarket bodywork was made by the Jack Olding firm in 1950. A Mark IV was offered in 1952 with the two-speed and telescopic forks standard. The Mark IV continued its career until 1954 when (slightly) more sophisticated cars took over the market.

Brumana Pugliese

BRAZIL/ITALY ★★

One of the world's most populated cities, São Paulo, got its own Lambretta do Brasil factory in 1955 to make the LD model and later the Series II. When the company changed its name to Pasco Lambretta in

Corgi

Originally serving the RAF as the Excelsior Welbike made by Brockhouse Engineering, this paratrooping putt-putt dropped from the sky striking fear into the hearts of the Luftwaffe. Postwar, its moniker was softened to that of the royal canines, the Corgi. Indian motorcycles even imported the odd little scooter slapping on their own stickers calling it the Papoose. Courtesy of owner: Hans Kruger

BSA Dandy

The Dandy Scooterette strayed from the macho image of BSA's motorcycles and catered to the dressed-up dandies of the day rather than the Lambretta mods. Four years later, BSA switched to the more powerful Sunbeam to complete its unsuccessful scooter line. Courtesy of the owner: Vittorio Tessera

1960, it began making the coveted TV Series III. In 1973, the company (now named Brumana Pugliese) built a Slimline Lambretta with an even narrower legshield and semi-exposed engine.

BSA UK

Birmingham Small Arms was one of the stalwart British motorcycle pioneers, but in 1960 it created a motorscooter. As part of World War II reparations, BSA had won the German DKW firm's prewar two-stroke engine design, which it shared with the lucky Harley–Davidson, Yamaha, WSK in Poland, MZ (formerly the DKW factory in East Germany), and Voskhod in Russia. The two-stroke design was used in BSA's Bantam and inspired the firm's first scooter, the Sunbeam, as well as the Triumph Tigress, since Triumph was owned by BSA at the time.

BSA BEEZA PROTOTYPE 1955 ★

The Beeza was based on a 198cc single-cylinder side-valve engine with a four-speed gearbox cast in unit and a finned muffler. Where the Beeza, or Beezer, failed, the Sunbeam succeeded with its sleek lines and power engine.

DANDY SCOOTERETTE 1955–1962 ★ ★

The Dandy finally started rolling off the production line in 1957, two years after the moped-like vehicle was promised in the form of a prototype. The gearshift for the 70cc engine was placed on the handlebars with an awkward levered chooser controlling a series of springs.

SUNBEAM B2 AND B2S 1959–1964 ★ ★ ★

The scooters were designed by Edward Turner, who up to that time had a great reputation based on his Triumph Speed Twin vertical engine. By 1959, nearly identical Triumph Tigress and BSA Sunbeams models were offered, each in two versions, a 175cc two-stroke single and a 250cc four-stroke twin.

The B2 250cc shared engine parts with the 175cc from the clutch back but the block and heads were cast in aluminum and were special to the four-stroke twin. The B2S added electric start and a second battery.

The 250cc engines zoomed the scooters faster than the 10in wheels and 5in drum brakes were made to handle. The front fork followed the Vespa design with a single-sided, stub axle with the damper and spring units enclosed.

SUNBEAM B1 1960–1965 ★ ★ ★

The B1 mirrored the Tigress 172cc TS1 with an engine based on the Bantam motorcycle although most engine parts were not interchangeable. The scooter had a foot shift and flywheel magneto fan to cool the ever-overheating two-stroke.

In 1960, the Sunbeam was garnished in the classic Vespa metallic green, but by 1961 it was offered in a choice of blue or red with an option of a cream weathershield.

BSA-Triumph built its scooters in an attempt to thwart the Italian-dominated scooter market, but it was too late. By 1960, much of the craze had faded away, and the Tigress and Sunbeam also died a quick death.

B. S. Villa ITALY ★

Based in Crespellano, near Bologna, B. S. Villa offered its 50cc AX and GZ scooters in the 1990s. At the 1992 Bologna show, Villa displayed a scooterone—larger scooter—with Buck Rogers styling and disc front brake.

Bug Engineering USA ★

Bug's Flea scooter was built at the firm's West Covina, California, factory in the 1960s. The Flea's 2½hp two-cycle Clinton was standard, but McCulloch or Yamaha engines were optional.

Cagiva ITALY ★

Founded in 1950 in the far northern Italian town of Varese, Cagiva was all about winning motorcycle races, especially motocross. The company grudgingly entered the scooter market in the 2000s but didn't survive.

Camille Foucaud FRANCE ★

Function over style described the 1951 Fastex FM 120 Modèle Standard. The exposed 118cc Jlo motor was surrounded by a bird cage to prevent singed

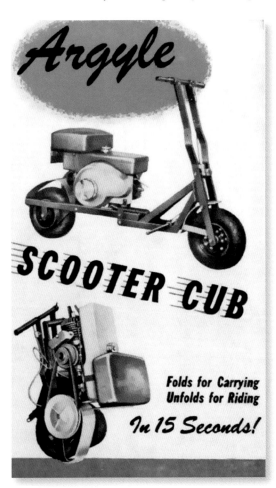

C & E Manufacturing USA ★★

The Argyle Scooter Cub was built at C & E's Memphis, Missouri, factory in the 1960s as a foldable scooter based on the 2½hp two-stroke Clinton.

Caproni Vizzola ITALY ★

This marque stuck mostly to motorcycles until a brief foray into the scooter world. Armed with an NSU engine, like all its bikes, Caproni Vizzola's economical scooter debuted in 1956 but the competition was already too fierce by that time.

Carabela MEXICO ★

The Acer Mex company began building Carabela motorcycles in the 1960s, but did not produce a scooter until the late 1970s when it offered its Pony-Matic with 60cc engine and automatic clutch. The styling was half mini-bike, half scooter.

Carnielli ITALY ★★

Carnielli's Vittoria scooters, named after the firm's home of Vittorio in Veneto, were based on tube frames. The bodywork had an odd feature: the engine covers ended below the pillion seat and a separate rear fender continued the lines.

The first Vittoria, Tipo 75, of 1951 was a lightweight scooter showing the firm's heritage of bicycle building. The engine was a 65cc two-stroke of 43x44mm giving 3.2hp at 5450rpm. Tires were 3.50x7in, later switching to 8in.

In 1952, Carnielli showed its Vittoria Luxe based on a 125cc NSU two-stroke. While many French, Germany, and English scooter makers used engines from other sources, the Italians almost always used their own engines, so Carnielli's NSU powerplant was an oddity—especially since it was based on a Lambretta C/LC engine.

The Luxe was soon replaced by the Grand Luxe with redone bodywork, chrome luggage rack, and 3.50x10in tires to carry it to 80-90km/h.

Carniti ITALY ★★★

Hooking up with Italy's premier auto designer, Ghia, Carniti ventured from its bread and butter in the boat business for a fantastic "Automotoscooter" with a three-cylinder, 200cc engine. Part scooter part jet ski, this two-seater could top 100 km/h as it floated

legs, a blatant gas tank was mounted on the front handlebars, and a boxy luggage space above the rear wheel all amounted to an unimaginative scooter. The S.53 with a 49cc or 70cc Lavalette engine was shown at the 1952 Salon de Paris with improvements such as hidden cables and side panels enclosing the engine. Sometimes this little putt-putt bore the label Bonin-Lavalette.

1949 Fold-Up Putt-Putt
The Argyle Scooter Cub folded up to 14-1/2 × 18-1/2 × 22-1/2 inches—and it took exactly 15 seconds to do it, according to Popular Mechanics. The layout of the Argyle was ingenious in its compactness: the horizontal two-stroke nestled under the seat with the carburetor feeding the crankcase at back. The frame and fenders were made from cast aluminum alloy.

Portuguese Scooter

The Iberian Peninsula had a scooter vacuum filled mostly with Italian imports. A few home-grown exceptions sprouted, however, such as the 170cc Casal Carina that, in pidgin English, "GIVES YOU ALL PLEASURE OF SPEED AND STRENGTH. A FINE TRIP!"

through the air with its wheels barely visible. The second attempt at a scooter in 1953 resulted in a more traditional style with a four-stroke 164cc engine. Neither bike made it into full production.

CAS CZECHOSLOVAKIA ★ ★ ★

In the 1910s, this Czech company made copies of the American Autoped with 155cc (56x63) engine mounted behind the steering column for better stability rather than attached to the wheel.

Casal PORTUGAL ★

The Casal Carina S170 scooter followed the classic step-through design with a tube frame covered by sheet steel bodywork. The two-stroke 50cc engine was 40x39.7mm delivering 5.2hp at 7500rpm. A four-speed gearbox was shifted by a foot lever giving power to the 3.00x10in tires.

The best thing about the Carina may have been the stilted English of its Portuguese ads. One brochure stated the scooter was "comfortable and clean, so you may drive it in your best suit. No parking troubles, that square inch between two cars is quite enough."

Casalini ITALY ★

Casalini began production in 1955 with its David scooter, believed to be the only scooter with a biblical name. Giovanni Casalini was known mostly for its bike frames, which it used for this 50cc covered moped. Most models were exported to Holland, Portugal and Greece, where the more successful David B. But Piaggio was the Goliath of the market, and Casalini lasted but a short time.

Cazenave FRANCE ★

Known for its mopeds, Cazenave decided to brave the scooter market with three models: the Belina, Super-Belina, and Alpina. The first two, in 1954 and 1955, resembled the Rumi Scoiattolo with an odd rear section overshadowed by a large boomerang-shaped chrome piece that was perhaps designed to reassure the quizzical buyers that the scooter would return them home as well as get them there. The two different models came with a choice of three different engines, a VAP, Mistral, or Ydral for a total of six possible combinations.

The Alpina appeared in 1960 with your choice of an Italian Demm or German Sachs motor.

Centaur USA ★

The Centaur fold-up scooter was powered by a Clinton engine and built by the American Motor Scooter Company and funded by the importer of Lambretta scooters into the US from 1960 to 1965.

CF Moto CHINA ★

Based in Hangzhou, China, CF Moto may specialize in motorcycles, but its scooters are equally pricey in hopes of going after a market that wants speed. With gas models such as Glory, the electric Charm, and the oversized lounge chair Fashion, CF Moto had a limited run in the US and pulled most of its scooters by 2011.

Changguang CHINA ★

Produced by the Changzhou Guangyang Motorcycle Company, these larger gas-guzzling scooters start at 125cc and top out at 275cc.

Chicago Scooter Company
USA ★

To release an inexpensive scooter without sullying its main brand, Genuine Scooter Company formed the Chicago Scooter Company for electric scooters.

Chuangxin CHINA ★

Jiangsu Chuangxin Motorcycle Manufacturing dabbled in scooters with 125 and 150cc sporting models.

Cimatti ITALY ★ ★

In 1957, Cimatti offered its two-stroke Scooterino 49. Marco Cimatti was known more for bicycles, but offered this attractive covered moped with a two-stroke HVM motor started with bicycle pedals. After little success for its Scooterino, Cimatti tried a little fold-up scooter dubbed the Pinguino (penguin) in 1963. In 1965, the sleek style of Lambretta was imitated in Cimatti's Denny scooter with the same 48cc engine, but still the scoot couldn't top 40 km/h.

CityCoco CHINA ★

The likely evolution of successful CityCoco scooters was after the German Scroosers were manufactured in China and—surprise!—the Electric Scooter Mobility CityCoco company produced nearly identical scooters soon afterwards. Numerous knock-offs, even in China, borrowed the CityCoco name, just as Vespa became synonymous with "scooter" for a while.

Apart from these big-wheeled low riders, CityCoco produces its electric City scooter for those "who enjoy going long distances." After all, "wouldn't you like to go alone or with your child and farther?" Be careful that this "long distance" must be under 60 km (37 miles), but at least CityCoco assures scooterists that you can take the battery "with you like a small bag."

CL WEST GERMANY ★

CL produced its 48cc mini scooter in 1951.

Claeys-Flandria BELGIUM ★

Based at Zedelgem, the firm showed its Flandria scooter in 1954 based on a German Jlo 175cc engine with four speeds. In 1956, Flandria started building the Italian SIM-Moretti Ariete scooter for Belgium.

In 1960, Flandria offered its Parisienne scooter with a 49cc two-stroke with four speeds. The 4.3hp Parisienne managed to survive until 1981 when competition from the Italians and Japanese overcame the little covered moped.

Clark Engineering USA ★★★

When the Powell scooter firm turned to war contracts during World War II, Clark Engineering of South Pasadena, California, bought the remaining stock of Powell's innovative A-V-8 scooter. Clark renamed its scooter the Victory Clipper in a burst of patriotic pride—and salesmanship as it offered the scooter during the wartime dearth of car production.

All Victory Clippers were leftover 1942 model A-V-8s: as Clark's brochure stated, "We cannot supply new Clippers," hinting, however, that "a very few near new ones [were] available!" And while you needed to be issued a buyer priority certificate by the US War Department as a war contractor to buy a new car or motorcycle, Clark noted that no priority was necessary to buy a used scooter. The Victory Clipper was doing its part to win the war.

In 1947, Clark was back, building the A-V-8 as the Clark Cyclone scooter.

CM ITALY ★

This factory out of Bologna built a peppy 150cc, four-stroke scooter in 1957. In spite of the fancy two-tone bodywork, CM's scooter was put atop scary 6 inch wheels, which were deemed too tippy for any Italian cobblestone strada.

Columbus Cycle Company USA ★

Named after its home base of Columbus, Nebraska, Columbus built the Discoverer scooter in the 1960s with a four-stroke 2.5hp engine. Suspension was by "frame and seat," according to Popular Science magazine. It was a sobering thought.

Comet Manufacturing Company USA ★★★

The Comet scooter was built prewar in Minneapolis, Minnesota, with four models available. The standard model had a rubber-mounted front fork, ½hp engine, automatic clutch, and two-tone blue and white paint scheme. A Pick-Up version had an extended tail section. An open-frame sport model was also available with a bicycle seat and a crossbar to stabilize the frame.

Condor SWITZERLAND ★

The famous Condor firm was known for its swift flat-twin motorcycles, but in 1954 displayed four scooters at the Salon de Genève. Instead of producing these prototypes, however, Condor built the Austrian Puch scooter under license and plastered "Condor-Puch" on the legshield.

Condor WEST GERMANY

From 1953 to 1954, Condor—not to be confused with the Condor factory in Switzerland—built a few small scooters with 48cc engines.

Blast like a Comet
Comet Manufacturing located on scenic Nicollet Avenue in beautiful Minneapolis built these early putt-putts. "Go Places!" boasted Comet's ads with a hand-colored woman.

Monark Powerbike Roadster

While first glance places the Monark Roadster next to Whizzers and other powered bikes, the second inspection reveals that the rear wheel is strictly scooter-sized with the covered engine of its two-wheeled brethren. Courtesy of the owner: Jim Kilau

Crescent's Svenske Skooters

The two scooters in Crescent's line were essentially rebadged Monark scooters with different paint schemes.

Continental Motors USA ★ ★

Looking more like a powered Whizzer than a putt-putt, the classic Monark Powerbike Roadster rode on a balloon tire in front and tiny motorized wheel in the back. This hybrid of classic bicycle powered by a scooter-like rear half was dreamed up in Chicago by Monark Silver King.

Cooper USA ★ ★ ★

Frank Cooper affixed his own decals to the Powell Aviate scooter to create his "decal-engineered" Cooper Aviate in 1941–1942.

When the US Army requested bids for a light-weight scooter to drop by parachute behind enemy lines, Cooper added a new engine to meet mil-spec, and offered the Army his Cooper War Combat Motor Scooter.

With such a belligerent name, the Cooper scooter should have won a Medal of Honor merely for striking fear into the hearts of the enemy. Alas, America's secret weapon was never built, as the Cushman Model 53 Airborne won out in bidding.

Still, Cooper's airborne was quite a machine. The 5hp Wisconsin engine was mounted in the chassis center with a long chain driving the rear wheel. The motor displaced 17.8ci or 290cc and created 5hp and 7.7lb-ft of torque at 3400rpm with a Wico magneto. The transmission was by Plymouth, although an Army Characteristics Sheet noted that it had been "altered."

But the chassis is what deserved the medal. With the aid of a welding torch, Cooper added a maze of triangulated reinforcing bars to the Aviate frame to stand up to the shock of a parachute drop. A single cantilevered saddle rode atop a sole coil spring with

an odd-shaped gas tank nestled on top of the frame rails. Mil-spec required 6.00x6in tires, interchangeable with USAAF training planes. Naturally no lights were needed.

While the Army rated the Cooper better than the Cushman 53, Army inspectors were unimpressed with the Cooper Motors, Inc.'s "factory," and awarded the bid to Cushman. A small number of Coopers were built circa 1944 for Army evaluation and probably destroyed in parachute testing

Cosmo USA–ITALY ★

Cosmopolitan Motors of Hatboro, Pennsylvania, sold Puch scooters under its own name in the late 1950s.

CPI TAIWAN

CPI offered two-stroke scooters, the 50cc Aragon and Oliver, for a time in the US—usually by mail delivery since dealers weren't convinced. Freaky and Popcorn models followed the same basic design.

Crescent SWEDEN ★

Crescent was a small bicycle maker starting production in 1954 in Varberg. It was soon bought by the Swedish Monark firm, which made bicycles and motorscooters as well as some of the world's great motocrossers. After the sale, Crescent sold Monark scooters under its name, usually in different color schemes.

The Monark Skoterett 901264 was renumbered as the 921264 and painted in yellow or blue and white two-tone for Crescent. It was powered by a 48cc Husqvarna two-stroke 1hp single.

Monark's version of the Honda Cub, the Skotermoped Model 901269, was also redesignated as the 921269 and sold by Crescent. Today both firms are part of Volvo.

Crocker USA ★ ★ ★ ★ ★

Albert G. Crocker was the builder of the great Crocker V-twin motorcycles of the 1930s that single-handedly caused Harley–Davidson and Indian more grief than any event up to the British motorcycle invasion of the 1950s. Crocker was a former colleague of Harley–Davidson's famed engineer William Ottaway when the duo worked for Thor motorcycles; Crocker was later an Indian dealer and racer, so he was well placed to be a thorn in everyone's side.

The high-performance Crocker V-twins put the other motorcycles to shame on the speedways and dirt tracks of southern California where they were bred. But neither Harley–Davidson nor Indian gave a hoot about Crocker's other endeavor of the late 1930s, his Scootabout motorscooter. In the end neither did Crocker himself.

The most interesting feature of the Scootabout was not its Lauson engine or solid front suspension but its flowing bodywork. Following the tenets of Salsbury's step-through design, Crocker added a further clause to the definition of a scooter: Styling.

The Motor Glides and Auto-Glides initially did not venture beyond single-plane folds in their bodywork; after all, scooters were built on a budget and sold as a utilitarian device. The Crocker, on the other hand, was formed of sinuous bodywork with two-tone paint that added a further dimension to the curvaceous lines. The tail section covered the wheels with fender skirts, the design coming together at the rear in a teardrop shape. The Scootabout foreshadowed the Vespa in spirit.

But the Scootabout never scooted about much. In fact, production probably numbered less than 100—as did Crocker's infamous motorcycle.

Csepel HUNGARY ★ ★

Part of a large steel works in Budapest, Csepel was once upon a time the largest motorcycle maker in Hungary. The firm offered its 175 Tünde scooter with 8.5hp based on the Puch Alpine of the early 1950s. A smaller 50cc Panni was offered to complete the line and was produced until the 1960s. Csepel was reorganized by the State as Danuvia and Pannonia in 1952.

Cushman BELGIUM ★ ★

In 1950, the Belgian Cushman firm was erected in Anderlues to build Cushman scooters for the Belgians under license. Cushman in the US supplied components including Husky engines, transmissions, wheels, and more to the firm as part of the European Recovery Act. The Belgian firm made its own frame, forks, bodywork, and other parts.

In 1951, Belgian Cushman offered its Single model with a 300cc Husky engine. The bodywork was odd when compared with the Cushman 50 Series of the day and weird compared with any other scooter.

The tail section was a standard rounded covering; the front legshield was a large sheet that looked like protective armor on an artillery cannon. A luggage compartment sat in front of the apron with styling that appeared to be based on a mailbox. As an early brochure tentatively offered, the Single could "perhaps by piloted by anyone without apprenticeship."

Belgian Cushman also offered a three-wheeled Delivery scooter with "robust construction."

Cushman USA

Cushman Motor Works' decision to build a motorscooter in the 1930s was a serendipitous afterthought from a company that was successfully producing industrial equipment and engines. Cushman played follow-the-leader into the scooter market, recognizing Salsbury's novel scooter as an economical option to a second car during the recovery years after the Great Depression. With the success of its first scooter, Cushman continued to construct the most long-lived American motorscooter in a dazzling variety of unique models. And as Vespa became synonymous for scooter in the rest of the world, Cushman stands for scooter to most Americans even today.

Cushman's Auto-Glide motorscooter was inspired by the innovative Motor Glide built by E. Foster Salsbury in Los Angeles. Looking for a more powerful engine to propel the Motor Glide, Salsbury sent blueprints of its scooter to Cushman and requested a bid in mid-1936 for 1,000 units of its renowned Husky engine. When Salsbury declined the bid, Cushman decided to use the 1,000 engines to build its own scooter.

Colonel Roscoe Turner, the famed Motor Glide–endorsing aviator, indirectly led to the startup of Salsbury's chief rival. In 1936, his barnstorming antics came to Lincoln, Nebraska, Cushman's hometown. In a 1992 interview, Cushman's former president Robert H. Ammon told the tale: Turner buzzed the airfield on his Evinrude-powered Motor Glide, prompting a local boy to fashion his own scooter out of angle iron, wheelbarrow wheels, and a Cushman Husky lawn mower motor. "We found out about this scooter by chance," Ammon recalled. "One day my dad looked out the window and he saw the kid on his scooter buying parts at our parts depot."

The writing was on the wall: Cushman built a scooter prototype that was to become the Auto-Glide Model 1-1.

"We were in the business of building and selling engines," Robert H. Ammon stated. "The idea of making a motorscooter was to build and sell more engines." It was that simple.

Salsbury's interest in the Husky motor was well founded: the Husky was a venerable, hard-working engine. According to a Cushman promotional history booklet published in the 1950s, Cushman was founded by cousins Everett and Clinton Cushman, who began building two-cycle gas engines in their basement

Belgian Cushman
As part of the European Recovery Act, Cushman helped start scooter production in Belgium by licensing its patents to the Belgian Cushman firm. This flyer shows what the Belgians could do with the American design, reworking the Cushman 50 series scooters into the oddly styled Single. Never imported to the United States, a Belgian Cushman would be the ultimate addition to an American Cushman collection.
Courtesy of the Vittorio Tessera archives

in 1901 to power pleasure and fishing boats. They were issued their first patent in 1902 for a two-stroke gas engine that was used on farms to drive everything from separators to washing machines. The duo later created several successful racing marine one- and two-cylinder two-stroke engines before venturing into a series of four-stroke, water-cooled engines.

In 1913, a full-fledged factory was built on the site that would become the current OMC works. In 1922, Cushman developed the Husky, its first air-cooled, four-stroke engine. The one-cylinder Husky ran on roller bearings, and was used to power its Bob-A-Lawn mower, aptly named for the Roaring Twenties era of bobbed haircuts.

But by the 1930s, Cushman Motor Company was in trouble due to the Depression and the hard-hit farm economy. In 1934, John F. Ammon and his son Charles, founders of The Easy Manufacturing Company, also of Lincoln, took over Cushman. The Ammons had a long relationship with the Cushmans, using Cushman castings and engines in their pipe layers, cultivators, and other industrial tools.

With this staid background in industrial equipment and no-nonsense engines, the creation of the Auto-Glide motorscooter by Cushman in Lincoln, Nebraska, was as far-fetched as a trip to the moon at the time. But "Uncle Charlie" Ammon had a son.

That scion, 19-year-old Robert H. Ammon, had heard tell of Roscoe Turner's barnstorming Motor Glide and seen the local boy's homemade machine. Robert and Charlie Ammon had a vision of a motorscooter.

AUTO-GLIDE MODEL 1-1 AND 1-2 1936
★★★★★

The first Auto-Glide was designated the Model 1-1, denoting the first scooter, first model. Robert H. Ammon built the first scooter in the Motor Glide mold with the 1hp Husky engine mounted directly below the seat in front of the rear wheel.

Ammon remembered that he copied the local boy's scooter in using 1¼in angle iron for the first frame but the angle iron soon broke. "So I used 2in

channel iron, which did the job," he said. "I learned early on that a rigid frame was essential, and the channel-iron frame lasted a long time for Cushman."

Pressed steel made up the step-through chassis with spindly fork tubes holding the fenderless front wheel and channel iron enclosing the engine and holding the seat aloft. There were no lights and no suspension. And as with the local boy's scooter, Ammon said he used wheelbarrow wheels on the prototype mounted with 4.00x8in tires.

Ammon's aim was to build "just a good, sturdy, two-wheel scooter," as he told The Lincoln Star for a retrospective article on June 21, 1984. "We finally had an engine in it and had it running in, oh, I'd say, 30 days. And it was a very crude-looking thing, of course."

A series of prototypes were built. Development continued, and by late 1936 the 1-2 was tested featuring similar mechanics to the 1-1 but with a front fender and simple bodywork made of welded steel sheets enclosing part of the tail section. The "styling" eschewed any compound curves, foreshadowing the familiar Auto-Glide shape.

After designing the rigid frame, Ammon worked on getting the steering geometry correct He recalled in 1992, "I had read an article at the Engineering School of the University of Nebraska about the correct geometry for a bicycle or motorcycle. I developed the first scooter's steering head angle so that the tail end of the steering head was at a point behind the point where the wheel first touches the ground. When I got the scooter stable enough so I could drive it without any hands, I knew it was ready."

According to Ammon, less than twenty Models 1-1 and 1-2 were built and sold.

AUTO-GLIDE MODELS 1 AND 3 1937–1938; 1T, 1V, 3T, AND 3V 1939 ★★★★★

By 1937, Cushman was serious about motorscooters. Production began at a pace with two models offered: the Model 1, called a Sport version, and the 3, which included the Kari-Pac, a bolt-on rear section with a 16x18x16in luggage box similar to Salsbury's Parcel Carrier attachment. And instead of Roscoe Turner's Salsbury endorsement, Cushman had more advanced technical support; one ad stated that "Prominent Engineers proclaim Auto-Glide the greatest advance ever made in low cost, motor transportation."

At the heart of the Auto-Glide was the Husky engine, as Cushman promotion always reminded buyers. But like E. Foster Salsbury before them, the Ammons had decided the 1hp Husky motor was not enough power for the prototype. With these first production models they stepped up to the 1½hp Husky based on a bored version of the 1hp motor. The 1hp engine had measured 2 3/8x2½in bore and stroke for 11.08ci; the 1 1/2hp engine was 2 5/8x2 ½in for 13.53ci.

At the heart of the Husky were Lincolnite aluminum-alloy strut-type pistons with three rings and a steel x-section drop-forged and heat-treated connecting rod riding on die-cast "high-speed" bearings. The cam- and crankshafts were both drop-forged and heat-treated steel with fully enclosed taper roller main bearings. A flywheel fan forced cooling air over the engine and an Eisemann magneto fired the 1937 models; by 1938, a variety of Wico magnetos was used.

Cushman expected to sell its scooters to novices with little mechanical or engineering skills and the Husky was an easy engine to use. Yet it did have its quirks, typical of most engines of the 1930s, that required expert care. The instruction book chided owners to de-carbon the cylinder head every 5,000–8,000 miles, grind the valve seats, and adjust valve-to-pushrod clearance by grinding the valve stem end with a margin for error of 0.02–0.03in. Scooter ownership in the 1930s was not for the faint of heart.

In an odd twist of marketing, early Cushman ads promoted the slow speeds of the Auto-Glide: "Low speed ensures safety. Auto-Glide is not a 'speed wagon.'" Instead, the ads promised economy: 30mph at more than 120mpg. As other ads featuring businessmen in suits speeding along atop Auto-Glides promised, "Operates for actually one tenth the cost of an auto!" And the ultimate sales point, "Cheaper than shoe leather."

Like the power curve, the chassis of the 1 and 3 was also strengthened over the 1-2. The frame was still of one piece from the engine mounts to the steering head. A side frame of 2×1/8in channel steel and five steel crossmembers braced the unit construction. As an ad promised, "It will stand up."

The 1 and 3 rode on disc wheels with "non-skid" 3.50x12in ballon tires filled by inner tubes, which supplied the scooter's "suspension." Operation was easy: the "smooth-as-velvet" clutch to the single-speed drive was operated by the left foot, the rear-wheel drum brake was controlled by the right foot, and the handlebar-mounted throttle by the right hand. For optional accessories, a bicycle light could be mounted on the handlebars.

The bodywork had developed slightly from the 1-2 to enclose the engine with louvers for venting—and was now painted. The paint was sturdy tractor paint and the colors were Ford blue or Farmall red.

For 1938, the 1 and 3 continued, supplemented by Deluxe 1T and 3T versions, which featured two-speed transmissions and a 6 volt lighting and horn kit with generator and battery. The generators were rebuilt Ford Model T units, according to the Cushman instruction and parts book: "The bearings, field windings, brushes and brush holders are usually new. The armatures are rewound. The commutators are new or newly sized." Call it built to a price point, but according to an ad, the lighting "Complies with all State Highway requirements."

The V suffix models denoted a v-belt clutch added to the two-speed 1T and 3T.

The Kari-Pac was optional for the Model 1. And either model could add on the Trail-It Attachment, which hooked the Auto-Glide backward to a car's rear bumper for towing. Yet, unlike Salsbury's Cycletow with its two-wheel attachment, Trail-It left the scooter to run on solely its front wheel, easy prey to things like potholes and corners.

AUTO-GLIDE R-1 1938 ★ ★ ★ ★

The R-1 was a stripper model of the 1. R stood for rental, and Cushman hoped to sell the model to what it foresaw as a blossoming scooter rental business.

The R-1 retained the 1½hp Husky but with a simplified starting procedure for novice riders. The unskilled simply pushed the scooter to start it, pulled in the compression release on the handlebar to allow the engine to turn over, released the release, and let the engine take off.

Standard color for the R-1 was green with an Auto-Glide logo decal on the frame side near the steering head.

AUTO-GLIDE MODELS 5, 5T, 7, AND 7T 1938 ★ ★ ★ ★ ★

Cushman continued to refine its scooters with each model change. As Robert H. Ammon stated in 1992, "I saw other scooters—Moto-Scoot, Salsbury, Powell, and others. We would buy them to look them over to see what good features they had that we could incorporate. We also had lots of suggestions from dealers and employees within the company."

In late 1938, Cushman introduced the 5 and 7 DeLuxe battery-ignition versions of the magneto-ignition 1 and 3; the 5 was the Sport and the 7 had the Kari-Pac. These models featured lighting via a 6 volt generator with a large headlamp mounted atop the steering head and an electric

1938 Auto-Glide
The "CHEAPER THAN SHOE LEATHER Auto Glide" was Cushman's debut into the scooter realm with ad copy that made true H.G. Wells' claim that, "Advertising is legalized lying." By the time this 1938 Auto Glide hit the pavement, most of the dangerous quirks of the first model no longer spelled certain disaster. Looking through rose-colored glasses at the poky 1 hp Cushman engine, ad copy assured that, "Low speed ensures safety. Auto-Glide is NOT a 'speed wagon.'" Courtesy of the owner: Jim Kilau

horn on the fork tubes above the fender. The 5 and 7 retained the 1½hp Husky, the T models grafted on a two-speed transmission.

The new models featured a two-tone paint scheme with the front fender, forks, and handlebars as well as the scalloped area down the back in the light color. Auto-Glide decals were glued to the rear above the taillight and the frame side near the steering head; a Husky decal was affixed to the engine fan cover.

AUTO-GLIDE MODELS 2-4 1938–1939; 2T-4T 1938–1939; AND 2V-4V 1939 ★ ★ ★ ★ ★

In 1938, Cushman went for more power, releasing the 2 and 4 as 2hp versions of the 1 and 3; the 2 was the Sport and 4 had the Kari-Pac. The 2 and 4 continued with the single-speed transmission and magneto ignition but had larger, 2 5/8in bore 13.53ci engines.

Along with changing the bore of the 2hp engines, a new cylinder head was introduced with a freer flowing exhaust exit angle and eight retaining bolts instead of the smaller engine's six bolts.

For 1938, the 2hp Huskys were fired by Eisemann magnetos; in 1939, both Eisemann and Wico were used.

T-suffix models added the two-speed transmission; V-suffix models added the v-belt clutch.

AUTO-GLIDE R-2 1938–1939 AND RV 1939 ★ ★ ★

With the arrival of the 2hp Husky, the rental model was also upgraded as the R-2. The RV added the two-speed transmission and v-belt clutch for 1939.

AUTO-GLIDE 6-8 AND 6T-8T 1938 ★ ★ ★ ★ ★

The 6 and 8 were 2hp, battery-ignition versions of the 5 and 7, respectively. Again, the T models added the two-speed transmission.

AUTO-GLIDE MODELS 12 AND 14 1940 ★ ★ ★ ★

In 1940, Cushman introduced its Models 12 and 14, the latter being the DeLuxe model. While both had 2hp and Wico magneto ignition, the 12 had the one-speed and the 14 the two-speed transmission. The clutch control moved from a foot pedal to a handlebar lever mounted on the same side as the throttle. Lights and 6 volt generator were optional.

The major change in the new models was a wheelbase lengthened to 54in and the move from 12x3.50in to 14x4.00in tires, which increased ride stability, as noted in the instruction book. The new front forks were reinforced by small section tubes at the front.

Cushman also recognized the advantage of suspension for the first time. A trailing-axle lever-action setup damped by a preloaded light-gauge coil spring held the front wheel; coil springs mounted in the center of the scooter cushioned the rear.

The bodywork of the new models was also updated. The squared one-piece rear section now completely covered the entrails of the Husky, lifting away for servicing. This cover incorporated the seat into the bodywork , adding a 1cu-ft package compartment to replace the add-on Kari-Pac. The styling update also included a full front fender featuring—for the first time—compound curves.

AUTO-GLIDE MODELS 22 1940–1942 AND 24 1940 ★ ★ ★ ★

The 20 Series Models 22 and 24 quickly replaced the 12 and 14 respectively, although changes were minimal. The 24 retained the two-speed transmission, which Cushman noted was ideal for use with the new optional Side-Kar.

The 22 came with Cushman's new Floating Drive, an automatic clutch and transmission. Salsbury had introduced its revolutionary Self-Shifting torque converter in 1937, and Cushman was not to be outdone. Its ads proclaimed the Floating Drive "just like a fluid drive on the latest models of automobiles," which was something of a simplified misnomer. Instead, the Floating Drive was a drum clutch with three shoes that pushed outward against the inside of the drum as speed increased their centrifugal motion.

As well as the optional lighting system, other Cushman accessories included a windshield and speedometer for 1940. The Auto-Glide was moving upscale.

AUTO-GLIDE ECONOMY MODEL 21 1940 ★ ★ ★

The 21 was a step forward and backward at the same time: it replaced the stripper R-2 but used the old 1½hp Husky with the new Floating Drive. It also retained the old-style 12x3.50in tires, it moved into modern times with the coil-spring suspension. And while the new body style incorporated a luggage compartment, the 21 did not; instead the Kari-Pac was once more available.

AUTO-GLIDE MODELS 32 AND 34 1942–1945 ★ ★ ★ ★

The 32 and 34 replaced the 22 and 24 respectively in 1942 as the 30 Series scooters. These were also the last to be called Auto-Glides; like Salsbury, Cushman chose to promote its own name as a scooter manufacturer following World War II.

The US Army formed much of the specifications for the 30 Series by requesting bids for military scooters. As part of the military requirements, the small Huskys were shelved and a new 4hp version was the sole engine available. While the 2 5/8in bore of the 2hp Husky was retained, the stroke went from 2½in to 2¾in for 15ci. Wico flywheel magnetos provided spark. The brawnier power output gave the Auto-Glides new life.

The 32 came with the Floating Drive while the 34 used the two-speed. Lights and horn were now standard equipment. The engine cover of the 30 Series was redesigned with a larger package compartment and louvers on the sides to cool the more powerful engine.

While the US Army had formed the 30 Series and was pleased with the outcome, it purchased only 495 Model 34s with Side Kars for use as administrative mules, according to Fred W. Crismon's US Military Wheeled Vehicles.

But the majority of 30 Series sales went to civilians. While production of civilian cars, trucks, and motorcycles was all but halted during the war to concentrate industry on war materiel, Cushman got an exemption from the War Department as its vehicles were deemed ideal for wartime civilian transportation: they were economical both to build and ride. During the war, Cushman was constructing up to 300 scooters daily.

"This was tremendous thing," Robert H. Ammon told The Lincoln Star. "We were making scooters when Ford couldn't get tires to make cars."

And when the war was over, Cushman would be in full swing for civilian production while other manufacturers had to retool. "That's when they really took off, right after World War II," Ammon remembered.

MODEL 53 AIRBORNE SCOOTER 1944 AND MODEL 53A CIVILIAN 1946–1948 ★★★★★

In the history of warfare, there have been few such fantastical strategies as the US Army's notion of parachuting motorscooters with the famed 82nd or 101st Airborne behind enemy lines so they could putt-putt their way to attack the nearest Tiger tank. Rank it up there with Hannibal's elephants and the Trojan Horse, both of which succeeded; the Army's plans for an airborne scooter did not.

None of which diminishes the fascination or collectivity of the Model 53. In fact, it was a great scooter.

In requesting bids for an airborne scooter, the US Army followed the lead of the Fascist Italian army and the British Red Berets. The Italians spawned the Volugrafo paratrooper scooter while the British built the collapsible Corgi Welbike.

The Army requested bids on April 29, 1943, for a lightweight airborne scooter, and received prototypes of the Cushman 53 and the Cooper War Combat Motor Scooter from Cooper Motors, Inc., of Los Angeles. The competing scooters were assessed by Army Ordnance in Detroit on Characteristics Sheets filed February 17, 1944. While the Cooper had a more antagonistic name, the better to drive the Nazis back into the Fatherland, it also outpow-

ered the Cushman Husky 5hp to 4hp. Overall, Army project engineers ranked the Cooper superior to the Cushman, but after inspection of the two factories, the Army recommended a contract be awarded to Cushman to build a first batch of 600 Model 53s. By the end of 1945, the Army had bought 4,734 Model 53s, according to Crismon.

The 53 was a Model 34 that had done the mail-order Mr. Universe course. Stripped down to shed unneeded bodywork, it showed off its muscle: a reinforced, rigid chassis and sturdy bracing surrounding the engine. It also shed the coil-spring suspension of the 30 Series; the tires were to handle the 53's heaven-sent arrival.

Cushman legend has it, according to Somerville's A History of the Cushman Motor Works, that to test the operational durability of the 53 dropped from C-47s by parachute behind the Normandy beachhead, prototype scooters were hoisted by rope over the branch of a tall tree out back of the Cushman workshop and dropped to make certain they could stand the impact.

Other military requirements dictated the design of the 53. The tires were 6.00x6in, interchangeable with USAAF spotter aircraft. And the nuts and bolts were the eccentric English Whitworth spec—as were lend-lease P-51 Mustangs—to standardize tools needed.

Along with its planned airborne duties, the 53 was drafted for flightline work in the USAAF. Mil-spec required the 53 to be painted olive drab green, but many were repainted yellow for airfield use.

Cushman 50s Series
Post-World War II, the name Auto-Glide was retired, and the scooters were called Cushmans. The name was changed, but the styling and mechanicals were largely the same. The 50s Series underwent a major advance with the new automatic clutch on the two-speed 54 model, although the 52 had the old two-speed gearbox. Courtesy of the Herb Singe archives

After the war, the 53 was just too good to be laid to rest with a twenty-one-gun salute, and so Cushman offered the 53A, a civvy version of the Army model with an honorable discharge. And the 53 was too good to be changed; the 53A merely added a lighting system with 6 volt generator, reinstalled the 30 Series coil springs to the forks, and added a Cushman decal to the gas tank. An optional Buddy Seat could be had that perched at the rear, supported by long barrel springs.

MODELS 52, 52A, AND 54 1946–1948; 54B 1948–1949 ★★★★★

Following the war, it was the Cushman rather than Auto-Glide motorscooter, but the 52 and 54 continued the lineage of the Auto-Glide Models 32 and 34 respectively. There was no 40 Series due to the 1940s war years.

Cushman regaled the new line as "The Family Scooter," and instead of the old Auto-Glide decals featured the script Cushman logo on the rear sides of the engine cover, termed the "tail sheet" in the instruction manual.

The chief update was the arrival of the automatic clutch on the two-speed 54 model. Cushman promoted the addition of the knee-action suspension to the rear wheel, which "gives a smooth velvety ride—that F-L-O-A-T-I-N-G sensation. . . . Road shocks and jars never reach the hands and arms." The main advance was the use of "moder"n barrel springs replacing the coil springs; with their different-size windings, the barrels were crude but (sort of) effective variable-rate springs. The 50 Series glided along on standard 4.00x8in tires or optional 6.00x6in tires leftover from the mil-specs for the 53.

But the most exciting item on the 50 Series was the new lighting system that could be turned on by tightening the generator belt with a control lever; all you had to do was lift the seat to turn on the Cushman Permalite generator. And the new scooters had a dazzling hi-low beam controlled by a "tilt-ray" foot switch.

The new Model 52A was a Sport version of the 52 sold without the engine cover "tail sheet" in the style of the 53A. The 52A was not widely promoted by Cushman, appearing only in rare ads. The instruction manual listed it, however, stating that the 52A and 53A had a special "sport-type frame," leading one to believe that the frame differed from the standard models, when in fact the frames were identical. As the 50 Series instruction manual noted parenthetically, "The frames of all machines are alike, allowing a conversion from one model to any other model." This can leave a black hole on the subject of scooter identity for restorers today.

The 52A and 53A were altered during their production runs as well. Later brochures show them with full rear fenders mounted with tail lamps and long dual leaf springs holding single or optional tandem cushion seats.

In late 1948, Cushman debuted its new belt-drive torque-converter automatic clutch and transmission, called the Variamatic and denoted as the B-suffix to the Model 54B. Cushman had attempted to do battle in the motorscooter marketplace with Salsbury's cutting-edge belt torque converter when it introduced its Floating Drive centrifigal automatic clutch in 1940, but it just wasn't the same. And neither was the new Variamatic.

Cushman's Variamatic was a trouble-prone design that "almost ruined the Cushman reputation for reliability," according to Somerville. Finding a 54B with the original Variamatic today is like searching for a proverbial needle in the proverbial haystack; most were retrofitted with the tried and true but less-sophisticated Floating Drive.

Cushman offered a variety of accessories for its 50 Series scooters as listed in ads of the era. Chromed "spill bars" were available that bolted to the chassis front to protect the paint finish on event of a rollover. A plastic windshield could be had with a snap-on "fabricoid" cover to serve as legshields. The speedometer was driven off of the front wheel by cable and bolted to the steering head; different speedo packages were listed for scooters with 6in, 8in, and three wheels. Two different tandem seats were offered, a saddle type and a cushion. A chrome headlamp was also available to add "glamour."

The most interesting and rare option was a front wheel brake, part number S22-456. The drum mounted to the right side of the wheel and could be used with the speedometer. The Cushman Side-Kar was also available. It was a box on wheels with a lid equipped with slip hinges that could be "removed in ten seconds," according to a brochure. A steel seat could be added to the Side-Kar but no one weighing over 200lb could ride.

MODELS 62 PACEMAKER, 62A SPORT, 64 ROAD KING, AND 64A ROAD KING SPORT 1949–1956 ★★★

Cushman advertised the new 60 Series as "Twice the Scooter!" depicting a monstrous Model 62 surrounded by diminutive people straight out of Gulliver's Travels. But for Cushman, the 60 Series ushered in a new era of gigantic scooter sales numbers.

The run of the new 60 Series was fraught with changes, alterations, and updates from year to year. Robert H. Ammon recalled examining the new Italian scooters as soon as they were imported to the United States, and as with the other American competition in the prewar years, Cushman compared them with its own products for updates and new features. "We got some ideas from Vespa and Lambretta," Ammon stated in 1992.

Bowing in late 1948, the first 60 Series scooters featured parts from the old 52 and 54. But by 1949, the style was defined until 1952 when a new, square-block engine was introduced.

The 62 Pacemaker replaced the 52 while the 62A was variously called a Sport or Super version of the Pacemaker but eschewing rear bodywork in the style of the 52A and 53A. The 62A was initially offered with only the Variamatic but soon switched to follow the rest of the 60 Series. Likewise, the 64 replaced the 54 but included a new two-speed sliding-gear transmission, and the 64A appeared in its Birthday Suit as a Sport.

The bodywork of the clothed 60 Series scooters was much like that of the 50 Series except it was smoothed over and rounded off. The rear was wider, with a turtle-back look.

The 60 Series were powered by a dazzling variety of engines all available from 1949 on. The 4hp Husky was the staple engine with bore and stroke of 2 5/8×2¾in for 14.89ci displacement. A 5hp version was optional according to ads based on a larger 2 7/8in bore for 17.80ci. The 5.4:1 compression ratio of the 4hp Husky also climbed to 5.9:1 for the 5hp.

Beyond that, the 60 Series continued in the Cushman tradition. The frame was still "sag-proof," as one ad proclaimed, and the automatic clutch still "has not four speeds, not ten, but actually hundreds of speeds," as another ad stated in purely technical terms.

In 1949, an updated Husky engine was quietly introduced, which revolutionized the Cushman. That the new engine design bowed without fanfare was probably an attempt by Cushman not to draw attention to any sort of change in the engine that may have cast doubts on its reliability among the non-mechanical buyers. Cushman ads simply denoted the new engine as the "heavy duty" Husky.

The square-barrel Husky engines still produced 4hp, 5hp, or the new optional 7.3hp, but they were better and cooler running as well as quicker in acceleration. The new Husky would power Cushmans until their demise, even after the 1960 introduction of the Super Husky.

And the 60 Series continued to sell. In 1950, Cushman produced some 10,000 scooters, including the new Eagle; by 1954, it was up to 12,000 units, according to Business Week.

MODEL 61 HIGHLANDER 1949–1950 ★ ★ ★

The new highlander carried on Cushman's old tradition of offering a stripper economy model alongside its regular line of scooters. The 61 was offered alongside the naked 62A Sport but used the old 3hp engine, which mounted directly to the frame without benefit of rubber bushings and caused more than its share of vibration.

Riding on 4x8in tires and fitted with a bare-bones tractor-like seat, the Highlander 61 was built for less than two years before being upgraded.

MODEL 711 HIGHLANDER 1950–1958 ★ ★ ★

The 711 was a refined 61 with the engine now mounted on rubber bushings and the fender bolted to the frame whereas it had been bolted directly to the engine of the 61.

MODEL 714 HIGHLANDER 1952–1953 ★ ★ ★

In 1952, Cushman released the 714, which was a 711 upgraded into a deluxe stripper model, a contradiction in terms to everyone except scooter manufacturers. The upgrades must have brought the 714 into conflict with the 60 Series as it now boasted the 4hp engine and full bodywork.

The bodywork was a curious blend of the 60 Series styling and the unclothed 61. An engine cover was added that was reminiscent of the early Auto-Glides.

MODEL 715 DELUXE HIGHLANDER 1953–1958 ★ ★

The 715 was a development of the 714 with added floorboards, a two-person padded cushion seat, and the new Cushman 100 tires.

MODEL 711-51 DELUXE HIGHLANDER 1958 ★ ★

The 715 was renamed as the 711-51 to bring it in line with the standard 711 Highlander that had lasted through three new DeLuxe models unchanged.

MODEL 721 HIGHLANDER SPECIAL AND 721-28 HIGHLANDER DELUXE 1958–1964 ★★

The 721 Series Highlanders were all new for 1958. As the brochure stated, "The Highlander proves you can have all you want in a scooter—sleek beauty, powerful performance and safe roadability."

The 721 Special continued with the 3.2hp engine and rode on 4.00x8in tires while the 721-28 had the 4.8hp engine and Cushman 100 tires.

The new Highlanders rode on a completely new frame (same frame from the 720 Series) with lever-action leading-link front forks, a splash shield, and fiberglass rear bodywork.

The DeLuxe was fitted with the 12 volt flywheel magneto, sealed-beam headlamp, and electric horn whereas the Special continued with 6 volts.

By 1960, the 3.2hp engine was shelved and for a short time just the 4.8hp Highlander could be had; by 1961, both the 4.8hp or 7.95hp Husky were available. At about the same time, the 721 Series moved up to Cushman 200 tires measuring 9.75x3.75in. An optional pillion seat was also available made of vinyl and polyurethane foam.

MODEL 722 AND 722-45 PACEMAKER AND 725 AND 725-46 ROAD KING 1957–1961 ★★

For 1957, Cushman turned its attention to a replacement for the 60 Series standard scooters. The new 720 Series Step Thru scooters featured the Pacemaker

and Road King models, carrying over the names form the 60 Series but little else.

The chassis for the 720 Series was completely redesigned and based on a large-diameter main steel tube that ran from the headstock to a rear subframe, which held the engine. The new front forks featured a knee-action leading-link design.

The 722s were clothed in bodywork that was either as "modern-as-tomorrow" or just boxy, depending on how you looked at it. Cushman said the new design had "eye-catching beauty" and termed the styling "streamlined". Whether you agreed or not, the value of any streamlining was dubious anyway at a 40mph top speed.

The bodywork was finished in bright two-tone paint schemes of Sapphire White with Castle Grey, Festival Red, Cascade Blue, Tahiti Coral, or Nugget Gold, or Safety Orange with Black; as an option, a clear overcoat of "reflective safety paint" could be had.

The seat was a monstrous padded cushion providing "arm-chair comfort" and finished in two-tone gray and white. It was redesigned in 1960 with contours but retained the color scheme.

The rear deck of the new 720s was hinged to tilt forward for access to the engine, gas tank, and a package compartment. The hinged cover could be removed by pushing a single button—no bolts held it in place. The Side-Kar was again offered for delivery or passenger use.

The Pacemaker was available in two models, both with single-speed transmissions: the 722 DeLuxe with the 7.95hp Husky and the 722-45 Special with the 4.8hp engine.

Likewise, the Road King was available in two similar models, but using the new two-speed sliding-gear transmission: the 725 DeLuxe with the 7.95hp and the 725-46 with the 4.8hp. The two-speed gearbox resulted in the Road King weighing in at 310lb, 35lb more than the Pacemaker.

The first series of 720 scooters had problems with engine overheating and in their second year, additional louvers were cut into the side panels.

In 1959, the front apron was redesigned in line with the styling of the new Super Eagle. A chrome plate with a C and M logo was placed just above the front fender and the new 12 volt sealed-beam headlamp was mounted in a chrome-plated bezel. A front shock was now also optional.

From 1959, the 720s were available in two-tone color combinations of Charcoal Gray with Starmist White; either Huntsman Red or Cascade Blue could be added to create a tri-tone scheme.

Starting in October 1959, a 725 Road King two-speed 7.95hp scooter without bodywork was offered as an economy model.

Biff, Skip and Chip

Buzz-cut boys have some good clean fun after class on their spiffy Cushman Highlander. "Eye-Catching Beauty… Arm-Chair Comfort… 'Life-Guard' Safety… Dollar-Saving Economy… 'Get-Up-and-Go' Ability," were the catch phrases on Cushman brochures for the new 720 Series. The Highlander was reworked in 1958 as the 721 Series as a 722 Pacemaker without the fiberglass bodywork.

CUSHMAN'S EAGLE SERIES

Along with the introduction of the 60 Series in 1949, Cushman split its motorscooter production in two further directions that would continue until the company's demise in the 1960s. The traditional step-through scooter symbolized by the 62 and 64 were supplemented by the stripper Model 61 Highlander. The 61 would develop into the 700 Series Highlander, and 720 Series Pacemaker and Road King before Cushman switched to carry the Vespa line in 1961.

In 1949, Cushman also unveiled its new Eagle, a radical departure from the step-through design to a scooter reminiscent of the big-twin motorcycles of the time that ruled the American roads: a Harley–Davidson E Knucklehead or Indian Chief. As Robert H. Ammon recalled in 1992, "Somebody in our sales department wanted a scooter that looked like a motorcycle with gas tank between your legs. It turned out to be a hell of a good idea."

The Eagle was a motorcycle in miniature. It laughed at the scooter design set in stone by Salsbury nearly two decades earlier. In creating the Eagle, Ammon and Jesperson looked back to the Powell P-81 and the Mustang lines: the workings of the engine were proudly on display without engine covers and owners were not afraid to get their hands dirty working on these "real" machines. And these were machines for real men, riders who weren't afraid to swing their legs over the gas tank.

All in all, historical hindsight has crowned the Eagle as the right scooter at the right time for the United States. Salsbury's 85 with its outrageous full bodywork died a quick death in the marketplace whereas the Eagle became the best-selling Cushman scooter ever.

MODEL 765 EAGLE SERIES I 1949–1954
★★★★★

The first Eagle was offered for sale by December 1949. It was a supreme example of styling selling the package. The mechanicals were largely carried over from the 60 Series scooters. It was the motorcycle look that sold the new product.

The frame was all new: a motorcycle-style tube frame with a rigid rear—hardtail in Harley–Davidson parlance. The front forks used the knee-action suspension of the 60 Series with barrel springs; the handlebars were welded to the fork tubes. Drum brakes were fitted to both the front and rear wheels.

Bodywork was at a minimum to show off the Husky's muscle. Front and rear fenders were curvaceous, continuing the lines of the motorcycle-style pea-shaped 2gal gas tank. The color was good old Farmall red. On the gas tank, a new decal had the Cushman script alongside the word Eagle superimposed over a bald eagle diving for prey.

The Eagle was powered by the round-barrel 5hp Husky engine with a chrome-plated exhaust pipe swooping down to the right. The two-speed transmission was operated by a handshift on the left side of the gas tank in the best Harley–Davidson tradition. Drive on the first 765 Eagles was shifted from the left side to the right, the opposite of all preceding Cushman scooters.

Cushman scooters were featured on the cover of Business Week on April 19, 1950, with a profile of Cushman's corporate expansion on the eve of the Korean War. "War talk has brought a sellers' market in automobiles, it had also started a boom in the motorscooter field," the magazine reported. Cushman production was going on a 48-hour six-day work week to meet demand; from 1936–1949, Cushman had made 200,000 scooters, and planned to build more than 10,000 scooters in 1950. Company President Robert Ammon stated that Cushman expected 1950 sales of $3.5 million—90 percent from scooters. And Ammon also boasted that Cushman controlled 90 percent of the United States' scooter market.

The debut of the Eagle was also the culmination of a three-year modernization effort within the Cushman factory. Ammon reported that efficiency was increased 50 percent by the new system of assembly-line production with roller conveyor belts and an overhead conveyor parts shipping from a central parts storeroom where one man supplied 165 machine-tool workers.

By November 1950, ads showed the "new" Eagle, now with a luggage rack over the rear fend-

The stylish suburbanite models

Pacemaker and *Road King*

Pacemaker

Road King

Suburban Scooters
An astronaut's haircut wasn't required to ride a Cushman, but the Nebraskan company always promoted a clean-cut image with its scooters. When the 720 Series made its debut in 1957 it was a modernistic vision of the scooter of the future with fiberglass bodywork and Jet Age styling. By 1961 the 720 Series was gone and— surprise of surprises— Cushman sold Vespas in its place...

er. Cushman now listed three further colors for the Eagle: along with red, you could have light blue, green, or cream. The 1951 ads and brochures also announced a "new" Eagle for 1951 but the scooter had carried over from 1950 with no change except the price, up from $282.50 to $344.70.

In April 1952, the new square-barrel 5hp engine was added as an option. In addition, the new 7.3hp engine was available based on a 2 7/8in bore.

In 1952, black was also made available as a color option.

MODEL 762 EAGLE 1952–1954 ★ ★ ★

In 1952, Cushman offered a stripper economy model Eagle as the 762. And it was truly bare bones. The 762 lacked any sort of transmission, running the drive chain directly to the rear wheel on the right side of the scooter, as with the step-throughs. There was no rear luggage rack available and the seat was bare metal.

The 762 could be had with either the 4hp, 5hp, or 7.3hp engine.

The Model was rarely listed in Cushman advertising and was built in only limited numbers, according to Cushman archives. Still, with the addition of a transmission and other minor parts, the 762 could have been upgraded to a 765—or vice versa, as today a 762 is rarer and more valuable.

MODEL 765 EAGLE SERIES II 1955 ★ ★ ★ ★

Ads again promoted a "new" Eagle for 1955 but while changes were actually minimal, they were important. As the Eagle's model, the Harley–Davidson big twin, now offered its Hydra-Glide and its chief competitor, the Mustang, came with telescoping forks, Cushman had to have one, too.

Ads listed numerous updates for 1955: the use of ball bearings for the steering head; a new kickstarter design; a new front brake design; and a new front fender.

The Eagle's new "air-cushioned ride" had nothing to do with air; short coil springs were mounted on telescopic forks and covered by rubber boots just above the front axle. The forks and steering head were clothed by a sheet metal apron with raised and painted Cushman script across the front; the headlamp mounted to a bracket above the logo.

Topping the fork apron was a small dash area for mounting the speedometer.

MODEL 765 EAGLE AND 765-27 SERIES III 1956–1958 ★ ★ ★ ★

For 1956, two Eagle models were offered, the 765 DeLuxe with a new 7.95hp engine (often termed the 8hp) and the 765-27 Special with the old 2 5/8×2¾in 4.8hp engine. Top speed of the DeLuxe was 50mph and 40mph for the Special.

The new 7.95hp Husky was based on a 3×2¾in bore and stroke for 19.40ci and used a new high-lift cam. In a 1956 Cycle magazine test it achieved a quarter-mile dragstrip run in 24sec. As another Cushman ad stated, you could now soar with the "dynamic speed and power of the eagle itself."

In addition, all engines now came with a new cast-aluminum exhaust manifold with colloing ribs as well as a new chromed straight exhaust pipe and muffler with removable baffles. The styling of the new exhaust system prompted Scoot magazine to report that the "new Cushman is a snappy looker."

An Oil Airbath air cleaner also became available as an option. The oilbath mounted on the frame below the gas tank with a long rubber tube running back to the carburetor.

On May 10, 1957, the Ammons family sold Cushman to Outboard Marine Corporation (OMC), the long-time maker of Johnson and Evinrude outboard motors. Robert H. Ammon would stay on, working with Herb Jesperson, who would later head Cushman.

In 1958, a new two-speed transmission was made standard on the DeLuxe. The gearbox was smaller and allowed the Eagle to revert to the right-hand chain drive. As Car Life magazine reported, "Cushman's automatic clutch duplicates the driving ease of automatic transmission on Detroit's proudest iron."

And the Eagle continued to push the sales records. Business Week, on Valentine's Day, 1959, reported that Cushman was up from building 10,000 scooters in 1950, the year of the Eagle's debut, to 12,000 total scooters in 1954 and 25,600 in 1958.

SUPER EAGLE MODELS 765-88 1959–1964 AND 765-89 1959–1963 ★ ★ ★ ★ ★

In 1959, Cushman gave the Eagle a facelift and produced a second line of Eagles, the Super Eagle 765-88 DeLuxe with 7.95hp engine and the Super Eagle 765-89 Special with 4.8hp engine.

Whereas the Series III Eagles had some of the brawn of a Harley–Davidson, the Super Eagle now took on the character of American car design of the late 1950s. Cushman yet once again called the new styling "streamlined," but that was just a stylish word at the time having little to do with aerodynamics; instead it stood for lots of bodywork and lots of shiny metalwork. The Supers were dressed up with a new fork apron featuring a polished aluminum nameplate with a large C and M logo.

But the main styling cue came at the tail end. A new squared-offender rose from the wheel to hold the luggage rack. A scallop—also known among Detroit designers as blood trough in honor of a knife—ran along both sides with the exhaust fitting handily into the right side. A chrome tail panel was crowned by a taillight, and a clutch cover enclosed the engine.

In designer lingo, the Super Eagle was all styling pizzazz. But there were also substantial mechanical updates, the most important of which was the move to 12 volt electrics. In honor of the voltage upgrade, the headlamps were now sealed beam. The engine also now breathed through an air filter mounted in an oval canister directly on the carburetor.

Cushman brochures of the time were at a peak of buzzwords to back the solid sales the Eagle line was turning in. "Just to look at the brand new Super Eagle and Eagle is to feel an urge to take to the road. Why not yield to that urge? Swing into the saddle, ease open the throttle, and learn a new definition of fun." Why not indeed?

In 1960, the Eagle line was given a second mild "tuck" to update the 1959 facelift. The gas tank was squared off and fitted with plastic knee pads. The front fender rear stay was enlarged, probably more for styling than support.

The seat support, however, was upgraded for luxury with rubber bushing mounts. Brakes were also updated with the lining now on the shoes rather than on the inside of the drums; ads stated that this change tripled the braking power.

Ads now listed a choice of four colors for the Eagle line: Black, Huntsman Red, Cascade Blue, and Starmist White.

The 1961 models continued the lineage largely the same as the 1960.

EAGLE SERIES IV MODEL 765 AND 765-27
1959–1964 ★ ★ ★ ★

The 765 and 765-27 Eagles followed the updates of the new Super Eagle with exception of the rear bodywork. As the ads stated, it was a new era of "dynamic roadability."

Cushman's large brochure in the early 1960s listed a number of accessories for both the Eagle and Super models. A plastic windshield was available as well as chrome safety bars. A chrome fender tip could also be had along with a speedometer/odometer unit. At the rear, a dual exhaust pipe was offered to split and run mufflers along both sides of the rear fender for a "full-throated exhaust tone."

The ultimate option of the era had to be the leather saddle bag set complete with white fringe, chrome bangles, and locks. The ads promised "Lots of room."

With the arrival of the Silver Eagle in 1961, the 765 models were to be phased out, but when the Silver Eagle was pulled from production late in 1961, the 765s got a new lease on life. It was to last only until 1964 when the revived Silver Eagle finally spelled doom for the old Husky line.

SILVER EAGLE SERIES I 1961 ★ ★ ★ ★

In early 1961, Cushman began the quiet promotion of an all-new, all-aluminum OMC Super Husky engine to replace the long-lived Husky engine. The promotion was quiet because the new Silver Eagle was to be a 25th anniversary model for the 1962 celebration. To some Cushman fans it was a sad moment; to others the new engine was full of promise.

The Super Husky was a radical, modern engine that would be superior to scooter engines throughout the world. Made completely of die cast aluminum alloy with a cast-iron cylinder liner, it featured a single cylinder angled forward with overhead valves and a new oiling system. The standard model was sparked by a flywheel magneto and kicked over by a side-mounted kickstarter.

Optional was a Cushman Permalite 12 volt alternator, rectifier, and 20 amp-hour battery, which powered the Folo-Thru Bendix turn-key electric starter.

The Super Husky was available in a 9hp version based on a 3½x2¼ oversquare bore and stroke for 21.65ci. The engine created the 9 horses at 4000rpm and 15lb-ft of torque at 2500rpm. A restricted engine was optional with 6hp.

The Super Husky was to power a 1962 silver anniversary model to celebrate twenty-five years of Cushman scooters; the model would be named, not surprisingly, the Silver Eagle. But it was not to be.

The Super Husky came about as a cost-saving effort by OMC, which had closed Cushman's foundry in 1959 and brought the aluminum engine in to replace the old cast-iron one. The new OMC was originally a two-cylinder industrial powerplant but the scooter version would only have one lung—and the crankshaft was not counterbalanced to make up for the missing piston assembly.

Thus, the first Silver Eagles literally shook themselves apart. Held taut in the rigid Eagle frame, the new, out-of-balance engine vibrated until the frame's welds cracked. Cushman quickly halted production until a new frame could be designed and returned to the tried-and-true Husky in the old Eagle and Super Eagle models.

SILVER EAGLE SERIES II 1962–1965 ★ ★ ★ ★

By 1962, the new Floating Power Chassis was developed with Power Frame rubber engine and transmission mounts to cope with a new Super Husky that included counterweights to balance vibrations.

1959 Cushman Eagle
While the crewcut scooterists in Cushman ads may look like brainwashed astronauts, the pep of their M9 19.4 cu. in. engines proved they weren't so dim after all. "Swing into the saddle of this real man's machine . . . and GO! Feel the breakaway power of nine husky horses in the rugged new aluminum engine," bragged the brochures for this Series IV 765 Eagle. Courtesy of the owner: Herb and Linda Letourneau

The Floating Power Chassis was at times given to dealers to fulfill warranty claims against the Series I Silver Eagles, so it's possible to find Power Frames fitted with the first Super Huskys.

Four Eagles were offered as of 1964: manual- and electric-start Silver Eagles as well as manual- and electric-start Super Silver Eagles. Updates included a restyled tail for the Supers.

With the Silver Eagle in 1963 came a new line of accessories. The windshield and speedometer/odometer unit were still available. But now you could turn your scooter into a full dresser with twin handlebar-mounted chrome mirrors, add-on white sidewalls, a chrome lean stand, chrome seat rail, chrome gas tank band, chrome battery cover, pillion cushion and foot pegs, as well as new fiberglass saddle bags. Cushman was truly "the big name in little wheels."

By late 1964, the Eagle was close to becoming extinct. In early 1965, production ceased.

TRAILSTER MODEL 723 1960–1965 ★

Half motorscooter, half Jeep, the Trailster was an attempt to broaden Cushman's appeal. In the end, however, it would be the firm's last new scooter model.

Based on a 720 Series frame and front forks, the 723 used the 4.8hp Husky; by 1962, the 7.95hp engine was optional. The Trailster was driven by the two-speed sliding-gear transmission, which was parlayed in ads into a high-low range gearbox for 12.3mph and 6.9mph respectively. An optional sprocket kit converted it to street speeds.

Interesting features of the 723 included the "tractor tread" rear tire and two brake pedals for either the right or left foot, a safety feature. And instead of a luggage rack, a "game and gear" rack was made for the rear frame section.

CUSHMAN'S DEMISE

By the dawn of the 1960s, Cushman was facing hard times in scooter sales. The writing had been on the wall for several years. Cushman had largely owned the scooter market at the dawn of the 1950s decade. By 1958, Vespas and Lambrettas infiltrated one-third of the US market, counting for 20,000 of the 60,000 scooters sold in the United States.

And with the boom in scooter sales in the late 1950s came a legislative backlash of laws limiting the minimum age for scooter jockeys. In what had always been largely a youth market, the laws were a tourniquet on sales. In Ohio alone, eleven deaths and 412 injuries were reported from scooter misadventures in 1958—although scooter industry spokesmen contended that twice as many youngsters had been killed on bicycles in the same year, according to Business Week.

In late 1960, a letter was mailed to dealers that sent a shock heard throughout the US scooter world: effective January 1, 1961, Cushman would distribute Vespa motorscooters across most of the United States. It was a move designed in one fell swoop to replace the aging 720 Series and cut manufacturing costs at the Lincoln works. While Sears, Roebuck and Co. were importing the Vespa 125cc as the Cruisaire, Cushman would sell the Vespa 125, 150, and GS from 1961–1963, merely adding a Cushman nameplate to the legshield.

According to sales figures from Cushman reprinted by Cushman historian Bill Somerville in his Allstate Scooters & Cycles 1951–1961, Cushman sold 1,341 Vespas in 1961; 3,005 in 1962; and 1,502 in 1963. The sales were a fraction of Cushman's annual sales of its own two-wheelers.

But most Cushman dealers didn't cotton to the Italian Vespa and many chose to drop Cushman and switch to the new rival, Honda. As Robert H. Ammon, who retired from Cushman in 1961, later said, "The Hondas were just frankly better machines than the Cushman Eagles—and they were cheaper." It was the end of an epoch.

It was not the end of Cushman, however. Throughout the 1950s, the firm had seen sales growth in a side market: its three-wheeled versions of scooters, and by 1957, the three-wheelers made up 16 percent of Cushman sales. With this data in the back of their minds, Cushman management prompted further production of the industrial Trucksters, Mailsters for the US Post Office, and a new Golfster for the grown-up kids in kelly green who had once buzzed Main Street on an Auto-Glide and could now tour the links in a Cushman golf cart. It was the dawn of a new Golden Age for Cushman.

Custer USA ★★

Custer scooters were built in Dayton, Ohio, in the late 1930s in two-and three-wheel form. The US Army tested the Custer alongside the Cushman and Cooper when looking for a paratrooper scooter in 1944 but decided its 2.5hp engine was too weak-kneed. The name probably did not inspire much confidence either.

Cycle-Scoot USA ★

Cycle-Scoots were built in Rockford, Illinois, from 1953–1955 and fitted with Cushman Husky and Briggs & Stratton engines.

ČZ CZECHOSLOVAKIA ★★★★

ČZ stood for the nearly unpronounceable Česká Zbrojovka, or Czech arms works, and began building motorcycles in 1932. After 1945, ČZ was merged with Jawa under state control, and in 1946, it was directed by the Communist board to build a scooter, which first appeared at the Prague Fair and was later distributed by Motokow with a 125cc engine and 16in (40cm) wheels.

Three basic models were made after the original 1946 scooter, beginning with the Čezeta Bohème. Although Puccini would have rolled over in his grave at the sight of this bathosphere-styled scooter, the Bohème was propelled by a decadent 175cc engine.

The impressionists influenced the next Čezeta of 1958, reflected in the name Manet. The Parisian's scooter had more understandable lines, especially after moving the Molotov-cocktail-like gas tank from the front fender. The two-stroke engine shrank to a 98cc producing 5.1 hp. Finally in 1965, the Manet became the Tatran, with a larger 125cc, 7hp engine.

With the renaissance of electric motors, the Čezeta was relaunched in 2018 and kept the singularly fantastic styling of the giant front fender as if it was half of a '57 Chevy. The first round of model 506 scooters were wildly expensive, but they were after an upscale market. By 2021, the prices were halved to be in line with the Vespa electric scooter.

Daelim (DNA) KOREA ★

This Seoul-based company was essentially a Honda offshoot. It has produced Japanese motorcycles for the domestic market since 1962. In 2018, Daelim officially split and became DNA a couple of years later. It produces a variety of scooters, from 50 to 250cc versions.

Dafra BRAZIL ★

Taking advantage of the relatively cheap manufacturing in Asia, Dafra imported scooter parts from China and reassembled them as its own scooters beginning around 2007. The company later expanded its partnership with other manufacturers in Italy, Germany, and India.

Danmotor INDONESIA/ITALY ★★

Between 1972 and 2001, Danmotor Vespa Indonesia built scooters under license from Piaggio.

G. W. Davis Corporation USA ★

G. W. Davis of Richmond, Indiana, built his Skat-Kat Jr. scooter in the 1960s. Skat power was a Koebler L-head single available in 3hp and 4hp versions started by a rope pull and backed by a V-Plex automatic transmission. Originally offered on 8in wheels, the Skat was soon upgraded to 12in tires. On the first models, suspension was absent but lights and a horn were standard. By 1960, telescopic front forks were standard.

Dayang CHINA ★

The Luoyang North Yichu Motorcycle Company jumped into the more lucrative scooter market with its Dayang (pronounced like a two-syllable "dang!"). Hop on the DY125-29 and "Keep worried away!" as the ad copy promises.

Dayton UK ★★

Dayton was a famous British manufacturer that decided to celebrate its fiftieth anniversary of bicycle building by offering a motorscooter, in 1955. The firm tempted fate in a volatile market by naming its scooter the Albatross; even if luck was with it, the name could not have been an effective marketing tool even to the most open-minded buyer.

Nevertheless, the Albatross was powered by a 224cc 1H Villiers two-stroke backed by a four-speed gearbox. The frame was of steel tubing with a rear swing arm, all covered by steel panels. But the bodywork ended abruptly below the steering head and front Earles forks were left bare-naked to fend for themselves.

Under orders from the Czech Communist Party, Česká Zbrojovka (Czech Arms Works) produced the boat-like Čezeta scooter in conjunction with Jawa. While the designers may not have been able to leave the country, their scooters sure did, and the scooters' names reflected artistic wanderlust: Manet and Bohème. This two-stroke 172cc Čezeta moved on 12-inch wheels and its nose was actually a gas tank, leading one to ponder whether it was a secret kamikaze Commie weapon. Courtesy of the owner: Léon Stevenart

the all British
DAYTON ALBATROSS

. . . combines short run convenience with long run comfort

In 1957, the Albatross Twin scooter was added with a two-cylinder 249cc Villiers 2T two-stroke. By 1958, Dayton designers finally admitted the error of their ways and covered the front forks.

Also in 1958, the model names were reworked: the Twin became the Empire, which was joined by a Continental Twin with new styling; and the single became the Single, now with a 246cc 2H. In 1959, the Single became the Continental Single and the Empire was available only on special order—and the Albatross name still remained as a prefix. In 1959, the line was joined by the Albatross Flamenco with a 174cc Villiers 2L engine. The frame and bodywork were shared in a joint venture with Panther and Sun.

By 1960, Dayton and the Albatross were no more.

Delaplace FRANCE ★★

Les Etablissements Delaplace exhibited its Horsy scooter at the 1952 Salon de Paris with a single-speed Le Poulain 85cc engine. The Horsy remained a prototype, never let loose from its corral.

Delius WEST GERMANY ★

The Gottfried Delius factory in Osnabrück sold its Cityfix 49 in 1950–1953 as a portable scooter with a bar between the rider's legs that doubled as a luggage handle. Although the Cityfix didn't fold up like early paratrooper scooters, it was light, weighing only 38kg with a dwarf 1.5liter gas tank. The standard engine was a 1hp Lutz 58cc engine that propelled the Cityfix to 30km/h on its spoked 20in bicycle wheels.

The Cityfix MR100 of 1952–1953 no longer doubled as a suitcase, weighing 55kg with a 3hp 95cc Fichtel & Sachs motor for a 60km/h top speed.

Herr Delius added an unenclosed frame around the engine and threw out the carrying bar over the legshield, but still the unattractive scooter appealed more to motorized bike aficionados than scooteristi.

DEMM ITALY ★

DEMM of Milan built a line of three-wheel commercial vehicles with 49cc two-stroke engines outside Bologna, a variety of carrying boxes, and scooter front ends in the 1950s and 1960s. In 1953, the two engineers, Daldi and Matteucci, teamed up to build the bizarrely named "Dik-Dik," perhaps due to the clicking of the engine. The 48cc engine came in either a two or four-stroke version and was covered with space-age styling on top of spoked white wall wheels.

Derbi SPAIN ★

Derbi's roots stretch back to 1922 when Simeon Rabasa Singla began building bicycles. In 1950, the firm showed its first motorcycle, named the Derbi, an acronym for Derivados de Bicicletus, or Derived from Bicycles. In 1953, the Masculino scooter was introduced, its name full of Spanish machismo—even with only 98cc. In 1955, a 125cc Masculino was added and both models continued until 1957.

In the 1960s, Derbi concentrated on two divergent markets: mopeds and Grand prix road racing. It was not until 1982 that another Derbi scooter was offered, the Scoot Derbi, with 12 volt electronic ignition firing a fan-cooled, reed-valve, near-horizontal engine with a torque converter transmission. From only 80cc, the Scoot Derbi produced 5.5hp at 7000rpm.

Into the new millennium, Derbi offered modern-looking two-wheelers for teenagers who love speed. The 49cc Atlantis two-stroke comes as the City, Bullet, and Wave with different flashy paint schemes to match even the flashiest of tennis shoes.

In the early 2000s, Derbi was bought out by Piaggio and went back into the scooter biz with models named Manhattan, Paddock, Predator, and Hunter. For a few years, Derbi hit the US market before pulling out.

Derveaux BELGIUM ★★

Derveaux of Gand (Ghent) offered its Miranda scooter in 1953 with a 175cc German Jlo engine and four speeds. Originally, the prototype was dubbed the Sagitta but later assumed the name of Miranda.

Dilecta FRANCE ★

While most German scooter makers were busy building airplanes and motorcycles prior to World War II, many French companies, like Dilecta, made bicycles. Its 50S Raider scooter was a copy of Monet-Goyon's Starlett with a FML (Fabrication Mécanique de Levallois) or VAP 110 engine. The Raider was also sold under the label of J-B. Louvet and de Dion Bouton.

DK DENMARK ★★

Svend R. Olsen and Svend Aage Mathiesen teamed up to build a true Danish scooter and surged with such Dansk pride that they closed their eyes and named if for Denmark, or DK. The two Svends used a 118cc Jlo engine with a two-speed gearbox and hydraulic brakes to stop the speeding scooter.

DKR UK ★★

DKR of Wolverhampton announced its Dove scooter in 1957 based on a 147cc Villiers 30C two-stroke with three speeds. The frame was of steel tubes with leading-link forks at the front. Wheels were 10 in.

The Dove's styling was anything but avian; the front end had all the grace of a well-developed beer belly. The tail section, on the other hand, was angular and awkward.

DKR launched two other scooters in 1958: the Pegasus with a 148cc 31C Villiers and three-speed gearbox and the Defiant with a 197cc 9E Villiers and four-speed. In 1959, the Manx joined the trio with a 249cc 2T Villiers, four-speed, and electric leg.

At the end of 1959, the Dove II replaced the original with a 148cc 31C engine. The Pegasus II was offered in 1960 with a 174cc 2L engine. In 1960, these two models were dropped to be replaced by the Cappella, which ran on until DKR end in 1966.

DKW GERMANY

Choose your acronym for DKW and they're all correct: Dampf Kraft Wagen (for its first steam powered engine), Der Knabische Wunische (the Schoolboy's Dream—of DKW racing motorcycles), and Das Kleine Wunder, (the Little Miracle).

In 1919, DKW was founded by the Danish engineer Jorgen Skafte Rasmussen in the town of Zschopau originally named JS Rasmussen. DKW began making two-stroke motorcycles in 1920, and by 1921 released the 122cc Golem and the year after, the 142cc Lomos. Both of these were hybrid motorcycle/scooters boasting all the luxury of an armchair. Unfortunately, it was too much too early, and sales were meager.

By 1930, DKW was the largest motorcycle producer in the world, but over-extended itself and merged with three other manufacturers to remain solvent. DKW, Wanderer, Horch, and Audi joined to become Auto Union AG in 1932 with the symbol of four interlinked circles still used to this day by Audi. Under the union, DKW continued to make motorcycles as well as two-stroke cars.

During World War II, DKW changed production to assist the Third Reich and supply the Wehrmacht with the RT125, which was later copied by BSA, Triumph TEC, Harley–Davidson, and Yamaha. Following the war, the DKW plant ended up in

the Russian sector, changing its name to Motorrad Zschopau or simply MZ, as the name of the town changed to Karl Marx to honor everyone's favorite Prussian.

The Auto Union, however, moved west, and DKW set up shop in Ingolstadt on the Danube and serviced old war vehicles until 1949.

HOBBY STANDARD AND LUXUS 75
1954–1957 ★

The 74cc Hobby boasted an elaborate system of drive belts creating an automatic transmission with a clutch for disengaging the gears. The single cylinder was inclined forward for 47x45mm bore and stroke, while the electrics skipped a battery and stuck with the simple flywheel magneto, more eloquently known as the Schwungradmagnetzünder. Many scooter riders didn't like the motorcycle image of a kickstart, so DKW opted for the coveted lawn mower image, placing a pull-starter by the scooterist's left foot.

The Hobby's 3hp at 5000rpm achieved 40mph getting 139mpg (as opposed to some earlier DKW two-stroke motorcycles that got as low as 15mpg). An automatic gas-oil mixer and the large, 16in wheels provided smooth operation.

The two-stroke scooter arrived to an anticipating public in a blitz of publicity with ingenious slogans like "smart people ride Hobbys." And also an advertising poem to bring tears to Whitman's eyes:

There was a young man named Bobby
who didn't have muscles or money.
Then daddy gave him a Hobby
to help him get friends and study.
He escapes the chaos of town
so elegant and debonair
and cools his studious head down
far away in nature.

If you have a Hobby, people want you as a friend. The Luxus version came with passenger handles on the rear cowling, a pillion seat, and deceptive go-fast horizontal chrome strips. Unfortunately, the added trim makes the rear section of the Hobby look suspiciously like a vacuum cleaner with seats.

In July 1956, an official DKW report stated "The DKW position is said to be far from happy." And so after producing approximately 40,000 Hobbys, DKW took it out of production. Then in November 1958, Mercedes–Benz gained control of the Auto Union and cut the number of DKW two-wheelers to three models, and by 1959 production halted altogether.

The Hobby lived on, however, being produced under license by the French company, Manurhin, and imported into England by AFN. Manurhin modified the styling, added wider tires, enlarged the engine, and improved the automatic gear change resulting in the scooter's new name, the Beltomatic.

DMW UK ★

DMW built numerous lightweight motorcycles for the British market based usually on Villiers two-stroke engines, including the firm's Bambi scooter of 1957 with its 99cc 4F and two-speed gearbox.

The Bambi's chassis was made from steel pressings like the Vespa, with a triangulated front fork sprung by a spring within the steering column. The rear swing arm was also made of steel pressings, as were the wheels, which carried 2.50x7.5in tires.

In 1961, DMW offered its 249cc two-stroke Deemster scooter in Standard and De Luxe versions, the latter with electric start. The Deemster resembled a motorcycle converted into a scooter, retaining the motorcycle riding position and engine placement while adding full bodywork and small 12in diameter wheels. The Deemster defied categorization, which was a problem in the market. It lasted, however, until 1967.

Douglas UK ★★★

The English Douglas firm bore a long lineage of elegant flat-twin motorcycles stretching back to motorcycling's pioneer days. But in 1948, Douglas chief Claude McCormack got religion. While vacationing in Italy, he was amazed by the Vespas and other scooters buzzing through the streets like nests of insects. Douglas saw a business venture, contacted Piaggio, and first showed an imported Piaggio Vespa with Douglas Vespa nameplate on the front legshield at the 1949 Earls Court Show in London. Plans were announced to build 10,000 Vespas in England.

Douglas launched its Vespa line on March 15, 1951. Built under Piaggio license at the Douglas factory on Hanham Road, Bristol, the first Douglas Vespa was almost a carbon copy of the current 125cc rod-control Vespa; Douglas termed its model the 2L2 with the major difference being that the headlamp was placed on the front apron just below the handlebars to meet British headlamp height laws.

Beyond the headlamp, Douglas followed Piaggio even down to the same metallic industrial green paint. But as they were made in Britain, many of the components were sourced in the UK, such as the Amal carburetors, Lucas electrics, Milverton saddles, British-made Michelin tires, and BTH magnetos.

In 1953, Douglas upgraded its Vespa with Piaggio's new cable-control gearshift; the new Douglas was termed the G. In 1954, Douglas again followed the leader, introducing its GL2 based on a new engine with revised cylinder head and barrel with twin transfer ports to feed the oil-fuel mix. The engine also had a new full flywheel and a square 54x54mm bore and stroke. A dual bench seat was optional.

In February 1955, Douglas announced its 42L2 Vespa, following Piaggio's lead in mounting the headlamp on the handlebars, where it was backed by a speedometer. The cooling cutaway on the engine sidecover was redone with simple louvers and a hydraulic damper was added to the front suspension.

In 1955, Douglas also offered a new model, the Piaggio Vespa 150 GS, or Gran Sport, which Douglas named the VS1 for Vespa Sports. With a 145cc tuned engine of 57x57mm and a four-speed gearbox, the GS represented a new stage in scooters. With the recovery advancing, buyers had extra money in their pockets and vacation time on their work timecards; the GS, like Innocenti's TV, were sporty, higher-speed touring models designed to meet this new, developing market.

Douglas' VS model designation was updated annually: the 1955 was termed the VS1; the 1956 was the VS2; 1957, the VS3; 1958, the VS4; 1959, the VS5. But oddly, while Douglas was building the 125cc Vespas, it only imported and never built the Piaggio GS, rebadging it as a Douglas model. The reason for this lay in the firm's growing financial troubles.

Despite the sales success of the Vespa line, Douglas was purchased by Westinghouse Brake and Signal. In 1955, the 42L2 was termed the Standard version and was joined by the Magna and Ultra versions with further options. In February 1959, the 42L2 was replaced by the 152L2. Later, the 125cc 232L2 and 150cc 312L2 rotary-valve models were produced.

British production of Vespas ended in 1963–1964, after which Douglas continued to import Piaggio models. Douglas had built a total of 126,230 Vespas and could even boast a 1967 Royal Warrant that read: "These are to certify that by direction of His Royal Highness The Prince Philip, Duke of Edinburgh, I have appointed Douglas (Kingswood) Ltd. Into the place and quality of Suppliers of Vespa Scooters to His Royal Highness."

Douglas Vespa Model Nomenclature		
Year	Piaggio Model Name	Douglas Model Name
1951–1953	125cc (Rod control)	2L2
1953	25cc (Cable control)	G
1954	125cc (Twin-transfer-port engine)	GL2
2/1955–2/1959	125cc	42L2
2/1959	125cc	152L2
1955	150 GS (Gran Sport)	VS1 (Vespa Sports)
1956	150 GS	VS2
1957	150 GS	VS3
1958	150 GS	VS4
1959	150 GS	VS5
1960	150 GS	VS
1961	150 GS	VS
1962–1964	160 GS	160 GS

Douglas Rotary-Valve Models 1959–1977	
Piaggio Model Name	Douglas Model Name
125	232L2
125	VMA1
125 Primavera	VMA2
90	V9A1
90SS	V9SS1
90 Racer	V9SS2
150 Sportique	312L2
150 Super	VBC1
150 GL	VLA1
150 Sprint	VLB1
180 Rally	VSD1
Rally 200 Electronic	VSE1

Ducati ITALY

Never mind horsepower ratings, power curves, or reliability, Ducati motorscooters were the only scooters blessed by the Pope.

The roots of Moto Ducati stretch back to 1922, when 19-year-old Bolognese finance student Adriano Cavalieri Ducati invented a radio transmitter, according to the family-written Storia della Ducati. He formed a company to make radio condensers, later branching into micro-spy cameras and Italy's first electric razor. During Benito Mussolini's rise, the Fascists charged Ducati to put a radio in every Italian house, the better to spread Il Duce's word.

Meanwhile in Turin in 1943–1944, Aldo Farinelli created a 1hp 48cc clip-on engine for bicycles, which he named the Cucciolo, his puppy. Following the war, Farinelli's engine began limited production at Siata in Turin.

Postwar, Ducati's factory at Borgo Panigale was leveled and production halted. The Ducati family looked for a new product and was introduced to Siata via the Istituto per la Reconstruzione Industriale (IRI), a governmental rebuilding agency. The IRI invested in Ducati with other capital coming from Opus Dei, the Vatican's investment arm. Ducati began large-scale production and sales of the Cucciolo, which, along with other clip-on engines, was to become as important to Italy's postwar recovery as its contemporaries, the Vespa and Lambretta.

CRUISER 1952–1954 ★★★★★

Inspired by the scooter's success, Ducati launched its Cruiser scooter at the Milan Fiera Campionaria of 1952. The Cruiser featured a 7.5hp 175cc overhead-valve engine with the cylinder transverse in front of the rear wheel, 12 volt electrics, and electric start. Following the lead of the American scooters, the Ducati also had an automatic transmission based

Douglas Vespa
This English Douglas brochure portrayed the Vespa GS 150 which cost considerably more than the Vespa 125cc but was worth every shilling. In the Gran Sport, Piaggio created its capolavoro, and the model sold well into the 1960s. Douglas built its own versions of the small-bore Vespas but imported the GS model, naming it the VS for Vespa Sports.

1956 Fairbanks-Morse Scooter
After building behemoth farm tractors and weight scales for decades, Fairbanks-Morse weighed into the scooter market in 1956 with this creation. Powered by a 2.75 hp motor, which was good power for the day, the Fairbanks- Morse could only reach 5 mph top speed, which was lousy in any day. With styling like a lawnmower, the firm missed the scooter mark and perhaps should have gone into the mower market.

on a hydraulic torque converter. With the powerful four-stroke engine, the Cruiser had to be detuned to meet the Italian government's maximum scooter speed limit of 80km/h.

The front forks were telescopic with a hydraulic damper mounted at the hub. The rear wheel was held by the massive aluminum-alloy gearbox case that doubled as a swing arm with a hydraulic damper mounted horizontally below the engine.

The Cruiser was stylish, like a metallic shark-skin zoot suit on wheels. Its step-through chassis was clothed in elegant, flowing two-tone bodywork penned and produced by the celebrated Italian carrozzeria, Ghia. The long right side cover swung open effortlessly on a front-mounted hinge.

Ducati believed that by offering a luxurious four-stroke scooter, it would steal the thunder from Piaggio and Innocenti's two-strokes. Ducati was wrong. The Cruiser lasted until only 1954.

BRIO 1964–1969 ★★

Ducati chose to concentrate instead on motorcycles, but built a second scooter series in 1964 that was what the Cruiser should have been for sales success.

In 1964, Ducati returned to the scooter fold with its Brio 48, based on a two-stroke 48cc engine pumping out 4.2hp. The Brio 100 used a two-stroke 94cc for 6hp at 5200rpm with ignition by flywheel magneto. To start either Brio, you were forced to a lowly kickstarter; to shift through the four gears, you had to use your hand. And the styling was as boxy as the Cruiser was sleek.

But the Brio was at least a limited success and continued in production until 1967 when it was superseded by the slightly updated Brio 50 and Brio 100/25 of 1968. By 1969, Ducati was moving from the two-stroke market, and the scooters were cancelled.

If Ducati's timing with the Cruiser had been different, the motorscooter world could have been changed dramatically. Instead, the Cruiser passed into history as a footnote.

Dürkopp GERMANY

Dürkopp called on the gods to assure its scooter's fortune and in honor of the goddess of forests, it named its two-wheeled temple the Diana.

Herr Nikolaus Dürkopp founded the company in 1867 as a bicycle manufacturer and by 1901 had designed its first motorcycle. After World War I, it produced clip-on bicycle motors and began making motorcycles again in 1949 after a thirty-five-year hiatus. In 1954, at the height of the scooter boom, it produced the attractive Diana scooter, which far surpassed the firm's motorcycle production.

DIANA 1954–1959; DIANA TS 175 AND DIANA TS 200 SPORT 1959–1960 ★★★

The Diana's introduction was splashed across Dürkopp ads when Miss Germany 1954 "won" a Diana and posed on her beloved scooter for a photo op. The Diana had sleek lines, obviously borrowed from the Lambretta LD while making some notable updates such as the smooth side panel line, an enlarged engine, and the headlamp attached to the handlebars.

The first Diana's 9.5hp zoomed it to an 80km/h maximum speed. The later 194cc Sport and 171cc TS had 12hp for 100km/h and 10.8hp for 95km/h respectively. The four-speed Diana had a large 3liter gas tank and was a solid scooter made for long distances in spite of its smallish 10in wheels.

Dürkopp produced a total of 24,963 of the two-seated Dianas, a relatively high number for the small manufacturer.

Elleham DENMARK ★★★★

Danish aviation hero Jakob Christian Ellehammer may be known to Norskies for his invention of the first engine used on a helicopter and his Ellemobile car in 1909, but to putt-putt historians he's known for his Elleham scooter. With a debut around the same time as the French Auto-Fauteuil, Elleham's attractive scooter dates back to 1903. Full production of the Elleham started in 1905 and the smokestacks didn't stop until 350 scooters hit the Danish roads by 1911. Armed first with a Peugeot engine then with a Zedel or Minerva motor, the Dansk scoot soon opted for a homemade powerplant. Scooter purists may nix the Elleham as one of the pioneer scooters because of the relatively large 20in spoked wheels, but the Ellehammer the aviator didn't listen to the critics and pumped out more than 1000 vehicles between 1904 and 1909.

Elvish FRANCE ★

Elvish–Fontan produced a semi-open-frame scooter with a four-stroke, 50cc Cucciolo engine made by Les Etablissements Rocher under Ducati license. The Elvish appeared at the 1950 Salon de Paris and disappeared by the following year.

Erla DENMARK ★★

Built in the 1950s in Copenhagen, the Erla used a Villiers engine that could push it along at 65-70km/h, at least according to ads. "Det nyeste nye paa motorcykler!" (The newest new in motorcycles!) boasted advertising copy for "the new Danish scooter" that could go 50km per liter along the flat land of Denmark.

Etablissements François

FRANCE ★★

The perfect gift for the businessman with everything, Les Etablissements François et Cie produced its 1952 fold-up Scooter-Valise F. R. with a 72cc Sotecma engine capable of 77km/h. Although more of a portable motorized bicycle with no bodywork, the Scooter-Valise (scooter-suitcase) was probably thrown into the scooter category as a sales gimmick in hopes that it would add prestige.

Etergo NETHERLANDS ★

In the 2000s, Etergo developed innovative electric scooters capable of going 240 km (150 miles) on a single charge. Ola Scooters of India bought Etergo in 2020 for a reported $92 million to produce the scooters in India.

Excelsior UK ★★★

Excelsior of Birmingham dated back to the 1870s when it began building bicycles. Through the prewar years, the firm sold large-bore motorcycles; following the war, it was reduced to churning out commuter machines.

The link between Excelsior's two periods was the Welbike, a lightweight, collapsible scooter built for the British World War II paratroopers. Harry Lester designed the scooter at a British Army R&D skunkworks, and the name came from the first prototype, built at Welwyn, England.

The 70lb Welbike was designed to fold into a canister to be dropped by parachute accompanying the British Red Berets into action. Based on a 98cc Villiers horizontal two-stroke that fit snuggly within the center of the scooter, its top speed was a poky 30mph.

According to English scooter historian Michael Webster, some 4,000 Welbikes were supplied to the British Army and used in Europe and the Orient as well as coming ashore at Normandy and braving the Eastern Front. After the war, the Welbike was civilized as the Corgi and produced by Brockhouse.

Excelsior returned to the scooter market in 1959 with its Monarch scooter, sharing body sheet metal with the DKR and Sun scooters but fitted with a 147cc two-stroke Excelsior engine. The KS version had a kickstarter and the EL an electric. In 1960, the versions were renamed the MK1 and ME1 respectively.

Faizant FRANCE ★★★

Jonghi, Ydral, Aubier–Dunne, and Jlo all provided various-sized engines for the AGF scooter through the years. In 1947, the Etablissements Faizant first showed off its scooter in France at the Paris Fair with a 98cc Jonghi motor and at the Salon de Paris with a 125cc Ydral motor. As a contemporary of the first Piaggio and Innocenti scooters, the AGF bore a resemblance to the foot-shifting Lambretta Model A. Faizant never quite found a niche in the market for its vehicle since it wasn't flashy enough for scooter goers and too small for motorcyclists.

Faka WEST GERMANY ★★

The Faka (short for Fahrzeugwerk Kannenberg) was built around one of the most stupendous of scooter styling cues: the rear section began with a jet tur-

Picking Flowers with a Faka
Two beauties out picking flowers on a weekend getaway.

bine-styled intake surmounted by a huge—and solely ornamental—chrome bulb. Walba initially presented these scooters designed by French engineer Louis Lepoix, who also designed the Bastert and worked on BMW motorcycles as well.

Faka built three models: the Tourist 150 of 1954–1957, Tourist Commodore 175 of 1954–1957, and Tourist Commodore 200 1954–1957. The old Walba Kurier wasn't continued while the Walba Tourists were only an inspiration for the new Fakas. The new-and-improved Tourist had a 147cc Jlo, 6.7hp engine with a choice of 8 or 10in wheels to help it reach 75km/h. The new, smaller Commodore had a 175cc Jlo motor and rode on 10in wheels. The bigger version sported a 197cc Jlo engine with a four-speed gearbox.

The larger Commodore weighed more (132kg.) than the Commodore 175 (126kg.) causing it to go 80km/h instead of 85km/h on its 8in wheels but with 9.6hp compared to 7.6hp.

Faroppa SWITZERLAND ★

Faroppa built a licensed copy of the Italian Casalini firm's David scooter as the Ticino.

Fat Bear USA ★

The fat tires on these low riders may seem unscooterlike to some, but these cruisers (similar to the German Scrooser) are electric scooters with a low center of gravity for more stability. No fat-shaming here, as all the models echo the obese moniker with the Fat Cub, the Fat Grizzly, and the Fat City. They still dub themselves a "scooter moped," even if a two-wheeled low rider is more apropos.

FB Mondial ITALY ★★★

The Fratelli Boselli Mondial firm of Milan produced its first motorcycle in 1948, a four-stroke racer in a field of two-strokes. Like MV Agusta, Mondial always concentrated on competition motorcycles, creating some of the most famous Italian four-stroke small-bore racers of the postwar era and ruling the 125cc class for years.

Mondial built two scooter models that were as odd as its motorcycles were graceful. Introduced in 1952, the first Mondial scooter consisted of a steel-tube frame with bodywork covering all save the engine, a 125cc two-stroke that propelled the scoot to 90 km/h. The front forks were telescopic, and a suspended swing arm cradled the rear wheel. But the Boselli brothers' souls were in racing, and the scooter was soon forgotten.

In 1959, Mondial tried again with its two-stroke 75cc Lady scooter and styling looking like the mirror image of the sleek Capri scooter. But once again, the Lady was in the competition machinery's shadow and quickly faded away.

Mondial also began to fade in the mid-1960s with the invasion of the Japanese two-stroke racers. Efforts to revive Mondial continued into the 1990s.

Fenwick FRANCE/ITALY ★★

Innocenti of Milan granted Fenwick of France a license to produce Lambrettas. Two hundred thousand scooters were built between 1951 and 1960. Soon after, the company switched to much more profitable forklift production.

Feiying CHINA ★

Not to be confused with the "Feiling," also from China, the Feiying are made by Guangzhou Panyu Huanan Motorcycles or Jiangsu Chuangxin Motorcycles, which also make their own models. The dizzying array of Chinese brands makes the models seem nearly the same.

Ferbedo GERMANY ★

In the style of certain American mail-order scooters, the Nürnberg-made Ferbedo R48 was an economical substitute for expensive larger scooters and a step up from bicycles "if you are tired of pedaling," according to its ads. In 1953, the R48 had such basic features as two barrel springs for the front suspension; it was discontinued by 1954. The 48cc Zündapp motor achieved 1.5hp for a maximum speed of 40km/h on this mini 32kg scooter.

Accessories included a luggage rack, a hand-powered rubber-bulb tooter, and what looked like a bird cage covering the engine to prevent burning flesh. As the ads advised, "Compare, choose judiciously and you can't help but become a happy owner of a Ferbedo."

FF GERMANY ★

The FF bowed in 1951 featuring a 43cc engine pumping out an unimpressive 0.8-1hp and mounted atop the front wheel in the style of the great French Velosolex moped. The FF was one of few front-drive scooters.

FIAMC ITALY ★★

Fabbrica Italiana Auto Moto Cicli from Parma built a two-speed, two-stroke 125cc scooter for two years: 1952–1953. The chunky FIAMC 125 debuted in 1952 at the Salone di Milano. The layers of sheet metal covering the engine looked like they were inspired by a Panzer tank, and the single bend in the flat legshield didn't dispel this image. Perhaps due to the lack of vision for the rather expensive two-stroke, FIAMC shut its doors a year later.

Fiame GERMANY ★

From 1951–1953, Fiame produced a 123cc scooter as well as a moped with the same engine. Sales were limited; perhaps customers were scared off as its Italian name meant "flame."

FIAT ITALY ★★★★

The huge Italian car maker ventured into the scooter world around 1938 under top-secret guise. With the success of its car for the masses, the Topolino (meaning "Mickey Mouse" in Italian), perhaps the auto giant didn't want to fare brutta figura (cut a bad figure) by showing that they delved into tiny little putt-putts.

Postwar, Piaggio followed FIAT to produce a putt-putt based on Mickey Mouse's feisty friend, Donald Duck, or "Paperino." Perhaps realizing that Walt Disney worked undercover for the US government, Benito Mussolini's language police kept Disney's Americanizing influence at bay by renaming all his cuddly cartoons. Benito chose to give his famous bare-chested tirade on top of the bonnet of a FIAT tractor, if only he'd opted for the more stylish little FIAT scooter perhaps his brutal black shirts would have ushered in the Italian scooter age a decade earlier.

The step-through design and the legshield of the FIAT followed the Cushman Autoglide, but high-minded Italian design made this early scooter the one for postwar manufacturers to follow. Louvers etched into the cowling provided air cooling to the 98cc Sachs two-stroke engine with a long-handled shifter.

With the Nazi blitzkrieg of Poland and Mussolini itching to annex Albania, FIAT was busy with other projects and its putt-putt barely made it out of the prototype stage before it was shelved.

Fimer ITALY ★★

With a debut at the Salone di Milano in 1950, Fimer's scooter legacy remains more impressive than its scooter sales. Two identical Fimers were offered, the L or N, with the only difference being the body shield over the scooter. This coincided with Innocenti's landmark decision to offer the covered and uncovered C and LC models. The other notable historical probability is the curvy lines of the fully-covered version most likely influenced Moto Parilla's much more successful Levriere scooter, which was released two years later.

Fiorelli ITALY ★

Moto Velo Fiorelli gave up its motorcycling ways in the late 1950s to focus on the Turismo model of its Microscooter. Powered by a 50cc two-stroke engine which could top 75 km/h, the Microscooter kept the gas tank elevated between the legs giving more of a mini motorcycle look than that of a cool scooter.

The 500 Industries USA ★

Fremont, California, was home to the Cub 520 and Cub 521 scooters in the 1960s. The 520 had a 2.5hp two-cycle while the brawny 521 boasted a 7.2hp two-stroke McCulloch MC-6. Deluxe trim included a headlamp, taillamp, generator, and fenders. Colors were metallic red or blue.

Flyscooters USA/CHINA ★

Not to be confused with the Piaggio Fly, Flyscooters are Chinese-built Znen two-wheelers imported and rebadged from 2006 to 2010.

FM ITALY ★★

F. Molteni's FM Tipo 50 and 52 scooters were an interesting blend of scooter and motorcycle with styling similar to the Mustang and Powell scooters. First shown in 1951 at the Salone di Torino, the FM was powered by a horizontal-cylinder 125cc two-stroke of 5hp with a three-speed gearbox.

The FM T.52 had new hydraulic shocks on the front and back, more chrome styling, and larger rear rack when it was displayed at the 1953 Salon de Bruxelles.

Fochj ITALY ★

In 1958, R.E.V.A. of Bologna tried to cash in on the burgeoning scooter market by adding the Fochj 75 to its line of Fochj motorcycles. The exotic unpronounceable name didn't contribute to the rather ordinary design of the covered-moped look on tall spoked wheels.

Foldmobile USA ★★

The Foldmobile was a license-built American version of the French Martin–Moulet Valmobile offered in the late 1950s and early 1960s with a 6hp engine.

FM Novelty
The FM T50 of 1951–1952 was bizarre, eccentric, and innovative, and all things that make a scooter fascinating. The horizontal 125cc two-stroke engine and its gearbox were cast in unit with the rear swing-arm and pivoted from the frame. They were suspended along with the rear wheel by a shock absorber mounted below the chassis. Courtesy of Vittorio Tessera

Forall USA ★★★

The Illinois Foundry Company of Springfield copied Beam's Doodle Bug with slight improvements from 1957 to 1959. The larger frame made for a smoother ride than its elfin cousin. The Forall was powered by a four-cycle Tecumseh Lauson engine that pumped out 2hp and was ignited with a lowly pull starter that did little to dispel the lawn mower look.

Forza NEW ZEALAND/ITALY ★

The giant Honda Forza has nothing to do with these smaller scooters. The Forza Capri LX is essentially a rebranded Moto Garelli scooter, starting in 2018 with a classic look harkening back to the 1950s Capri scooters. The 50cc Forza Ciclone scooter is a rebranded Baotian scooter.

Frera ITALY ★

Frera of Milan was a long-established Italian make of bicycles and motorcycles with roots stretching back to 1906. Following the war, Frera was reduced to building small-capacity two-stroke motorcycles and its 125cc Confort scooter debuted in 1952. The Confort had a 52x58mm engine mounted in the center of the scooter creating 4.75hp at 5000rpm. Only a few of the two-stroke scooters made it into production due to financial difficulties at Leonardo Frera's company.

Frisoni ITALY ★★

In 1952, Elettromeccanica Luigi Frisoni of Cedrate di Gallarate christened its 125cc Superba scooter at the Milan Fiera Campionaria based on an NSU 125cc engine with four speeds. Production started with a 160cc two-stroke engine of Frisoni's own making at

the end of the year to push the putt-putt to more than 85 km/h. Only a small number were produced of the Superba with its design inspired by Iso and looking surprisingly like the Parilla Levriere.

Fuji Heavy Industries
JAPAN ★★★

Fuji of Tokyo created Japan's first motorscooter, the Rabbit. Emerging from World War II, Japan was in ruin similar to Germany, and like the other European countries, economical transportation helped pull Japan out of the war's destruction. Fuji introduced the first Rabbit in 1946, the same year as the first Vespas went into production on the other side of the world. In that year, only eight Rabbits were built.

The Rabbit was a rustic little scooter, similar in style to prewar American models; Fuji had done its homework. A padded cushion provided seating and suspension; a luggage rack was mounted behind. The Rabbit was based on a 135cc four-stroke single of 57x55mm producing 2hp at 3000rpm. Top speed was 55km/h.

In 1950, the Rabbit was updated as the S-23 with luxury features: pillion pad seat, spare tire, and twin klaxon horns. Barrel-spring suspension was added front and rear.

Two new models were introduced in 1950. First came a 170cc Rabbit S-41 based on a larger bore for 61.5x57mm for 3hp at 3400rpm with 4.00x8in tires. Second was the Jack Rabbit S-31 based on a longer wheelbase and a Cushman-like tail with luggage compartment. The 270cc engine was a doubled-up 135cc Rabbit creating 4.5hp at 3500rpm.

The three models continued until 1954 when they were superseded by the restyled and more-powerful S-48 and S-61. The first was based on the S-41 but with a longer stroke, 61.5x67mm 200cc engine producing 5hp at 3600rpm. The S-61 was the luxury flagship featuring electric start on the 225cc engine, which produced 5.9hp at 4000rpm.

The styling was cutting edge Japanese design of the time, based on the philosophy of more is better. Thus, the Rabbit's flowing front apron was set against slab-faced legshields; the boxy tail was softened by adding multiple curved bodylines, contours, and air inlets. To make sure it all caught the eye, the whole affair was bejeweled by miles of trim work and the debut of the circular chrome Rabbit logo.

In 1955, a small bare-bones 125cc S-71-I Rabbit was added to the line with a 52x58mm engine for 5hp at 5000rpm. The S-71 was updated as the Junior S-72 in 1957 with refined bodywork featuring even more chrome trim work and air ducts on the side covers. In 1958, the S-82 arrived making 6.2hp at 5600rpm from its 125cc engine; this was updated in 1960 to the S-82S.

Forall Doodlebug

After seeing the popularity of Beam's Doodle Bug distributed by Gambles Department Stores, the Illinois Foundry Company decided to copy the little scooter from Iowa but enlarged the frame and engine. A four-cycle 2 hp Tecumseh engine was popped under the seat for a Forall for all. Courtesy of the owner: Jim Kilau

In 1957, the Rabbit Superflow S-101 replaced the luxury S-61. The Superflow featured a torque converter automatic transmission and a 250cc engine of 68.5x67mm for 5.9hp at 4000rpm. Bells and whistles were everywhere on the Superflow: electric start, front and rear turn signals, instrument dashboard with gas gauge and warning light that lit at excessive riding speeds, parking brake, foot-operated headlamp dimmer, and stylish two-tone paint.

The Superflow was updated for 1959 as the S-101 D-2 with cleaner styling and 7hp at 4000rpm from 250cc. This was followed in 1961 by the 125cc S-300, which was redesigned in 1962 as the S-301 based on the Superflow styling. By 1965, the 125cc had matured to 150cc.

In 1961, Fuji introduced a 50cc Rabbit with a single seat and minimalist styling. Based on a square 40x40mm engine for 3hp at 6500rpm, the 50 rode on 3.00x10in tires.

Inspired by the success of Honda's Cub, Fuji began producing a series of 90cc moped-scooters in 1958, continuing through the 90cc S-202 of 1964, a dead ringer for the Honda.

Fulgur FRANCE ★★

The Fulguretta appeared at the 1952 Foire de Paris with a 50cc VCT or three-speed 49cc Lavalette engine and probably never made it beyond the prototype stage, the same fate as many of Fulgur's projects. The covered style, a developed version of a child's push scooter, had some speed and even brakes but lacked a headlamp or any other electrical "luxuries."

GAOMA ITALY ★

GAOMA of Lodi created its Daino 65 scooter in 1951. A lightweight scooter with 20in wheels, the Daino (meaning "buck" in Italian) was powered by a two-stroke 65cc. In 1954, the Daino 75 was born with 45x45mm delivering 2.5hp at 5500rpm via three speeds on top of slick spoked white wall wheels. Gas consumption was 2 liters per 100km and the 60kg scooter could reach 55-60km/h depending on the girth of the passenger. Belgium and Luxemburg received the bulk of this Italian export through Etablissements Decomotor de Bruxelles.

Garelli ITALY ★★

Known for its buzzing mini Mosquito motor, Garelli tried its hand at scooters together with Agrati in 1961. The Scooter 98 debuted at the Fiera di Milano as a middle-of-the-road option between the Capri 80 and the Capri 125. Although the scooter design borrowed the tried-and-true Lambretta style, the market didn't respond even though Garelli's great motor produced 4hp.

In 2018, Garelli made a comeback with the Capri LX, which looks like a smaller Vespa, just as its classic Capri did.

Garrison Manufacturing USA ★

Garrison of Chicago made the By George scooter with a 3hp four-stroke engine, automatic clutch, recoil cord starter, and Ezyglide spring forks. George—his last name has been lost to scooter posterity—signed his scooters like a Modigliani.

Gasuden JAPAN ★

The Gasuden motorscooter was built primarily for the Japanese market in the 1950s and 1960s.

Genuine Scooter Company Stella USA ★★★

Aiming toward the loyal Vespa market that wanted the old lines without the price of the new Vespas and reliability to boot, the Genuine Scooter Company contracted to have the old Piaggio P series Vespas built again. "Designed with great style in Italy, assembled with great skill in Asia . . . and sold in the US by folks who have a love affair with classic scooters" reads the brochure copy.

With a new market swamped with modern plastic scooters with retro styling, Stella simply uses the old Vespa design and has it stamped in metal by LML in India. Stellas even made it into the British market.

Genuine Scooters is a "sister company" to Scooterworks from Chicago, a Vespa shop that has fixed so many quirky two-strokes that it knew what to use and what to avoid in remaking a classic. Therefore, the Stella features fancy Grimeca front disc brakes and Bitubo gas shocks with the tried-and-true four-speed transmission.

The Stella ended its stellar run in 2014, with the last one being a 125 automatic.

GenZe by Mahindra USA/INDIA ★

Though parent company Mahindra is located in Mumbai, the construction of these electric scooters was in Ann Arbor, Michigan. Its name is a play on Generation Zero Emissions. Perhaps unknown to them was that the book *Generation X*

Ready for a Picnic
The seafoam green Stella soon became a collector's item once Genuine stopped making them. The Stella delivered on essentially being an improved P-series Vespa without the headache of fixing.

Best Buddy
Surprisingly during the COVID-19 pandemic, the Genuine Buddy sold out of showroom floors across the country. This go-to scooter just proved to be the best bang for the buck, and it came in lots of cool colors.

Un po' di Brio!
For those who just want to hop on a scooter as quickly as possible, the Genuine Brio has the 50cc power to get them around the block. Sure, brio means energy, spunk, and panache, but it also means noise, so saw off the end of the muffler for speed and to turn heads.

(not the Douglas Coupland copy) was about anti-establishment British Mods who would likely scoff about trying to save the environment and told the authors, "I'm rude to my mum and ignore my dad, and that's how it should be."

Regardless, GenZe began its scooter run in 2013 with a plucky mobile that could zip along at 30 mph (48 km/h) for 30 miles (48 km) on a charge. Just plug it into any outlet.

An offshoot of Über called Postmates utilized a fleet of these scooters for those too lazy to fire up their Lambretta to go to the local café. GenZe scooters could also be picked up in many cities as part of a rideshare program, Scoot Networks. Alas, the COVID-19 pandemic took its toll, and the company's scooter business seemed doomed in 2021.

Gianca ITALY ★★★★★

Gianca's Nibbio was the first Italian scooter. Built in Monza, the Nibbio used a standard tube frame covered by sheet steel bodywork with telescopic front forks. A swing arm was used at the rear with an avant-garde monoshock mounted beneath the engine, as later developed by Harley-Davidson for its "revolutionary" Softtail.

The Gianca engine was a 98cc two-stroke of 48x54mm creating 2hp and cooled by flywheel fan. The multi-plate clutch fed power to a two-speed gearbox, which was shifted by a heel-and-toe foot lever. Tires were 3.50x8in, and the Nibbio was available in dark green, dark red, or ivory.

In 1949, Nibbio construction was transferred to the San Cristoforo firm of Milan on Via Borgonuovo.

The rear of the scooter was extended and the engine was enlarged to 125cc with a three-speed gearbox.

In 1952, the Simonetta took the place of the Nibbio, but held on to its 125cc engine. The gearbox, as well, remained the same with the gear shifting via the right foot. The two-seater weighed 85kg and could supposedly reach 75km/h, probably downhill. The French firm Ravat acquired a license from Gianca to produce an identical scooter on the other side of the Alps.

Giesse ITALY ★★

The Furetto debuted at the Fiera di Milano in 1947 to much fanfare in their ad campaign as "lo scooter perfetto," the perfect scooter. Built in the workshop of Ottavio Quadrio by engineer Scarpa and his technician partner Valerio, Giesse's Furetto had telescopic front forks holding larger spoked wheels that were later imitated by Guzzi's Galletto. Perhaps the questionable name of Furetto, meaning "ferret" in Italian, wasn't as successful as hoped. In 1948, Giesse sold the two-tone polecat to Isothermos S.p.A., usually known simply as Iso.

Gilera ITALY ★★

In 1962, Gilera, one of the long-lived Italian motorcycle marques, decided to also enter the scooter fray. Gilera offered its G50 scooter based on bodywork and engine designs that were so similar to the Vespa it is surprising the scooter did not end up doing battle in court instead of in the marketplace.

But the Gilera G50 offered several differences and advantages over the 50cc Vespina that also appeared in 1962. The layout of the G50 engine was almost identical to the Vespa—except that it was mounted on the scooter's other side. And the G50 was a four-stroke with overhead valves.

The 50cc engine had a 38x44mm bore and stroke, creating 1.5hp at 4800rpm via three speeds shifted by a hand twist. In 1963, a 80cc G80 version was added with a square 46x46mm delivering 3.65hp at 6000rpm. Whereas the G50 had a sole saddle seat, the G80 had a two-person bench. Both models remained in production until 1966.

In 1969, Gilera was purchased by Piaggio, so this storied marque is kept alive through the factory at Pontedera with sporty brands like Runner Black Soul or White Soul in 50 or 125cc models. The bizarre-looking Fuoco (fire) is a microcar/scooter chimera with two wheels in front powered by a 500cc engine reaching 90 (!) mph (145 km/h). Gadzooks.

Gitan ITALY ★★

Gitan (short for Gino Tansini) began when bicycle manufacturers put the Italian people on self-propelled two-wheelers in the 1920s. Just outside of Piacenza in the flat Po Valley, Gitan saw how Piaggio's

wasp, the Vespa, flooded the market, so he named his scooter after a more likeable insect, the cricket, or Grillo. Available as a 50cc two-stroke step-through moped, the Grillo hit the market in 1958. Deemed too slow, the Grillo was accompanied by the Poker 70 the following year. Then in 1963, the more scooter-like Joligri with the still slow 48cc engine debuted but could still keep up with traffic because the bodywork was light-weight fiberglass, not metal.

Glas Isaria GERMANY ★★

Glas publicity read, "Everyone is amazed about the new Goggo," whether by its beauty or audacity is in the eye of the beholder. Der Goggoroller was in the style of the Maico and Bastert scooters except with the smaller 8in wheels typical of the Italian makes. Three models were offered: the Goggo 125 of 1951–1956, and Goggo 150 and 200 of 1952–1956.

The extended front fender was embellished with a front bumper and large winged Goggo label. The scooters were armed with 123cc, 148cc, or 197cc Jlo engines, to let you "go with the times" at a fast clip.

The Glas factory at Dingolfing, Bavaria was known, however, more for the Goggomobil midget car, which Innocenti later produced under license in Venezuela. Instead of Goggo going the way of financial misfortune like so many other companies, Hans Glas Isaria sold his company to BMW while its sales were still turning a considerable profit. BMW, in turn, shipped the Glas tooling to South Africa to set up a plant there.

Glenco Products USA ★

Glenco of Fort Wayne, Indiana, built its Little Gen scooter in the 1960s with your choice of a two-cycle 2.5hp or four-cycle 2.25hp engine.

Gianca's Nibbio
The Nibbio predated the Vespa as the earliest Italian scooter. One of two Nibbio designs, this version's stinging wasp abdomen probably influenced the Vespa. Courtesy of Vittorio Tessera

Globe USA ★★★

Globe Corporation of Joliet, Illinois, built two- and three-wheeled Globester scooters, beginning in 1948 and running into the early 1950s, based on a centrifugal clutch and "torque-shifting" V-belt Maximatic transmission. Power came from a Continental Red Seal 2hp four-stroke of 2 1/8×2in, sparked by a flywheel magneto.

The Globe chassis was made of cast aluminum, which was considered a futuristic "miracle metal" at the time. A basket was mounted atop the fender, which held the 6in wheel.

Two models were offered: the solo Globester Runabout with a red body and gray "metallescent" frame and the Pick-up three-wheeler in red and grey or yellow and brown frame.

Gloucestershire Aircraft Company UK ★★★★

While most early scooters seem primitive compared to today's jetpod styling, the Unibus of Gloucestershire Aircraft Company of Cheltenham, England went beyond just crossing a child's scooter with a motorcycle, and melded not just a motorcycle with a car, but added the third design element: the airplane.

The scooter's design was very advanced for its age and was powered by a 269cc two-stroke engine with a two-speed gearbox. The Unibus rode on 16in wheels to reach 40km/h. With a sleek covered body hiding the dirty engine, the 1920 Unibus finally set the stage and drew the design for scooters to come. While the name would suggest a one-person bus, ad copy claimed that "To see the Unibus is to want one," and called it the "Car on Two Wheels," a motto later taken up by German Maico scooters in the 1950s as "Das Auto auf 2 Rädern."

Gogoro TAIWAN ★

About 23 million people live in Taiwan, and 15 million scooters provide them a ride. This is the capital of the scooter world, so it's little wonder the electric Smartscooter by Gogoro is such a hit. The price tag may be a bit steep, but the swappable battery stations make this sleek ride a winner. The catch is that riders must rely on battery charging stations, so look to see if you have a special charging station before hopping on.

Göricke Germany ★

Göricke's Gö-Mo 100 of 1951 was less than glamorous with an unenclosed 98cc Jlo engine. The one-seated scooter appeared to borrow from the design of the early Lambrettas without the speed.

Although Göricke was one of the innovators of the German motorcycle industry, its Görette stadtroller (town scooter) of 1955–1956 was less than noteworthy. Available with either an Jlo 49cc or Sachs 47cc engine, the Görette sold at the same price for either motor. The nearly identical versions zipped along at a top speed of 40km/h on the 20in wheels, the 1.7hp Jlo engine having a slight power advantage over the 1.5hp Sachs.

GOVECS GERMANY/POLAND ★★

Manufactured in Wroclaw, Poland, with an HQ in Munich, the Go electric scooters sport a Bosch battery and boast they are "climate neutral" but still reach up to 75 km (46 miles) per charge. The Go Flex scooters come in various sizes and even include a cargo carrier.

More interesting is the revival of Simson's Schwalbe (sparrow) scooter in 2015, which brought back an East German classic but in an electric version.

Grasshopper USA ★

A Grasshopper scooter was tested by the US Army in 1944 as a possible paratrooper scooter.

Griffon/FMC FRANCE ★★

This French firm produced Peugeot scooters but stamped their own label on the legshield. These early scoots changed the numbers slightly: Peugeot's S.55 became Griffon's S.555; the S.57 turned into the S.557; and the S.157 was the S.657 under the new marque.

Gritzner–Kayser GERMANY ★

Sewing machines, three-wheelers, an occasional motorcycle, and the KTM "Gritzner de Luxe Special" scooter was Gritzner–Kayser's renown. It built the two-toned Austrian KTM scooter under license with the motor between the driver's feet. The white-walled tires and the sharp, but tacky, styling gave it the scooter-of-tomorrow look, yesterday.

Guiller FRANCE ★

In 1951, the Fontenay-le-Comte moped maker opted to produce the Italian Moretti Gran Lusso scooter under license from SIM rather than pen its own scooter design. In 1952, Guiller came out with four other scooters with different engines, including the 125cc AMC, 170cc four-stroke AMC, and 125cc and 175cc Aubier-Dunne. Although Guiller later showed off prototype scooters for posterity, it didn't delve back into production.

Guzzi ITALY ★ ★ ★

Moto Guzzi's roots stretch back to the 1920s. It remains in the market in the 1990s, one of the few motorcycle makers to survive the onslaught of Japan.

After decades of building sophisticated road and race motorcycles, Guzzi turned in 1950 to build a scooter, the Galletto, or Rooster. Just as Guzzi had bucked tradition in the design of its horizontal single-cylinder motorcycles, its scooter broke many of the established tenets and found a market niche that kept it alive until 1964, when many other scooters had long since come and gone.

The most striking feature of the Galletto was not its crude, agricultural bodywork; rather it was the large wheels, 17in—larger than the standard scooter's but at least an inch smaller than the smallest motorcycle's. These wheels, along with other motorcycle-type features such as the foot-operated gearbox and especially the taller stance, made it a "serious" scooter. It was almost an enclosed motorcycle and had the dignity of a motorcycle with the protection of a scooter; the Galletto was a scooter adults did not feel was beneath them to ride.

The prototype Galletto was based on a horizontal four-stroke 150cc engine, but production ran from 1950–1952 with a 160cc of 62x53mm for 6hp at 5200rpm via three speeds.

For 1952–1954, the Galletto was offered as a 175cc with a larger, 65mm bore and 7hp. More importantly, the gearbox now had four speeds.

In 1955, the stroke of the Galletto's engine was increased to 58mm giving 192cc and 7.5hp. In 1961, Guzzi decided to further motorscooter esthetics and practicality. The wheel covers were enlarged, the light was incorporated into the headset, the suspension was now an adjustable hydraulic shock, and an electric starter was added. The only problem was the whole shebang now weighed a hefty 137kg. Nevertheless, the Galletto continued in production until 1964.

Haojin CHINA ★

Guangzhou Haojin Motorcycle Co. makes three-wheeled rickshaws, motorcycles, and gasoline-powered scooters that come in mostly 100 or 125cc versions and are primarily for the Chinese market.

Haojue CHINA ★

Made by the Jiangmen Dachangjiang Group or the Jiangsu Xinxi Nanjue Motorcycle Company, these sporty scooters generally run on gasoline, with most of the motors 100 to 125cc.

Hap Alzina USA–GERMANY ★

In the late 1950s, famed California Indian and West Coast BSA distributor Hap Alzina sold his Playboy scooter from his shop in Oakland. Made in Germany, the Playboy was powered by "the famed Pranafa" 1.5ci two-stroke, pumping out a whole 0.7hp. A 1956 Playboy flyer showed Junior in the backyard with his diminutive scooter—"Small Fry's newest sport."

The flyer also assured Mom the Playboy was safe. As Popular Science noted in 1961, the "42-pound Alzina Playboy can be driven by a seven-year-old or a 200-pounder." Top speed was 15mph (presumably with the seven-year-old).

Harley–Davidson USA ★★★

The Harley-Davidson Topper was a Hell's Angels starter scooter—or at least a putt-putt for the crew-cut sons and daughters of Harley-Davidson motorcycle owners. But The Motor Company entered the scooter market just as Cushman, Mustang, and Lambretta were getting out—and getting out with reason. By 1960, the fad had largely faded in the United States, and the Topper would never sell to its potential.

The first Topper was released in 1960 to fanfare promoting it as "Tops in beauty and tops in performance." The Topper boasted a pull-start two-cycle 10ci (165cc) engine laying on its side with the 2.38x2.28in single cylinder facing to the front, which was supposed to eliminate the need for a cooling fan. Spark was by magneto with a generator supplying lighting.

Harley–Davidson got its two-stroke technology from the German DKW as the spoils of World War II. The Motor Company first used the DKW two-stroke in its S-125 and its Hummer models; the Topper's engine was largely new but the lineage was old.

The Scootaway automatic transmission used a centrifugal clutch and V-belt with final drive by chain. Ratios were "infinitely variable" from 18:1 in low to 6:1 in high range. With front and rear brakes, an Earles-style triangulated front fork, and 4.00x12in tires, the Topper was good for 45mph and 80mpg.

The Topper's frame was a standard tube chassis. The slab-sided body was made of fiberglass and even the two-tone paint scheme could not hide the scooter's mystifying resemblance to a refrigerator on wheels.

According to a June 1959 Popular Science preview, the Topper "has three main features that Harley–Davidson figures will appeal to American males: styling, automatic transmission, and those 12-inch wheels." The styling has already been discussed, the automatic transmission had its share of woes, but the 12 inchers were nice—2in more than the Vespas and Lambrettas of the day. The other feature Popular Science failed to mention was the Topper's parking brake. Why a scooter needed a parking brake was a question not worth asking.

The Topper's moment in the sun came when Ed "Kookie" Byrnes combed his hair and blasted away on his Topper in TV's "77 Sunset Strip." Promotional ads wheedled fans with "Advice to Teenagers: When it comes to combs and scooters, never a borrower or a lender be. Instead, start dropping hints to Mom and Dad about the new Topper."

From the start, two Topper models were available: the A was the 9.5hp standard and the AU was a de-tuned 5hp version with a carburetor restrictor to meet new state laws for minimum driving ages. In 1961, the models were upgraded: the A became the AH (touted in ads as simply the H) and the AU retained its designation. By 1962–1963, colors included

Birch White, Tango Red, or Black with Birch White trim. The seat was made of fabulous Hypalon.

By the end of 1965, the Topper was but a memory. Harley–Davidson chose to follow the road traveled by Cushman in canceling its scooter and shifting to golf carts.

Harper UK ★★

Harper Aircraft in Exeter embarked on a scooter in 1954 based on a hefty tube frame covered by full fiberglass bodywork. The Scootamobile was first created with a 125cc Villiers and body styling that looked like a dustbin racing fairing in front with built-in panniers at the rear, copying the Maicomobil concept. Development continued through 1957 with a 197cc Villiers, but few production models were ever built.

Hartford TAIWAN ★

These four-stroke, four-valve scooters proudly bear the Italian tricolor flag on the front legshield and the name Cappuccino despite their Taiwanese origin. Regardless, the 125cc engine and sleek design make for a decent scooter.

Hawk Tool & Engineering USA ★

Hawk built its Special scooter in Clarkston, Michigan, in the 1960s with a 2hp four-stroke engine. Many accessories were available, including 3hp or 4hp engines. The more-powerful engines were probably worth the money.

HDR THE NETHERLANDS ★★

German Binz scooters were released into the low countries with the new logo HDR on the legshield.

Heinkel GERMANY

In 1922, Ernst Heinkel founded his company in Stuttgart and became one of the primary forces that helped Nazi Germany's Luftwaffe rise to be the world's most powerful air force at the time. Like many other German companies, Heinkel turned to two- and three-wheeled vehicles as they were forbidden to produce aircraft after the war. By 1965, after building 100,000 Tourist scooters, Heinkel returned to making solely airplanes.

TOURIST 101 1953–1954;
TOURIST 102 AND 103 1954–1965 ★★

As the scooter became more and more an instrument of teenagers, Heinkel thought the Tourist could appeal to both the youth and wannabe youth with slogans like "On two wheels you stay young" and "For young people who know what they want." Complete with front bumper, the Tourist was a reliable four-stroke scooter that was a common sight on German roads in the late 1950s. Even German police used Heinkels when law breakers were on scooters or micro cars, before they switched to Porsches to chase speeders on the autobahn.

For added incentive to drive a Tourist into the ground, Heinkel offered gold plaques to be mounted on the front fender if the scooter surpassed 100,000km. A silver plaque was awarded after 75,000km, and the bronze plaque was discontinued because every self-respecting Heinkel owner should be able to achieve 50,000km. The 150cc Tourist 101 had 7.2hp for 85km/h and the 175cc Tourist 102 and 103 had 9.2hp for 92km/h.

The Tourist scooter was so successful that Heinkel tried to pass off their three-wheeled, front-entrance car as a "cabin scooter" since one version had the 174cc Tourist engine. The "cabin scooter" was later produced in Ireland and imported to Britain under the name of Trojan.

112 1957 AND 150 1960–1965 ★★

The 125cc Heinkel 112 was one of the few scooters to ever have a model number less than the size of the engine. The 6.25hp Heinkel Roller 112 was an attractive scooter but unfortunately stayed in production for only one year. The 150, on the other hand, took a stab at new innovative scooter lines and failed miserably. The engine put out a decent 9hp for a maximum speed of 85km/h, but the lines and excessive two-tone make for a gaudy, at best, exterior.

Hercules GERMANY ★★

"You can fall in love with this scooter and every way you look at it, it's beautiful!" read a Hercules ad for the R200 of 1955–1960. Just as Triumph GB made a scooter with BSA, its owner at the time, so did German TWN Triumph produce a scooter with Hercules. The TWN Contessa and the Hercules R200 had nearly identical bodywork, used a four-speed 191cc Sachs with 10.2hp for a maximum velocity of 100km/h, and had different emblems on the paneling. Kieft of Britain announced the R200 under its own name for importation, but the project was quickly abandoned. Soon after, its name changed to Prior when the British BP Scooters of The Airport became the importer.

The later Hercules Roller 50 and 50S from 1964 were KTM scooters made under license. As with the Gritzner–Kayser scooter designed by KTM, the paint job displayed a garish two-color scheme.

Hero INDIA ★

Originally Hero banded together with Honda to make motorcycles and scooters but slowly severed the bond beginning in 2010 as long as Hero stayed in India and neighboring countries in the beginning. The Hero Duet played for a few years, followed by the four-stroke Hero Maestro, Hero Destini, and the questionably named Hero Pleasure. The Honda technology made this company a force.

Hildebrand-Wolfmuller
GERMANY ★★★

While more of a powered bicycle than scooter, the Hildebrand had a 1500cc steam engine, that's right, steam. Debuting in 1889, this Teutonic beast had a step-through design with a larger front wheel and a springy leather seat for suspension. With boiling water between the legs, the Hildebrand is a more of a collector's dream than a daily driver.

Heinkel 150
"No Hill Too Steep, No Road too Rough, Nowhere Too Far!" declared Heinkel ads. Not surprisingly, the Heinkel 150 debuted in 1960, the decade when design and architecture went awry. Hoping to hit up the teen market, the firm's ad proclaimed, "The Heinkel 150 is the ideal companion for the young, the not so young, and the young in heart who know what they want."

Hirano JAPAN ★

With the Pop, Hirano entered the scooter market in the early 1950s. Riding on 16in wheels, this little putt-putt was followed by the 80cc Popet and the 165cc Popmanlee in 1956, which both seemed strikingly similar to the Honda Cub. In 1958, Hirano opted to follow the lines of the more stylish Lambretta.

In 1961, a version of the fold-up Valmobile was produced. This 50cc suitcase-sized scooter was invented in France by Victor Bouffort where it was constructed by Martin-Moulet and also sold in the US as the Foldmobile.

Hirundo ITALY ★★

Built by Michele Porrera, a designer from Turin, just a few copies of the scooter made it to market in 1950 and 1951. The Hirundo (Latin for the winged swallow) was pushed by a 125cc engine or the optional 150cc split cylinder motor.

HMW AUSTRIA ★

Halleiner Motorwerke of Salzburg offered, in 1954, its 75R Bambi scooter with a 75cc two-stroke of 3.8hp. Riding on medium-sized 12in white-wall wheels, the red Bambi with chrome galore allowed happy Tyroliennes to scoot to the hills alive with the sound of music and yodel to the fawns.

In 1959, HMW sold its 50cc Conny scooter, which was a spitting image of the DKW Hobby. Its pokey engine, however, couldn't carry as well as the Hobby, even though it featured two seats.

Hoffmann GERMANY ★★★

Hoffmann was licensed in mid-1949 to begin production of the Vespa 125, which the firm called Die Konigin, or the Queen, for the German market. The 124.7cc Hoffmann Vespa A had 4.6hp at 4900rpm, 0.6hp more than the Italian 125 at the time. The Hoffmann was also 5km/h faster, which Piaggio matched the following year and surpassed in horsepower. In 1951, Hoffmann offered an official Vespa sidecar with a windshield as well as floorboards. By 1953, some 1,800 Konigin Vespas were manufactured monthly.

In 1954, the Vespa Die Konigin was replaced by the Vespa 54, which had 5hp. On some of the Hoffmann models a second, larger headlamp was mounted on the bicycle-style handlebars for extra safety.

By 1955, Hoffmann was looking to switch from scooters to motorcycles and cars, and so the Piaggio-Hoffmann license was cancelled.

Honda JAPAN

Siochiro Honda's story is classic Horatio Alger rags to riches. Born the son of the Komyo village blacksmith, he got his start producing a radical new piston

ring pre-World War II. During the war, his fledgling company built wooden propellers for the Japanese air force. After the war, Honda turned his hand to designing economical motorbikes and scooters.

Honda first created a motorized bicycle, the Model A, in 1947 and built it in Honda's 12x18ft shed that housed thirteen employees. In 1953, the motorbike gave way to the first Cub clip-on motor, which developed into the Cub moped line that continued all the way into the 1980s as the Passport. By the end of its run, some 15 million Cubs had been built.

JUNO KA 1954 ★★★

Inspired by the success of the major Japanese makers, Fuji with its Rabbit scooter and Mitsubishi with its Pigeon, Honda built its first scooter in 1954, the Juno KA. It was based on a 189cc overhead-valve engine measuring 65x57mm bore and stroke and creating 5hp at 4800rpm. The rear drive was by enclosed chain.

The Juno was available solely in metallic green—a color not far from the early Vespa green—and had two pad seats, enclosed handlebars, and a headlamp on the front apron. The styling of the Juno line would always be bizarre or futuristic, depending on your point of view. It continued the Japanese scooter design philosophy of more is better, and was dressed up with miles of molding running from the front turn signals to the rear turn signals.

JUNO JB 1955 ★ ★ ★

In 1955, the KB replaced the KA with a 220cc engine of 70x57mm for 9hp at 5500rpm riding on 5.00x9in tires. And the styling had grown even more outrageous.

JUNO M80 1960–1961 AND
JUNO M85 1962–1964 ★ ★ ★ ★

In 1960, Honda introduced a new scooter in its M80 based on a flat twin engine that was unique in the scooter universe. Each cylinder measured 43x43mm and together made 10hp at 9000rpm. The accessories followed the styling: turn signals, electric start, gas gauge, glovebox, and more.

The styling was again futuristic, but it was now minimalist or boxy, again depending on your viewpoint. The elements never quite fit together, looking like a tool-room special made up of not just Honda spare parts but parts from every other Japanese scooter make as well. Even the flashy two-tone paint could not save the lack of styling.

In 1962, Honda offered its M85 scooter powered by a 168.9cc overhead-valve flat twin engine of 50x43mm bore and stroke. Power was 12hp at 7600rpm riding atop 10in wheels. The M85's career lasted until only 1964, after which Honda concentrated on its Cub series and motorcycles.

AERO, ELITE, SPREE, AND HELIX ★

Twenty years later, Honda returned to the scooter fold, introducing its Aero series of 50cc and 80cc scooters in 1983 as well as an Aero 125cc in 1984. The Aero plastic scooters mimicked the styling of the Vespa Nuovo Linea, and were the first Honda scooters to be imported to the United States.

Simultaneously, Honda released its Spree 50cc line in 1984 as well as the modernistic Elite series with 125cc in 1984; 80, 150, and 250cc in 1985; and 50cc in 1987. In Italy, Honda sold its Vision scooter. The little 80cc Elite has the illustrious career stemming back to advertising of DEVO and Adam Ant when MTV first hit the small screen.

In 1986, Honda created its Helix 250cc armchair motorscooter, a step back in time to the Ner-A-Car style. Based on a potent four-stroke liquid-cooled single-cylinder engine, the Helix was the original Barcalounger-cum-UFO to hit the scooter line that all the maxi-scooters have sought to copy.

The Honda Joker (known as the Shadow in the US and UK) had a customized Harley wannabe look that didn't quite appeal to the classic scooter crowd nor the motorcycle gangs who wouldn't want to be caught dead on a scooter. The Joker/Shadow was built from 1996 to 1999 and later essentially copied in China as the Znen C Artemis.

Around the same time the Vespa returned to the US, Honda responded with its classy Metropolitan as part of its new line of sport, maxi and classic models. Although the 50cc four-stroke Metropolitan draws from classic styling of early Italian models, the Metropolitan uses a plastic body for the two-tone covering. This automatic scooter even features a combined braking system, so when the scooterist clutches the left handlebar lever, both front and rear brakes stop the little two-wheeler. To appeal to a broad market, Honda offers edible paint schemes of: kiwi, blue hibiscus, juice and salsa.

At the same time, Honda is trying to broaden the scooter market with the Honda Ruckus, a bizarre mix of two-wheeled ATV and mini Humvee. The fat tires and camouflage design on this 49cc scooter make it perfect for dragging dead deer out of the woods.

The other stretch of the word scooter comes from the 582cc Silver Wing. With a four-stroke, fuel-injected engine, this beast is more like a 100mph sofa with ABS than motorcycle. Due to its step-through design and relatively small wheels, the Silver Wing gets lumped in with the scooters, but relates more to its big brother Gold Wing than an Autoped. Honda lists its prestigious line of scooters on its website just below water pumps and right above snowblowers.

LEFT:

La-Z-Boy Scooter of the Future
Part Goldwing part Lambretta, the 1998 FB-S Future Concept Design scooter by Honda practically floats down the streets of Tokyo like a hovercraft. This futuristic prototype is hot on the tail of the outrageous success of the top-of-the-line Helix scooters called by a 1994 Consumer's Digest, "the sexy, low-slung two-passenger Honda Helix, virtually the 'stretch limousine' of the scooter world . . . it will effortlessly cruise at interstate speeds." In fact, the 250cc Helix could easily reach 65 mph, and this new space-age design of motorcyclecum-scooter could leave Helix loungers in the dust.

RIGHT:

Honda Brochure
Sugoi! The Juno KA was originally released as 189cc scooter, but Honda upped the ante before the Italians by plopping in a 220cc engine in this 1955 KB model—not even Piaggio or Innocenti dare make such a powerful putt-putt. Courtsey of the François-Marie Dumas Archives

TOP:

Scooter Spree!
Just as Innocenti called it quits and Piaggio left the US, Honda released its tiny Spree in the mid-1980s and found a market for this glorified covered moped. Suddenly Sprees were everywhere as teenagers went way too fast on the mini bikes that gave little protection with the plastic legshield that often cracked under duress.

BOTTOM:

Plastic Elite
Honda's incredible engines are some of the best ever made, so why cover them in plastic? Still, the Honda Elite kept running despite the inevitable cracking of its outer shield.

Horex GERMANY ★

Horex's motto was "Built by motorcyclists for motorcyclists," so it's no wonder that in 1956 when it built its scooter it failed and ended up being a waste of time for the company. Motorcycle makers often fell into the same trap making scooters not as an option to motorcycles, but as small motorcycles—as opposed to other factories that made typewriters, sewing machines, and plumbing who viewed the motor scooter as another appliance to get from point A to point B.

The powerful 16hp Rebell was so rebellious that Horex didn't sell a single one. Perhaps Horex mixed up the name of its scooter with one of its motorcycles, the Resident, which would seem much more appropriate for a scooter. Although not by any means a hideous scooter, the 249cc was a catastrophe for Horex.

Humblot FRANCE ★

Famous for its mopeds, this Châtillon-sous-Bagneux-based company stepped up the two-wheel ladder with the Paloma 705 scooter in 1954. Even with a larger-than-moped Lavalette 3hp engine and mostly covered body, the large spoked wheels gave away its heritage. The 705 model was replaced in 1954 by the Paloma 1250 (also available in a Luxe model) with a 125cc René Gillet engine. Unable to reach a large size in its scooter, Humblot ceased making scooters in 1956, except for a brief return when, in 1962, SNE Paloma produced the Paloma 50cc, looking like a dwarf version of the Lambretta TV.

Hummel–Sitta GERMANY ★

The Hummel 120G, 125G, and 150G looked like early Lambretta LCs that had been blasted with a cannon. Holes in the legshields covered by grates to let in cool air for the engine gave the impression of mistakes and last-minute remedies. Made from the late 1940s to early 1950s, all the Hummel scooters used Jlo engines.

Hunter AUSTRALIA ★

These Australian scooters skipped the girly side panels and any other covering for the bike to make mini choppers with wide tires. Boasting that the idea for Hunter scooters "originated in the alleyways and chop shops of Tokyo in the early 2000s," these bikes defy the ho-hum mini sport bike look, but, alas, ceased production in the 2020s.

Husqvarna SWEDEN ★ ★

Husqvarna is one of the grand old motorcycle makes, starting production in 1903. Through the years, it built myriad graceful large-bore motorcycles before concentrating on innovative motocrossers postwar.

In 1955, Husqvarna purchased a small number of scooter chassis from Parilla and fitted them with HVA engines and the Husqvarna crown nameplate. The 120cc HVA two-stroke engine created 4.3hp at 5000rpm. Riding atop 3.00x12in tires, top speed was 70km/h.

In between chainsaw and sewing machine production, Husqvarna developed its own scooter in 1958, the Corona Model 3842. Powered by Husqvarna's own two-stroke 0.8hp engine, it rode on 2.50x20in tires. In 1986, the Husqvarna motorcycle division was bought by Cagiva.

IFA EAST GERMANY ★

The IFA Rico-Roller was a spiritual predecessor of the great Trabant automobile. It was part motorcycle, part bicycle, and part scooter with its 19in wheels and springer rear suspension belying its heritage. But its 125cc engine covered by swooping sheet metal bodywork made one think of a motorscooter—or a medieval steed decked in jousting gear.

IGM ITALY ★★

Impresse Generali Meccaniche of Milan was a metal-stamping firm that decided to try its hand at scooter production following the lead set by Piaggio in the late 1940s. IGM offered its 125cc Bantam scooter of classical design; the firm's brochure hailed it a true gran turismo scooter. To show that the Lambretta and Vespa had early competition, the IGM Bantam was presented at the Salone di Milano in 1947, but only a few copies were ever produced.

Il Motore ITALY ★★

With a sleek single metal piece covering the whole back of the bike, Il Motore's scooter called Giorgino (little George) debuted at the Salone di Milano in 1950. The Giorgino stands out not only for the space-age styling, but the little 75cc had a split cylinder to push the 55kg scooter to 65 km/h.

IMN ITALY ★

Known more for its mopeds and light motorcycles, IMN of Naples tried to expand its market with the Scooter 65 in 1956. Produced mostly for export, the scooter followed IMN's other bikes except it was covered with metal bodywork and a legshield.

Imperial Motor Industries UK ★★★★

Seeing the success of the American Autoped, this British company made copies of the original for Britain in the 1910s.

Indian USA ★★

In 1949, the famed Indian Motorcycle Company made several odd decisions. After decades of buildings its great V-twin motorcycles, it decided to develop vertical twins in the English style and sell motorscooters in the Cushman style. Both were ill-fated projects.

Indian contracted with Lowther to build its scooters; no less than twenty-four two- and three-wheeled solo and tandem scooters were offered. Among the array were the Spartan, Vagabond, and Stylemaster with varying degrees of bodywork from none to completely clothed, respectively. The styling left a lot to be desired; a kind word would be "agricultural."

TOP:
Multihued Metropolitan
The Metropolitan caught on because of the motor that just wouldn't stop and the colorful plastic bodywork. Sure, it cheapens it, but metal is much heavier, even if it could save your life in an accident.

BOTTOM:
Swedish Scoot
The 1958 Husqvarna Corona, or Crown, was named for Sweden's national image of three crowns, one of which also rested atop Husqvarna's own logo. The Corona Model 3842 was powered by Husqvarna's own two-stroke engine with its compelling 0.8 hp.

Innocenti ITALY

Ferdinando Innocenti was a plumber before starting his company in 1931 to produce steel plumbing pipes and tubing. From this background, it was thus no surprise that Innocenti's Lambretta scooter would be based on a tube frame versus the avant-garde pressed-steel unit chassis of its chief rival, Piaggio's Vespa.

During World War II, Innocenti produced artillery shells and pontoon bridges, and was lovingly declared "a model of fascist establishment" by the blackshirts. While the Lambrate factory was busy making bullets for Mussolini and the Nazis, Ferdinando Innocenti played both sides by supporting the partisan resistance as well. This way, when the Fascists were defeated, Innocenti escaped the Allied purges. To cover his back, he'd generously given to both sides, much as Enzo Ferrari to keep his automotive dreams intact.

Inspired by scooters dropped from the heavens by British paratroopers, Innocenti knew these little two-strokes would be a hit in Italy. In Guidonia, Innocenti arranged a meeting with Colonel Corradino d'Ascanio to see if this engineer would be interested in creating a scooter that every Italian could afford to own and operate. D'Ascanio and Innocenti didn't see eye to eye, perhaps because of the bitter political postwar climate in which people wouldn't forget if you supported the other side.

Instead, Ferdinando Innocenti and his general director, Giuseppe Lauro, looked for a way to turn swords into plowshares. In 1945–1946, the duo assigned engineer Pierluigi Torre to create a scooter, which they named the Lambretta after the factory's site in the Lambrate quarter of Milan. The quarter was named for the bubbling brown Lambrate River that runs through the suburb, a river that is now one of the most polluted in all of Italy.

Innocenti never restricted itself to just scooter production. Through the years it continued the production of steel tubing as well as making milling machines and presses. The Innocenti factory also manufactured parts for most Italian car makers as well as Ford of Europe and Volkswagen. In 1961, Innocenti began producing the British Austin cars under license.

Due to a decline in the scooter market, Innocenti ceased Lambretta production in 1971 after building some four million scooters. As a consequence of further financial problems, it fell into the hands of the Italian government in 1975. In 1975, Argentine-Italian magnate Alejandro de Tomaso added the Lambrate factory to his empire. The factory continues production to this day, including engines for the De Tomaso–owned Moto Guzzi.

Lambrettas had been built in Spain by Messrs Serveta Industrial SA (formerly Lambretta Locomociones SA) since 1954 and the Innocenti tooling was sold to Scooters India in 1972, both of which have kept the Lambretta in production into the 1990s.

LAMBRETTA A 125 1947–1948 ★★★★

The first Lambretta 125 m (later called the A) could have been ready by the summer of 1945, but the Allied occupation of Italy caused Innocenti to delay production for two years. The first Vespa was for sale in April 1946; by October 1947, the race with Piaggio was on as the first Lambretta scooter rolled off the production lines. Within a year, Innocenti would manufacture nearly 10,000 of its Model A.

The Lambretta's launch was preceded by months of advertising to ready the market for Innocenti's radical new vehicle. Italy's RAI radio played a Lambretta commercial day and night throughout 1947 with a ditty that became the Shave-and-a-haircut-two-bits of Italy, still subconsciously whistled by Italians. "Sono le ore venti e trentacinque è ora della Lambretta," (the time is twenty thirty-five (8:35 p.m.) and it's time for Lambretta).

The Lambretta was radical not in design but in its concept of providing inexpensive transportation with easy operation. The chassis was a traditional tube frame lacking bodywork. The frame was built in two sections: the front consisted of a pressed-steel main section connecting to the steering head, which held the front fork; the rear section consisted of two chrome tubes surrounding the gas tank and connecting to the pressed-steel toolbox.

The A lacked bodywork to cover the engine and had scanty legshields compared to its chief rival, but what it fell short of in covering, it made up for with a larger 125cc engine compared to its 98cc counterpart. The A's two-stroke, single-cylinder measured 52x58mm with its upright cylinder inclined slightly forward. A 16mm Dell'Orto carburetor fed the fuel, which was sparked by a Marelli flywheel magneto; power was 4.3hp at 4500rpm with a top speed of 65–70km/h or 40–44mph.

Drive to the rear wheel was via an enclosed shaft with bevel gears turning the axle. A foot-operated rocker pedal controlled the three-speed gearbox with an indicator on the inside right footboard to tell which gear had been selected.

Alongside the larger engine, the Lambretta's most important feature was a second seat for carrying a passenger, marking it in buyers' minds as a more social scooter than the more functional, one-seated 1946 Vespa. The front saddle seat sat above the gas tank with the rear pillion perched above the toolbox. The gas tank held 6 liters with 0.8 liter reserve for an incredible 300km on one tank of miscela.

The Model A was not received enthusiastically; buyers lacked confidence in the elfin 3.50x7 in. tires. Thus, in December 1948, Innocenti created a revised version of the A, called naturally enough, the B.

LAMBRETTA B 125 1948–1949 ★★★

The A evolved into the B with further comfort due to its larger, 3.50x8in wheels, a left-hand twist-grip gearchange using a push-pull cable system rather

than a foot lever, and, in an effort to keep up with Vespa, rear suspension. The suspension worked by a swinging knuckle on the rear of the shaft drive case controlled by a coil-spring damper mounted horizontally under the engine. And the Lambretta was a hit; by 1950, Innocenti was building up to 100 scooters daily.

LAMBRETTA C 125 AND LC 125 1950–1951 ★★★★

The new C was based on a completely redesigned chassis fitted with the tried-and-true 4.3hp shaft-drive engine. The A/B chassis with its twin-tube construction was replaced by a single large-diameter main tube wrapped around the engine and gas tank to support the two seats. Trailing-link front suspension eased the ride, and would become characteristic of almost all subsequent Lambrettas. Other features were updated as well: a horn was added above the redesigned front fender, which fit snugly inside the front forks; and the Lambretta decal was now affixed to the gas tank.

Even with its extra seat and more-powerful engine, the Lambretta trailed the Vespa in popularity, primarily due to Piaggio designer Corradino d'Ascanio's bodywork that saved riders from road spray and engine grime. Innocenti finally recognized the importance of bodywork for a scooter and gave the public a choice of the "undressed" C or its new "dressed" LC, or Lusso C model, which made its debut in April 1950 following the C's February arrival.

With the LC, Innocenti finally had a winning combination. Piaggio met the challenge by enlarging its engine to 125cc to compete.

On the now-covered Lambretta engine, meanwhile, a fan was added to the flywheel magneto to blow cooling air over the cylinder—a design that Vespa had perfected years earlier. The side panel also featured a door to allow access to the carburetor.

LAMBRETTA D 125 AND LD 125 1951–1956; D 150 1954–1956; AND LD 150 1954–1957 ★★★

The D and LD sported a redesigned frame, front fork tubes that enclosed the front suspension springs, larger tires of 4.00x8in, and a new rear suspension setup, with the engine hung by pivoting links and suspended at the rear by a single damper. The unenclosed D was offered as an economy model alongside the Lusso LD.

The D engine measured 52x58mm, fathering 4.8hp at 4600rpm via a larger, 18mm Dell'Orto carburetor for a 45mph top speed. On the dressed LD, a two-piece sheet-steel housing was added to direct cooling air over the cylinder and head.

In 1954, Innocenti manufactured its most powerful scooter to date, a 148cc based on a longer-stroke, 57x58mm D engine that created 6hp at 4750rpm via a more-powerful magneto of 36 watts compared to the 123cc model's 25 watts. Although the 150 added 5mph to its top speed, gas mileage dropped from 193mpg to 140mpg. And Piaggio quickly responded with its own 150cc model.

The dual-porthole side panel trim of the LC was changed to a single oval grille on the LD. The access door to the carburetor, carried over from the LC model, continued for a short time on the first LDs.

As an added feature, electric-start LD 125 and LD 150 models were offered. These machines were not a great sales success as the cost of the started raised the scooter's price above many buyers' means.

As a precursor to the primped scooters of the mods, Innocenti marketed extras for the LD including chrome trim pieces, extra driving lights, a clock, fuel gauge, and radio, all of which often ended up costing a scooterist more than the original scooter. The Lambretta was marketed in Britain as the "sports car on two wheels," and with all these luxurious extras, one need not have suffered any inconvenience while riding a Lambretta.

Lambretta Model D

When the D appeared at the end of 1951, the fate of the "uncovered" Lambrettas was already sealed since the previous year the "sheathed" LC (L for Lusso, or Luxury) with a larger legshield and metal side panels completely enveloped the engine. Many loyal Lambrettisti scoffed at Innocenti's attempt to copy the Vespa's full covering of the engine, but the Italian people loved the style and the more powerful Innocenti engine. When Italian scooter aficionados look back on Innocenti's zenith, inevitably they get teary eyed for uncovered models like this D (even though it's missing the horn). Innocenti straddled the fence trying to please both sides, and continued to manufacture the open style scooters until 1956 with models A through F. Courtesy of the owner: Vittorio Tessera

BOTTOM:

Lambretta LD 125

The scooterization of the United States in the 1950s was complete with the introduction of the LD and the resulting hubbub in the press for the economical and stylish putt-putt. Available for a mere $379.50 (or $329.50 for the stripped-down D model) when it first entered at Ellis Island to Barkas & Shalit distribution in New York, the LD soon hit showrooms across the country. Popular Mechanics raved in 1957 about its 100mpg but still hesitant about the Lambretta's Italian heritage, "that's economical traveling in any man's language." Courtesy of the Robert Donati archives

In 1956, Innocenti tallied $43 million of Lambretta sales, including 6,000 scooters shipped to the United States as well as additional exports to a total of ninety-six other countries.

LAMBRETTA LD 125/57 1955–1958 AND LD 150/57 1957–1958 ★ ★ ★ ★

Seated in Milan, Italy's fashion capital, Innocenti recognized the value of annual updates to keep its scooter en vogue. For 1957, the front area was redesigned to add a sleek cowling over the handlebars that incorporated the speedometer/odometer and horn while leaving the headlamp on the front apron. An optional battery for the 125cc was available that sat alongside the gas tank. These two-tone luxury models with a grey and blue color scheme came in both the 125cc and 150cc models.

Popular Science magazine in the United States got a chance to test one of the first 57 models and wrote of the Lambretta in July 1957 in purple prose that echoed Innocenti's own ads: "Once warm, its superb engine starts at first kick, responds jauntily to the throttle. Like other two-cycle power plants, it's fond of revs, and the constant-mesh three-speed transmission lets you take full advantage of this at all times."

The 6hp LD 150/57 came standard with such luxuries as a speedometer, pillion seat, white sidewall tires, and a mechanical marvel that made Italy great, according to Popular Science: "a clock that works." The 150 needed a 12volt batter to power all these appliances.

The Series IV LD was sold alongside the new TV and Li but was soon dated next to their advanced features.

LAMBRETTA E 125 1953–1954 ★ ★ ★

The E for Economico was released as entry-level scooter with bare-bones features that were much simpler than the C or D. Since flashy fully-enclosed scooters had become the rage, few scooterists wanted to be seen on this uncovered Lambretta; the E never sold well, was not exported to all markets, was only kept on the mark for one year.

In spite of these checks against it, the larger-diameter frame tube of the E strengthened it far more than the other models, but added weight. The hand-recoil, cord-pull starter mounted in front of the engine near the magneto only added to the idea of this scooter as a working tool while the covered Lusso models gave the handsome appearance of a modern scooter in an age when people thought technology could actually alleviate all work.

The rear suspension equaled the D and LD, while the front suspension relied on elastic instead of the trailing-link of the C or the enclosed springs of the LD. The engine, with a gas tank of 6.7 liters, differed little from the D except for the prestigious pull start.

LAMBRETTA F 125 AND F125 SERIES II 1954–1955 ★ ★ ★

The F replaced the E with a kickstart replacing the pull start. Although this abolished the outboard motor look, top speed still kept well within trolling parameters.

The F II updated the front forks and several other features but couldn't spark any further sales.

LAMBRETTA TV 175 SERIES I 1957–1958 ★ ★

In 1952, Ducati created its Cruiser, a luxurious four-stroke scooter with hydraulic suspension and all the accessories a rider could handle. Ducati believed its scooter would steal the thunder from Piaggio and Innocenti's no-frills tow-strokes, but the Cruiser was too much too soon. Its price was too high for the floundering Italian economy and it was gone within two years. But the idea was sound.

By the mid-1950s, Italian automakers such as Ferrari and Maserati had created gran turismo cars that blended sport with luxury and began to sell to a new, more affluent class of Italians as well as to a strong export market.

Looking back to the Ducati Cruiser and at the new success of the GT cars, Piaggio decided in 1955 to create an upscale scooter with sports and touring features, the 150 GS, or Gran Sport. Locked horn to horn in battle for the scooter buyer, Innocenti responded in April 1957 with its TV 175.

TV stood for Turismo Veloce, or Touring Speed, a scaled-down translation of gran turismo into scooter-speak. Innocenti believed that while its earlier models had sold well as utilitarian workhorses, the times were changing; Italians now had some extra money in their pockets and the dawning of leisure time. That extra pocket money could buy a more stylish scooter that could drive to work during the week and be loaded up for a trip to the sea or a picnic in the country on weekends.

The TV1 was a completely new design from the wheels up. The 170cc two-stroke engine measured 60x60mm and delivered a powerful 9hp, significantly more than any earlier Lambretta or Vespa.

The addition of a fourth gear to the transmission erased perhaps the LD's sole shortcoming. And the shaft-drive of all earlier Lambrettas was shelved in place of a radically modern enclosed duplex chain drive that required no adjustment, lubrication, or cleaning. Wheels were now 10in with 3.50x10in Pirelli tires.

The bodywork that was wrapped around the TV1 was like fluid metal. The curves followed the scooter's function with rich expanses of flowing steel that made the new Lambretta look more modern than Piaggio's GS, which only a trained eye could differentiate from the first Vespa of 1946.

A wider, fixed front fender shaped like a zucchetto replaced the pivoting fender of the LD, allowing the wheel to move independently. The headlamp was perched on the front apron with a peaked visor above it and the horn behind a grille just above the fender. The handlebars were covered by a cowling with the speedometer/odometer on top.

The Turismo Veloce concept was right, the timing was right, but Innocenti's execution was wrong. Whereas Piaggio's GS became its best scooter of the 1950s and 1960s, the first series Lambretta TV 175 was a dismal failure. It was underdeveloped and won a reputation for poor reliability that haunted Innocenti into the 1960s. Never mind that in January 1959, the redesigned TV2 would be a world beater.

LAMBRETTA LI 150 AND LI 125 SERIES 1 1958–1959 ★ ★ ★

In early 1958, Innocenti launched its new Li line based on a completely new engine from the preceding TV, although with similar bore and stroke dimensions to the old D. The Li featured a single horizontal cylinder with enclosed duplex chain drive to the rear wheel via a four-speed gearbox. The 148cc measured 57x58mm and created 6.5hp; the 123cc was based on 52x58mm for 5.2hp.

The Li Series 1 scooters were clothed by a body identical to the TV Series 1 with the apron-mounted headlamp and a small cover over the handlebars to dispel the bicycle look.

The Li was as great a success as the TV1 was a failure. It was modern, powerful, and reliable whereas the TV1 was modern, powerful, and fragile. The Li line would dictate the direction of Lambretta scooters until 1971 when Innocenti halted production—and even then Serveta in Spain and Scooters India would continue building Li and Li-based models.

LAMBRETTA TV 175 SERIES 2 1959–1961 ★ ★ ★ ★ ★

Innocenti rushed to fix its TV and repair its image. After just sixteen months of production, the TV1 was

pulled to be replaced by the TV2, which was a new scooter based not on the TV1 but on the successful Li line. The only items carried over from the TV1 were the name and the body style, which was also updated.

The new 175cc engine was a wider-bore version of the Li engine at 62x58mm, creating 8.6hp. Midway through TV2 production, the early 23mm Dell'Orto carburetor was swapped for a 21mm that provided for smoother performance throughout the powerband.

The bodywork was redone with the headlamp moved to the handlebars and fitted beneath a streamlined cowling that also incorporated the speedometer unit.

With the TV2, Innocenti had its flagship sporting scooter that it should have had in the TV1.

LAMBRETTA LI 150 AND LI 125 SERIES 2
1959–1961 ★★★★

The Li line was modified in 1959 with the headlamp moved from the apron to the handlebars as on the TV2, creating a much more stylish scooter. The 125cc Series 2 engine breathed via an 18mm Dell'Orto whereas the 150 was fed through a 19mm carburetor. In addition, a wide variety of gear ratios were used to match the powerband of 125cc versus the 150cc engine.

LAMBRETTA LI 125 SERIES 3 SLIMLINE
1962–1967, LI SERIES 3 150 SLIMLINE 1962–1967 ★★★

In 1961–1962, the bodywork of the Li and TV lines were redrawn. The new Slimline styling was sleek and angular with flash replacing the fleshy look of the earlier Lambrettas. The Slimline replaced the curvaceous Marilyn Monroe styling that characterized the 1950s Lambrettas with the thinner Twiggy look of the 1960s.

Power was now up as well: the 125 created 5.5hp whereas the 150 made 6.6hp. In 1963, Innocenti released the 150 Li Special with 8.25hp putting the machine at more than 95km/h. The 125 Li Special hit the market in 1965 and had 7.12hp to help the scooter reach the impressive 86km/h.

LAMBRETTA TV 175 SERIES 3 SLIMLINE
1962–1965 ★★★★

The TV3 wore the new go-fast Slimline styling over a high-performance 8.7hp engine and front hydraulic dampers for a smoother ride. With the TV3, a 20mm Dell'Orto replaced the late TV2's 21mm.

The TV3 dropped anchor with a mechanical disc front brake that pressed a full-circle pad against the rotor via the cable-operated hand lever. The rotor was prone to uneven wear or warping if heated by continual use.

The Lambretta's disc brake was an early use of what was considered a radically new—as well as complex and untrustworthy—braking system. The first use of disc brakes on a motorcycle was on the 1957 Maserati motorcycle; the first use on a scooter was the optional disc brake offered in 1961 on the American-made Midget Motors Autocycle. Still, the TV3's disc brake was the best-known system and the most influential, leading the way for motorcycle and automakers in the mid-1960s.

LAMBRETTA TV 200 (GT 200) 1963–1965
★★★★★

The TV 200, aka GT 200 for Gran Turismo, was a TV3 hot-rodded with a 200cc engine with an overbore of 66x58mm fathering 12hp at 6200rpm and reaching a top speed of more than 70mph or 113km/h. This high-performance TV was created for the large and enthusiastic British market, and specifically for the Isle of Man Scooter Rally, the most important scooter rally in Europe in the late 1950s.

The GT soon replaced the 175cc Lambretta in Britain, and was not initially available in any other market. It was built in relatively small numbers, only 14,982 units.

LAMBRETTA 150 LI SPECIAL PACEMAKER
1963–1966; 125 LI SPECIAL 1965–1969;
150 SPECIAL X (SX 150) AND 200 SPECIAL X
(SX 200) 1966–1969 ★★★★

The Li Special and Special X Series were performance versions of the basic DL line that carried the hot image of the Turismo Veloce. In 1968, three Pacemakers, as the 7.1hp 150 Li Special was termed in Britain, swept first through third places in the Isle of Man Scooter Rally.

By 1969, the 125cc was up to 7.4hp, the updated 150cc was at 9.4hp, and the hot-rod 200 SX created 11hp. The SX series rode on 3.50x10in tires and the 200 SX featured a revised version of the TV3 mechanical front disc brake.

LAMBRETTA DL 125, DL 150, AND DL 200
1969–1971 ★★

The De Luxe (or Di Lusso) Series updated the Li Series and soldiered on as Innocenti's no-frills commuter scooter. Power for the 125 was up to 7.4hp whereas the 150 created 9.4hp. The 200, meanwhile, had only 7.3hp but retained the disc brake and used electronic Ducati ignition.

With the DL, Innocenti created an updated bodywork styling with racing stripes on the side panels and a rectangular headlamp. The DL line continued through to Innocenti's decision to end scooter production in 1971.

LAMBRETTA 50, CENTO, J50 20/1, J98, AND J125 1961–1966; J125 STAR STREAM 1966–1969
★★

At the 1961 Milan Show, Innocenti bowed a prototype 50cc economy scooter, which it followed with a 100cc production version, named the Cento, first shown at the 1961 Amsterdam Show. The line was based on a unitized steel monocoque chassis fitted with a vertical-cylinder engine, three-speed gearbox, and chain drive to the rear wheel. The Cento pumped out 4.7hp at 5300.

Later in 1961, the Cento gave way to the J, or Junior, Series with 49.8cc, 98cc, and 122.5cc versions. In 1966, the three-speed J125 was upgraded with a much-needed fourth gear and built primarily for export as the Star Stream.

LUNA SERIES: LUI 50CC, LUI CL, LUI 75S, VEGA 75CC AND COMETA 75CC
1968–1971 ★

The famous Italian designer Bertone slimmed the space age lines on this new Innocenti series. In spite of other beautiful projects he accomplished, these scooters' designs insulted the earlier classic Lambrettas. The 49.8cc Lui, meaning "he" in Italian, debuted in 1968 with 2.5hp. In the same year, the 75cc Vega was released with a 5.2hp at 6000rpm and a top speed of 55mph (89km/h). Although not exceptionally attractive, the elevated boy and fast engine rivaled the Vespa 90SS on the race track. The 75cc Cometa possessed a special feature called the Lubematic system, boasting a separate oil pump that automatically mixed the two-stroke oil with the gas.

LAMBRETTA LN125 2012–2013 ★

After numerous promises and false starts, the new Lambretta finally made its debut in 2017 with a design based on the Slimline series—not the wider and equally classic Series II. These single-cylinder, four-stroke Lambrettas were the first new scooters to carry that label for decades, but purists were skeptical.

Yes, many modern modifications ensure a smoother ride, but gone are the days of controlling your ride with a clutch and gears. The automatic twist-and-go gears don't ensure that you can blow by souped-up café racers off the line. Still, the paint job is colorful, and the side panels are actually metal. The realities of the market made production in Taiwan necessary, but what would this Lammie be if it had been a fully Italian-produced new Lambretta?

LAMBRETTA V-SPECIAL 2017–PRESENT ★

This Lambretta reboot is definitely a step up from the 2012 version with a 50, 125, and 200cc version. (Rumors even tell of a 300cc version in the making).

Most important, many of the infamous Lambretta quirks are gone because the scooter borrows many, if not most, of its parts from the SYM Fiddle. Even so, the Austrian (KTM) and Swedish (Husqvarna) designers tried to stay as true to the original Slimline lines as possible, despite this being a Taiwanese-built Lambretta.

Rather than the bright colors of Mod scooters or even the 2012 LN125, the V-Special went with "the fashionable hard colours of the current era like lead, brown and orange." Well, at least the company thought of those who love two-tone scooters and produced "Carbon+" sets to Mod-out the Lammie with aftermarket bodywork. As of 2021, these new Lambrettas only were in the European market.

ABOVE:

Oodles of Scooters
Just the scooter for the dapper man about town: the Lambretta Li125 had class, styling, and a single-cylinder 125cc two-stroke engine. Vittorio Tessera archives

RIGHT:

Super Lambretta
Badged as a Lambretta, the Grand Prix series was built by Scooters India and not Innocenti, who offered its SX series as competition. This GP 200 was exported throughout the world into the 1980s, offering a high-performance scooter in the best Lambretta tradition. The engine was based on the influential Li, now at 198cc and pumping out 12.4 hp for an astonishing 71 mph or 114 km/h top speed. The racing stripes were essential at those speeds.

Iso ITALY

Iso's history followed the ups and downs of the Italian postwar economy in textbook fashion. Isothermos of Bresso near Milan—changed in 1948 to Iso Automotoveicoli SpA—entered the scooter market in 1948 with a background not in aviation, as did Piaggio, but in refrigerators.

Like Enrico Piaggio and Ferdinando Innocenti, Iso owner Renzo Rivolta saw the need for economical transportation. After the success of the Iso scooter and along with the country's gradual recovery, Iso developed the Isetta minicar—a stepping stone to a full-sized car such as the Fiat 500. The Isetta—which was truthfully inspired by a watermelon—was never a production success for Iso but was licensed throughout the world, including to its most famous maker, BMW.

With the Isetta royalties, Iso created a gran turismo car line—the Iso Rivolta, Grifo, Fidia, and Lele—to do battle with Ferrari. And at the company's zenith, it failed along with the economy in the mid-1970s recession.

FURETTO 1948–1949 ★ ★

Iso's first scooter was the 65cc Furetto, which goes down in history as the scooter that so enraged Rivolta that he dug a big hole and buried his own Furetto as deep as possible. The Furetto inspired Rivolta to build a better scooter.

ISOSCOOTER AND ISOMOTO 1949–1956 ★ ★

In 1950, Iso baptized the Isoscooter and Isomoto, both sharing the same specifications of a 125cc two-stroke split-single-cylinder engine based on a Puch design. The engine had two bores of 38mm and a single stroke of 55mm creating 6.7hp at 5200rpm backed by three speeds. The Isoscooter went through three series with slight updates, for example to simplify changing tires. Despite its name, the Isomoto was half scooter, half motorcycle with ample, 3.00x12in tires and substantial bodywork. The Isoscooter was all scooter but with awkward, homely styling.

ISO DIVA (MILANO) 1957–1960 ★ ★ ★ ★

In 1957, Iso created its masterpiece, the Diva scooter, also known in export countries as the Milano. The styling was graceful with bodacious, flowing curves from the front fender to the side covers. The look was half Vespa, half Lambretta TV1; the effect was inspiring.

The Diva's engine was a two-stroke 146cc single of a square 57x57mm. With four speeds, 6.5hp at 5000rpm was possible. Like a Vespa, the Diva had one-sided lug axles holding the wheels and 3.50x10in tires.

Like the TV Lambretta, the Diva was a large-bore luxury scooter designed for touring. The scooter market had grown from basic, boring transportation to buyers with extra cash in their pockets and free time to spend; they wanted a scooter that could take them to the beach on holiday as well as about town. The Lambretta TV, Vespa GS, and the Iso Diva were the scooters of a new Italy.

Through the years, Iso played a key role in the postwar Italian recovery as one of the largest Italian scooter manufacturers, although its two-wheeled vehicles are virtually unknown in the rest of the world. But by the 1960s, Iso had forsaken the scooter market to concentrate on building gran turismo cars. It was a sad day for scooter aficionados.

Italemmezeta ITALY ★ ★

Leopoldo Tartarini is famed with building perhaps the first plastic scooter ever in 1964. Italemmezeta's Scooter 50 had a little 48cc MZ motor from West Germany, so it needed the lightest possible scooter to push. Tartarini ushered in the plastic scooter age and continued the tradition as Italemmezeta became Italjet.

Italjet ITALY ★

The Italjet firm was formed in Bologna in 1966 by famed racer Leopoldo Tartarini. Besides building numerous racing and sports bikes, Italjet built the Pack-A-Way in 1969, a fold-up 50cc scooter. The Pack-A-Way, sometimes just called the "Pack," was designed to be stowed away in the trunk of a car and unfolded for city driving. Italjet raves the Pack was the first fold-up scooter—a claim obviously refuted by many other makers from the 1920s on. Regardless, the MOMA (Museum of Modern Art) in New York put the Pack on permanent display as part of Italian design

In the late 1980s and into the 1990s, Italjet offered three plastic scooters for three different careers: the Shopping, Reporter, and Bazooka, all based on 49cc two-stroke engines.

Iso Diva

Iso's scooter masterpiece was its Diva, introduced in 1957 and known in some parts of the world as the Milano. Although largely forgotten today, in the 1950s Iso competed head on with Innocenti and Piaggio for the scooter buyer; Iso had more than 2,500 concessionaires and scooter service stations in Italy and Europe. Iso had come a long way from making refrigerators.

The most revolutionary scooter of the early 1990s, however, was the Velocifero. As one of the first scooters to re-adapt the classic rotund Vespa styling of the 1940s and '50s. The success of the scooter put other marques on notice that much of the public didn't care for miniature sport bikes but wanted a rehash of Corradino d'Ascanio's original vision.

At the 1992 Bologna show, Italjet announced a collaboration with Hyosung of Taiwan and displayed its Cruise scooter, a rolling sculpture of plastic.

Plans in 2004 were unfolded for another maxiscooter on the market, the Marcopolo with a powerful 500cc engine with automatic transmission travelling on 17in wheels. More shocking is the Italjet Scooop as a hybrid between a scooter and a three-wheeler. Two wheels on the front of the space pod make it impossible to tip and give worried parents a piece of mind when junior hits the road.

James UK ★

James of Greet concentrated on building lightweight utility motorcycles, so it was only natural that the firm should try its hand at a scooter. James scooter debuted in 1960 based on an AMC 149cc two-stroke with a horizontal cylinder allowing it to be mounted directly under the floorboards. This also placed the spark plug inches behind the front wheel and in a direct line for mud and water spray, symbolic of the James' trouble-prone existence.

In 1963, the James scooter, designated the SC1, was updated to a four-speed gearbox, becoming the SC4. The scooter lasted until James' demise in 1966.

J. B. Volkscooter USA-GERMANY ★

The Volkscooter was planned as a two-wheeled version of the four-wheeled success of the 1960s, the Volkswagon. Two models were offered in 100cc and 125cc form. But part of the VW's success was due to Hitler's support; the Volkscooter lacked Hitler's endorsement and never made a dent in the volks' market.

Jet JAPAN ★★

Taking on the lines of the Mitsubishi Silver Pigeon and Fuji Rabbit, Jet built a total of 13,029 scooters primarily for the Japanese market from 1951 to 1956. To push its hefty 250cc J-7 on the Japanese market, Sumo wrestlers rode without crushing the metal puttputts with their folds of fat.

Jialing CHINA ★

Made by Guangdong Jialing Motorcycle Company, these scooters come mostly as 125cc in both gas and electric.

Jiangsu Dalong Jianhao

CHINA ★

You could be forgiven for confusing the seemingly endless array of Chinese scooter manufacturers with similar names. Here, the brand's name just rolls off the tongue: Jiangsu Dalong Jianhao New Energy Industry Company Limited, which makes the Yizhu gasoline-powered scooters.

Jianshe CHINA ★

These brightly colored little plastic scooters are 50cc for the most part and are run by an electric engine.

Jinan Dalong CHINA ★

Different models of the Xianfeng scooter were built both by Taizhou and Jinan Dalong Motorcycle Company.

Jinan Qingqi CHINA ★

Qingqi began in 1956 with its first moped/motorcycle and soon worked with Suzuki to make its motorcycles and scooters. The TB50 from 1987 was essentially a Suzuki Love. The company focused on the motorcycle and boasted that in 1999 it officially became "Famous Trademark in China." By 2006, the company entered a partnership with Peugeot and used both its base in Japanese technology from Suzuki and

Many-Splendored Velociferos
Midnight Black, Salmon, Seafoam Green, Cobalt Blue, British Racing Green, Bordeaux, and Citrus Yellow were the two-toned color schemes available for Italjet's Velocifero based on Piaggio's classic

now French expertise as well. Cheap labor in China allowed the company to sell many modern Qingqi scooters into France as Peugeots and into the UK as Sinnis, with the retro-styled Encanto and the more modern 50cc Twist and 125cc Shuttle.

Jincheng CHINA ★

Following the line of other Chinese plastic scooters, Jincheng manufactures both gasoline- and electric-powered bikes with that lean-forward look to appear to go fast even when halted in excruciating Beijing traffic. A notable departure is the JC-1TDR167Z (not exactly a catchy name), with a look like a cute pink Pokémon.

Jinyi CHINA ★

The Jinyi Vehicle Industry Company built the Jinyi, Jinfu, Yufeng, and Shuangqiang scooters that follow the standard sport models with gasoline engines. A notable exception is the JF125T, which has a more classic look in bright colors, including pink.

JoeBe USA-GERMANY ★

Joe Berliner's JoeBe line of scooter were actually Glas Goggo-Isaria scooters featuring the Glas emblem on the army helmet-styled front fender and the JoeBe script emblem on the legshields.

Jonghi FRANCE ★★

The brainchild of Italian designer Giuseppe Remondini, the Jonghi scooter sported a similar look to the Guzzi Galletto without the spare tire in front of the legshield. Perhaps tired of other scooter makers using its engines for themselves, Jonghi jumped into the game.

Jonghi refused to lower itself to the apparently pejorative appellation of "scooter" for its vehicle, never mind that the name "Jonghi" is bad enough. "A motorcycle conceived as an automobile," the firm boasted to deaf ears. In spite of all this vanity, the Jonghi made a decent, if ultimately unsuccessful, scooter riding on 19in spoked wheels.

Jonway CHINA ★

With both gas and electric engines, Jonway scooters are made by the Zhejiang Jonway Motorcycle Company. The 50cc and 150cc models use the same engines as Kymco and SYM, whereas the large 250cc engines are exclusively on the Linhai and Roketa models.

Junak POLAND ★

The Motorower Junak e-Vintage had a distinct chrome Nike swoosh from its legshield to floorboard. That said, it inevitably evoked comparisons

to the new Vespa, just as the Soviet Vjatka copied the classic Vespa behind the Iron Curtain. The 50cc and 125cc versions offer a sporty electric engines with all the extras, or as the ad copy put it, "tarczowe hamulce, które zasługują na pochwałę" ("the disc brakes deserve praise").

Juneng CHINA ★

Juneng Motorcycle Technology Company offered 75cc to 125cc gasoline-powered scooters. While most are the typical modern look, the Bravo line (in 50cc to 150cc) is an obvious nod (or "borrowing") of Piaggio's new Vespa design. Perhaps this is why it is named the Evasion model.

Kawasaki JAPAN ★★

Although Kawasaki is known for its famous motorcycles, in 1954 it tried to make a dent in the scooter market with a 60cc two-stroke that rode on large, spoked wheels. Only 200 of the model were made before Kawasaki realized that small motorcycles were its calling.

With the scooter boom of the 2000s, Kawasaki reentered the scooter market with its J125 and J300 in bizarrely titled colors: Metallic Moondust Gray, Metallic Flat Anthracite Black and Candy Flat Blazed Green. Wow. The bikes are more of a step-through motorcycle than a full-on scooter.

Keen Power Cycle USA ★★★

The Keen Power Cycle was first offered by the Keen Manufacturing Company of Madison, Wisconsin, in 1936 as a basic step-through scooter following Salsbury's contagious design. Power was a ½hp Lauson engine with direct drive and no clutch. By 1939, four models were available based on a two-speed transmission. As a 1936 flyer asked, "Can you think of anything more thrilling?"

By the early 1940s, the manufacturing rights were sold to the J. A. Strimple Company of Janesville, Wisconsin, which carried on the legend.

To meet the onslaught of Nazi Germany's panzer divisions head on, the Strimple Company created a military Keen Power Cycle. The Tiger tank had 23,000cc twelve-cylinder engine and 88mm cannon;

Kawasaki Prototype
Known more for enduros and motocross, Kawasaki tried to enter the scooter market in 1954 with its KB2 prototype. Alas, the sukuta, Japanese for scooter, lacked the umph to appeal to a Japanese youth market obsessed with speed. Courtesy of the François-Marie Dumas Archives

the Keen had a Lauson 8.9ci (146cc) single-cylinder engine and a bathtub-like sidecar to hide in.

Strimple's scooter still followed in the design style of the Motor Glide almost to a tee. But military requirements dictated aspects of the design, such as the 6x6in wheels, interchangeable with USAAF spotter aircraft. The US Army tested the Keen with sidecar in January 1944 and it was procured in limited numbers.

Keeway CHINA ★

Qianjiang (QJ) scooters originally came with two-stroke engines but switched to 50 and 150cc four-strokes.

Kenilworth UK ★★★

Propelled by a 142cc four-stroke Norman engine, the Kenilworth was built by the Booth Bros. ltd. in Coventry. This early scooter had large diameter wheels, a seat (unlike the Autoped), and was born around 1920 and survived until 1925.

Kieft UK ★★

In 1955, Kieft of Wolverhampton jumped into the scooter world with a 200cc model with electric starter to bring the two-stroke Sachs engine to life. While the clutch was operated by the left handlebar control, a left-foot rocker switched gears. All appendages of the scooterist were utilized since the right handlebar controlled the front brake and the right foot pedal controled the rear. Nevertheless, "the scooter, which, irrespective of technicalities of the kind that interest pukka motorcyclists, surely cannot fail to sell on its good-appearance value," raved Motor Cycling in 1955 about the Kieft scooter with "eyeability" and "advanced Continental design."

Kinetic INDIA/JAPAN ★

This joint venture began as Kinetic Honda in 1984 with the Japanese scooters made in India. Honda's revolutionary automatic transmission and electric ignition proved popular, but Honda pulled out in 1998. Kinetic ceased operations in 2008.

Kingsbury UK ★★★★

This early scooter from London took the design of the American Autoped and moved the two-stroke 150cc engine from the side of the front wheel to behind the driving column. This improved the stability on the Kingsbury scooter produced by a British aviation company.

KR SOUTH KOREA ★

KR Motors began as part of Hyosung, which produced Suzuki motorcycles—Japanese bikes for the Korean market. Hyosung mostly made powerful motorcycles but jumped into the scooter market in the 2000s with four-stroke engines, with everything from the Exceed to the Grantus 125.

Kreidler GERMANY ★

Although little more than a moped, the Kreidler R50 was definitely "ein Roller mit Charme." Located in Kornwesteim, Kreidler at one time produced more motorcycles than any other company in Germany. In 1953, it grew into the scooter business after making the K50 and K51 mopeds. The Union of Bicycle and Motorcycle Industry (VFM) restricted the maximum speed to less than 25mph in 1955, so in 1956 Kreidler released the R50 scooter with the same 49cc two-speed engine as its moped. The scooter had 2.5hp for a top speed of 50km/h, but added a pillion seat, smaller 19in wheels, an enlarged rear fender, and an enclosed engine, thereby constituting a scooter.

According to publicity material from Kreidler, "Women prefer this scooter because it meets your wishes for a well-groomed, well-cultivated exterior without lacking a sporty, elegant feel. To go with this scooter gives one a feeling of being chic and charming."

Kroboth GERMANY ★★★

Second only to Maico Mobil for outrageous design but unfortunately much less common, the Kroboth 100 of 1951–1955 was surrounded with a gigantic front fender and numerous air ducts in the paneling, giving it the appearance of a forklift with no lifting ability. The Kroboth had many attributes of an enclosed motorcycle, but it still had the small wheels, floorboard, and leg protection of scooters that is also an attribute of all the finest tanks.

1945 Keen Power Cycle
First weld a metal box to some tubes, drop in a 1/2 hp Lauson engine (skip the clutch), and borrow some of junior's 6-inch wagon wheels. Paint it blue and call it "Keen." This later four-cycle, two-speed wonder from Madison, Wisconsin, was nothing to be scoffed at, however, with an expanded 3 hp Lauson motor the Keen lasted through the war with its parent company (then Strimple of Janesville) making tanks. Ad copy claimed not just transportation, but existential bliss since Power Cycles "actually cast monotony and every-day cares 'to the winds'" Eat your heart out Albert Camus. **Courtesy of the owner: Jim Kilau**

The Kroboth scooters all used Fichtel & Sachs engines, and the Truxa's 175cc motor was strong enough to carry a sidecar. The Truxa's style had 9hp for a top speed of 85km/h whereas the 100 achieved 3hp for 60km/h and the Cabrio of 1951–1955 upped it with 6.5hp for 75km/h. The design of the Truxa of 1953–1955 was considerably refined from the bar functionalism of the earlier Kroboth scooters.

Krupp GERMANY ★★★★

Back in the 1910s, Krupp made copies of the American Autoped with a 185 or 198cc engine.

KSR AUSTRIA ★

"Classic without kitsch" boasts the ad copy, so the Italian style doesn't have any gaudy two-tone but the Classic 50 and 125 comes in matte black with a four-stroke engine to comply with European emission standards. Other models, such as the Cruzer, Quip, Generic, and TTX come in various sizes and some electric bikes too.

KTM AUSTRIA ★★

Known mostly for its motocross bikes, KTM made an attempt at scooters with the 49cc Mecky in 1957. The two-tone scooter looked like the real thing up front, but the presence of pedals gave away that it could only manage 40km/h. A new Mecky was released in 1962 with a 50cc Sachs motor to push the scooter along on its 12in wheels.

Kumpan GERMANY ★★

The Kumpan electric scooters don't cut corners. The more expensive models have all the bells and whistles of the high-end Vespas, plus all the touch-screen technology, ABS, and halogen lights. This Teutonic reliability comes at a cost, however, but Kumpan scooters can fit up to three batteries for long trips to Italy and boast a top speed of 100 km/h (62 mph). While touring through pastoral Alpine passes in Bavaria, just remember Kumpan's utopian environmental vision: Kumpan ist unsere gelebte Vision einer grünen, vernetzten Mobilität der Zukunft! ("Kumpan is our lived vision of a green, networked mobility of the future!").

Kymco Taiwan ★

Established in 1963, Kyong Yang Motor Corporation, or Kymco for short, had already produced more than three million little two-strokes within two decades. "Looking over the past, we must attribute our accomplishments today to the hard work of all Kymco employees, now and then," Kymco brochures proclaim as though their labor force doesn't always work so hard. No wonder this Asian marvel offers a large line of plastic putt-putts including the "Grand Dink," which could produce quite an uproar if it lands on the US market.

While not quite as sport-bike looking as the other new scooters on the racetrack, Kymco's ZX50 still has the downward angular slant that gives it go-fast lines even when parked at WalMart. The price on Kymco's scooters are relatively cheap for these 49cc oil-injected two-strokes.

The more classic lines are left for the People scooters that are reminiscent of Aprilia's Scarabeo, which is in turn a copy of Guzzi's Galletto. Translators for Kymco's scooter names to English must moonlight on early Jackie Chan Hong Kong Kung Fu movies. Apart from the long line of Dinks, Kymco has the Bet & Win, the Yup (for yuppie or yes?), the Movie, the DJ Refind, and a series of active names: Vitality, Agility and Xciting.

LaRay USA ★★

LaRay Cycle of Los Angeles was a bicycle builder that decided to try its hand at the fledgling scooter market, offering its LaRay scooter in the late 1930s.

Lacombe FRANCE ★

Presented for the first time in 1948, the FL 22 of Les Etablissements Comindus (Lacombe) seemed to have forgotten that scooters had made huge steps forward. The FL 22 was an ABC Skootamota replica thirty years after its debut. Armed with a 49cc P. P. Roussey two-stroke engine, this sidewalk scooter could reach 40km/h since it only weighed 28kg. Built by M. F. Lacombe who gave his initials to the scooter, but also gave it the important-sounding Latinate name "Comindus," as if this scooter were the new Caesar.

Lance USA/TAIWAN ★

Some SYM scooters produced in Taiwan are brought into the US as Lance scooters with tropical names such as Cabo, Havana, and the Cali Classic.

Laverda ITALY ★★

The Laverda family began building agricultural engines and farm machinery in Breganze in the 1830s. Founded near Vicenza, a town famous for its recipes for cat during the lean times of WWII and beyond, Laverda formed in 1948 and established a distinguished motorcycle racing history.

The Laverda Mini-Scooter made its debut at the 1959 Milan Fiera Campionaria with a diminutive four-stroke 50cc engine measuring 40x39mm with a two-speed gearbox shifted by twist grip. The Mini-Scooter was designed to meet a 1959 Italian regulation lifting taxes on one-rider 50cc mopeds and scooters that were a maximum of 1.5hp and 40km/h top speed. Ignition was by flywheel magneto and the scooter rode atop dwarf 2.75x9in tires.

Laverda followed Piaggio's lead in creating a unit body-chassis from stressed steel. The styling was simple; the scooter was so small there was little room for flourishes. A single saddle seat sat atop the engine and gas tank.

In 1962, Laverda decided its 40km/h top speed was not enough. A third gear was added to the transmission, and with tuning work to the 50cc engine, power was up to 2.5hp at 6000rpm for a top speed of 57km/h.

Along with the 50cc version, a 60cc model was added in 1962 based on a larger, 47mm bore delivering 3hp at 6000rpm for a 65km/h top speed. The 60cc model was dressed up by a modern two-person bench seat with Wild West fringe around the edging, spare wheel with vinyl cover, and small luggage rack.

The Mini-Scooter never took Laverda far. Piaggio and Innocenti controlled the market and left little room for others. Laverda, however, struck an exportation deal to bring great numbers of its scooter into Great Britain.

Ironically, the most successful Vespa of all time would be the 50cc Vespina, also introduced in 1962. Piaggio's might was far greater than Laverda's; it was modern-day story of David and Goliath warring on motorscooters.

In 2000, the Laverda brand appeared for four years on rebadged Chinese scooters.

Lefol FRANCE ★

In 1954, La Sociéte Lefol et Cie released its Scoot-Air as a civilian parachutist's fold-up scooter. Made of lightweight metal and moved by a 98cc Comet engine, the Scoot-Air dissembled into three pieces to make sky diving a snap.

LeJay USA ★★★

The LeJay Electric Rocket was the world's first electric motorscooter, arriving on the scene in 1939 from LeJay Manufacturing of Minneapolis, Minnesota. LeJay's kit added an electric motor to a Motor Glide-inspired scooter chassis that beat them all in economy and operation: 100 miles for 5 cents, according to ads. But there was no mention of how far the batteries would last.

Lenoble BELGIUM ★★

Lenoble had factories in Brussels and Charleroi where in 1952 it made its Kon-Tiki scooter, in honor of Thor Heyerdahl's reed boat expedition. In spite of the inspired name, the Lenoble goes down in history as the scooter with the silliest bodywork. Styling looked like a coffin on wheels with a headlamp and windshield on top; power was from a 150cc two-stroke Sachs engine and four-speed gearbox.

In 1953, Lenoble was back with its Phenix scooter with Sachs 150cc and 175cc engines offered.

Lexmoto UK/CHINA ★

The British branch of the Chinese company Znen, Lexmoto is based in Exeter, bringing into the UK a line of modern scooters, including Yadea electric scooters. Most interesting was the Lexmoto Milano, essentially the same bike as the AJS Modena, as a retro Vespa (pre-PX series) at a good price. Yes, it may not be authentic, but why not?

Liberia FRANCE ★

Known more for its bicycles than scooters, Liberia from Grenoble decided to join the putt-putt battle in 1951 with a little scooter armed with a 98cc Sachs engine on 10in wheels. Not until 1954, however, did Liberia begin production in earnest of a covered moped named the Alouette after the bird and the song that it could use in songs. The little 2.75hp Alouette disappeared from Liberia's line at the end of 1955.

Lifan CHINA ★

Located in Chongquing, China, Lifan mostly builds automobiles but has dabbled in the world of wine and sport shoes. Its line of scooters are four-stroke, 125 and 150cc bikes for the sporting crowd.

Lohner's Sissy

While Lohner was more of a covered motorcycle than an actual scooter, no self-respecting rocker would be caught dead on one of these little putt-putts, especially with a name like "Sissy."

Lilac JAPAN ★★

The bulbous headlamp/dashboard/gas tank is the prominent feature of the 90 Lilac Baby SF from 1953. No legshields or covering hide the little engine, but nevertheless the Lilac still carries many scooter traits

Linhai CHINA ★

Offering the Aeolus scooters from 50cc to the giant 400cc, Linhai uses Yamaha technology that makes the larger scooters nearly indistinguishable from the Japanese brand's Majesty.

Linlong CHINA ★

Shanghai Jianshe Motorcycle Co. makes a 125cc gasoline-powered scooter with an oversized front fender.

Lohia (LML) INDIA ★★

Lohia Machinery Limited (LML) struck a deal with Piaggio in 1984 to produce Vespas. The partnership faded and eventually ended in 1999, but Lohia still produced the Star, which was sold as the Stella in the US, and a version finally made it into the UK once it complied with European emission standards.

The company released more modern scooters but finally declared bankruptcy in 2018 and dismantled the factory and sold everything in 2020.

Lohner AUSTRIA ★★

Lohner of Vienna showed its first scooter in 1951, the L98T with a 98cc Sachs two-stroke with two-speeds. In 1953, it offered its Super-Roller L200 with a Rotax 199cc of 62x66mm creating 8.3hp at 5000rpm via a Famo four-speed gearbox and 4x10in tires.

Lohner continued in 1956 with its Rapid 125 and 200 based on a Sachs 125cc and a Jlo 200. A Rapid 200 was also offered with an integral sidecar that was built into the bodywork of the scooter. This fantastic duo of scooter and sidecar formed an aerodynamic three-wheeler with full windshields and smooth bulbous surfaces all around.

In 1957, Lohner returned with its Sissy, a motorcycle in miniature with full bodywork and power from a Sachs 47cc and three speeds.

Loncin CHINA ★

Its four-stroke, air-cooled scooters are built in China and then distributed around the world with new Italian-sounding names such as Zanella in Argentina or Italika in Mexico. Manufactured by Longxin Motorcycle Industry Co., these scooters managed to make it into Russia as the Minsk and into Ukraine as the ominous Viper.

Longjia CHINA ★

Clearly going for the Dolce Vita vibe in its advertising, Ningbo Longjia Motorcycle Company has its share of multicolored mini sport scooters with names like Grido, meaning "shout" or "cry." Still, its brightly colored Estate (summer) is a bit more fun in a four-stroke 50cc or 125cc engine. The Insetto (insect) clearly wishes it were a full-fledged wasp (*vespa*). These are rebranded as TNT and sold in France and several other countries.

Lowther Manufacturing Company USA ★★

Lowther of Joliet, Illinois built a wide range of motorscooters in the 1940s, which the company called "The 'Park Avenue' Scooter with the 'Main Street' price" in a 1948 flyer.

Lowther offered each model with a wide variety of "artistically created" body styles and a range of engine sizes, spawning a whole variety of scooters. The Stylemaster was an Art Deco vision on two wheels with read and black two-tone paint and a massive chrome Jet Age bumper on the rear that looked like a cowcatcher or 'roo bar gone wrong. It came in three bodies and with 3hp, 4hp, and 6hp.

The Lightin' was "as stylish as next year's fashion," according to a 1948 dealer letter. Power came from a Briggs & Stratton 4.5hp or 6.7hp engine; a rear hydraulic brake from a Plymouth car did the stopping. Two versions were available: the Model 600ZZ1-P Airflow and the 600ZZ2-P Playboy. A sidecar with 16cu-ft carrying capacity was optional. The three-wheeled Commercial came in an array of six bodies with 4, 6, and 8hp engines.

Lowther also sold its scooters to Indian, who rebadged them as its own line.

Lucciola ITALY ★

Armed with a 48cc Ducati Cucciolo four-stroke engine, the Lucciola (firefly in Italian) was a bare-bones fold-up scooter from Oscar Manzione in Naples. In spite of the spartan design, the firefly still weighed anywhere from 25 to 35kg.

Lumen FRANCE ★★★

In 1919 and 1920, the Etablissements Lumen of Paris based their scooter on the ABC Skootamota but had a little carpet on the floorboard and larger wheels for more stability. The Lumen used a four-stroke engine of 143cc with the single cylinder nearly horizontal. Even though the handlebars were larger than the Skootamota, the top speed was only 20-25km/h compared to the ABC's 40km/h.

The 'Park Avenue' Scooter with the 'Main Street' price

The LOWTHER STYLEMASTER

THE THRILL RIDE OF 1949 LOWTHER LIGHTNIN'

TOP:

Park-Avenue Stylemaster
While tame compared to the outrageous Lightnin' scooter, the Lowther Stylemaster still carried an eye-catching two-tone and oversized rear metal bumper when Tin Lizzies tailgate a bit too close. Courtesy of the Herb Singe archives

BOTTOM:

Lowther Lightnin'
With a design unique to the scooter world, the Lightnin' seemed more like a covered pony with monkey bars than a putt-putt. In brochures, Lowther put the woman in the front with the Fedora-toting dude hanging on in back. Courtesy of the Herb Singe archives

Lutz GERMANY ★

"Economical" described the Lutz R3 scooter of 1949–1954 since the 58cc Lutz engine had only 1hp and a top speed of 40km/h. Styling, if it can be called that, was definitely unique with a triangular front fender and wire-mesh side panels instead of typical molded sheet metal. Four exposed front cables added to the spaghetti design of the R3.

Lutz made up for lost ground, however, with the R175 of 1951 of 1951–1954 with excessive rounded covering and dual seat, a design likely inspired by the fantasies of Dr. Seuss. The 174.3cc Lutz engine pumped out 6hp for a top speed of 75km/h on its petite 8in wheels.

Mahindra INDIA ★

See GenZe.

Maico GERMANY

"In the shadow of the Wurmling Chapel, made famous by the well-known song by Ludwig Unland, lies an extensive factory, animated by the spirit of progress, and staffed by men who take an intense pride in their work. This is the birthplace of Maico."
—1955 Maico Information Bulletin

Maico's publicity made the factory seem godsent. And judging from the dustbin design of the Maicomobil, some paranormal influences had to be at work. During World War II, the Fatherland turned to Maisch & Co.'s (aka Maico) aviation expertise to supply the Luftwaffe, while DKW, BMW, and Zündapp were in charge of motorcycles. Following the conflict, the factory ended up in the French section of a divided Germany where manufacturing aircraft parts was banned, and so Maico began making children's toys. Maico soon relocated to Herrenburg in the American sector where tools and materials were readily available to again produce motorcycles.

MAICO MOBIL MB 150 1951–1953;
MB 175 AND MB 200 1954–1958 ★★★★★

Maico's own brochures said it best: "With its latest product, the Maico-Mobil, Maico have introduced a completely novel type of machine which lies midway between the conventional motor cycle and the scooter; it may be that this will prove to be the true touring machine of the future."

While the micro-car fad swept Germany, Maico believed it could convince the public that two wheels were better than three for a touring vehicle. At the Reulingen Show in June 1950, Maico introduced its "car on two wheels" with a tank-like frame to support the armor-plated paneling, needed for weather protection and incorporated enough luggage space for a few suitcases. Its dashboard featured a speedometer that indicated the gear engaged, and a radio in the 1955 model.

Underneath the bodywork, the Maico Mobil was more a motorcycle than scooter due to its 14in wheels, duplex-tube frame with a crossbar between the rider's legs, telescopic front forks, and its sheer size.

The first Maico Mobil of 1951 was powered by a 148cc single-cylinder engine. The air-cooled two-stroke measured 57x58mm and fathered 6.5hp at 4800rpm via a three-speed gearbox, which was not quite enough power to push along its 115kg or 253lb mass. In 1954, Maico updated the Mobil with two new models, a 173cc (61x59.5mm) and 197cc (65x59.5mm) for 8.5hp and 10.9hp respectively with a new four-speed.

Not until the gigantic high-class German 197cc Maico Mobil hit the market would his illustriousness the King Hussein of Jordan be satisfied. (Just don't call the scooter its nickname "Dustbin" in his preeminent presence). The royals admitted that the Mobil provided motorcycle handling with scooter performance and weather protection with styling like the Hindenberg zeppelin on wheels.

MAICOLETTA M175 1955–1966 AND
MAICOLETTA M250 1956–1966 ★★★

The Maico design team of Pohl and Tetzlaff created the Maicoletta in secrecy in their basement away from the prying eyes of the cut-throat German scooter industry. It was unveiled at the 1955 Brussels Show, with classic scooter lines, although many of the Mobil's attributes carried over, such as the dashboard with an illuminated clock and the 14in wheels. Maico publicity bragged that "Even the most discerning rider will find that everything a modern scooter can offer in the way of comfort has been incorporated."

Although the Maicoletta's looks were undoubtedly scooterlike, several features such as the foot shifter, telescopic front forks, and hydraulic damping for the rear suspension gave it the advantages of a motorcycle. The powerful 174cc and 247cc engines gave 9hp and 14hp for top speeds of 85km/h and 105km/h. In autumn 1957, the Maicoletta was offered with a 277cc engine, one of the largest engines ever shoehorned into a scooter.

Maico underwent financial problems in 1987 from which even the shadow of the Wurmling Chapel couldn't protect it. By summer the factory was sold.

Maiolina ITALY ★

In 1949, Officina Meccanica Ciclotecnica Maioli produced a bare-bones little scooter on spoked moped tires propelled by a 48cc Alpino engine. The Microscooter Maiolina had scooter characteristics, such as the step-through design with a flat floorboard and two-stroke engine set under the saddle. Perhaps the name fell flat with the Italian public as it sounds painfully close to "maialina," or little sow.

Mako SWITZERLAND ★★

In 1953, Mako offered its scooter with a Jlo 125cc and three speeds. Styling almost replicated the Lambretta LC—even down to the two portholes on the side cover.

Malaguti ITALY ★

Malaguti originally made bicycles beginning in 1923, but then switched to scooters in 1965 with Lambretta-inspired designs. The Scooter 50 topped out at 40 km/h and even the angular design and the loss of the back rack of the 2nd Series of the Scooter 50 in 1967 could push it much faster.

At the same time as the Scooter 50, Malaguti released the Scooteretto with a Morini 48cc motor, but the look tended towards the covered mopeds. More interesting was the 1965 Gaucho scooter styled after the South American cowboys. The gaudy uncovered Gaucho sports a frilly fake leather seat with studded stars and matching pack in the back.

Malaguti kept in the game, though and made uncountable numbers of mopeds in the 1980s, 1990s,

and 2000s some with plastic legshields and enclosed bodywork. With an obvious hats-off to earlier Italian design, Malaguti unveiled the Yesterday with modern updates such as electronic ignition, no pesky shifting, and a front disc brake as first appeared on the Lambretta. Although the Yesterday may look classic, the fiberglass body and fake spare tire, that's actually a mini glovebox reveal the sheep under the wolves clothing.

The sport scooter in the new Malaguti line is the F12 Phantom Digit looking more like a donor bike/crotch rocket than a Lambretta. The liquid-cooled 50cc two-stroke is covered by a sharp F15-style plastic covering and digital dials on the dashboard bring the Phantom into the 21st century.

Malanca ITALY ★★

Following the sleek design of the Lambretta Series 2, Malanca released a diminutive version in 1962 dubbed the Vispetta, perhaps in hopes that people would mistake it for a small Vespa. A slightly updated Malanca scooter was offered in 1963 called the Super Vis with only slight modifications and a higher price tag.

Mammut GERMANY ★

In 1954, the 47kg Mammut Solo-Roller sported the coveted feature of wing bolts to hold on the side panels covering the 50cc Sachs or optional Jlo engine. Mammut-Vertriebsgeschaft of Bielefeld's scooter cruised to a 40km/h top speed on its 20in wheels.

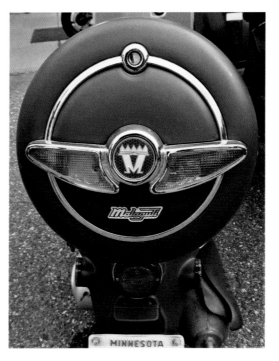

LEFT:

How I Long for Yesterday
Building on its storied history in bicycles and motorcycles, Malaguti entered the market with its nostalgic Yesterday to ride the scooter revival in the late 1990s. With the onslaught of Asian bikes, Malaguti began its slow decline.

RIGHT:

Fool Me Once . . .
The tire rack on the Malaguti Yesterday looks impressive and lends the idea that this scooter actually could go on road trips across the continent. Alas, it's a ruse! The tire rack was merely a plastic storage bin!

Manurhin FRANCE ★★

Known for its production of munitions, pistols, and other weapons of destruction, Manufacture du Haut-Rhin began producing a two-wheeled weapon, the MR 75 scooter, in 1957. Riding on 16in wheels, the MR 75 was a French version of the DKW Hobby scooter although many parts differed, such as the Gurtner carburetor instead of the German Bing, and a French Morel flywheel magneto, but the motor remained a 3hp DKW. In 1958, DKW joined the Zweirad Union at which time it gave up on the Hobby leaving Manurhin as the sole producer of the MR 75.

Mar-Max Products USA ★

In Salem, Ohio, Mar-Max built its Lil-Injun scooter in the 1960s with the good old Clinton 2.5hp two-stroke. The Lil-Injun was also available in do-it-yourself kit form; plans were $2.50.

Marinavia Farina ITALY ★★★★

The Marinella scooters claim to fame is that Pinin Farina designed the bulbous putt-putt. Pushed along by a 125cc two-cylinder two-stroke, the 1948 Marinella drew its inspiration from the Nibbio and other early makes.

Mars GERMANY ★

The Mars factory in Nürnberg originally made airplanes before turning to scooters in 1955 with its Stella 200 model. The Stella ran on a 175cc Sachs two-stroke engine giving it a hefty 9.5hp.

Martin-Moulet FRANCE ★★

The Martin-Moulet was the perfect briefcase for the commuter to work because thirty seconds later, abracadabra! it would transform into a scooter (albeit unattractive). Imagine carrying a small purse loaded with 25kg of gold bullion, now that's the Valmobile. The original prototype carried a 60cc Alter motor with a top speed of 50km/h on the miniscule wheels and by 1953 had changed to a 98cc British Villiers for 65km/h.

The Valmobile's Parisian designer, M. Victor-Albert Bouffort, proved his scooters worth by traveling from Paris to Geneva in a day, and from Paris to Madrid in three days. Produced by Martin-Moulet, this new round of Valmobiles were offered with two models, the 125B with a 125cc three-speed engine, and the 100 FS with a two-speed 98cc engine. Still, these scoots could carry two people and could be folded up in less than half a minute.

Production of the Valmobile was licensed to makers in the United States (called the Foldmobile), Japan, and Great Britain as well as tested by the French army for parachuting.

MAS ITALY ★

Known in the 1930s in Milan for its speedy motorcycles, MAS tested the waters with a 50cc scooter armed with a German Sachs engine in 1956. The two-tone paint scheme on large spoked motorcycle wheels couldn't save the scooter and caused the company to close its doors.

MBK ITALY ★

MBK of Gerno di Lesmo offered its CT50S and Booster scooters in the 1990s.

MBM ITALY ★★

Strangely, MBM of Bologna named its 48cc scooter "Maggiolino" (beetle) in 1961, even though the name was already widely used for the Volkswagon Beetle in Italy. The Lambretta-inspired scooter's biggest selling point was "Senza patente, senza targa" (without driver's license, without license plate) for the younger set to meet their friends in the piazza.

MDS ITALY ★

A builder of small-bore motorcycles, MDS also produced its Motoretta 65cc four-stroke scooter in 1955. While the uncovered bodywork made the scooter and esthetic mess, the little engine jet the scooter easily to 70 km/h. After one year, the Scoccimarro brothers gave up on this utilitarian scooter.

Mead Cycle Company USA ★★★

Mead of Chicago was established in 1889 by the Mead family and had long been famous for its balloon-tired Ranger bicycle, which went head to head against Chicago's Schwinn. When Schwinn turned to motorized bicycles with its Whizzer engine, the envious Mead firm followed suit.

Across town, Mead management had seen the Moto-Scoot of upstart manufacturer Norman Siegal. In 1938, Mead contracted with Siegal to build badge-engineered Moto-Scoots as the Mead Ranger scooter.

Throughout the Ranger's history, it would follow the style and specs of the Moto-Scoot, but sometimes with lesser features. The first Rangers of 1938 were basic step-through scooters with two speeds and 1hp engines good for 30mpg. Two models were initially offered: the basic 80-1 and the C-80-1, which added a clutch and kickstart.

The Ranger was available in the same variety of models as the Moto-Scoot from 1939 on but with different names. The 1½hp Standard line included the Model 100 Solo and 101 Carrier. The 1½hp De Luxe with Vari-Torque Drive featured the 103 Solo, 104 Carrier, and 105 Tandem. The 2½hp Rocket line was the 106 Solo, 107 Carrier, and 108 Tandem. The Rocket Special added the Vari-Torque Drive to the

Rockets and an S suffix to the model numbers. A Sidecar was advertised in Popular Mechanics ads as a three-wheel miniature auto.

Fuel consumption was always the key to 1930s scooter sales, and Mead ads usually headlined the figures. In 1938, the Ranger got 129mpg; by 1939, the Ranger was up to 130mpg, probably based on extensive engine reworking, or a reworking of arithmetic. As one Mead ad tantalized tourists: "Go across USA for $6.00 gas money!" There was no mention of how long the trip would take at 30mph top speed—never mind the Continental Divide.

Following World War II, the Ranger was extensively reworked along the lines of the new Moto-Scoot with a two-tiered rear bodywork design and a larger engine. By the 1950s, the Mead Rangers had ridden away into the sunset.

Meijer THE NETHERLANDS ★★★★

As one of the earliest scooter-type two-wheelers, the Meijer used a wicker chair for comfort and round steering wheel to turn the front wheel. Appearing first in 1908, the Meijer was pounded out by J. W. Meijer & Co. of Arnhem with a advanced front telescopic forks with suspension, but no front legshield. The large white-wall tires spun round large spoked wheels and a little floorboard made for an easy step-through design. No Meijers are known to have survived the years, but would surely fill in the gaps in any scooter museum.

Meister Fahradwerke GERMANY ★

In 1955, the Meister M41S boasted a 47cc Fichtel & Sachs engine, and was also sold under the brand names of Phenomenon and Mammut. The Meister scooterette used chrome to make up where styling left off, especially the hood ornament on the front fender of the 20in wheels with a chrome bust (a precursor to the bowling and baseball trophies on front fenders). The M41S had 1.5hp pushing the Meister to a top speed of 40km/h.

Mercier FRANCE ★

Known mostly for bicycle construction, Mercier started with scooters in 1954 with Le Vacances putt-putt for French holidaymakers to enjoy their five weeks of summer vacation. Powered with a two-stroke Comet 98cc Le Poulain (or "pupil"), Le Vacances had a sister with the same motor but was more of a moped named the Côte d'Azur for the rich Riviera jet set. Already by 1955, Le Vacances took time off from Mercier sales list.

Mercury UK ★

Mercury of Birmingham was another British bicycle builder that decided to construct a scooter. At the 1956 Earl's Court Show, it unveiled its Dolphin scooter with a Villiers 98cc two-stroke of a modest 2.9hp with a two-speed gearbox riding atop 2.50x8in tires. In 1957, Mercury added its Pippin scooter with the same mechanicals as the Dolphin and a face-lifted front fender.

Neither the Dolphin nor Pippin went far in the market, although attempts were made to export them to the United States.

Messerschmitt GERMANY ★★★

Following World War II, the famous aviation firm of Messerschmitt was restricted from building aircraft, so Fritz Fend's design of the Kabinen Roller, or Cabin Scooter, was put into production to keep the firm in business. The Kabinen Roller was a three-wheeled micro car that looked like little more than an overgrown scooter.

When Hoffman Vespa moved onto production of larger vehicles, Piaggio licensed Messerschmitt to manufacture Vespas beginning in 1955.

The German Vespas differed little from the Italian versions except for the Messerschmitt emblem added under the Vespa logo. Messerschmitt later produced seven different models of Vespas including the Gran Sport. By the mid-1960s, scooter sales were slowing so Piaggio opted to revoke Messerschmitt's diminishing scooter production and export Vespas to Germany from the Pontedara factory in Italy.

Meteora ITALY ★

Using a 49cc NSU Quickly engine or Demm motor, Meteora presented its Pony scooter with large wheelbase and bicycle pedals to rev it up. The public wasn't crazy for the covered moped with telescopic front forks and production didn't last much beyond its 1955 debut.

Mead Ranger
Post-World War II, the Mead Ranger returned with an odd two-tiered rear section with gothic styling; why the louvers were needed as well as the open section was not clear. Mead continued to offer its badge-engineered Moto-Scoot into the 1950s.

VESPA MESSERSCHMITT GMBH
AUGSBURG

Vespa G.S.

Messerschmitt Vespa
The sleek lines of the GS make it the quintessential Vespa and arguably the best scooter ever put into production. In a wise business move, Piaggio eventually pulled Messerschmitt's production license to keep Piaggio's heads above water during the years of waning scooter sales of the 1960s.

MFB-Telaimotor ITALY ★

With a strange moniker like Telaimotor (frame-motor), MFB produced its Scooter in 1957. By 1960, a two-stroke 75cc engine was plopped under the cowling.

Micro Manufacturing USA ★

From Tulsa, Oklahoma, the Micro Cycle MC-3 Rebel was a mini-bike with a 6hp engine available in the 1960s.

Midget Motors Corporation
USA ★

The aptly named Midget Motors built its Autocycle in the 1960s in Athens, Ohio. Styled like a Mustang or Cushman Eagle, power was 5hp from a four-stroke engine and two-speed gearbox with passing gear. Amazingly, disc brakes were optional on the Autocycle as early as 1961 as well as a 12 volt electrical system and electric starter.

Militaire USA ★ ★ ★

While jury is still out on whether the Militaire fits into the realm of scooters, this step-through vehicle was important in the refinement of the scooter. Built in the 1910s in Cleveland, Ohio, the Militaire's design avoided the bulky gas tank between the legs and improving stability.

Minerva-Van Hauwaert
BELGIUM ★ ★

The old Antwerp firm of Minerva was sold in the 1950s to Van Hauwaert of Brussels; the new firm of-fered its Minerva scooter in 1953 with a 150cc two-stroke of 9.5hp. At the same 1953 Brussels show, it also displayed a prototype "triscooter" based on the Minerva with two front wheels and two seats covered by bodywork. In 1954, the firm launched its Motoretta scooter with a Jlo 175cc two-stroke.

Minneapolis USA ★

The Minneapolis firm offered its 2.75hp Sportster scooter in the late 1950s.

Mitsubishi JAPAN ★ ★ ★ ★

During World War II, Mitsubishi was one of several builders of the Zero-San for the Japanese air force. Like Piaggio, postwar Mitsubishi turned its talents in aircraft structural engineering to the field of motorscooters. Fuji had built Japan's first scooter in 1946 and Mitsubishi followed its lead, introducing its first in 1948. From the late 1940s and into the 1960s, Fuji and Mitsubishi would control the Japanese scooter market as a Far Eastern Piaggio-Innocenti zaibatsu duo.

The Japanese appetite for scooters was as strong as the Italians. In 1946, only eight scooters were built in Japan, all by Fuji; by 1954, more than 450,000 scooters were on the road with the country's total production at 50,000 annually. By 1958, total annual production was 113,218.

Mitsubishi named its scooter "the Pigeon" from its debut in 1948 with the 115cc C-11 two-stroke. The styling was pure Motor Glide, following the design tenets set down by the Americans in 1936 almost to a tee. The engine was 57x44mm bore and stroke, creating 1.5hp at 3500rpm for a 50km/h top speed riding on diminutive 3.50x5in tires.

The Pigeon was updated in 1949 as the C-13 with a larger, dutiful headlamp and the Pigeon emblem on the front fork apron, a Nazi-esque symbol that would continue to be used into the 1950s. The overall styling was agricultural, shaped more by a blacksmith's hammer than a stylist's hand, a "look" the line would keep until the mid-1950s.

In the 1950s, the Pigeons began breeding offspring models. The C-21 was introduced in 1950 with a 150cc engine of 57x58mm for 3hp at 3800rpm. It was available with a passenger or delivery sidecar, following the lineups of the American scooters once again. In 1951, the C-22 took over from the C-21 with even more bizarre styling featuring air ducts over almost every available space on the tail section.

In 1953, the C-35 175cc Pigeon arrived with a four-stroke engine, three-speed transmission, and 4.00x8in tires. But the look was still blacksmith chic.

In 1954, the Pigeon got styling. A new 200cc C-57 model led the way with a 65x58mm four-cycle engine producing 4.3hp at 3800rpm with an automatic transmission and 4.00x8in tires. The design work

was a blend of curves and slab sides that gave the scooter a weird elegance, all set off by the usual chrome trim, turn signals, covered handlebars, and so many air ducts that you worried for the scooter's structural rigidity. A C-57 II arrived in 1956 with further chrome trim. In 1957, a new 200cc model bowed as the C-90 with sleeker, minimalist lines and 5.7hp from the same engine.

The small-bore Pigeon got styling in 1955 by copying the lines of the current Lambretta LC—even down to the Italian's three ports on the side covers, which must have impressed the Japanese by given their love for air ducts. This two-stroke 125cc C-70 was up to 3.6hp at 4200rpm with a new 55x52.5mm engine and 4.00x8in tires.

In 1958–1959, the C-73 took over from the C-70, retaining the Lambretta LC lines, and was followed by the 192cc four-stroke C-74. The four-stroke 125cc C-83 complemented the Standard C-73 with lines similar to the new Lambretta TV1! The 5.5hp C-83 was nicknamed the Bobby De Luxe in a curious bit of Japanese-English. This was superseded by the four-stroke C-200 in 1960 as well as the C-90, which was advertised for the US market as being "heavy-duty, long-range luxury," as well as having "johnny-on-the-spot performance." Along with the Bobby De Luxe came the Peter De Luxe of 1959, a four-stroke 210cc luxury scooter.

In 1960, two new high-end models were unveiled with styling similar to the Maicomobil's dustbin front end. The C-110 was an overhead-valve 175cc good for 8.5hp; the C-111 was a larger-bore, 210cc version with 11.5hp and a 95km/h top speed.

In 1963, the 125cc was redesigned as the C-135 Silver Pigeon with curvaceous, multi-angled styling and 8hp from a small-bore version of the C-110 en-gine. In 1964, a facelift created the C-140 as well as the four-speed 150cc C-240.

Beginning in the late 1950s, Pigeons were imported into the United States by Rockford Scooter of Rockford, Illinois, which labeled the Rabbits as its own. Into the 1960s, Rockford imported the C-73, C-74, C-76, and C-90 models, which were wholesaled to Montgomery Ward and sold through its mail-order catalog as the Riverside.

Mi Val ITALY ★ ★

Made outside of Brescia, the stylish Mi Val Scooter 50 had only 1.5hp to scoot up the Lombardy hills on the 8in wheels. The scooter debuted in 1961, but couldn't keep up with the market ruled by Innocenti and Piaggio.

Mochet FRANCE ★

"Its great gas mileage, its impeccable road handling makes it the ideal engine for the modern man and woman," read the ad for the Vélostyle Luxe. Perhaps Mochet's scooter was the ideal vehicle in 1949, but its pedals and small 49cc VAP-4 engine soon dated it. Mochet gave up on scooters and stuck to its destiny of building "voiturettes," such as its Vélocar with dual pedals for the two passengers to start up the 100cc Zurcher engine.

Molteni ITALY ★ ★ ★

The Molteni brothers may have been known for their micromotor Minimotor, but the T 50 earned them fame as one of the most original scooter designs. Fratelli Molteni (FM) used a beam construction of aluminum that incorporated the gas tank into the unusual triangular construction. The 125cc T 50 lasted from 1950 to 1953.

LEFT:

Mitsubishi Silver Pigeon
Just like the Italians, the Japanese scooter makers marketed their wares to women and with the added advantage of having a buriko babe on the putt-putt to appeal to the male market. The Silver Pigeon was imported into the American market with the Rockford badge since Japanese fighter plane manufacturers had a postwar image problem in the US.

RIGHT:

Mitsubishi Gale Pets
The Silver Pigeon Gale Pet models were like little pets to the larger scoots. Their styling was equally strange, though. Perhaps someday they too would grow up to have whitewalls and chrome.

Monark SWEDEN ★

Monark got its start in 1920 making bicycles but soon ventured into motorcycles from 49cc to a 998cc overhead-valve v-twin. In 1957, the firm ventured into the scooter market with its Monarscoot M33. Dressed in full bodywork, the M33 rode atop tall 20in wheels.

In the 1960s, Monark created its Skoterett Model 901264, powered by a 48cc Husqvarna two-stroke single of 39x40mm with 1hp at 4500rpm riding atop 3.00x10in tires. The bodywork styling was pure Lambretta Slimline. The fixed front fender and covered handlebars as well as the tail section belied the Innocenti influence. A scalloped section on the sidecover bore the Monark script in chrome.

Monark also developed a Honda Cub-style moped-scooter called simply enough the Skotermoped Model 901269 and powered by a two-stroke Sachs.

Monark purchased the Swedish Crescent firm and sold its Skoterett and Skotermoped under the Crescent name as well as its own. Today, Monark is owned by Volvo, the General Motors or Fiat of Scandinavia.

Mondiale BELGIUM ★★

Constructed in Brussels in 1919, the Mondiale Tourisme appeared more of motorcycle than scooter, but carried some important scooter-like characteristics early in the evolution of these vehicles. The covered 308cc engine was placed under the seat allowing for a near step-through design, one of the key components of scooterdom, and an ample floorboard for the feet. However, the lengthy beast rode on 19in wheels and couldn't be mistaken for the Autopeds and Skootamotas putsing around the sidewalks of Europe.

Monet-Goyon FRANCE ★★

As early as 1919, Monet-Goyon of Mâcon designed something of a scooter called the Vélauto type T with a 124cc engine. In 1921, a new Vélauto with double suspension replaced the model T, but the engine was shrunk to 117cc under the seat. In 1922, the Super-Vélauto was added to the line run by a two-stroke 270cc Villiers that was kick started to turn over. The regular Vélauto was updated in 1923 with a 147cc 2hp Villiers engine.

Monet-Goyon built these scooter-like mobiles until 1925 with attractive wicker seats for the true gentleman or lady. Remember this was the age of dirigibles that had to use all wicker furniture for passengers to be as lightweight as possible.

When the first age of scooters came to an end, Monet-Goyon kept the spirit with the Automouche named after the insect, the fly. The strong tubular frame held the Villiers engine available as a 147cc, 175cc, and 250cc.

The firm began making scooters again in 1953, twenty-four years after taking over Koehler-Escoffier from Lyon. Monet-Goyon produced the 52GDC Starlett with a 98cc Villiers MK1F engine with 2.9hp. Later models were the S2s and S2L Luxe and Grand Luxe, keeping the same design of a covered bicycle with paneling giving away the location of the chain.

Monark Skoterett

monarscoot → M 33

Monarscooten är fordonet med de tusen och en finesserna —— »toppen» bland Monarks modeller. Monarscooten förenar smidig elegans med robust styrka, den fordrar nästan ingenting av sin ägare men ger mycket tillbaka! Monarscooten är morgondagens modell i dagens Sverige.

In 1956, Monet-Goyon produced two evolved prototype Starletts called the Starlett Record 53R as well as Le Dolina painted in Eiffel Tower gray.

Montesa SPAIN ★★

Montesa began building small commuter motorcycles in the years following World War II under the guidance of co-founders Pedro Permanyer and Francisco Bulto and under the watchful gaze of Fascist Generalissimo Francisco Franco.

Montesa built a strong racing reputation but by 1958, the founders split apart: Permanyer sought to return Montesa to building commuter cycles; Bulto wanted to continue racing, and left to start Bultaco. Later that year, Montesa's first scooter was unveiled.

The Montesa scooter was an oddity in a scooter market full of oddities. Instead of a step-through design as with Derbi's Masculino scooter, Montesa opted for more of a motorcycle-like design with two seats atop the fiberglass bodywork. The end effect was a scooter that looked like a two-wheeled car.

The seats and luggage rack were mounted on rails and could be adjusted fore and aft. It was an interesting feature on a scooter that lacked many normal features that buyers expected. Production started in 1959 and ended in 1960.

For 1962–1965, Montesa returned to scooters, building its version of the Laverda Mini Scooter as the Montesa Micro Scooter. With a three-speed gearbox and 60cc four-stroke engine, it was the sole four-stroke Montesa ever built. Riding atop 2.75x9in tires, the diminutive overhead-valve engine pumped out 3hp at 6000rpm. From 1966–1969, the Montesa's scooter was called the Micro 66.

Mota EAST GERMANY ★

In 1955, Mota built a prototype scooter featuring a curvaceous front fender and unusual front leading-link suspension. The 3.6hp 98cc engine moved the Mota to a 75km/h top speed.

Mota-Wiesel's small-wheeled scooterette was available with either a 74cc or 98cc engine. In 1956, it also produced the Wiesel SR 56 Pitty scooter with an 125cc IFA engine for 75km/h, a copy of the three-speed DKW. Not surprising considering that IFA and MZ were housed in the old DKW factory.

Motobécane/Motoconfort (MBK) FRANCE

SCC/STC 1951 ★★

Géo Ham designed the first Motobécane/Motoconfort scooter, which was shown at the Salon de Paris in 1951 with a four-stroke 125cc engine for 5hp at 5000rpm. The Motobécane version came un-

Lo scooter Montesa a due posti del 1958

MOTORROLLER

VEB VERLAG TECHNIK BERLIN

der the name of SCC and the Motoconfort was the STC, but all their scooters were affectionately known as "Mobyscoots."

SB/SV 1954–1956 ★ ★

The SB/SV (again SB=Motobécane, SV=Motoconfort) was a French version of the "undressed" Lambrettas as opposed to the "dressed" SCC/STC. This latest Mobyscoot had an air-cooled engine producing 5hp on 10in wheels up from the SCC/STC's 8in wheels.

SBH/SVH 1956 AND SBS/SVS 1957 ★ ★

Following Innocenti's lead, the Mobyscoot went back to "dressed" scooters with SBH/SVH and SBS/SVS, the "gran luxe" versions of the SCC/STC four-strokes. Updates were made in the engine, including a fan-cooled engine and the rubber "Flexi-bloc" suspension to eliminate vibrations. The SBS/SVS were the latest Moby-Montagne versions with two-tone paint jobs. In 1959, Motobécane's naming changed again to M Montagne-Standard and M Montagne-Lux (substitute and O for the M to get the Motoconfort name).

In 1974, Motobécane bought the classic French mopeds VéloSoleX, and ten years later, MBK and Yamaha took over the company. This brought in a whole new era of scooters with the Ovetta, Nitro, and the unfortunately named Doodo.

Modenas MALAYSIA ★

While the name seems to stem from Modena, the Italian city of Ferrari and Maserati, it's actually short for Syarikat Motosikal Dan Enjin Nasional Sdn. The wide range of scooters are often more like step-through motorcycles, many of them rebranded PGO scooters from Taiwan.

Motobécane
The SC Mobyscoot made by Motobécane added fancy reverse hand levers for one of the sportiest French scooters by a company known more for their mopeds than their limited engagement in the world of putt-putts.

SCOOTER MOTOBÉCANE

BLOC-MOTEUR 4 TEMPS
125 cm³   3 VITESSES
Graissage intégral par circu-
lation intérieure automatique

Motobi ITALY ★ ★

Moto B was formed in Pesaro when one of the six Benelli brothers, Giuseppe, left the Benelli firm in 1952; by 1955, the new firm's name had been settled as Motobi.

Wasting no time, in 1956, Motobi displayed a scooter prototype at the Milan Show based on a tube-frame chassis covered by sheet steel bodywork. By 1957, Motobi had entered into production with a full line of scooters based on the one prototype and 3.50x12in tires: the Ardizio with 125cc and 150cc two-strokes; the Imperiale with 125cc four-stroke delivering 5.5hp; and the Catria with a 175cc four-stroke giving 11hp.

The Catria was a stylish scooter along the lines of the Lambretta LD, with two saddles and full body-work. As the Motobi flyer stated of the Catria, it was "Lo scooter per l'intenditore"—the scooter for the one who understood.

In 1959, Motobi introduced a scooter-moped called the Pic-nic with a 75cc four-stroke engine; by 1963, the Pic-nic was available at 98cc and 125cc. Simultaneously with the new update, Motobi released its Cicloscooter 48 that also hit the market under the Benelli marque.

Motobic SPAIN ★

From 1963, the Motobic firm built the Italian Capri 98 scooter under license.

Motoflash ITALY ★

At the 1956 Milan Show, Motoflash presented the Clipper scooter with the option of two engines: 48cc or 75cc. The Clipper had large spoked wheels, a covered body but exposed engine and comfortable bench seat for two.

Motom ITALY ★ ★

Motom Italiana SpA of Milan created a 49cc over-head-valve clip-on bicycle motor in 1946–1947, following the route to recovery also traveled by Ducati and Garelli.

By 1950, Motom offered its Delfino, of Dolphin, model that was half scooter, half motorcycle. Introduced with an overhead-valve 147cc four-speed single, it soon grew to 163cc.

In 1955, Motom brought out its 98 TS model that was a lightweight scooter-motorcycle with a pressed-steel frame and extensive bodywork. The engine was an overhead cam 98cc backed by a four-speed gearbox.

Motor Industry SA BELGIUM

Under license from Piaggio, Motor Industry SA assembled scooters for the market in Benelux.

Moto-Scoot Manufacturing Company USA ★ ★ ★ ★ ★

In 1936, 27-year-old Norman "Abe" Siegal grew tired of racing Fronty-Fords on the dirt track chitlin circuit, reformed his ways, and rolled the dice to go for broke where he envisioned the big money was: motorscooters. Siegal sold his share in a Chicago Loop garage for $1,090, hired three workman, rolled up his sleeves, and set to work constructing the Moto-Scoot in the corner of a West Side Chicago factory.

Siegal's legs ached and he was sick of dropping two bits to take the streetcar across Chicago in 1934. While Al Capone was busy bullet-proofing his limousine with steel, Siegal "got an engine from a gasoline-powered washing machine. He used two-wheels from my baby buggy," recalls his son Burt. "He rigged it up so he could hook it to the rear bumper of the car. People saw him riding it during the depths of the Depression and asked him to make one for them." Although zoot-suited gangsters probably scoffed at this makeshift contraption, Siegal's invention made him a millionaire while Al was doing time for a slight tax problem.

Siegal had obviously done his homework and studied E. Foster Salsbury's Motor Glide when he designed—and named—his scooter. The first model of 1936 used a 1½hp Lauson engine with direct drive and no clutch, all mounted on a step-through chassis. Suspension was by a padded seat at the rear. Lighting and a rear drum brake were standard as was a spiffy two-tone paint job.

Norm soon rented a Chicago storefront promising to pay rent as soon as he sold his first batch of ten scooters. Using his old-fashioned American ingenuity when he "ran out of metal, he broke a hole in the wall of his store, and pulled out a lead water pipe," recalls Burt Siegal. Thus the very first Moto Scoots were born. "When he got paid, he just replaced the pipe."

In 1936 when Norm was only 24 years old, he officially set up shop in part of a west-side Chicago factory and "by the end of the year he had sold 186 of them at $109 apiece and had taken over the whole factory. In 1937 the output was 2,700," according to a 1939 Time article.

Also by 1937, the headlamp had been built into the handlebars. In 1938, the engine was enclosed by a Space Age, rounded cover set off by two-tone lines.

Surpassing retail sales of $500,000 in 1938, Moto Scoot moved to 8440 South Chicago Ave. with a banked gravel race track running around the building so employees could let off steam by taking a couple of laps around the building. (The winged Moto Scoot logo graced the marquee in the now run-down factory until 1996.) In a 1938 Chicago Daily Times article, Siegal was surely misquoted as saying that "he recommends it for the gent too indolent to walk to work and too anti-social to ride a street car."

The Magic Carpet of Bagdad!

Just imagine owning this remarkable little vehicle that gives you a new motion, rivaled only by the mythical "MAGIC CARPET OF BAGDAD."

Imagine possessing the power to step on the platform and almost at the expression of a wish to be able to GO .. through the heavy mazes of traffic into the open spaces and into the countryside .. Relax with the MOTO-SCOOT!

Thrill with the MOTO-SCOOT. Get out into the open road .. open your throttle wide .. and away you go .. ahead of the line of traffic .. Thrill to the instantaneous response of your throttle .. the steady purr of the engine .. as it sweeps you to your destination.

IMPROVED ...
KICK-STARTER . . . MOTO-CLUTCH
MOTO-FLEX . . . GREATER HORSE-POWER
the NEW ORIGINAL *Moto-Scoot*

By 1939, Moto-Scoot offered several lines: the De Luxe line was powered by a 1½hp Briggs & Stratton and included the basic Solo, Delivery, and Tandem. The upgraded Century line with 1½hp and Vari-Torque Drive in Solo, Delivery, Tandem, and Side-Car models. The ultimate Moto-Scoots were the Imperial line with a 2½hp engine in Solo, Tandem, Delivery, and Side-Car models. As a 1939 brochure warned, the Century and Imperial models were identical in outward appearance. A Moto-Scoot Trailer was available for all Solo models.

An early brochure promised, "The 1939 Moto-Scoot is the sensation of the highways." Top speed was 30mph but more importantly—and probably the source of the scooter's sensation versus its speed—was the fuel consumption: 120mpg.

Siegal began advertising his wares in back-of-the-book one-column Popular Mechanics ads—the nationwide sales tool for motorscooter upstarts of the 1930s and 1940s. Here, the Moto-Scoot did battle for the techno-minded reader's eye with the Rock-Ola, Zipscoot, Constructa-Scoot, Trotwood, and others long lost to the junkyards of America. Siegal persevered.

Since Siegal had been on the county fair dirt track circuit racing "Fronty-Fords" before he pounded out his first puddlejumper, he souped up a three-wheeled racing Moto Scoot and rented it to tourists at Navy Pier to let them feel the power of a two-stroke. He also worked on a rentable, two-seater "quarter-in-the-slot" scooter to zoom gawkers around the futuristic 1939 World's Fair.

1938 Moto-Scoot
For a mere $111.50, this beautiful faux-wicker-covered puddle jumper could have been delivered to your doorstep in 1938. Or for another forty greenbacks, a side car would be tagged on complete with fancy Moto-Scoot decals. "Make this your Declaration of Independence," announced early ads, and went on to say, "Keeping old friends and making new ones, the new 1938 MOTO-SCOOT, mechanically perfected, gives more satisfaction than ever before." Mead Cycle Co.—also of Chicago—bought up a whole slew of Moto Scoots, slapped on some Mead Ranger stickers, and added these putt-putts to their line of "velocipedes" and "sidewalk bikes."

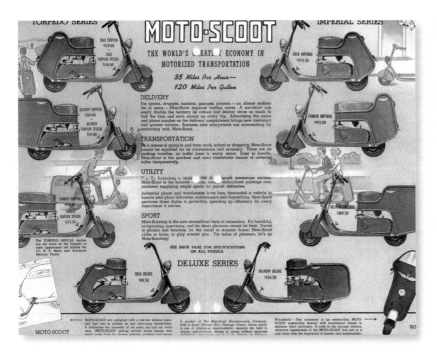

Complete Line of Postwar Moto-Scoots
By the time Moto-Scoot entered the forties, the welded tubular steel frame and optional Lauson, Clinton, or Briggs & Stratton engines made these putt-putts into speedsters. "More Fun than Flying—And Far Cheaper," claimed early Moto Scoot ads as well as "The Magic Carpet of Bagdad!" Unfortunately, when the war hit, capitalist scooter entrepreneurs forced Norm Siegal to sell his beloved Moto-Scoot factory, which became the short-lived "American Moto-Scoot."

On April 3, 1939, Time magazine did a profile of Siegal and the motorscooter mogul's success. The article offers a list of production figures, presumably from Siegal's mouth: In 1936, the first year of production, 186 Moto-Scoots were built and sold; in 1937, 2,700; and in 1938, 4,500. For 1939, Siegal had high hopes of selling 10,000 Moto-Scoots from his new factory at 8428 South Chicago Avenue where he then had seventy-five workers. According to the magazine, Moto-Skoot (sic) was the largest American scooter maker in 1939, which may or may not have been true. Regardless, Time crowned Siegal "the Henry Ford of the scooter business."

Still having racing fever from his "Fronty-Ford" days, Siegal built a half-sized racing Moto Scoot with a two-cycle Villiers engine and four-speed transmission that put the competition to shame with its speed and maneuverability that it was banned from motorcycle races. To celebrate his success in sales and racing, Siegal built a gold-plated Moto Scoot in 1941.

Part of Siegal's success was due to the badge-engineered scooter he built for Mead Cycle Company of Chicago, long famous for its Mead Ranger bicycles. Mead had seen the potential of the scooter and contracted Siegal to build Mead Ranger scooters beginning in 1938 and lasting until World War II.

With the start of World War II, Siegal turned his manufacturing expertise to war materiel, but postwar a redesigned scooter appeared. Siegal signed a chattel mortgage on his patents and machinery to make payroll. He ended up losing the Moto Scoot dies to "American Moto Scoot" which didn't begin scooter production again until 1945. This American Moto Scoot had stylish new bodywork wrapped around a Lauson engine in a two-tiered affair punctuated by

rows of louvers. The rear end now rose up to enclose the gas tank and offer a small luggage compartment as well.

Even if Siegal lost his Moto Scoot, his vision of getting off the tram and onto a putt-putt was confirmed by Popular Mechanics in 1947, "[Scooters'] low cost of operation means it can be used for commuting to work daily at about the same expense as streetcar riding."

MotoTec USA ★

Based out of Plover, Wisconsin, MotoTec clearly delved into the scooter market as an afterthought since its bread and butter is in ATVs. The Knockout and Fat Boy lines are low-riders with fat tires and no front legshield. Even its cute, mini scooter-like bike is a called a "moped." Well, it does only reach 15 mph (24 km/h) and is the "ultimate kids ride." No trips to the store, though: "great for driveway and parking lot fun, cruise around cones and speed through trails with ease."

Motovespa SPAIN ★★★

In 1952, Enrico Piaggio began construction on his huge factory in Madrid that would make 100,000 Vespas by 1959. The difference between the Italian-made and Spanish-made Vespas was minimal.

Mowag SWITZERLAND ★

Mowag, short for Motorwagenfabrik, launched its Vroller scooter in 1958, a contraction of the scooter's full name of Volksroller. Power was a 50cc Mowag engine of 1.5hp at 5000rpm, riding atop 2.50x8in tires. Styling followed the Lambretta A and B but with added fenders and legshield.

Mustad NORWAY ★

Trying to follow in the footsteps of the relatively successful Swedish Crescent Skotereet, Mustad produced putt-putts for Norway but couldn't match the competition from imported Vespas and Lambrettas.

Mustang USA

The story of the Mustang began in the garage of a budding young engineer named Howard Forrest. Growing up in southern California, Forrest loved to race anything with an engine. In the early 1930s, he built and ran midget sprint cars, which formed the source of two mainstays of Mustang design: powerful small-bore engines and small wheels.

Forrest loved small wheels. Midgets typically raced on dwarf wheels, and under Forrest's hand Mustangs would keep to 8in and 12in wheels through thick and thin. It was to be one of their great features, making them competitive in Class C dirt-track racing against Harley-Davidsons and Indians. It was also one of the reasons for the firm's eventual undoing; the small wheel always denoted a motorscooter rather than a motorcycle.

Much of the background information here comes from Michael Gerald's excellent self-published history, Mustang: A Different Breed of Steed.

HOWARD FORREST
FOUR-CYLINDER MOTORCYCLE

Forrest built one of the first ten or twelve midget cars on the West Coast, according to his son and keeper of the flame, Jim Forrest. His midget was powered by an Ace motorcycle four-cylinder with his own home-built water-jacket for cooling. But in the 1930s, Forrest was also bitten by the motorcycling bug; he acquired an Indian big twin and later a Salsbury Motor Glide. The Motor Glide had small wheels but its engine, while small, was not powerful. Forrest began work.

In 1936, Forrest, then 22, fabricated his own in-line four-cylinder engine to power a midget, but as these things always happen, he eventually stuffed it into the modified chassis of his Motor Glide, building his own version of what a motorcycle should be.

The Forrest four-cylinder bore looked like a miniature version of the famous Offenhauser engine that ruled sprint car racing and the Indy 500. Forrest's 19ci or 311cc engine breathed through a single carburetor mounted on the right side and run via an overhead camshaft. Forrest machined the crankshaft himself from billet, as well as the connecting rods, camshaft, and pistons. As Jim Forrest told Classic Cycle Review magazine, "The only things he didn't build on that engine were the spark plugs and the carburetor."

Stuffed into the light-duty Motor Glide chassis, Forrest's four was cramped. In 1940–1941, he built his own frame by hand, as well as his own two-speed gearbox, a right-angle bevel-drive unit. Since a suitable radiator was not at hand, Forrest bought a car radiator and a new saw. And the wheels were small, 8in whitewalls.

Just before World War II, Forrest was hired on as an engineer at Gladden Products based at 635 West Colorado Boulevard in Glendale, California. John N. Gladden started the firm with backing from the Los Angeles Turf Club to manufacture small airplane parts, a business that boomed with the coming war.

Forrest commuted to work on his four-cylinder scooter and on lunch hour it was a conversation piece; one day, John Gladden saw the scooter and was amazed to learn that Forrest had built it himself. The scooter sparked the development of a Gladden motorcycle.

MUSTANG COLT 1945–1947 ★ ★ ★ ★

John Gladden was far-sighted. He knew of the success of the Motor Glide and other scooters conceived as alternatives to a second car for working families

during the hard times that led up to the war. With Gladden's wartime business devoted solely to government contracts, he wisely was scanning the scenery for postwar success. In 1944, Gladden set up a motorscooter skunkworks with Forrest and fellow engineer Chuck Gardner.

Walt Fulton, who later started as a Mustang dealer in Kansas City, Missouri, and eventually became a Mustang sales rep and racer, remembered the inner workings at Mustang in a 1992 interview for this book. "Howard Forrest was very capable, very imaginative, and he did not hesitate to experiment. He was energetic, completely dedicated, and an enthusiast."

By 1945, Forrest and Gardner built five different prototype scooters on 12in wheels and powered by English prewar Villiers single-cylinder two-stroke engines. Based on a 59x72mm bore and stroke, the engine breathed through a rear-facing Amal carburetor and exhausted through twin ports with exhaust pipes running out along both sides of the frame to end in distinctive English-style mufflers of the time. The engine was built in unit with an integral Villiers three-speed gearbox shifted by a long-throw "suicide" hand shifter.

Photos of the prototypes show a simple scaled-down motorcycle chassis similar in lines to Forrest's homemade chassis for his four-cylinder. The tail was rigid but the front used a short-throw leading-link suspension with long coil springs running up both sides of the front forks all the way to the headlamp bracket. A single saddle seat was placed behind the pea-shaped gas tank.

The invention was to be named the Mustang after the P-51 Mustang fighter that had proven itself during World War II and for which Gladden had supplied landing struts. And it was to be called a motorcycle, not a motorscooter.

Harley on 12-inch Wheels
The Mustang may look like its big brothers, Harley-Davidson and Indian, and strive for the look thanks to the tasseled leather sidebags, but the vehicle was dubbed a scooter thanks to its relatively little wheels. With a long line of breeding—from Colt to Pony to Bronco to Stallion—the Mustang could outhandle the big bikes thanks to its small size and was eventually banned from these races for fear of upstaging the big boys.

In late 1945, Gladden ordered 100 Villiers 197cc engines but the English firm had been bombed during the war; only a limited supply of its small vertical single 122cc engine was available. Gladden requested the shipment and a scaled-down Mustang was readied for production using the 122cc and 8in wheels.

The smaller Villiers two-stroke was a truly prehistoric design dating back to 1937. Overall, it was similar to the 197cc with twin exhaust ports, a rear-facing Amal carb, and Villiers unit three-speed gearbox. But the 50x62mm bore and stroke was based on a built-up crankshaft riding on a roller-bearing big end and firing through a cast-iron barrel; power was only 4hp, barely half that of the 197cc.

The Colt carried the styling of the final prototypes with the addition of stylish fishtail mufflers and a Mustang script decal on the gas tank. Lighting was blamed on Lucas, the infamous English electrical system manufacturer disdainfully nicknamed the Prince of Darkness.

For the name of the first model, Gladden added the wild horse Mustang image, calling it the Colt as plans for larger machines were in the works.

The first series of Colts were largely handbuilt. The first production Colts are believed to have been sold in 1946 and continued through early 1947 when the supply of engines dried up. Between 235 and 237 Colts were believed to have been built, depending on different sources.

MODEL 2 1947–1950 ★ ★ ★ ★

In the postwar years, Gladden bought the local Kinner Motors Company, which had built a radial five-cylinder Army Air Corps training engine and before running into financial trouble, switched to producing a 19.4ci or 317.6cc single-cylinder side-valve industrial engine quaintly named the Bumble Bee, previously used to power airborne generator units.

America was the land of four-stroke engines; two-strokes were for lawn mowers, and the two-stroke Villiers never satisfied Forrest. With some modifications, the four-stroke Bumble Bee became the new powerplant for a revised version of the Mustang Colt, called the Model 2 with the engine and other changes.

The Bumble Bee cranked out 9.5hp, which was much more "American." Bore and stroke measured 2 7/8x3in.

The engine still breathed through a British-made Amal carburetor and an English Burman three-speed gearbox now with a foot-change backed up the engine and housed the kickstart; early Burmans had exposed lever return springs until this was changed on the Model 4 Mustang. For ignition and lighting, a Wico generator was driven by a belt from the exposed flywheel.

In 1947, the Mustang became the first American motorcycle to use telescopic forks. Walt Fulton was

kind in calling the forks "unsophisticated," but they did the job, and the Mustang now rode on 4.00x12in disc wheels.

Ads of the time from the factory and its major distributor, Johnson Motors of Los Angeles (which was the West Coast Triumph importer), reflected the two-faced image of the Mustang. On one hand, the firm promoted the 70mpg fuel efficiency; on the other, it promoted the 9.5hp and a top speed of more than 60mph.

With the success of the motorcycles, Gladden separated Mustang as a division with Forrest as chief engineer and Chuck Gardner as production manager.

MODEL 3 DELIVERCYCLE 1949 AND
MODEL 5 1950–1956, 1963–1965 ★ ★

Salsbury had its Cycletow, but this was only an adaptation—"training wheels"—added to the basic two wheeler. In the world of big motorcycles, Harley-Davidson built its three-wheeler Servi-Car and Indian its DispatchTow, both of which fit the market better and sold well for years. Thus it was little surprise when Mustang followed suit with a tricycle-chassis delivery scooter.

With the addition of trunk and a Crosley miniature automobile rear end, the Model 3 became a commercial delivery machine; a tow bar attachment allowed auto dealerships to deliver cars with the Model 3 in tow and then have their drivers return on three wheels. They were hardy enough that oil well service companies also used them.

The Model 5 updated the Model 3, soon with a Burman four-speed gearbox to handle the heavier loads. A later option was electric starting, which was never offered on the Mustang cycles.

By 1956, Delivercycle production was discontinued. But in 1963, new Mustang management revived the Model 5 and continued to build it until Mustang's last days.

MODEL 4 STANDARD AND SPECIAL 75
1950–1958 ★ ★ ★

The Model 2 was updated in 1950 as the Model 4 and offered in a Standard and Special model.

The chief modification marking the Model 4 was the reversal of the Bumble Bee engine in the frame, placing the intake and exhaust manifolds to the front of the chassis. This promoted airflow to the carburetor and cooling air for the exhaust manifold.

In addition, the exposed flywheel was now enclosed as a flywheel magneto replaced the belt-driven generator. The clutch was a multi-cork plate type lubricated by engine oil mist. The Burman three-speed gearbox mounting was also changed, bolting directly to the engine versus to the frame—a change that shaved 15lb from the cycle, according to Michael

Gerald's history. The four-speed Burman that had been used to handle the extra workload of the Model 5 was soon to be optionally available on the Special.

The gas tank capacity was enlarged to 2.4gal by converting to two tank sections in the style of the Harley-Davidson and Indian big twins of the time.

The Model 4 Special added features to the Standard, including a front brake, higher, 7.0:1 compression cylinder head, and high-lift camshaft as well as a high-level exhaust pipe and higher price. The Special breathed through an Amal 7/8in carburetor and produced 10.5hp at 5000rpm.

With this "speed equipment," a Model 4 Special could truly gallop. The power-to-weight ratio for a 215lb cycle with a 19.4ci engine was pure hot rod. The acceleration made you hold onto the reins, and while the hardtail and early telescopic forks didn't always hold the road, it was a spirited beast. Top speed was advertised at 70-72mph.

Fulton began racing a Model 4 Special in the late 1940s and lauded its handling and ride. "The frame was designed for stability. Early on we had problems with the frame breaking but that was fixed with the tube framing. Everything worked in harmony and the engine was well placed in the chassis. It didn't have the comfort of the big motorcycles but it was adequate for its size, power, and the types of riders.

"The Mustang was far superior to anything else available at that time in the lightweight motorcycle or scooter class."

MODEL 8 SPECIAL 1957 ★ ★ ★ ★

The Model 8 was a short-lived Special based on the Model 4 Special with the same 10.5hp 19.4ci engine but with a cast-aluminum primary case. The 8 added the heavy-duty four-speed gearbox of the Model 5 Delivercycle in place of the three-speed Burman of the 4, which was a great advantage.

The 8 was also finished in a deluxe color scheme. The frame and forks were Lustre Black while the fenders were black with white striping, and the gas tank was black with a red panel outlined in white. The Mustang decal was gold and black.

A Mustang Model 8 flyer promised the future arrival of a Model 8 Standard with the same paint scheme but using a low pipe, standard cylinder head, and without the front brake. The 8 Standard never went into production as such.

COLT 1956–1958 ★ ★ ★

With the Model 4 as the deluxe model, Mustang decided to create scaled-down economy cycle and chose to look back to its beginnings and named it the Colt.

This new Colt continued with the Bumble Bee side-valve engine but detuned to 8hp; a 5hp throttle governor could also be specified, making the Colt legal for young riders in certain states.

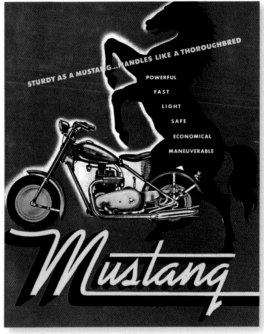

Instead of the standard clutch, an automatic centrifugal clutch was used as on the Cushman automatics. Use of this clutch was possible as the new Colt eschewed a gearbox for economy of production and lower sales prices.

The new model featured a new triangulated Earles-type front end, similar to that used on the Cushmans of the time with a lever-action linkage that had a longer reach than that used on the first Colts. A spring damped the forks.

The new Colt was available in two-tone Banner Green and Silver Grey.

The package was aimed at kids. Ads read, "Hit the Trail! . . . to school, paper route or just good fun."

TOP:

Mustang Stallion
The most collectible breed of Mustang is the Stallion built from 1959 to 1965. Using a fancy four-speed Burman gearbox plucked from a Delivery cycle, the Stallion pumped out 12hp thanks to its Bumble Bee powerplant. Courtesy of owner: Jim Kilau

BELOW:

Thoroughbred Mustang
With a name synonymous with a wild horse, the Mustang featured a bucking bronco behind the plucky putt-putt. While motorcyclists may scoff at the little wheels of the minibike, they're silenced when reminded of Walt Fulton's record setting on a souped-up Mustang lying flat with his belly on the seat.

PONY 1959–1965 ★ ★

In 1959, Mustang reorganized its lineup giving equine names to variations on the old Model 4 versions. The Model 4 Standard became the Pony with the base 9.5hp engine and three-speed gearbox.

By 1960, the complete line would shelve the old Amal carburetors and switch to Italian-made Dell'Ortos, which were more easily adjusted and longer lasting than the older English units.

Mustang began offering a full line of accessories to keep its cycles as well dressed as Cushman's now line of Super Eagles. Options included a chrome luggage rack, crash bars, folding kickstart lever, speedometer, and high-level exhaust system. A 5hp engine conversion was also optional, replacing the old throttle governor; the special engine was fitted with a sleeve and new pistons to decrease the bore, giving a 14.7ci displacement.

BRONCO 1959–1965 ★ ★ ★

With the change in 1959 model changes, the Bronco was created as deluxe edition of the Pony, with a 10.5hp engine and the three-speed.

Ads in 1959, show the complete line riding on the old disc wheels, but soon after only the Pony kept the discs as the Bronco came with new Italian-made 12in spoked wheels and full-hub-width brakes.

STALLION 1959–1965 ★ ★ ★ ★

The Stallion replaced the former Model 4 Special, riding now on spoked wheels and using the Burman four-speed transmission that had originally been used in the Model 5 Delivercycle. In addition, the Stallion lived up to its name with a special high-lift camshaft creating a 12hp, high-torque Bumble Bee engine featuring a chrome-plated flywheel.

THOROUGHBRED 1960–1965 ★ ★ ★

Harley-Davidson had followed Mustang's lead in the use of telescopic forks; now Mustang followed The Motor Company in moving away from the rigid hardtail and developing a new frame with a rear swing-arm suspended by dual shock absorbers. Walt Fulton led the way, adding a swing-arm and suspensions to the tail of one of his racing creations, as he recalled; Mustang's new chief engineer Chuck Gardner added the swing-arm to create the new Thoroughbred that became Mustang's top of the line model in 1960.

The Thoroughbred used the 12hp Bumble Bee of the Stallion and the new wire-laced wheels. But the new frame design allowed for the addition of a two-person bench seat with an optional toolbox hidden below.

TRAIL MACHINE 1962–1965 ★

In 1962, Gladden stockholders voted in a new general manager at Mustang, Ralph L. Coson. In the next few years, the company was shook up as John Gladden and Chuck Gardner resigned, followed by many other key personnel. Times were tough and the market was taking its toll.

In 1965, Coson supervised the production of the Mustang Trail Machine as an attempt to take back market share. The off road mini-bike seemed to be the hot item in the US market; Cushman had recently offered its Trailster, and Mustang was not to be outdone. The Trail Machine had been Gardner's last design for Mustang. It used a Briggs & Stratton engine in a basic, no-frills frame. Two models were offered: the Rigid Frame Model and the Rear Suspension Model with their differences readily apparent.

The Trail Machine took Mustang off the right track. The firm's specialty had been in building a unique motorcycle cum scooter, and the monies paid to developing the Trail Machine ultimately spurred on Mustang's demise.

MUSTANG'S DEMISE

Just as availability of the English-made Villiers engine had stumbled the Mustang at its birth, availability of the English Burman gearbox spelled its doom twenty years later. The English motorcycle marques such as Matchless that had used the Burman boxes shifted to redesigned unit engines; suddenly the Burman was obsolete.

And then came Honda. The new line of inexpensive and reliable Japanese motorcycles hobbled Mustang where it hurt most: sales. Buyers needed to lay out $500 for a Mustang and Honda undercut them.

The year 1965 was a sad one for American motorscooters. Cushman curtailed production on its Silver Eagle line, and Mustang production was limited in 1965. In 1966, production ceased, with the new owners continuing to stock Mustang replacement parts.

Fulton remembered Mustang's last days: "John Gladden was purely a business man. He expanded his company into something that was totally foreign to his main line of building industrial engine and airplane hydraulics, and he got in over his head.

"I contend to this day that if Gladden had both pulled the plug on Mustang Motorcycles and Forrest had been allowed to use his imagination, Mustang could have cornered the whole lightweight motorcycle market."

It was not to be.

DON ORR STALLIONS ★ ★ ★ ★

In 1971, Los Angeles chopper customizer Don Orr bought the rights to the Mustang name and began production of custom-built Mustangs. He named his new creation the Stallion, but while it used many original parts, it also differed from the original Mustang Stallion—and differed from unit to unit due to parts availability. Many had extended chopper forks. During the one year, Orr was estimated to have built between thirty to fifty Stallions, according Michael Gerald; others state that less than a dozen were made.

By the end of the year, Orr's Mustangs were mavericks, according to the California DMV. Orr ran onto the wrong side of the law's paperwork bureaucracy; his new Stallions failed to meet legal lighting requirements and so he did not have proper ownership titles for the cycles when they were sold.

As quickly as he had arrived on the scene, Orr was gone. But a few of his rare custom-built Stallions have survived, a collectible blend of exclusivity and outlaw history.

THEY SHOOT HORSES—OR DO THEY?

In 1972, Circle Industries of El Monte, California, bought the Mustang rights with plans to revive the old warhorse. But the plans failed to materialize into motorcycles, and Circle soon auctioned off more than 20 tons of components to former Mustang dealer Roy Stone of Waco, Texas.

Stone has done more than anyone in carrying on the Mustang heritage. He continued to supply replacement parts into the 1990s. Stone sold the frame-making jigs to Alan Wenzel of Dallas, Texas, who manufactures replacement Stallion frames. Other parts suppliers have also continued the Mustang tradition to this day.

MV Agusta ITALY

In 1945, an odd scenario was unfolding. At the Piaggio factory, Enrico Piaggio was turning from wartime aviation production to a novel peacetime venture: a motorscooter to be called the Vespa. At the same time at the new MV Agusta firm, Sicilian aristocrat Count Domenico Agusta was switching from his aviation love to a novel peacetime creation: an economical, basic motorcycle to be called the Vespa.

MV, soon to be called MV Agusta, stood for Meccanica Verghera, the latter being the name of the factory site near Milan. MV's Vespa was based on a 98cc two-stroke single, wet clutch, unit construction, and two-speed gearbox. The specifications could have easily been for the Piaggio Vespa.

But Piaggio registered the name first, and Agusta's cycle went on the market as the MV 98. And the two went their divergent ways from there: Piaggio to fame with the Vespa scooter; and MV to fame with its numerous racing motorcycles that would win thirty-seven manufacturers world championships. Alongside its racing motorcycles, MV always produced street bikes as a way to finance Count Agusta's love of competition—much like Enzo Ferrari did.

MODEL B 1949 ★★★★

After developing a prototype Model A scooter, MV introduced its Model B 125cc scooter in 1949 with full monocoque bodywork and one-side front and rear lug axles—again, specifications shared with the Vespa scooter.

The engine was a two-stroke single of 53x56mm creating 5hp at 4800rpm. Cooling was by fan with a flywheel magneto giving spark; a wet multi-plate clutch connected to the four-speed gearbox. The tires were 3.50x10in.

POPOLARE, NORMALE, AND CGT
1950–1952 ★★

In 1950, the B was accompanied by the Popolare scooter, a bare-bones economy scooter that looked like a Lambretta from the seat backward and a Vespa from the seat forward. Renamed the Normale, by 1951 it was renamed again as the CGT, or C Gran Turismo; in 1952, the CGT was available in 150cc form.

MODEL A 1949 ★★

MV Agusta released its A after its B by a few months. Although the A had almost all the same specs as the classier B, the price was significantly less due to the unsheathed rear of the scooter. The A followed the design of the early uncovered Lambrettas, while the B resembled the early bulbous Italian Nibbio and FIAT scooters.

MODEL C, AND CSL 1950–1951 ★★★

Also in 1950, the Model C replaced the B with a tube-steel chassis covered by unstressed bodywork bearing similar styling. In 1951, the CSL, or C Super Lusso, was offered. Production was halted by the end of 1951.

MV Agusta Line-up
The original Model B from 1949 was MV's first scooter effort, fitted with a two-stroke 123cc engine in a Nibbio influenced pressed-steel unit chassis and carrying its wheels on single-sided stub axles. By 1950, the B was replaced by the tube frame model C. While MV's first scooter followed the Vespa ancestral lineage of the Nibbio and SIMAT, its second scooter design, the restored CGT in blue, was influenced by Innocenti. The open bodywork and single large-diameter backbone frame all spoke of the Lambretta C. MV Agusta, however, concentrated its energy on racing motorcycles and built scooters and road bikes just to fund the factory race team. Courtesy of the owner: Guido Delli Ponti

OVUNQUE 1951–1954 ★ ★

In 1951, the CGT was replaced by the Ovunque, translated as Everywhere. Using a tube frame, portions of the body were still uncovered. And while the engine was the same as the CGT (Gran Turismo), the gearbox was a three-speed. The first model, the Ovunque Tipo 51 for 1951, had one exhaust pipe; it was followed by the Ovunque Tipo 52 from 1952 with twin pipes and the Ovunque Tipo 53 in 1953. Production ended in 1954.

CHICCO AND BIK 1960–1964 ★ ★

MV held itself back from the scooter market until 1959 when it showed the Bik and Chicco scooters. The Bik had a four-stroke 166cc with semi-hydraulic tappets, but unfortunately never went into production.

The Chicco was built from 1960–1964 with steel monocoque bodywork that was easily mistaken for a Vespa but with a Lambretta's fixed front fender. The horizontal two-stroke 155cc engine created 5.8hp at 5200rpm with a four-speed gearbox and 3.50x10in tires. The Chicco was widely exported, coming to the United States via Cosmopolitan Motors, the Parilla importer.

MV's scooters, while interesting, were always second place to the Vespa, Lambretta, and Iso. The firm's winning motorcycles meanwhile command monstrous prices and the scooters are often weighted down under price tags that are proportionally high due to the name recognition.

MZ GERMANY ★

Sprung from the ashes of the Industriewerke Ludwigsfelde (IWL) that made airplane engines for the Luftwaffe and was later flattened by Allied bombs, MZ's factory in Zschopau took up the slack to make scooter engines in the 1950s in East Germany. The *Neue Kurs* agenda, or "New Course," of the DDR communist government included scooters for the masses. Working with other government-controlled companies, MZ provided essential parts and engines to the other East German scooter manufacturers, such as the Troll, which is often considered the MZ Troll—not to be confused with the ill-fated Norwegian Troll car.

After taking part in such fantastically bizarre and collectible East German scooter manufacturing, MZ joined the scooter renaissance in the 2000s with the 50cc Moskito.

Alas, the factory in Zschopau closed in 2008 after eighty-eight years of producing motorcycles and scooters. The factory was turned into a nightclub, since now is the time when we dance.

Nassetti ITALY ★

Specializing in flywheel magnetos and mopeds, Nassetti took a stab at scooters with the strangely-named Dilly 50 in 1956. The four-stroke 49cc engine sat atop large spoked wheels. The Dilly died just a few months after production began.

Neco BELGIUM/CHINA ★ ★

Neco offers a line of modern scooters and somehow manages to make a line of new Vespa near clones. The Borgia (taking the name of the notoriously depraved and murderous Italian family) and especially the Azzuro (azure, the color of Italy's national team) will fool many into believing it is a bonafide Piaggio but at half price.

More interesting is the Neco Abruzzi, dubbed the "poor man's Vespa," which recreates the classic Piaggio style in plastic with modern updates (and it's much cheaper). Gone is the gearshift in favor of an automatic, and the rear tire case is not that at all, but a storage bin. As with many retro scooters, too much chrome (or chrome-like plastic) can diminish the sleek stock lines, but this is a good stab at a classic while Piaggio was too busy focusing on the future.

Negrini ITALY ★

The area around Modena is the land of Ferraris, Maseratis and Stanguelini race cars, so when Pietro Negrini began his workshop in the town of Vignola, the Modenesi expected great things. In 1959, the Negrini Scooter 48 started zooming through the Apennine hills on the 18in spoked wheels. The little Negrini pushed by its 1.3hp to 40km/h and the newer Motorscooter 75 pumped out 3hp to allow a passenger to ride on the bench seat. In 1963, Negrini launched its 48cc Farfallino (little butterfly) with much more aerodynamic lines on 10in wheels, but the little Negrini putt-putts couldn't be heard over the Formula One Ferraris blasting around the race track at Maranello.

Chicco
The first MV Chicco imported into the United States, pictured in front of the Cosmopolitan Motors showroom in 1960. The Chicco's horizontal two stroke 155cc engine created 5.8hp at 5200rpm with a four-speed gearbox. The 10-inch wheels were carried on stub axles of the Chicco, Italian for coffee bean.

Nera GERMANY ★

Wolfgang Neuscheler designed the Nera scooter, of which just a few were built, offered with either a 149cc Sachs or a 120cc Jlo from 1948–1950.

Ner-a-Car USA-UK ★★★★

Carl Neracher took his turn in inventing cars, and opted for his "Near a car" scooter which debuted in 1921. Neracher put in a 221cc two-stroke engine, but the Ner-a-Car fell prey to criticism that it was too frail. The famous Cannonball Baker quieted the skeptics when he traversed the country from New York to Los Angeles in 174 hours.

The Ner-a-Car used dual headlamps and was originally intended just for women since it had a low center of gravity and dual springs to ease the ride. To push this "nearly-a-car," sultry flappers slinked back on the lengthy motorcycle/scooter as the perfect vehicle to show up in at fancy shindigs on Long Island. The Ner-a-Car was built in Syracuse, New York from 1921 to 1924 and under license in Britain from 1922 to 1926.

Neue Amag SWITZERLAND ★★

Sited at Baden, the firm offered its Piccolo, or Small, scooter in 1950, a miniature scooter motorcycle in the style of the American Mustang. In 1951, the Piccolo was renamed the Ami, or Friend, and was fitted with a Sachs 98cc. Also in 1951, the Ami A3 was launched with full bodywork, a two-person bench seat, and 150cc Sachs.

In 1953, the Ami Achilles A6 was offered as a Sport model with full bodywork; a 175cc Sachs was optional.

New Map FRANCE ★★

With a British-sounding name, this French firm was found in the 1920s in Lyon to produce motorcycles and by the 1950s stooped to mopeds. In 1954, New Map took a step back up with the Mascoot that was essentially a copy of Monet-Goyon's Starlett. The engine, however, was a 98cc Sachs putting out 2.75hp at 5000rpm.

The following year, the Escapade replaced the Mascoot with a 125cc AMC Isard engine. The large spoked wheels on the Escapade were soon complemented with a two-tone paint scheme, but the scoot only survived until 1957.

Niu CHINA ★★

Made in Changzhou and now close to doubling its capacity to two million scooters a year, the Niu boasts its ride as a "smart" electric scooter. Rather than the traditional lead-acid batteries, Niu used more expensive lithium-ion batteries for more efficiency and lon-

ger distances. Niu's design thankfully broke from the ho-hum sport scooters seen everywhere and opted for a futuristic, minimalistic design. The company also built mopeds to Lime Scooters, which could be seen in just about every major city for a while for ride-sharing schemes. Clearly Niu broke from the past with new technology, interesting design, and promising eco-friendly scooters.

Norlow UK ★★★

Sir Henry Norman and Major A. M. Low combined their names to form Norlow and their efforts to produce one of the first motorscooters. The engine was square 60x60 for 170cc and a dry battery was used rather than a magneto. The wheels measured 35cm and carried the 25kg to 36km/h. Sir Henry Norman pulled an early scooter publicity stunt by riding his Norlow scooter to his position in the Parliament.

NSU GERMANY

The history of NSU dates back to April Fool's Day, 1880, when Christian Schmidt founded a company to build strickmaschinen—sewing machines. The firm was soon set up in the village of Neckarsulm in the

New Niu

In 2020, suddenly scooter showrooms across the US were filled with the new electric scooter that was going to change it all: Niu. The future had arrived as something out of WALL-E, faceless yet comforting. Instead, the company skipped the too-cool mini crotch rocket design in lieu of something completely, well, new.

NSU Prima

The cover of the spare parts manual only begins to do justice to the miles of chrome and accessories the Prima boasted. With a dashboard often more intricate than cars of the time, the NSU Prima wowed riders with an array of gauges, knobs, and buttons that would make a jet fighter pilot green with envy. Technology of this kind marked the Funfstern as one of the fanciest scooters of its day.

Baden-Württemberg region of Germany. The name NSU stood for Neckarsulm Strickmaschinen Union. In 1887, a new owner, Schmidt's brother-in-law Gottlieb Benzhoff, took the reins and started production of bicycles. By 1901, NSU expanded to construct its first small motorcycles powered by Swiss-made 234cc Zédel engines. By 1955, NSU was the largest motorcycle maker in Germany.

During World War II, NSU built its amazing HK101 Kettenkrad tank-tread motorcycles for the Wehrmacht. After the war, Germany was in need of economical lightweight transportation, the fertile breeding ground for motorscooters the world over. Italy had gone through a similar history but had recovered more quickly than Germany postwar, so it was a far-thinking NSU that approached Innocenti to build Lambrettas under license.

NSU-LAMBRETTA 125 1950–1954
AND 150 1954–1956 ★ ★ ★

In 1950, NSU began fabricating Lambrettas in Neckarsulm under a five-year contract. The first NSU scooters used Innocenti C/LC engines shipped from the Lambrate works; bodywork was stamped out at the nearby Volkswagen factory.

The Lambretta C/LC 125 engine had a 52x58mm bore and stroke for 123cc. Running through a three-speed gearbox and shaft drive, the 125 was good for 4.5hp at 4500rpm and a top speed of 73km/h.

But the Germans had no patience for certain features of the Lambretta that they found lacking in good Teutonic over-engineering. Soon, NSU was building the majority of components for its scooters, and the NSU models surpassed the Innocenti

Lambretta in the quality of brakes, Bosch 6 volt horn, Magura seats, and higher-output, 30 watt flywheel magneto at a time when the Lambretta LC had only 25 watts. The Germans also added a glovebox behind the legshield topped by a small dash featuring the ignition switch, speedometer with odometer, choke, and a handy clock.

The styling of the NSU retained the lines of the LC with open handlebars. On the left legshield, NSU added its logo above the Lambretta nameplate. Colors available were beige, mittelgrau und hellblau.

At the 1953 Frankfurt Motorcycle Show, NSU unveiled a new 12 volt electric-start scooter powered by two 6 volt batteries wire in series; ignition remained 6 volt. This Luxus-Lambretta also included parking lights!

In 1954, NSU introduced a 150cc version with 6.2hp at 5200rpm. Top speed was 81km/h but the scooter retained the three-speed gearbox when a four-speed would have done it well.

In 1950, only 743 NSU-Lambrettas were built; in 1951, a mere 1,100. By the end of its life, however, production of the NSU Lambretta in all versions was prolific—117,045 units—but never approached the success of Innocenti's original.

In 1953, NSU cobbled up a prototype car made from two NSU-Lambretta 125 scooters welded together side by side. Bathtub-like rear bodywork was added on to allow for four saddle seats. The handlebars on the left-side scooter had a bar running across to the steering rod of the right-side scooter so the two front wheels could be controlled by the one set of handlebars. Two complete the automobile styling, a single chrome front bumper stretched across both front fenders, presumably with a pivot system to allow it to move with thee wheels as they leaned into turns.

A photo from the NSU archives show a beaming family of four out for a spin in the NSU-Werbeabteilung with a Volkswagen Bug in the background; presumably this was the family's second car, a "convertible" for Sunday putt-putting along the autobahn.

The world remains a poorer place as the NSU-Werbeabteilung never went into production.

PRIMA D 1956–1958 ★ ★ ★

The NSU-Innocenti contract expired in 1955 and was not renewed. Instead, in 1956, NSU introduced a Lambretta that was not a Lambretta; this was NSU's version of what a Lambretta should be.

Always competitive and class-conscious, NSU chose to call its new scooter the Prima, Italian for First.

The styling of the Prima D belied its Lambretta LC heritage but it was masked beneath gaudy chrome work, including side-cover trim, a single-piece headlamp/horn bezel, and a bulbous front fender bumper. The handlebars were now covered in a sheet metal sleeve and electric start was standard.

Colors included jade green, wine, polar blue, and several two-tone schemes: green and black, and ivory white paired with turquoise or racing red.

The engine was NSU's version of the shaft-drive Lambretta LC, still producing 6.2hp at 5200rpm with the one-cylinder two-stroke engine of 57x58mm bore and stroke. With a three-speed transmission, the Prima ran on 4.00x8in wheels and tipped the scales at 123kg.

The only substantial difference between the Prima D and the new Lambretta LD of 1954 was in NSU's use of pressed-steel front forks versus Innocenti's tried-and-true steel-tube forks.

The Prima D was only ever planned as a stopgap scooter to serve NSU's faithful during the year when the contract with Lambretta was finished and a new NSU scooter could be made ready.

PRIMA FÜNFSTERN 1957–1960 ★★★★★

In 1957, NSU created an original scooter, the Prima Fünfstern, known variously throughout the world as the Five Star or by the roman numeral, V.

NSU engineers were schooled in Lambretta design, and the Prima V carried on with a central large-gauge tube frame covered by sheet metal bodywork; the old Lambretta LC styling was still visible underneath the new, smoothed-out lines. Chrome hid the similarities along with a bulbous new front fender that was derisively said to be styled from a leftover Wehrmacht army helmet—which was in truth being kind.

The most fascinating feature of the new NSU was its exotic engine design. It was still a one-cylinder two-stroke but the cylinder was horizontal and transverse to the chassis. The flywheel magneto was at the front of the engine with the new four-speed gearbox to the rear of the crankshaft with a single-plate clutch mediating between the two. Final drive was via bevel gears.

The complete engine unit was suspended from the frame by a front pivoting mount and damped at the rear by a shock absorber with well-cushioned preload to handle the best German beer drinker. In an ironic twist of NSU and Innocenti's interwoven fates, the Italians would later use a similar design with their 125 Li Series of 1958.

The electric-start Prima V engine was of 174cc from an oversquare design of 62x57.6mm and a four-speed gearbox. Power was now 9.5hp, all electrics were 12 volts, and the wheels had finally grown to 3.50x10in but with an overall weight of 138kg, top speed had climbed to only 90km/h.

Much of that weight was due to the luxury equipment. Along with speedometer, horn, and electric start, the V also had an electric fuel gauge and fog light.

The Prima V was exported worldwide and imported into the United States by Butler & Smith, Inc. of New York City, which also imported the later Prima III as the Deluxe. Butler & Smith was a renowned promoter, also carrying the BMW line—it even got a Prima V on the "Price is Right" TV game show in June 1959. The correct, winning price was $555.

Five stars was recognized worldwide as the highest rating; the Prima Fünfstern was NSU's two-wheeled answer to Mercedes-Benz. This was the scooter that the good German plutocrat could love, a blend of world-class engineering, luxury features, and power.

PRIMA III K 1958–1960 AND KL 1959–1960 ★★★

The Prima III was a simplified, democratic version of the V with two stars-worth of features deleted. This included a smaller, 57mm bore engine of 146cc producing 7.4hp and a top speed of 84km/h. The bodywork was also revised with a new, modernistic rear-end treatment. And of course, the III cost less.

The standard K model featured bare-bones trim work, black saddle seats, and any color of paint as long as it was ivory. The K stood for "mit Kickstarter," according to the ads.

In 1959, the Luxus version was offered with electric start, chromed trim, two-tone color scheme, and an optional dual bench seat.

MAXIMA PROTOTYPE 1960 ★★★★

In 1960, NSU engineers began work on a prototype of the ultimate scooter, the Maxima. Designed as an alternative to the high-class Heinkel Tourist and Maicomobil, its name reflected its quality as the top-of-the-line Prima model, blending the words Maxi and Prima.

The Maxima was powered by NSU's exotic Prima V engine still at 175cc but now producing 10.5hp for a 95km/h top speed.

Instead of going ahead with the Maxima, NSU curtailed scooter production in 1960. By the end of its production life, some 69,000 Prima V and III units had been constructed. NSU now chose to concentrate on building automobiles using the avant-garde Wankel rotary engine instead of motorscooters as the German economy had rebounded figuratively from two wheels to four.

NV Progress SWEDEN ★★

Around 1957, the German Strolch Progress was built in Uppsala, Sweden by Nymanbolagen. The Swedes opted for a different engine from the original and renamed it the NV Progress.

Oscar
The English Oscar made its stage debut in London in 1953, but the curvaceous lines of the curious two-stroke reminiscent of the Maico Mobil or Pitty never made it out of the prototype stage.

N-Zeta NEW ZEALAND/ CZECHOSLOVAKIA ★ ★ ★

JNZ Manufacturing in New Zealand assembled the fabulous Czech Čezeta scooters in the early 1960s.

Ola Scooters INDIA/NETHERLANDS ★

According to *Fortune* magazine, India is the world's largest market for scooters, and Ola is slated to have the largest factory of two-wheeled vehicles in the world. With headquarters in Bangalore, Ola bought out the Dutch company Ftergo and will make its innovative electric scooter in 2021.

OLD FRANCE ★

Age had nothing to do with the name, although the OLD's Miniscoot could hardly be called modern. The Levallois-based company was known more for its luggage racks than mobiles, and its 75cc Miniscoot bore a striking resemblance to a ski rack with a pull-start engine. The 3hp motor was covered with a slick metal pod under a bizarre suspended trapezoidal luggage rack. OLD forgot the front legshields and fender exposing the tiny wheels.

Olmo ITALY ★

Just as many other Italian marques wanted a piece of the scooter action, Olmo put the Scooter 48 on the market with large spoked wheels. The 2.1hp two-stroke engine pushed the scooter to 65km/h—impressive for just a 48cc engine.

Orix A. Prina ITALY ★ ★ ★

At the Salone di Milano in 1950, a sleek new scooter showed the other makes that designing two-wheelers is all about innovation. The Orix Mod. b had a powerful 173cc two-stroke engine for 8.2hp and 85km/h. The air intakes on the side panels looked like horizontal rocket ships that shot the Orix through the air. Gas and air mixed in a Bing carburetor, as opposed to the ubiquitous Dell'Orto and the four-speed gearbox was shifted via a pedal. The Orix Model b ran through 1953 and was once displayed alongside the 123cc Orix Utilitario model C prototype in 1952.

ORLA ITALY ★ ★ ★

The ORLA goes down in history as one of the boldest bodywork ever conceived on a scooter. The one-piece aluminum covering was attached to the frame with easy to remove fasteners to expose the underside. ORLA named the rotund putt-putt after the sleek bird the swallow, Rondine, but perhaps a pelican would have been more appropriate due to its gigantic beak. The final production version of the Rondine dropped the steering wheel of the prototype and was propelled by a four-stroke 125cc engine that pushed the aluminum beast to 87km/h.

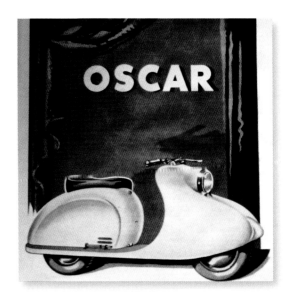

Oscar UK ★ ★

The Oscar scooter was created by Projects and Development Ltd of Blackburn. It appeared as a startling prototype at the 1953 London Show; yet while production was promised for several years, the Oscar ended its life in prototype limbo.

Based on either 122cc 4.8hp or 197cc 8.4hp Villiers two-strokes with fan cooling and a foot-shifted three-speed gearbox, the Oscar rode atop 3.25x6in tires with 5in brakes front and rear. Suspension was by bonded-rubber units with adjustable preload.

The frame was of steel tubing with a rear swing arm. The whole affair was covered by two pieces of fiberglass with bulbous and bloated styling; The Motor Cycle called it "up-to-the-minute," which may have been true.

Paglianti ITALY ★

Paglianti offered 48cc and 75cc two-stroke scooters with 12in wire-laced wheels from 1959 to 1963. The two-toned 48cc Paglianti took on the name Cip in 1963 at the end of its run.

Pak-Jak USA ★ ★

Produced for only one year (1971), the Pak-Jak rivaled fellow Wisconsin-based company Harley-Davidson in the scooter realm in a race to the most bizarre. A mere 125 were made of this three-wheeled mini-bike/scooter—with all wheels in a line!

Palmieri & Gulinelli ITALY ★ ★

Palmieri & Gulinelli from Bologna was a moped builder that decided to make the step up to scooter production in the late 1950s. The firm offered its Guizzo 150cc two-stroke scooter with 6hp at 5400rpm and zaftig bodywork at the 1957 Salone di Milano. The unusual 14in wheels compromised between large diameter moped wheels and those of tippy scooters. With the success of the first Guizzo (mean "flash" in Italian), the company tried to update the scooter, but ended up losing its original design to the influence of the Lambretta. By the early 1960s, sales plummeted, forcing the company to close.

Pannonia HUNGARY ★

Pannonia motorcycles and scooters were built at the Mogürt factory in Budapest, sharing the assembly lines with the Czepel Danuvia motorcycles—and often design and parts. Pannonia's Panni R50 scooter was inspired by the Nicki Victoria and powered by a 48cc two-stroke of 38x42mm giving 1.8hp.

Panther UK ★★

The famous Panther works in Cleckheaton dated back to the pioneer days of motorcycling. In 1959, it released its Princess scooter based on a 174cc Villiers 2L engine with either kickstart or optional electric leg.

By 1961, the Princess was available in four models: 174cc kickstart and electric start versions and 197cc kickstart and electric start. The Princess lasted until 1963, by which time Panther was in receivership.

Parilla ITALY

Moto Parilla was created in the back of a truck diesel-injector repair shop on the outskirts of Milan in 1946. Whereas most of the immediate postwar motorcycle firms built scooters and small cycles to capitalize on the need for economical transportation, founder Giovanni Parrilla went with his heart. He began by handcrafting a limited series of beautiful 250cc overhead-cam racing motorcycles; only later did he mass-produce motorscooters and then merely to provide funding for his racing effort.

At one time in the 1950s, Moto Parilla was one of the major Italian makes, ranking fourth behind Piaggio, Innocenti, and Gilera in production.

Founder Giovanni Parrilla opted to drop one r from his Spanish name for easier Italian pronunciation of the motorcycle marque. But like Iso, which produced thousands of scooters in its time, Parilla has largely been forgotten in this age of Honda and Yamaha.

LEVRIERE (GREYHOUND) 125 AND 150 1952–1959 ★★★

Moto Parilla's motorscooter was introduced in January 1952 at the Milan Fiera Campioniara. As Parilla's logo was a racing greyhound, the scooter was named the Levriere or "Greyhound."

Giovanni Parrilla chose to give the scooter buyer the option of a more refined scooter with a powerful engine, telescopic forks, large, 12in wheels, and stylish bodywork. The Levriere was built in large numbers and sold well through its history, but it never challenged the inexpensively efficient Vespas and Lambrettas.

The chassis was primarily that of a motorcycle with a central duplex tube frame covered by sheet-metal bodywork. The bodywork was used not only to shield rider from the engine and road grime but also for aerodynamics: the central step-through section channeled cool air from behind the front wheel back to the engine and transmission and then out through side vents.

The first Levriere was offered with a single-cylinder two-stroke 125cc with square internal measurements of 54x54mm. A three-speed gearbox was shifted by a twist grip. Secondary drive was to be chain.

A unique feature of the Greyhound was its 3.00x12in wheels, which were again of motorcycle design featuring Borrani aluminum-alloy rims laced to 112mm hubs with drum brakes front and rear.

In 1953, a 150cc version was offered based on a large, 60mm bore engine capable of producing 7hp at 5700rpm. The 150 model ran via a four-speed gearbox but all other features were identical. Top speed was advertised at 85km/h.

SLUGHI (RAMJET) 1959–1961 ★★★

In 1957, Parilla showed its new Slughi 99 at the Milan Show. Unorthodoxy prevailed: the backbone of the Slughi—named for a breed of desert racing greyhounds—was of pressed steel with other sheet steel body panels covering the engine and much of the 2.75x17in rear wheel. The Deluxe version had legshields, panniers, and windshield.

Original plans called for a horizontal single-cylinder 98cc overhead-valve four-stroke but production finally commenced in 1959 with a 125cc two- and four-stroke offered.

All things considered, the Slughi was a motorcycle version of the Vespa. And while it never sold as well as the scooter, the poor sales were due more to Parilla's financial health at the time than to the Slughi's failure.

Imported into the United States, the Slughi was renamed the Ramjet and fitted with a jet ornament launching from the front fender. A copy of the Slughi was also sold on the Japanese market beginning in 1959.

OSCAR PROTOTYPE 1960 ★★★★★

Moto Parilla created one of the most fascinating scooter prototypes in 1960, but like the Rumi prototypes of the same year, the Oscar was fated to prototype limbo.

The bodywork of the Oscar was sleek and stylish, like a refined Lambretta. But it was the engine that was the most unique.

While Rumi was looking at a V-twin, Parilla created a horizontal two-stroke twin similar in layout—but little else—to Rumi's classic powerplant. The electric-start Parilla engine displaced 160cc and featured double cooling fans drawing air through channels between the inner and outer walls of the crankcase. Backed by a four-speed transmission, the motor-gearbox unit pivoted on a front mount and was suspended at the rear by shock absorbers. Primary drive was by duplex chain, whereas secondary drive was by gears to the rear hub.

Development of the promising Oscar came at the wrong time for Parilla. In 1961, Giovanni Parrilla was forced to sell out to a holding company, SIL, to avoid bankruptcy. Moto Parilla soldiered on for two more years but its soul was gone.

Parillas were imported into the United Kingdom and the United States through much of their run. The US importer, Cosmopolitan Motors of Hatboro, Pennsylvania, even purchased the factory's stock in 1963 and continued limited Parilla assembly in the United States until 1967.

Pandra JAPAN ★★

This lengthy little one-seater debuted in 1959 and tried to rival the Japanese powers of the time: Fuji with its Rabbit and Mitsubishi with its Silver Pigeon. Pandra was able to find enough of a market niche to survive until 1962.

Patimo FRANCE ★

The tiny Patimo 49cc scooter appeared at the 1947 Salon de Paris and was discontinued by the following year. The miniscule VAP-4 engine produced 0.65hp at 3500rpm, possibly enough to move the scooter with a passenger.

Paul Vallée FRANCE

Paul Vallée productions distributed and marketed by SICRAF (Société Industrielle de Construction et de Recherches Automobiles de France), made scooters that were essentially borrowed Lambretta designs but under no contract with the Italian company for extra profits.

The engine was small enough to skirt French driving laws for motorcycles and offered the opportunity for garçons et femmes without a permit (or car) to get to town. Sales brochures blared "Tous sur scooter P. Vallée sans permis de conduire!" (Everyone on a P. Vallée scooter without requiring a driver's license!).

S.149 1949 ★★

The first model, the S.149, was essentially a 125cc Lambretta A or B with a darker paint job in metallic blue. The engine was a 125cc Aubier-Dunne AL with three-speeds that gave 3.6hp. Apparently Innocenti didn't mind, possibly thinking that imitation is the truest form of flattery, that is as long as Paul Vallée didn't try to sell them in Italy. In 1952, Paul Vallée's second scooter was nearly identical, chrome trim and all, to the dressed Lambretta LC except for the mechanics with a 125cc Ydral with four speeds.

BO.54L AND BO.54 GT 1953 ★★

Possibly while designing his three-wheeled car, quaintly named the Singing Cleric, he got away from the Italian influenced design and came up with the decidedly French BO.54. Appearing at the Salon de Paris in 1953, the BO.54 had sleek lines with a front fender like a retriever's nose, and was available in a tasteful two-tone (the BO.54L). An Ydral 125cc or 175cc powered the BO on its 8in wheels. Just when M. Paul Vallée had an originally design, he ceased coming up with any further scooter ideas.

Pawa GERMANY ★★★

In 1922, Kurt Passow designed an odd motorcycle with long U handlebars, a reclining seat, and a 226cc engine between the driver's feet covered with metal siding and plenty of air ducts. Riding on 15in wheels, the Pawa boasted 60km/h under ideal conditions. Passow soon took his designs from his home in Berlin and settled in Braunschweig for his new PER motorcycle/scooter.

Peirspeed USA/TAIWAN ★

Taiwanese TGB scooters were badged as "Peirspeed" and sold in the US.

Peripoli ITALY ★★

In 1961, Peripoli introduced its Giulietta scooter named for Romeo's better half. The scooter was a jolly blend of fanciful styling, brilliant color, and chrome jewelry.

The Giulietta was powered by a Morini two-stroke motor of 125cc with 38x42mm and 2.8hp at 7200rpm. Top speed on the dwarf 3.25x8in tires was 80km/h.

Peugeot FRANCE

Peugeot threw caution to the wind in breaking from the other large European automakers that were monomaniacally focusing on cars and risked a scooter.

S.55 1953, S.57 1954, S.57 AL 1955 AND S.157 1955 ★★★

Unlike many French scooter makers, Peugeot got it right the first time with a classic design and optional 125cc or 150cc engines atop 8in wheels. The enlarged front fender borrowed directly from the bizarre Scootavia, this time actually using the space for storage and space on top it for strapping down extra luggage. Although protruding luggage space off the front didn't detract from the lines, one can't help make a correlation to a hinged toilet seat.

Two brave French Air Force quarter marshals proved the longevity of their Peugeot scooters enough to venture from Saigon to Paris, leaving April 21, 1956. They arrived back in Paris On August 25, 1956 parading down the Champs Elysées to almost as much fanfare as Lindbergh's transatlantic flight from New York. After traversing eleven countries, their beat up Peugeots were displayed at the Salon de Paris in 1956.

S.57B 1956 AND S.57C 1957 ★★★

With a new day dawning, Peugeot updated its earlier scooters, the C with larger 10in wheels and 5.1hp, up from the 4.6hp of the B.

Peugeot scooters were also sold under the name of Griffon/FMC with only different labels and names. The S.55 was the S.555, the S.57 the S.5577, and the S.157 became the S.657.

Peugeot returned to building scooters in the 1980s and 1990s, offering a variety of modern plastic scooters, including its basic ST50L and SC50L Metropolis models as well as its Rapido with red and white two-tone graphics that made up for its lack of rapid speed. At the 1992 Bologna show, Peugeot displayed its Fox 50 scooter with Buck Rogers styling, a large purposeful-looking muffler, and neon graphics.

Peugeot then introduced its Scoot'Elec, boasting a quiet electric battery that will bring the driver 28 miles (45 km) from home before needing a recharge (and a ride back home). Peugeot offers, among others, the macho-sounding Jet Force Compressor, the Trekker, the Elystar, and the scrappy Speedfight2. While the names evoke gang fighting in the 'hood, Peugeot brags about its Police Patrol Vehicles that are "the number 1 choice for law enforcement organizations."

In 2014, Mahindra and Mahindra of Mumbai, India, bought a controlling percentage of Peugeot but kept part of the production in France and the rest in Jinan, China. Peugeot kept producing modern scooters and some three-wheeled scooter-like vehicles.

PGO ITALY-TAIWAN ★

The PGO Star 50 scooter was made in Taiwan in the 1990s and imported into Italy by Rimoto of Palermo, Sicily. PGO was an obvious takeoff on Piaggio's name; its scooters also paid homage to the Piaggio line. With a 49.4cc engine of 40x39.3mm, the PGO was a typical modern-day plastic scooter of sharp-angled design.

Piaggio's collaboration with PGO lasted ten years and ended in 1982, but the company continued making bikes for Genuine Scooters, such as the Buddy, Roughhouse, and Hooligan, and its own versions, such as the Bubu.

Phoenix UK ★★

The H. B. Engineering firm arose from the ashes of Tottenham, London post World War II with its Phoenix scooter. Spearheaded by Ernie Barrett, the company concentrated on a line of scooters with different-size Villiers two-strokes in a common chassis with similar bodywork.

In 1956, the first model was launched at the Earl's Court Show with a 147cc 30C backed by a three-speed gearbox in a standard tubular frame with a swing-arm rear and leading-link front forks holding 3.50x8in tires. The bodywork was svelte and stylish, jeweled by chrome trim. In 1958, the range expanded to Standard and De Luxe 147cc versions.

In May 1958, the four new models were launched with face-lifted styling and a fiberglass rear body section. New models included the Standard 100; 150 Super de Luxe with the kickstart 147cc 30C and dressed up by whitewall tires; the S150 with electric-start 148cc 31C; the S200 with electric-start 197cc 9E; the T250 with the Villiers 249cc 2T twin-cylinder engine with electric start and 10in wheels; and the gussied-up 250 Super de Luxe.

In 1959, the range was further expanded to fourteen models with the S prefix denoting single-cylinder and T marking the twins. The 150 De Luxe was dropped, but sidecars were available for the other three 150cc models.

New T325 and fancy 325 Super de Luxe models were offered with an electric-start 324cc Villiers 3T twin with 17hp at 5800rpm. The large-bore models were designed as mules to pull sidecars. As the 325 models' flyer promised, "The Phoenix Scooter is an accumulation of the best ideas and suggestions of a great number of people in the trade and also scooter owners themselves, and we feel sure that many happy and safe miles will be covered by the proud owners of this very British product."

In 1960, three new models were added: the Standard 200 with kickstart and the kickstart Standard 175 and the electric-start S175 both with the 174cc 2L. For 1960, the 150 Super de Luxe was upgraded to the 31C engine.

Production continued until 1964, when the Phoenix scooter died.

Piaggio ITALY

Throughout the world, scooter is synonymous with Vespa. In many European countries, the names are interchangeable: in Paris, parking signs refer to all scooters as Vespas; in Italian, there is even a verb meaning "to acquire a Vespa," vespizzare."

Piaggio named its scooter the Vespa not for the ancient Roman emperor Titus Flavius Sabinis Vespasianus, but rather for the buzzing of its two-stroke engine that sounds like a wasp, or vespa in Italian. The styling of the scooter's tail also bears an odd resemblance to the wasp's abdomen.

Piaggio's scooter began its career in 1946 as the two-wheeled "car" upon which the Italian postwar recovery rode. By the 1950s, the Vespa brought freedom of mobility to large sectors of the population—and became a symbol of Italy in many foreign minds. And by the 1960s, the Vespa, along with Innocenti's Lambretta, had become a counterculture statement.

The changing image of the Vespa was chronicled in film. The 1953 William Wyler movie, Roman Holiday, starred Audrey Hepburn as an Italian princess who escaped the humdrum royal life of the palazzo to cavort about fairy-tale Rome on a Vespa with dashing American journalist Gregory Peck. The Who film, Quadrophenia, told the tale of the Mod-Rocker wars of 1960s Great Britain; the subtext was a scooter-motorcycle war, although both vehicles stood for the same thing: rebellion.

By 1993, Piaggio had built 10 million of the archetypal scooters worldwide, millions more than its closest rival, Innocenti's 4 million Lambrettas. Besides merely creating an industry, the omnipresent and omnipotent Vespa created a youth culture that was, to rework John Lennon's words, more popular than Jesus Christ or The Beatles combined.

Società Anonima Piaggio factory was founded in 1884 by Rinaldo Piaggio in Genoa, Italy, to make wood-working machinery and later, railroad cars. In 1915, Piaggio delved into aviation, inventing such innovations as cabin pressurization. The firm also built a remarkable aviation engine that set twenty world records; in the 1920s, Piaggio constucted a series of remarkable racing seaplane prototypes in hope of contesting the Schneider Trophy. Rinaldo Piaggio died in 1938, leaving the factory to his sons Enrico, born in 1905, and Armando.

During World War II, Piaggio produced Fascist Italy's only heavy bomber, the P108B, which killed Benito Mussolini's son, Bruno, during a test flight crash. In the waning years of the war, the Piaggio factory at Pontedera was bombed and destroyed by the Allies; the remaining machine tools were confiscated by the Nazis. The factory was rebuilt after the end of hostilities, and Piaggio began looking for a new product to construct and sell.

Enrico Piaggio described those immediate postwar days to American Mercury magazine in 1957: "Our over 10,000 employees were thrown out of work by the bombings and by the fact that, as soon as the war was over, our production fell to zero. In fact, we were prohibited from making airplanes by the peace treaty. So you see it was essential that we find a new peacetime product for the sake of the Piaggio Company and our employees."

Enrico Piaggio had witnessed the lightweight Aeromoto paratrooper scooter built for the Italian Army in World War II by Volugrafo, and believed that there might be a market for a civilized version of such a scooter to provide transportation, primarily for women. He instructed his chief designer, Corradino d'Ascanio, to begin work.

The abruzzese engineer d'Ascanio led the firm's aeronautics division and was an authority on helicopter design, aircraft engines, and stressed-skin bodywork where the body was designed to serve double duty as the frame in a monocoque unitized design. Such advanced monocoque structures had been used on airplanes prewar, but their adaption to scooters was indeed cutting edge; today this design is used throughout the world in automobiles.

After a false start with a first prototype, called the Paperino, d'Ascanio created the Vespa, which made its debut in 1946. D'Ascanio's Vespa was truly revolutionary, incorporating features of motorcycles (two wheels, easy-to-use handlebar-mounted controls, and saddle seats), airplanes (monocoque unit design and single-sided stub axles), and automobiles (protective bodywork, covered motor, and floorboards). After a rocky introduction, the scooter won acceptance, and soon Vespas were everywhere.

Since the majority of Italians couldn't afford a motorcycle, let alone a car, most of them had to settle for a "two-wheeled car," as Piaggio promoted its scooter in the postwar years. And they soon came to love the wasp. It was ideal for driving down the narrow Italian streets in cities and hilltowns from Genoa to Palermo where cars could not fit. For personal transportation, the scooter was ideal. "I'd give up my car, only the Vespa won't hold my trombone," quipped American Dixieland jazz artist Wilbur de Paris to The New Yorker in 1956.

Because of its small, 8in wheels, the first Vespas were not designed for touring any significant distance, but competition for the scooter came not from the motorcycle companies as much as from the car manufacturers who were producing three wheelers and micro cars, such as Iso's Isetta and Fiat's revived prewar 500 Topolino. Piaggio's marketing focused on the working class, who needed inexpensive transportation; according to a poll of the Italian market by Business Week in 1956, "2% of all Vespa owners are priests, 2% doctors, 3% students, 7% other professionals, 10% skilled laborers, 16% merchants, 30% white-collar workers, and 30% laborers."

Enrico Piaggio confessed that the success of the Vespa was due to its affordability. "Just like Henry Ford put the workers on wheels in America," he told Newsweek in 1956, "we put automotive transport within the reach of people who never expected to travel that way." Scooters were available, affordable, operable, and desirable to everyone—even the Duke of Edinburgh had an affection for Vespas and ordered a fleet in 1956 to cruise the grounds of Buckingham Palace.

PAPERINO 1945 ★★★★

Fiat called its 500cc midget car the Topolino, or Mickey Mouse, so d'Ascanio's first creation was nicknamed the Paperino, or Donald Duck, trading on the Italian love for Walt Disney's cartoon characters, which are almost as popular as images of the Madonna in Italy.

The Paperino was powered by a single-cylinder 98cc two-stroke engine of Piaggio design mounted alongside the rear wheel with direct drive via the in-unit gearbox. The gearbox was shifted by rod linkage from the left twistgrip; the throttle was cable-operated from the right twistgrip. This basic engine-gearbox-controls layout would carry over to the Vespa.

The Paperino's body design foreshadowed that of the Vespa. A central tunnel housing ran from steering head back to the engine cover, which would have made it difficult for Piaggio's female target audience to straddle the scooter. This, along with other details, doomed the Paperino. "Admittedly," Piaggio said, "the first motor scooter was a horrible looking thing, and people ridiculed us to our faces."

After creating the single Paperino prototype, it was back to the drawing board for d'Ascanio.

VESPA 98CC 1946–1948 ★★★★★

In creating the Vespa, d'Ascanio refined many of the ideas set forth by the Paperino. He outlined his parameters in creating the scooter to an Italian magazine: "Having seen motorcyclists stuck at the side of the road many times with a punctured tire, I decided that one of the most important things to solve was that a flat should no longer be a large problem just like it wasn't for automobiles.

"Another problem to resolve was that of simplifying the steering, especially in city driving. To help this, the control of the gearshifting was placed on the

Handlebar Vespa

Realizing the importance of scooters to the devasted Piaggio factory, Enrico Piaggio recruited his top aeronautic engineer Corradino d'Ascanio to design the MP6 prototype. D'Ascanio was a regular da Vinci designing planes and helicopters, and now the 3.2hp Vespa that could reach 60 km/h. "And this was how the Ugly Duckling (Paperino), as in Hans Christian Andersen's fable, became a swan, or rather a wasp (Vespa)," as La Vespa e Tutti i suoi Vespini put it. **Courtesy of the owner: Hans Kruger**

WHO BUYS IT... *never looses-always gains...*

handlebars for easy shifting without abandoning maneuverability making its use intuitive for the novice.

"Another large inconvenience with traditional motorcycles was oil spraying on clothes, so I thought of moving the engine far from the 'pilot,' covering it with a fairing, and abolishing the open chain with a cover placing the wheel right next to the gearchange.

"Some solutions came from aeronautical technology, with which Piaggio was obviously familiar, such as the rear tubular wheel holder borrowed directly from the undercarriage of airplanes. The single shell frame surpassed even the most modern automobile design since the stamped bodywork of strengthened steel was a rarity."

The Vespa prototype was first shown to the public at the 1946 Turin Show, and 100 pre-production prototypes were built before the production lines started rolling.

The Vespa was powered by the single-cylinder 98cc two-stroke measuring 50x50mm bore and stroke. A cable-operated throttle controlled the Dell'Orto T2 16/17mm carburetor. Cooling was by ambient airflow. The engine was backed by a three-speed gearbox with rod gearchange controls that provided direct drive to the rear wheel. The single-sided stub axles held the bolted-up stamped-steel wheels fitted with 3.50x8in Pirelli tires; the wheels were interchangeable front to rear.

Power from the little engine was 3.3hp at 4500rpm, enough to propel the Vespa to a 60km/h or 35mph top speed and still return 100mpg, according to Moto Revue magazine of July 1946.

As on the Paperino, d'Ascanio opted for handlebar-mounted controls for the gearchange, throttle, clutch, and brakes, making it easier for the uninitiated rider than the foot levers of motorcycle; he left the handlebars uncovered to give them the look of being taken from a bicycle and therefore familiar and easy to ride.

In 1946, the Vespa's styling was strikingly modernistic—almost to the point of exaggeration. Prior to World War II, the Italian Futurist movement lead by poet and gourmand Filippo Tommaso Marinetti preached a philosophy of cleansing society through speed, power, and war. After Italy's defeat, war was no longer so appetizing, but speed and power still reigned to mobilize the people. Inevitably, Piaggio was influenced by the Futurists since the smooth, streamlined design of the wasp gave the (mistaken) image of a super-fast scooter.

The most unique feature of the scooter was the step-through frame, flat footboards, and full bodywork to protect the rider from the elements. The large front fender carried the headlamp and turned in unison with the wheel that it all but covered.

The Vespa boasted a toolbox that was housed within the body under the curve of the single saddle seat; a luggage rack rode behind the seat. The left sidecover housed a glovebox by the spare tire which balanced the right leaning motor leaning off to the right. The interchangeable spare and the muffler exiting on the left didn't weigh as much as the motor on the right, forcing Vespisti to learn to lean to the left to compensate, which became a characteristic trait and you could spot the arrival of a Vespa from afar by the silhouette.

The Vespa was immediately derided by the Italian motorcycle industry. Pundits put down the scooter's near-vertical front fork and elfin, 8in wheels, insinuating for all potential buyers to hear that the setup made for a dangerous ride on Italy's war-torn roads and that it was unsafe on wet cobblestones. The front knee-action suspension was criticized as being too soft, forcing the scooter to dive frontward under even the lightest braking. In the end, the erratic sparking and the simple pump lubrication caused motorcycle companies to dismiss the scooter on the grounds of engineering faults.

Piaggio rebutted these attacks, claiming that the Vespa was not a small cousin of the motorcycle, but rather an entirely novel form of transportation made for slower speeds and short distances. In the end, the Vespa proved Piaggio and d'Ascanio's concept was a success.

By 1948, the front fender was redesigned to allow the wheel to be more easily removed. A fan was introduced to cool the engine; a horn was added on the front apron.

VESPA 125CC 1948–1950 ★ ★ ★

In 1948, after less than two full years of production, the Vespa was updated. Innocenti had introduced its Lambretta scooter in 1947, and the firms would be locked in competition until 1971, when Innocenti finally threw in the towel. In the intervening thirty-four years, updates and changes– as well as completely new models—would be added to both firms' lines largely in response to real or imagined threats from the other maker.

The Lambretta was powered by a brawny (in relative terms) 125cc engine, so Piaggio quickly created its own 125cc, which bowed in 1948 to replace the original 98cc. The 125cc measured 56.5x49.8mm and created 5hp at 4500rpm via a new Dell'Orto TA 17 versus the 3.2hp of the smaller Vespa engine and the Lambretta's 4.3 at 4000rpm. The top speed of the 125cc scooter reached a full 70km/h or 44mph.

The other major change to the Vespa in 1948 was the redesigned suspension, giving a smoother ride and combating the front braking squat.

In 1949, the old-fashioned, though functional rod control system was updated to become more flexible. In 1950, the rear body was redesigned with an added egg-shaped muffler.

These early models are sometimes called "wide body" Vespas due to the rounded rump that was slowly put on a diet. Just as plump Marilyn Monroe "jiggled like jelly," according to Some Like it Hot, her curvaceous lines were replaced by androgynous, some would say anorexic-looking, Twiggy in the 1960s.

The early "Fenderlight" Vespas ran from 1946 to 1957 with the distinctive headlamp plopped on the fender and the handlebars left lightless.

VESPA 125 '51 1951–1952 ★ ★ ★

In 1951, the Vespa's cable gearchange control was finally replaced by cables; Innocenti had always used cables—as did most other manufacturer in the world—and Piaggio's stubborn refusal to use cables had probably cost them some sales.

By 1951, the right sidecover was hinged upward with a catch (that inevitably broke) to hold it for easy engine access. Unlike the Lambretta with its glovebox under the seat, the Vespa's glovebox was a small panel on the left sidecover, and the panel under the seat accessed the carburetor. The carb's long manifold routed the fuel on a long path through the monocoque bodywork.

The gearbox still had only three speeds but the direct gear final drive of the first models was replaced by a chain secondary drive. The updated rear suspension with hydraulic damper also smoothed the ride. The handlebars remained essentially the same with the 150mm headlamp still perched on the front fender; the '51 boasted a new rectangular tail lamp.

VESPA 125 '53 U 1953 ★ ★ ★

In 1953, Vespa unveiled its 125 U, or Utilitaria, economy model with the headlamp now mounted on the handlebars, which were partly covered by a steel cowling. The headlamp's ascension was due to laws that regulated its height; Vespas made in other countries followed suit, although some makers waited until 1955 before making the change, as with England's Douglas.

The single-saddled Utilitaria (also know as the Vespa Junior) was exhibited at the 1952 Milan Show but did not go into production until 1953, priced below the Normale model to combat the (unsuccessful) Lambretta E and F economy models. The Utilitaria had front suspension harking back to the simplicity of the early models as well as a bare-bones front fender. Piaggio cut out the baggage compartment on the top of the left side cover and exposed part of the engine on the other side with a cutaway around the top of the fan.

VESPA 125 '53 1953–1957 ★ ★

In 1953, the 125cc engine was upgraded with a revised cylinder head and barrel with twin transfer ports to feed the fuel-oil mix. The compression ratio was now at 6.4:1 fed by a Dell'Orto TA 18mm carburetor; power was up to 5hp at 4500rpm. The gas tank was enlarged to 5.25 liters and by 1946, it would be at 8.2 liters; meanwhile the wheels remained 8in with 3.50x8in tires.

While the headlamp was moved to the handlebars on the 125 U for safety concerns, the Normale retained the fender-mounted light—and it had been switched to a smaller, 130mm diameter.

Under Modena's Porticos
The early Vespa featured its headlamp mounted on the front fender and was typically painted in Piaggio's classic metallic green, which became the quintessential Vespa color even though other colors were available such as a dark maroon. The metallic green is believed to have been a war surplus rustproofing industrial paint. Piaggio added an extra seat on its scooter to compete with Innocenti's A 125 two-seater, but the added weight of a second rider required an increase in engine displacement to 125cc in 1951.

The Vespa's front fender was redesigned, however, bearing a bulge to clear the right-side forks and shock. In later models, Piaggio cut out the baggage compartment on the top of the left sidecover and exposed part of the engine on the other side with a cutaway around the top of the fan.

In 1953, the classic metallic gray-green of the Vespa was changed to a new nonmetallic gray-green, although other colors were still available, albeit rare. In 1955, a light gray color was added to the Vespa line as well as stronger front suspension and the saddle pushed forward to allow easier access to the gas cap.

In 1954, a sidecover made its debut that completely covered the fan and flywheel magneto, approaching the definitive Vespa design used on all future models.

In describing the Vespa 125, Piaggio ads proclaimed that the "Vespa's Always In Style—the basic design of this handsome machine doesn't change from year to year. This means that your Vespa will be slow to depreciate, will never become obsolete." Unfortunately, the conformity of style aged the newest Vespas and no matter how hard Piaggio tried to promote its scooter, the new model looked much the same as the old one.

VESPA 150 1954–1958 ★★★

A new 150cc Vespa made its debut in 1954 based on a square 57x57mm engine that fathered 5.7hp. Not surprisingly, Innocenti had introduced its LD 150 in 1954 as well. The very first Vespa 150s didn't have a battery to support the electrics, but this soon became a standard feature. The headlamp followed the Utilitario model's lead with the placement on the handlebars, which were updated in 1957 with an entirely enclosed handshifter.

Overlapping the 98cc and 125cc Fenderlights were the "Handlebar" Vespas which ran from 1955 to 1958. The distinctive feature was an open bicy-cle-style handlebar with the headlamp perched in the middle. The VB1 Vespa still had the wide body, but finally enclosed the headset to set the standard for the modern scooters.

The American Popular Science magazine tested a 150 in 1957, commenting on its "horn like a Model T's with a foreign accent." The threat of Vespas becoming widespread in the United States led to a media assault on the loud noise of the scooters' two-stroke engines—there was no qualms about the four-stroke noise of the American-made Cushmans—and later to exaggerated claims against their safety. Popular Science described a new Vespa's sound in 1957 as a "vacuum cleaner" with "a polite but busy whisper," while a 1956 Fortune article claimed it was "the sound of riveting guns."

Piaggio claimed the Vespa had the lowest decibel level of all scooters—except when Italian hot-rodders sawed off an inch or more of the muffler for better gas mileage and about a 10 percent power increase, essential for piazza cruising. Piaggio, however didn't condone the decibel increasing muffler adjustment, but still got blasted in the American press for the noise when Vespas were first sold in the United States. Fortune reported, "Not content with making the Italian night hideous, Piaggio & Co. of Genoa, which manufactures one of Italy's most popular scooters, the Vespa, has launched a determined assault on the American market."

In April 1956, the one-millionth Vespa was produced worldwide, combining the production of all factories in France, England, Germany, and elsewhere that were building Vespas under license. A celebration was held in Pontedera and Vespa Day was declared throughout Italy with festivities held in fifteen Italian cities, including a convoy of 2,000 Vespas traveling en masse through Rome and halting all traffic. The Piaggio factory in Italy now manufactured 500 scooters a day, and by this time, the French Vespa firm, ACMA, had produced a total of 100,000 Vespas.

VESPA 150 GS 1954–1961 AND 160 GS 1962–1964 ★★★★★

Beginning in 1949, Piaggio created a series of sport, racing, and speed-record prototypes and factory works machines. Piaggio saw winning races and setting speed and endurance records as a way to prove its product and sell more machines.

In 1949, the firm built a special prototype for a Sport scooter backed by a belief that as the economy recovered, there would be demand for a high-performance sporting model. The Sport was based on the 125cc model but bore a radically reworked body. An enlarged front fender covered most of the wheel to provide better aerodynamics; a slotted vertical opening on either side allowed cooling airflow to the brake. The legshield was narrowed, again to cut wind resistance, and no horn or headlamp was fitted. The right sidecover was cut away from the engine even more than standard to let in more cooling air. A gas tank was mounted between the rider's legs to form a bridge to the handlebars; a pad was strapped to the gas tank's top so the rider could lean on its for long-distance races.

The timing of the Sport was too early, but the idea was sound, and Piaggio would return to the sporting theme six years later in creating its Gran Sport model. Some of the Sport prototype's features would be used in designing the GS, while others would carry over to the later 90 SS.

By 1954, the time was right. Italians had extra money in their pockets to buy an upscale scooter that offered extra power and luxurious accessories. Piaggio beat Innocenti to the punch in creating a gran turismo scooter in the image of the Ferrari GT cars of the same era, albeit on a different scale.

The 150 GS first appeared at the Salone di Milano in late 1954. The GS design stunned all; Piaggio had refined and perfected its scooter into a high-performance touring and sporting model. The engine was a square 57x57mm with a compression ratio of 6.7:1, pumping out 8hp at 7500rpm via a UB 23 S 3 Dell'Orto carburetor. Backed by a four-speed gearbox, the GS reached 100km/h or 62mph on the new 3.50x10in wheels.

The 150 GS came with a bench seat for two people and was available exclusively in metallic grey. On early models, the spare tire was mounted on top of the central tunnel behind the legshields as the left sidecover now housed a luggage trunk.

In 1958, the 150 GS featured a new speedometer as well as wheel and saddle design. Although the GS reigned as the most powerful Vespa, its lack of fuel efficiency compared to the other Vespas was criticized. To put these worries to rest, Joan Short and Tommy Behan of the Vespa Club of Britain loaded up their GS with a mere £1 worth of gas and rode all the way from London to Paris in 1959.

In 1957, Innocenti responded to the Gran Sport by offering its Lambretta TV 175. With a 175cc competitor threatening to steal the thunder created by the 150 GS, Piaggio created its 160 GS in 1962. "Vespa's powerhouse," the 160 GS enlarged both the bore and stroke of the 150 GS engine to 58x60mm, making it capable of 8.2hp at 6500rpm via a Dell'Orto SI 27/23 for a top speed of 65mph. Fuel consumption dropped to 80mpg due to the 160 GS's heavier weight of 232lb.

Although the 160 was a steadier ride than the smaller GS, it didn't conquer the market the way the quicker 150 did. Distinguishing features of the 160 were the added metal trim on the front fender, a mat on the center bridge, a smaller saddle seat with glovebox behind instead of in the left side panel, and a new exhaust system.

VESPA 125 VNAI, VNA2 1957–1959
AND VESPA 125 VNB 1959–1965 ★ ★

The classic Vespa 125 was reborn in 1957 with a sleek, new body and entirely enclosed handshifter like its more powerful cousin, the GS. The new 125 featured a revised engine based on the 150, with a square 54x54mm bore and stroke creating 4.5hp at 5000rpm and pushing the 81kg scooter to 75km/h.

By 1960, a distinguishing factor of the 125 from the 150, look to the legshield where the larger scooter boasted "Vespa 150" and the 125 simply said "Vespa." Also, the bigger scooter had the classier clamshell speedo while the 125 was left with a square little dial.

In 1962, the 125 offered a left side panel that hid the spare tire and battery; the side cover could be removed completely instead of the former hinged version with the small glovebox. In 1963, the modernized design with new bodywork smoothed the edges of the old style making the slicker bench seat standard. In 1964, a fourth gear was added.

VESPA 150 VBA 1958–1960 AND VESPA 150
VBB 1960–1965 ★ ★ ★

In October 1958, the Vespa 150 sported a new look, following the 125 of the previous year, and an improved engine with 5.5hp at 5000rpm. The square 57x57mm engine wasn't as fast as the GS—it topped out at 51mph—but got better gas mileage and cost considerably less.

The Vespa 150 VBA no longer had the wide body of the early VB1 Vespa 150, but had a new engine design and large frame that was the basic chassis for all further big Vespas. The holdover from the old model, however, was the three-speed gearbox, but now had the classic clamshell-shaped speedo.

By 1960, the standard Vespa 150 had four speeds and was tuned to 6.9hp at 5000rpm for a 56mph top speed and 100mpg. The no-frills 150 VBB kept to the small, 8in wheels.

In the 1960s, both Piaggio and Innocenti (separately, of course) sponsored international beauty contests on scooters noting that a well-tended putt-putt added much to a tidy image. In Britain, famous movie stars presented the Silver Rose Bowl award to the Miss Vespa Darling. At the English Lambretta National Rally held in Portsmouth, the winner of the Miss Lambretta contest would go on to compete in the prestigious Miss Lambretta International contest.

By this time, Piaggio and Innocenti both financed massive advertising campaigns to promote "scooter culture" in general, and their respective vehicles in particular. The Vespa was advertised as the second conquering of the New World by a Genovese (the first being by Italian Christopher Columbus, not Leif Erikson). Owners magazines funded by the companies were published in a different languages, containing articles on the latest updates, movie stars on

With the dawn of the Vespa Gran Sport at the end of 1954, Piaggio proved to the world that scooters were more than mere gadabout toys. Scooters are for racing. While Innocenti's early Lambretta was viewed as quicker—albeit less stylish, Piaggio put that theory to rest with the top-of-the-line GS. At least until 1957, when the Lambretta TV 175 took back the crown, which of course prompted Piaggio to release the souped-up GS 160, the king of Vespas, and this slick GL in 1962. Courtesy of owner: Aaron Harp

scooters, and continental tours. These publications pushed the idea of the sleek, attractive scooter that was fashionable but functional. Fashionable, because no bar between the rider's legs allowed the latest style instead of riding clothes and the covered engine prevented oil spotting clothes. Functional, because a scooter could tour the world but still be parked anywhere.

Piaggio and Innocenti were no longer advertising a product. They were promoting a lifestyle.

VESPA 150 GL 1962–1965 ★★

In 1962, the 150 Gran Lusso was announced with two saddle seats to counter the Lambretta LD 150. The 150 GL had a different engine from the basic 150; it was an oversquare design of 58.5x54mm delivering 6.2hp at 5500rpm for a 53mph top speed via a four-speed gearbox.

Although not quite as sporty as the GS, the GL sat atop more stable 10in wheels than the previous Vespa 150. The denominations VLA and VGL are assigned to this scooter that set the style for the later Sprint, Super and Rally scooters.

VESPA 50, 50 N, 50 S, AND 50 L 1963–1966 ★

In 1962, Piaggio launched its entry-level economy scooter, the 50cc Vespa, nicknamed the Vespina, or little Vespa. Piaggio's ads described the 50 in Futurist-like prose as "a brand new Vespa created to allow everyone to enter unhesitatingly the sphere of motorization." Never mind the poetic ad language, the 50 became an instant hit and Piaggio's best-selling scooter. By 1993, with a revised 50cc 50S Vintage and 50A with automatic transmission still in production, more than four million 50cc Vespas had been built.

The Vespina was powered by an entirely new motor with rotary port induction requiring a mere

2 percent oil content to the fuel, thus allowing increased performance and power from the elfin engine. The new cylinder was inclined forward at 45 degrees, measuring 38.4x43mm and delivering a faithful 1.5hp. Top speed was 40km/h or 25mph. The three-speed Vespina brought Piaggio's scooters back to Enrico Piaggio's original philosophy of reliable, inexpensive scooters to mobilize every class, every age, everywhere.

The following year two models were offered, the 50 N "for the whole family," and the 50 S "for professional and leisure time," although background checks were not made. The N's three speeds brought it to a top speed of 40 km/h while the 2.5hp S's four speeds made for a top speed of 60 km/h or 37mph. It was a heady speed for the midget 8in wheels.

During these years, stiff competition with Innocenti prompted a policy of allowing foreign dealers to only sell Vespas or Lambrettas. A tale of two cities was being played out between Milan's Innocenti and Genoa's Pontedera mirrored by the intense automobile competition between the Milanese Alfa Romeo and Turinese Fiat. Gone were the days of catapulting plague-infested carcasses over rival city-state's walls; loyalty to one's local scooter maker took the place of sieging thy neighbor.

Piaggio and Innocenti constantly pushed film directors to feature a shot of their scooter somewhere in movies instead of the opposition's latest model. Rival gangs of Vespisti and Lambrettisti were formed in scooter clubs with intense competition throughout Europe.

VESPA 180 SUPER SPORT 1964–1968 ★★★

The engine of the 160 GS was enlarged to make the 181.1cc Super Sport, which replaced the GS as the top-of-the-line Vespa. The 181cc engine was based on 62x60mm, creating 10.3hp at 6250rpm. Although the SS 180 took over where the GS 160 left off, almost no parts could be swapped from the old speedster.

The 180 Super Sport obtained a new body-chassis, straying from the classical rounded styling of the GS to the angular look of the mid-1960's Rally and Sprint models. The crown of the fastest Italian scooter was once again obtained by Piaggio with this scooter zooming at up to 63mph.

A large built-in glove box was added on the passenger-side of the legshield that became the favored spot for mounting a boombox to blast out your own soundtrack as you flashed by the coffee shops.

VESPA 90 1964–1971 ★

Scooterists often suffered under a subconscious phobia of their Vespa being branded as feminine, especially by the British Rockers. The Vespa 50 and 90, as smaller and easier-to-handle scooter, were often considered sissy models whereas the larger scooters offered the horsepower necessary to console the fragile macho self-image. To assuage this imagined shame, Piaggio developed its Primavera, but a smaller performance scooter was still needed.

VESPA 90 SUPER SPRINT AND VESPA 50 SUPER SPRINT 1965–1971 ★ ★ ★ ★

In the early 1960s, the three-speed Vespa 90 offered maneuverability that the larger scooters lacked, but the small scooters didn't have a sporting character. In 1965, Piaggio created a Super Sprint, or SS, version of its 90 with a high-performance 90cc engine shoe-horned into a lightweight chassis creating a hot power-to-weight ratio.

The body of the 90SS was reworked with a narrower legshield to cut wind resistance, as used on several of Piaggio's racing prototypes in the early 1950s. The spare tire rode between the rider's legs, capped by a dummy gas tank that served as the toolbox. The tank wore Super Sprint badges on both sides.

Although the Vespa 90 Super Sprint had a smaller engine and weighed slightly more than its 125 Primavera counterpart, it boasted a higher maximum speed by 8km/h, topping out at 88km/h or 55mph. The four-speed SS series scooters were designed for competition, often providing better performance than many 200cc competitors.

The 90 provided the added advantage of the engine size falling conveniently short of the new laws in the United States requiring motorcycle licenses for two-wheelers over 100cc. One of Piaggio's original concepts for having the scooter's open area between the legs was for women wearing dresses, but now that the raging style was slacks, this space was unnecessary. Instead, Piaggio gave the scooter a racy motorcycle look while retaining the Vespa design.

Vespa's competition tried to have the SS banned from competition because the area between the rider's legs was closed off with a spare tire and a gas tank-looking glovebox. The Federation of

British Scooter Clubs ruled in favor of the SS since the dummy gas tank was not structural and allowed the Vespa to keep on conquering its competition.

One German ad for the Super Sprint announced the added benefit that "Die Vespa 50 Super Sprint ist steuerfrei!" meaning it's tax-free. Prior to the establishment of foreign firms that license-built Vespas, importation of the Italian scooters into Germany, France, and other countries was stiffly taxed for fear that the Italian ingenuity would ruin domestic production of vehicles. When early Vespa imports were totally banned, a black market scooter trade developed into Switzerland and France with tourists begging the custom agents to let them cross the border for the weekend on their scooter. The "vacationers" would meet their contacts on the other side, sell the Vespa at a profit, and then head back on the Mediterranean or Lago Maggiore under cover of night.

VESPA 150 SPRINT 1965–1969 AND 150 SPRINT VELOCE 1965–1977 ★ ★ ★

Piaggio replaced its 150 GL with the 150 Sprint VLB riding on 10in wheels and a 150cc (57x57mm) engine that put out 7.1hp at 5000rpm. Four speed was by now standard as well as the bench seat.

In the summer of 1969, the Sprint's engine was modified to produce 7.7hp and 97km/h, the body was updated to be the same as 125 GTR except for the chrome piece on the sidepanels, and they called it the Veloce.

VESPA 125 SUPER AND 150 SUPER 1965–1977 ★

As the Sprint replaced the GL, the Super replaced the standard 125 and 150 Vespas. The Super was the economical model but still used the sleek design of the faster scooters to make a practical form of transportation, but still on 8in wheels. The 125 had a 52.5x57mm engine for 85km/h, and the 150 had the square 57x57mm engine for 90km/h.

The 150 Super VBC and the 125 Super VNC both lost the curvy classic Vespa look for the new angular style that was all the rage. A battery was added in 1972 and turn signals in 1974, but electrical problems still tormented their loyal owners.

VESPA 125 PRIMAVERA AND 125 ET3 1966–1983 ★ ★

In 1965, Piaggio enlarged the 50cc engine to 125cc and retained the 50 chassis to create the 125 Primavera, or Spring; Botticelli would have been proud. Piaggio's pride was a hot-rod scooter with a four-speed gearbox capable of hitting a shaky 80km/h or 50mph—a mere 5km/h short of the 150 GL's top speed. An improved gear ratio meant the

Swiss Super Sprint
Both the 90 Super Sprint and the 50 Super Sprint (pictured) were Piaggio's challenge to the diminutive motorcycle market aimed at teens looking for speed. When Piaggio gave birth to the Vespa 50 in 1962, the "Vespina" instantly became the best-selling scooter in their lineup. Now the souped-up Super Sprint, like this Genevamade SS50, with narrow handlebars, front legshield, the sporty extra gas tank and spare tire between the legs would make even the quietest Italian piazza a mini-Monza for teenagers. Courtesy of owner: Hans Kruger

Modern Stone-Age Scooter

This bizarre Piaggio photo ran in a Japanese motorcycle magazine with all sorts of symbolism that begs to avoid being analyzed. What the Nuova Linea P Series Vespas lost in traditional styling, they more than made up for in reliability with a modern overhaul of Corradino d'Ascanio's original design to keep it current into the 1990s. The P200 was the top of the line offering rotary-valve induction, electronic ignition, hydraulic shocks, turn signals, and optional turn-key electric start. Pictured is the Nuova Linea Vespina 50cc scoot.

125 took only 47.9sec to travel 1km from a dead stop while the 150 managed it in 46.1sec. In the 0-75km/h dash, the smaller Vespa clocked 18.5sec versus 18sec for the 150. In other words, these scooters could beat almost any car off the line for at least the first ten feet.

In 1967, the 121.17cc Primavera became the ET3 packing a potent 5.4hp for an 85km/h or 53mph top speed. The ET3 was so popular, Piaggio revived the model for the 1980s and 1990s as the ET3 Vintage with a 121.16cc engine of 55x51mm now creating 5.6hp via a four-speed gearbox. Wheels were 10in with 3.50x10in tires.

By the mid-1960s, Piaggio was no longer content with graphically avant-garde advertisements, so an ad campaign launched into another art form, poetry. Dante would have rolled over in his grave:

> The convulsive traffic, the jammed parking lots,
> the crowds in the public transportation system
> are real problems
> for all who, forced to be continually on the move,
> do not possess the proper vehicle.
> With Vespa the traffic problem
> is not a problem.
> With Vespa there is always a place
> in every parking lot.
> With Vespa each trip, long or short, is a
> thrilling parenthesis of joy, of freedom.

VESPA 125 GT 1965–1969 AND 125 GTR 1969–1977 ★ ★

Piaggio announced yet another version of its 125, the Gran Turismo version with 6.27hp for 88km/h that was essentially an updated version of the Sprint. The GT had essentially the same motor as the 125 Super with higher compression adding to the velocity.

Piaggio modified the GTR with a round headlamp, more power (7.8hp), more speed (95km/h), a new taillight (borrowed from the 180 Rally), and an R for rinnovata (renovated). A Vespa TS was also released from Piaggio with the same shape as the Rally.

VESPA 180 RALLY 1968; RALLY 200 AND RALLY 200 ELECTRONIC 1972–1978 ★ ★ ★

During the late 1960s, interest in scooters waned as higher standards of living in the western world allowed families to now buy automobiles. This downward swing hurt Piaggio but doomed Innocenti, which ceased scooter production in 1971. Scooters largely became a thing of the past, remembered as a necessary evil in the tough times following the war. Vespas and Lambrettas were stowed away in the backs of garages and barns throughout the world to make way for the shiny new car; it would be at least another decade before anyone recalled their scootering days with nostalgia.

At the same time, the market for scooters shifted. Vespas became a cult symbol of the growing youth market, winning an image as a mode of transportation primarily for teenagers before they could afford a motorcycle or car. For this growing market, Piaggio created a new speedster, the Rally 200.

The Rally was the hot Vespa of the day. Its brawny engine fathered 12hp at 5700rpm reaching a staggering 101km/h or 63mph (a questionable 1km/h more than the GS, P200E, and the PX200E, according to certain graphs). Piaggio boasted the Rally as the most reliable Vespa thus far, making it perfect for long distance touring.

The Rally 200 was supplanted by the Electronic model, which added electronic ignition to replace the decrepit mechanical points system. The benefits of the new electronic ignition can hardly be overpraised.

By 1977, six years after Innocenti had given up on the Lambretta, the Piaggio factory at Pontedera produced 613,805 vehicles, ranking fourth in the world behind Honda, Yamaha, and Suzuki, but ahead of Kawasaki. In the same year, Piaggio exported 289,000 Vespas and three-wheeled Apes to 110 countries.

VESPA 50 N, 50 N SPECIAL, 50 N ELESTART, AND 50 SPRINTER 1972–1977 ★

These 50cc models updated the 1963 versions with a new look. The Special and the Elestart had squared-off headlamps for that particular 1970s appeal; whereas the 50 N and 50 Sprinter were "obviously classic with timeless elegance," at least according to Piaggio's own view, it was a tough choice. All four of these models came with a bench seat, but lacked much of the power needed to haul two human bodies. The Elestart's battery for an electric start sat on the left side of the scooter, opposite the motor.

VESPA 100 SPORT 1978–1984 ★

This small frame scooter had the updated 12volt electrical system, but still had the three-speed gearbox of the V90.

VESPA NUOVA LINEA P125X, P150X, AND P200E 1977–1985 ★★★

On April 17, 1978, the Nuova Linea, or New Line, with the Vespa P125X, P150X, and P200E made its debut in Florence with a grand celebration marking the most major update to the Vespa since the first 98cc model more than thirty years earlier. The P Series was the brainchild of Piaggio's managing director, Ing. Giovanni Squazzini. The P stood for Piaggio, the X for extra qualities, and the E for electronic ignition. Vespas purists lamented, however that the P stood for plastic as Piaggio opted for the cheaper material on these new steeds. The suspension, lighting, and performance were all significantly improved making for a reliable form of transport. The updated electrics produced 12volts with 80watt output from the flywheel magneto and electronic regulator.

The P Series engine featured rotary-valve induction via three piston ports. Riding on two main bearings, compression for each model was 8.0:1 at minimum, offering superior top-end power and smoother delivery throughout the powerband. And now that service stations rarely offered miscela, or premixed gas with two-stroke oil, each Vespa had separate reservoirs that automatically mixed the fluids for the engine.

Top of the line was the P200E, based on a 198cc measuring 66.5x57mm with 8.2:1 compression ratio and fed via a Dell'Orto carburetor. Power was up to 12hp at 5700rpm; ignition was completely electronic.

Backed by a four-speed gearbox, the P200E could do the American quarter-mile dragstrip dash in 20sec. The 231lb P200E returned 65mpg.

The new body design strayed from the curvaceous lines of the original Vespa to become stunningly modern with angular fenders and sidecover lines. Turn signals were built into the bodywork.

Piaggio took over Moto Gilera in 1979, and reported an annual production of 450,000 scooters in 1980.

VESPA PK50S, PK80S, PX80E, PK125S, PX125E, PX150E, AND PX200E 1982–1990 ★★

At the 1985 Milan Show, the new Vespa two-stroke direct-injection engine, developed over the previous ten years, was introduced. In that same year, the P Series was updated with two model lines, the K and extra-features X line. The PK125 came with an automatic progressive hydraulic transmission, and a 125 supersports version of the PK was released called the T5.

The PK models all had four-speed automatic transmissions, which caused an uproar in Italy since

"La Nuova Vespa"
Piaggio still lives on the edge when the "New Vespa" cruised into the piazza, like this one parked in Modena. Italians were split. How could Piaggio improve on a classic? The design harks back to the height of scooterdom when BSA and British Triumph teamed up to produce the Tigress/Sunbeam scooter in 1959, alas at the end of the scooter boom. While Corradino d'Ascanio's muse inspired him to create the first Vespa in 1945, "All the designers were trying to get their name on the new Vespa," said a young Piaggio designer in 1997.

Vespa ET2
Just as Piaggio released the Vespa ET4 (for four-stroke) in 2001, the company also released the ET2 50 pictured here. Sure, the big motor got all the attention, but the ET2 two-stroke was the result of years of tweaking these little engines for maximum performance and avoiding the breakdowns of the early models.

Vespa LX 150
As part of the 60th anniversary of the Vespa—get it? LX in Roman numerals—Piaggio released this four-stroke in 2006 and continued production until 2014.

Spring Is Here!
The Vespa Primavera was iconic for Piaggio during the 1960s, continuing its successful run of some of the best scooters ever made. In the 2020s, Piaggio relaunched the Primavera as part of its 75th anniversary in a kaleidoscope of colors, just like the original. This is the special 150 gold model.

automatics were considered for people who weren't competent enough to shift. Piaggio knew this might be a problem and offered the PX series as well with a four-speed manual transmission.

In Paris, the reliability of the P Series prompted the founding of Scooter Express, a scooter taxi service that could carry passengers through the crowded streets faster than car cabs and for less money. The scooters were all 1985 white P Series Vespas with a "chrome bar between driver and passenger [to prevent] any possible promiscuity. All drivers are males in their thirties. So far, there are more women clients than men," according to New York magazine. The business wasn't all glamour since jealous cabbies assaulted them with tear-gas bombs for taking their business.

The PX200E continued through 1993 with the remainder of the Piaggio Vespa line made up of the 50A automatic, 50 S Vintage, 100 Vintage, 125A automatic, and 125ET3 Vintage.

COSA 125CC, 150CC, AND 200CC
1985–1990; COSA II LX200 1990 ★

The Cosa arrived on the scene as the Vespa's replacement in 1985; it brought sighs and tears from throughout the world, and while the Cosa was an excellent scooter, the public outcry prompted Piaggio to reinstate the Vespa in the lineup.

The Cosa revised much of the Vespa's design underneath the skin while retaining its exterior styling lines, although it was now a rolling sculpture in plastic. The stressed-steel unit chassis was retired in favor of a more traditional tube frame covered by unstressed plastic bodywork. Piaggio called this "new technology," and stated that it was based on new advances in the automobile world; it forgot to mention the Lambretta.

The engine was an air-cooled, rotary-disc induction two-stroke in your choice of 125cc for 8.3hp at 6000rpm, 150cc for 9hp at 6000rpm, and 200cc for 11hp at 6000rpm, all backed by a four-speed gearbox. Each model came with an automatic gas and two-stroke oil mixer, denoted as the MA miscelatore automatico model; a 125 Cosa was available without MA. Electric start was optional.

Luxury features were plentiful. Turn signals were sculpted into the front legshields and tail and instrumentation went so far as to include a tachometer. And when Italy enacted a helmet law, which immediately cut into scooter sales, the Cosa offered an under-seat hook to hang your helmet from so you wouldn't have to carry it with you while you bought your cappuccio.

In 1990, the Cosa line was updated to just one model, the Cosa II LX200. The 197.97cc engine was based on a 66.5x57mm bore and stroke. With 12 volt, 100 watt electrics and riding on 4.00x10in tires, the LX200 could top 110km/h or 68mph.

Six Days of Speed
Another special-edition Vespa recalled the days when the little wasp overtook the competition in the mountains of Varese near the Swiss border. The cool styling cue of dropping the headlamp back to the front fender harkens back to the earliest Vespas and will appease Italian collectors who only will buy these scooters with the lower headlight.

Power, Power, POWER!
The most powerful Vespa ever made hit the streets in 2020, perhaps to compete with the motorcycle market. The GTS 300 is a four-stroke, liquid-cooled Vespa with all the bells and whistles. The question remains, however: Is power what a Vespa is all about, or is it cruising through the piazza at a slow enough speed that everyone can see you?

Sprint to the Finish
In homage to the highly collectible Super Sport and other racing Vespas, Piaggio released the 50cc Sprint in 2021 to prove, once again, that big engines don't mean more speed—the racing stripes don't hurt to remind the skeptical!

Cigar on Wheels
Attempting to cash in on the English lust for anything Italian, in 1952 Cyclemaster (Britax) put into production Vicenzo Piatti's mini hovercraft in two models, a two-speed 98cc and a three-speed 125cc. Les Anciens Establissements D'leteren of Belgium also took up the design boasting, "Total Stability either with or without a passenger." Wow! **Courtesy of the owner: Vittorio Tessera**

SFERA 50 AND 80; AND QUARTX AND ZIP 1990 ★

The Sfera, or Sphere, scooter was introduced in 1990 as the economical entry-level scooter, a modern steel-frame, plastic-bodywork counterpart to the Vespa 50. The engine was a 49cc rotary-disc two-stroke of 40x39.3mm with automatic gas-oil mix, electronic ignition, automatic gearbox, and electric start. The Sfera was Piaggio's scooter of the future.

The styling was like a spaceship on 2.15x10in wheels with angular, modernistic lines. The seat pivoted forward with a helmet storage area hidden below.

Piaggio continued scooter production into the 1990s with no end in sight and its advanced scooters selling as well as ever. It had come a long way since the Donald Duck scooter prototype of 1945.

VESPA ET2 AND ET4 1996–2005 ★ ★

Vespa reentered the US market with a bang at the end of the millennium. Vespa boutiques opened across the USA and Piaggio insisted that these dealers open only in major metropolitan areas and sell only Vespas. The slick new Vespa was high priced compared to the competition, but its name made customers line up to get the coolest new ride in town. Two basic models were offered, the ET2 with a 50cc engine (the first fuel-injected two-stroke in the world, according to Piaggio) and the luxurious electric starter, and the ET4 four-stroke 150cc Vespa.

Piaggio attempted to cash in on the craze for a villa in Tuscany by reminding customers that its factory is in Pisa and by offering Tuscan color schemes: Giotto Orange, Olive Green, Livorno Blue, and Etruscan Red. While purists recoiled at the idea of trying to remake a classic, the new Vespas kept the curvaceous form of the original with much of it in metal.

VESPA ET4 GRANTURISMO
2003–PRESENT ★★

What the Granturismo gained in power (200cc engine and 14.7hp), sturdiness (12in wheels) and speed (115km/h), it lost in style. With lines similar to the doomed Cosa and other modern plastic scooters, the Granturismo still retains much of the ET4 updates but opts for practical over cool. Then when you compare the Granturismo to other mini crotch-rocket scooters in Piaggio's line, like the Derbi Atlantis, the 460cc X9 Evolution or LT50, the Granturismo looks like a classic.

VESPA LX, LXV 2005–PRESENT ★★

As the evolution of the ET series, the LX (for the 60th anniversary of la Vespa) came in a slightly smaller body but offered four different engine sizes. The LXV updated the LX in 2006 and harkened back to many of the classic elements of the '50s and '60s Vespas.

VESPA GTS IE, GTV 2005–PRESENT ★★

When Piaggio released the Vespa GS, the first "sport" scooter, it caused a revolution in souping up the little Vespa to be a speedster. Still, the GS is the most collectible Vespa to this day. In homage to this classic, Piaggio assembled the 250cc GTS fifty years after the GS for those who demand performance. Soon after, the GTS 300 was released with an even more powerful engine.

VESPA SPECIAL EDITION SCOOTERS ★★

To mark various anniversaries and other landmark Italian brands, Piaggio released tricked-out Vespas in limited numbers with a hefty price tag to boot. An ET Vespa Ferrari was even offered in 2001 in Ferrari red with a special saddle out of leather and signatures from famous race car drivers, such as Michael Schumacher. (Remember that Fiat owns Piaggio and Ferrari.) In 2015, Piaggio collaborated with Giorgio Armani for a specially designed (and a bit odd) Vespa 946 that looks more like the 1940s models— all in black, of course. Piaggio relaunched the iconic Primavera in a rainbow of beautiful colors, even one in "gold." In honor of the Super Sport mini racing Vespas, Piaggio released the speedy Sprint with racing stripes but no number. Instead the number 6 appeared on the Vespa GTS Sei Giorni in honor of the six-day races in Varese in 1951, when the little Vespa swept the competition.

Piatti UK ★★★

The Piatti was a truly international scooter. Piatti scooters were an attempt by a British manufacturer to break into the Italian-dominated scooter market, and what better way than with an Italian designer? Designed by the London-based Italian engineer Vicenzo Piatti, built in Britain by Cyclemaster (Britax), as well as in Belgium by Les Anciens Establissements D'Ieteren.

In spring 1952, after having created the Minimotor for the British Trojan firm, Vicenzo Piatti designed two Piatti scooters: the three-speed 125cc with a top speed between 70 and 78km/h and the two-speed 98cc (built by Vincent, according to certain sources).

The Piatti's saddle could be raised and lowered as on a bicycle, and the nearly vertical front fork was similar to a child's push scooter. However, the Space Age design gave the impression of a hovercraft, and the wheels almost disappeared under the body as though it was crawling on a cushion of air. The vertical lines of this cigar-shaped scooter did not merely give the impression of breakneck speed, but also facilitated airflow over the engine preventing two-stroke seizure. Elaborate cooling systems were telltale to Italian scooter design and the Piatti with its bridge between the rider's legs and the front and rear grille was no exception.

Picot ITALY ★★★

Halfway through 1947, Piscitelli and Cosso (Picot) presented a completely different vision of how scooters could be. While Piaggio and Innocenti had just begun convincing the world how a scooter should look, Picot's two 148cc four-stroke scooters looked like a Picasso cubist painting with aggressive folds in the body paneling that only an artists could dream up. If only the world had followed these two visionaries, the scooter world would be very bizarre indeed.

Pirol GERMANY ★★

The Dortmund-based Pirol-Fahrzeugfabrik GmbH was originally called Firma Schweppe and came up with one of the great ugly scooters in a rarified strata that can include only the Piatti and a select few others.

The headlamp erupted from the front fender like a pig's snout from a mudpit with the styling carried through to the tail. The rounded front legshield displayed the Pirol logo mounted in the center in the shape of a large crucifix.

Each scooter had a different company's engine, the Pirol 145 of 1949-1951 a 4.5hp Jlo, the Pirol 200 of 1951-1954 had a 6.5hp Küchen, and the Miranda of 1953-1954 had a 9.5hp Sachs. The Pirol 200 was the continuation of the Pirol 145, both with an actual rubber front bumper evoking images of bump 'em cars. The entire rear fender of these scooters hinged up to expose the engine. As Pirol's ads promised, "Der Pirol 200 ist Daher das Fahrzeug für Alle!"

Pointer JAPAN ★

The Pointer Bike Let hit the Japanese market in 1960 with its extensive two-tone covering and large spoked wheels. The 125cc two-stroke couldn't survive the onslaught of the more popular Honda Cub.

Polaris USA ★

Polaris, a northern Minnesota snowmobile manufacturer, built a variety of products in the 1960s to keep production lines active year-round. In 1962, it offered the Trail Tractor, a heavy-duty, industrial-strength mini-bike scooter. What it lacked in styling or bodywork it made up for in strength and durability with its all-welded tube frame.

Power was a 3.5hp Lauson, via an automatic clutch similar to the Polaris snowmobiles at the time, and a V-belt drive. Top speed only hit about 15mph. Not much for cruising between coffeehouses but enough torque to pull stumps. A cargo basket up front made the Trail Tractor look like Dorothy's ride in the off-road remake of The Wizard of Oz.

Pop Nanlee USA ★

The Pop Nanlee scooter was offered in 175cc form in the early 1960s for a price of $479.

Postlaufer GERMANY ★★★

Like the English Kingsbury scooter, the Postlaufer (sometimes called the Postler) from the 1910s took the design of the Autoped and placed the engine behind the steering column for better stability.

Powell USA

Channing and Hayward Powell built vehicles to the tune of a different plumber. The brothers were based in Los Angeles, the Mecca for eccentricity in two-, three-, and four-wheeled vehicles; it was the home of hot rodding and the birthplace of the modern scooter, E. Foster Salsbury's Motor Glide. It was only natural that the brothers would be inspired to build their own brand of hot-rod motorscooter.

[Much of the information in this chapter comes from the research of Wallace Skyrman, who started the Powell Cycle Registry in 1981.]

STREAMLINER 40 1939-1940 AND 41-J 1941 ★★★★

The first Powell scooter arrived on the scene in the late 1930s and followed the commandments set by the Motor Glide: step-through frame, small wheels, automatic clutch, and a rear-mounted engine. Named the Streamliner Series 40, it used a Lauson 2.3hp four-stroke engine, Tillotson carburetor, and Eismann flywheel magneto ignition. The engine measured 2¼×2 1/4in bore and stroke with 6.0:1 compression. Lighting was initially by magneto but altered in 1941 for the 41-J model to a motor-driven generator. Engine cooling was by flywheel fan—"forced blast cooling," according to one brochure.

The Centri-Matic automatic clutch touted in ads was a centrifugal clutch with only one speed; a planetary transmission was optional. Final drive was by chain to the rear wheel, which featured the sprocket built integral with the wheel hub.

The front forks rode on ball bearings in the steering head, a feature that was a long time in coming for most American scooters. The Streamliner also had front and rear suspension before many others. Springing was knee-action on the front forks and on a rear subframe similar to a swing-arm. Ads also touted its "spring steel frame," probably referring to the natural flex of overextended steel bars.

Options listed in a 1940 flyer included a rear luggage rack, Package Carrier, Tow Back to attach the Streamliner backward to a car's rear bumper, and commercial sidecar. With the 41-J, a tandem seat was offered.

As with the Motor Glide, Powell promoted the ease of scooter operation: one flyer promised that "Everyone who can ride a bicycle can ride a Powell Motor Scooter!" Two foot pedals were all that was needed: one for throttle, the other for the rear wheel's drum brake. Options for the Streamliner included a tandem seat with luggage rack, package carrier, sidecar, and tow hitch for 1941 models.

A-V-8 (AVIATE) 1940–1942 ★★★

In 1940, Powell moved to a new factory in Compton, California, and released its new A-V-8 or Aviate scooter, styled as a Harley-Davidson or Indian big twin that had been shrunk in the laundry. This Powell creation would later spark a whole series of such scooters modeled after motorcycles including the Glendale, California, Mustang and Cushman's Eagle line, both of which came postwar.

The A-V-8 was designed for riders who were not afraid to swing their legs over their machine versus the step-through design, which had often been laughed at by true motorcyclists as being effeminate. The A-V-8 featured the motorcycles' rigid hardtail, saddle seat, a separate gas tank, and 4.00x8in tires.

Power was 5hp—a whole lot of horses at the time in a motorscooter—from an odd engine built by Powell from Ford V-8 parts stuffed into Powell's own cast-iron block. As Powell's flyer stated: "Important—pistons, connecting rods, valves, springs, guides, push rods, and fibre timing gears are replacement parts of a popular low-priced automobile." It was difficult to say if that was meant as an enticement or a warning.

Powell's engine measured 3 1/16×2 7/8in bore and stroke for 21ci with 5.0:1 compression. The single-cylinder version of the Ford Flathead was fired by battery ignition—and oddity for scooters at any time. The engine was turned over by kickstart, although the first push-button electric start for a motorscooter was optional.

The first A-V-8s were built with a variable-speed V-belt drive similar to what Salsbury had developed several years early. The clutch was a three-shoe centrifugal automatic driving a variable-speed transmission via a rubber v-belt, which could be manually shifted into any of four speeds plus a fifth-speed overdrive. Final drive was by roller chain. Yet while Salsbury's variable-drive was a great success, Powell's was not, and most machines found today have been converted to some other type of transmission.

Standard color was harbor green, and a range of options was available: buddy seat, luggage rack, package carrier, windscreen, tow hitch, and delivery and passenger sidecars, the latter with side door.

Powell built the A-V-8 from 1940-1942, during which time a number of other entrepreneurs attempted to make it famous—under their own names. Frank Cooper silk-screened his own decals and sold the A-V-8 as the Cooper Aviate. When the US Army requested bids for a lightweight airborne scooter to drop by parachute behind enemy lines, Cooper took a welding torch, added a maze of reinforcing bars to the Aviate chassis, and offered the military his own Cooper War Combat Motor Scooter. While the Army liked the Cooper better than the Cushman 53, Army inspectors were unimpressed with the Cooper Motors, Inc.'s "factory," and awarded the bid to Cushman.

When Powell turned its machinery from plowshares (as it were) to swords for World War II rocket and shells production, the Clark Engineering firm bought the remaining stock of 1942 A-V-8s and sold them as its own Victory Clipper scooter. In 1943, the firm of L. Ronney & Sons built A-V-8s as the Ronard Jeepette. And following the war in 1947, Clark was back building A-V-8s as the Clark Cylcone.

LYNX ★★

Following the war, Powell introduced its economy Lynx scooter with a Wisconsin AKN 6hp engine, Wico magneto, and disc-style automatic clutch, riding atop odd-sized 4.00x7in tires.

The Lynx followed the style of the Series 40 but eschewed any bodywork or suspension. The scooter was painted green, the engine gray. As Powell's flyer announced, "Dreams do come true!"

C-47 1947 ★★

The C-47 scooter, built in 1947, returned to a Powell-built powerplant; this design would continue with modifications through 1951 in other Powell models.

Powell's new engine followed true motorcycle lines with a split die-cast aluminum crankcase, a built-up crankshaft, and a cast-iron flathead cylinder. Powell even made its own carburetor and ignition and generator system in an effort to keep costs down. Folklore has it that the piston and some valvetrain parts were again from the Ford V-8, but Powell never made mention of this in its ads. The pistons used were identical to Ford and Mercury pistons except that the Powell's used a flat-top piston whereas the Ford's was domed.

Bodywork now covered the front wheel and ran from the steering head over the rear wheel, but not covering the engine. A saddle seat sat atop the engine trailed by a luggage rack.

DAS starke wettergeschützte ZWEIRAD-MOTORFAHRZEUG

P-48 1948 AND P-49 1949 ★★

In 1948-1949, Powell produced respectively its P-48 and P-49 scooters with a refined version of the Powell C-47 engine but lacking that scooter's bodywork. The new 7hp 24ci engine used a cast-iron cylinder barrel with 3 1/6×3 1/4in bore and stroke, a die-cast aluminum crankcase, and a built-up crankshaft. The engine was sparked by a Powell magneto with the kickstart working directly to the camshaft. The Power-Matic automatic clutch transferred power to the rear 4.00×7in wheel via two rayon-cord v-belts.

Powell continued its tradition of eccentric creativity in the dry sump oiling system, which scavenged oil via crankcase pressure from an oil tank mounted to the floorboards. And the lucky rider sat on a seat formed by the aluminum gas tank.

Two models were offered: the Standard with solid front forks, crash bar seat cushion, floor mat, luggage rack, and rear foot rests; and the Deluxe with all of the Standard's features including telescoping front forks, chromed luggage rack mounted on springs so it could double as a buddy seat, headlamp, and taillamp. A side car was also available for either model.

The P-48 and P-49 were odd-looking scooters, an indestructible maze of solid bar stock that made up for its lack of grace by being sturdy—and heavy at more than 200lb for the complete machine. As a P-49 flyer hinted, "It Looks Custom Built," a polite way of saying it was not streamlined, to coin the other buzzword of the era.

P-81 1949–1951 ★★★

In 1949, Powell returned to its miniature motorcycle styling from the A-V-8 in creating its new P-81. This new scooter was half Whizzer, half Indian Chief, arriving on the market at the same time as Cushman's new Eagle. But the Powell offered more power than the Eagle, and rode atop 4.00x12in wheels.

Two P-81 models were offered: the Deluxe and the Special (called the Custom for 1950). The Deluxe engine was based on a 3 1/16×3¼in bore and stroke for 24ci, creating 8hp at 3200rpm and a 45mph top speed. Fitted with a larger-bore piston, 10hp at 3400rpm was possible from 26ci. Both models used the automatic clutch but resorted to the tried-and-true chain drive; some last models reverted to the dual V-belt final drive. Continuing its exotic tradition, Powell used the furnace-brazed frame as an oil supply tank to the dry sump system.

For 1949, the P-81 was available in black baked enamel set off by chrome trim with an optional luggage rack. By 1950, you could have a Custom in red, blue, green, or black. As the ads promised, "BIG motorcycle features throughout and at an unbelievably low price!"

During the Korean War, Powell turned away from scooter production and back to war contracts. In 1954, the brothers began building economical pickup trucks and sport wagons designed with hunters and campers in mind. Working with 1940s era Plymouth chassis, they added fiberglass front end, wood bumpers and funky options like a pop-up camper top, fishing pole compartments and more.

From 1967-1972, the final Powell scooter series was built, the 3½hp Model M and 5hp Model L Challengers and 7hp Model J and JL Phantom minibikes, using Briggs & Stratton or Tecumseh engines.

It was the end of a long line of fascinating scooters. Like Salsbury, Powell had been innovative. The Powell had an influence on other scooters that went far beyond the small size of the firm and the number of scooters it built. The brothers set the style for miniature motorcycle scooters, offered the first scooter with electric start, and experimented with a broad range of eccentricities. The Powell scooters are rare and collectible today.

Prior UK ★

B. P. Scooters of Wolverhampton offered its Prior Viscount scooter in 1957 based on the German Hercules R200 and built under license. The motor was a 191cc Sachs providing 10.2hp at 5000rpm via a four-speed gearbox.

Ironically, the Hercules had been based on the German TWN Contessa, and when that scooter was imported to the UK, English buyers were confused by the two nearly identical scooters.

Progress GERMANY ★★★

By 1954, Heinkel had already claimed "Tourist" for its scooter, Progress stuck with the wanderlust idea and opted for "vagabond", or strolch, and "Tempo." The most impressive feature of the Strolch 150 and 175 were their headlamps mounted on the front apron but moving separately with the wheel. The Stuttgart company chose 16in wheels for added hill-climbing ability in the mountainous region. The engines were made by Sachs with 6.5hp for the 147cc, 9hp for the 174cc, and 10hp for the 1955 191cc Progress 200. The Strolch roller was also available with a 98cc Fichtel & Sachs engine. The Progress 200 didn't have the pivoting headlamp of the Strolch, and from 1958-1960 all Progress' scooters erased this interesting feature as well.

Progress 200
While the largest version of the Progress lacked the pivoting headlamp of the smaller versions of the Strolch, the plucky 200cc engine zoomed this German roller at speeds almost enough to enter the autobahn.

ing 4.5hp at 5100rpm with three speeds and 3.25x12in tires. The R was sparked by flywheel magneto; the RL by battery ignition.

In 1954, Puch sold RL scooters to the Swiss Condor firm as well as working together to develop a three-wheeler with two rear wheels driven by a differential. In 1955, the Puch R disappeared, the RL continued, supplemented by the RLA with electric start.

In 1957, the SR and SRA 150 Alpine line made its debut with a 150cc engine of 6hp at 5500rpm and completely updated bodywork. Again, the SRA added electric start.

In the early 1960s, Puch developed its DS 50 and DS 60 Cheetah scooters; in 1965, it offered its R50 Pony.

Qianjiang CHINA ★

Previously called the Zhejiang Qianjiang Motorcycle Group, but now known mostly as QJ, this company began in 1985 and became one of the largest two-wheel vehicle makers in China with its Qjiang line of scooters. In 2005, Qianjiang bought out historic scooter and motorcycle company Moto Benelli.

Rabeneick GERMANY ★ ★

In the town of Bielefeld, August Rabeneick founded his company in 1933, and by 1963 was bought out by Hercules. The Rabeneick-Roller R50 was therefore built under Hercules with the design of the Austrian company KTM. The R50 had a 50cc Sachs engine that produced 4.3hp for a top speed of 65-70km/h.

Radior FRANCE ★

Founded at the beginning of the century in Bourg, France, and manufacturing mostly mopeds and motorcycles, Radior realized in 1954 that between their two two-wheelers lay a third vehicle, the motor scooter. The Mouette scooter's paneling offered extensive protection for the driver but the 4hp 98cc NSU Quick engine was left mostly exposed to the elements.

Raleigh UK ★ ★

Raleigh was famous for its bicycles dating back to the high times of Queen Victoria. In 1960, however, the firm decided to risk its reputation by selling a scooter. It contracted with the Italian Bianchi firm to sell its 78cc Orsetto scooter to the English market as the Raleigh Roma—never mind that Bianchi was situated in Milan. The Roma continued through 1964.

Rapier GERMANY ★

Rapier of Bielefeld introduced its Rolly scooter in 1950 with your choice of 100 or 120cc Jlo FM motors. Running on 4.00x8in tires, top speed was 65km/h.

At the 1955 Geneva show, the scooter was shown as a set with a Strolch-emblemed Steib sidecar. A trailer was also optional for extended touring. The Progress scooters were imported into Britain by Carr Bros. Garages in Surrey and sold in the United States by Phillip Phillips Inc. in New York City.

Progress UK ★ ★

Carr Bros. Ltd. of Purley in Surrey built German Progress scooters under license beginning in 1956. Three English Progress models were offered, all with Villiers two-stroke power: the 148cc Anglian, 197cc kickstart Briton; and the 197cc electric-start Britannia.

Puch AUSTRIA ★ ★

The grand old Steyr-Daimler-Puch firm of Graz offered its first scooters in 1952, the Puch R and RL. Power was from a 125cc single of 52x57mm deliver-

Ravat FRANCE ★

Ravat showed off their prototype scooter at the Salon de Paris in 1952 on a marble stand "très Arts Déco" in hopes of making their scooter an instant artistic classic. The 125cc Ravat motor was mounted in the Lambretta style body, but unfortunately never went into production even though the scheduled release date was March 1953.

Renmor USA ★

Renmor Manufacturing of Chicago offered its Constructa-Scoot kits mail-order in the late 1930s and up until the start of World War II. The Renmor scooter was a bare-bones affair lacking any bodywork. Prices were $29.50 less motor or $59.50 with motor. According to Popular Mechanics ads, the kits could be quickly assembled by anyone.

REX SWEDEN ★★

Having pieced together motorcycles since 1908, REX deemed scooters too pricey to begin from scratch. Instead, this Swedish company simply imported the German Röhr Rolleta and simply added its own REX badge to the legshield from 1954 to 1956.

Reynolds UK ★★★

This very early British scooter took the design of the Autoped one step further by placing the engine under a seat. The Reynolds Roundabout featured a two-stroke 269cc Liberty engine with a two-speed gearbox. The hefty scooter weighed in at 100kg and could hold two passengers, but surely couldn't reach its top speed of 65km/h with someone on the rear.

Rico GERMANY ★

The Rico-Roller was part motorcycle, part bicycle, part scooter. Its 19-inch wheels and springer rear suspension belied its heritage. But its 125cc engine, covered by swooping sheetmetal bodywork, made one think of a motorscooter—or a medieval knight in jousting gear.

Riedel GERMANY ★

Not afraid to try new designs, Norbert Riedel first developed an "Imme" motorcycle with a bizarre rear suspension pivoting directly below the seat instead of at the axle. In 1950, Riedel created his first scooter, the Till prototype, bearing an obvious debt to the Vespa. The 99cc prototype engine had 4.5hp for a top speed of 70km/h.

By 1951, the firm began production of a reworked scooter bearing the same name, the Riedel-Ideen Till. The styling now looked like a bunch of balloons on wheels for a bulbous blend of zaftig sheetmetal.

AUF
ZWEI RÄDERN
BLEIBT
MAN JUNG!

Rabeneick

Rabeneick Roller
Harkening back to the famous photo of Amelia Earhart zooming around on her Autoped, Rabeneick pictured a blonde fraulein picking up her man at the airport. He sits on back. Courtesy of the Hans Kruger archives

Rieju SPAIN ★★

Reiju built several scooter designs strictly for the Spanish market. The 1959 Isard scooter is a fantastic scooter/moped hybrid completely covered with a 50cc or 125cc engine.

In 2010, Rieju jumped back into the scooter market after focusing mostly on motorcycles with the MIUS (Movilidad Individual Urbana Sostenible), an electric scooter that could reach up to 50 kilometers on one charge.

Rivero GERMANY/CHINA ★

These bikes are rebranded *motorrollern*, or scooters, from Zhejiang Taizhou Wangye and sold in Germany in the 2000s.

Riverside USA ★★

Montgomery Ward came late to the scooter market but it came in style and force. As Sears Roebuck named its scooter line the Allstate, Monkey Ward named it the Riverside.

In the late 1950s, Monkey Ward bought Rockford Scooters, which were actually Mitsubishi Silver Pigeons, and were renamed Riverside scooters. Ward sold the scooters mail-order via its nationwide catalog and outlet stores. The scooters were given further model names: the Nassau, Waikiki, and the Miami, which started its life as the C-74 Pigeon.

The identity crisis didn't end with Rockford-Mitsubishi; in the early 1960s, Montgomery Ward sold Lambretta scooters for several years, adding its nameplate to the legshield of the Li Series.

Rizzato-Atala ITALY ★

In the 1960s, the firm offered its 70cc two-stroke Atala Scooter 115A.

Rockford Scooter Company

USA ★★

Beginning in the late 1950s, the Rockford Scooter Company of Rockford, Illinois, was the US importer of Mitsubishi Silver Pigeons, which were relabeled as the Rockford Scooter. Into the 1960s, Rockford imported the Pigeon C-73, C-74, C-76, and C-90 models.

Rockford in turn wholesaled its scooters to Montgomery Ward, where they were sold as Riverside scooters.

Rock-Ola USA ★★★★

Canadian David C. Rockola sparked his Rock-Ola firm in Chicago in the early 1930s building penny scales for the weight conscious. With Prohibition's repeal, Rock-Ola created its first jukebox in 1935 and spun disks on its way to success in the jukebox dance craze of pre-World War II days. Rock-Ola's jukeboxes were attired in brilliant lights, chrome frou frou, and Buck Rogers cool, and when the firm turned to scooters in 1938, it brought along its eye for style.

The Rock-Ola scooter followed the basic tenets of scooter design set down by the Salsbury Motor Glide with its small wheels, step-through design, and rear-mounted engine. Rock-Ola power was a one-cylinder 5.8hp Johnson Iron Horse engine. Clutch action was by tightening a belt.

The Rock-Ola's styling appeared in the engine cover, which was subtly curvaceous with its compound curves—something other makers were wont to invest in. The scooter was set off by two-tone paint, a headlamp, and a taillamp.

All told, the Rock-Ola looked like a roller skate dressed up in a swank metal zoot suit. Popular Mechanics ads pictured young girls at speed on the Rock-Ola—showing off both the ease of the scooter's use and more than a fair share of leg as their flouncy dresses were lifted by the breeze of a full 30mph top speed.

Rock-Ola also offered a three-wheel Delivery model based on the scooter rear end but adding a two-wheel front axle and large carrying compartment.

During World War II, Rock-Ola gave up scooter production to punch out ammo boxes and rifle parts for the war effort. Postwar, the firm returned to jukeboxes and forgot about scooters.

Röhr GERMANY ★

Röhr turned to scooters from farm machinery in 1952, and its Roletta always bore agricultural lines. Equipped with a roaring 197cc Jlo engine, the Roletta had 10hp with a top speed of 90km/h on the 12in wheels and was made until 1957. One of the most distinctive features of the Roletta was the boar's-snout headlamp that looked like an overgrown, lighted zucchini resting on the front fender.

The Roletta was built from 1952-1957 with a 200cc two-cylinder engine creating 10hp.

L. Ronney & Sons USA ★★★

The influential Powell firm created an innovative new scooter in 1940 known as the A-V-8, or Aviate. This scooter was a miniature motorcycle, setting a style that would continue with the Mustang and Cushman Eagle. And since it was such a success, numerous firms either purchased Aviates and sold them as their own or built their own versions under license.

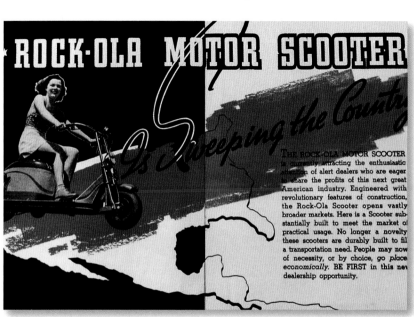

In 1943, the Ronney firm of Los Angeles offered its version of the Powell as the Ronard Jeepette with 4.00x8in tires and a 21ci engine delivering 5hp.

It's not clear whether the Ronneys simply resold A-V-8s or built their own. A Ronard Jeepette instruction and parts book noted that the scooter was "manufactured by L Ronney & Sons," but that statement could have referred to the complete scooter or just the new nameplate.

P. P. Roussey FRANCE ★ ★

The frères Pierre and Paul Roussey displayed their elegant scooter in 1952 with long, sleek lines reminiscent of a two-wheeled Citroen. Water cooled the two-stroke motor available in two sizes: 125cc for 5hp or 170cc for 9hp. The design was revamped by les frères with updated models for 1953 and 1955.

Royal Alloy UK/CHINA ★ ★

Based on the Lambretta Slimline series—and close enough to make scooter snobs look twice—the Royal Alloy scooters are a dream for those who want that classic look without the headaches of pushing around a "Lambroken." For purists, the design is frustratingly close but not quite there. The body is just a bit too hefty and not quite the thin of the Slimline, and the handlebars are a bit too busy. Still, the trade-off is avoiding the frustrations of pushing a classic, kaput Lambretta as Vespa riders chuckle.

RSI FRANCE ★

The 65cc Sulky scooter was initially made under the label Motobloc and later RSI (Riva-Sport-Industrie). The Vichyssoise company displayed the Sulky in 1953 with a SER two-speed engine producing 2hp

and 50/60km/h. The following year, the Sulky received a 98cc AMC Mustang engine, and the year after that a 125cc AMC Isard.

Rullier FRANCE ★ ★

In a blitz of publicity, M. René Rullier's Le Scot with a 70cc Lavalette engine traveled from Patras to Athens to Paris, 3800km in a masochistic feat to prove the scooter's worth. The front fender shaped as a paisley, housed the sole suspension and white-walled tires.

Rumi ITALY

There's a certain exquisite poetry in moving from manufacturing miniature submarines to building motorscooters. And Moto Rumi's Formichino scooter is perhaps the one motorscooter respected by motorcyclists—probably because it can melt the paint off many 250cc motorcycles of the era with its amazing horizontal two-cylinder two-stroke 125cc engine.

Moto Rumi was gone as quickly as it had arrived. The firm created its first motorcycle in 1949 and left the market by 1962. In those twelve years it built a reputation based on the power of its trademark engine, used across the line in its production motorcycles and scooters. It also created a series of exotic prototype racing machines.

Rumi's motorcycles and scooters were always unique. The engineering was avant garde and innovative; the styling was unlike any other two-wheelers. The features were created by a different mindset—unorthodox frames and forks, handy clocks mounted in gas tanks, odd fittings often individually stamped with Rumi's logo. The Rumi motorscooter was a totally unique creation compared to the Vespa, Iso, or Lambretta of the day.

Officine Fonderie Rumi was created before World War I by Achille Rumi as a specialized foundry based in the center of the city of Bergamo, Italy; after Achille's death, it was headed by his son, Donnino. During World War II, Rumi constructed two-men midget submarines as well as torpedoes for the Italian Navy. For the Italian postwar reconstruction, Rumi turned its engineering skills to the manufacture of motorcycles and scooters. Inspired by the success of Lambretta and Parilla, both located in nearby Milan, it built for the street; envious in rivalry with the four-stroke MV Agustas and Mondials, it built for the racetrack.

The Rumi engine was an engineering masterpiece, a race-winning two-stroke a decade ahead of the dominant East German MZ and the myriad Japanese designs. It was also a masterpiece of efficiency, weight, and size, as was the Vespa powerplant.

The crankcase was cast in four parts: two central sections that bolted together on the horizontal to hold the gearbox and crankshaft, and two side cases that bolted to the center block on the vertical to hold the clutch and Nassetti flywheel magneto. Separate cylinder barrels and heads bolted to the block, each held in place by four studs.

Bore and stroke of the 125cc was 42x45mm, with the two cylinders timed to fire at 180 degrees. A variety of single or dual carburetors and mufflers or megaphones were available for Standard, Sport, or Competizione models.

This engine premiered in the 1949 Rumi motorcycle, and soon appeared in race tune in the 1951-1954 Competizione Gobbetto, or Hunchback (nicknamed for the mounting of the magneto atop the engine like a humpback), and the long-lived Junior Gentleman production racer. In 1951, Rumi created its first scooter.

SCOIATTOLO 1951–1956 ★★★

The Scoiattolo, or Squirrel, scooter was introduced at the Milan Fiera Campionaria in 1951, the same year the Lambretta D and fully enclosed LD models bowed. Certainly Rumi was lured to the scooter market by the success of Innocenti and Piaggio, but its Scoiattolo was more of a motorcycle than a scooter, lacking the compactness, efficiency, and simple operation of the Vespa.

Like the Vespa, the chassis and body were a stamped-steel unit without a frame. But the wheels were 14in and gave the Scoiattolo an identity crisis: on one hand, it was an overgrown moped; on the other, a weak-kneed motorcycle.

The engine was Rumi's great 125cc twin with 6.5:1 compression and a single UA 15S Dell'Orto, creating 6hp at 4800rpm. The three-speed foot-change gearbox belied its motorcycle roots; a four-speed was offered from 1953. Top speed was 80km/h.

In 1953, an electric start version was offered with two 6 volt batteries run in parallel and mounted beneath the long saddle seat. In the same year, an aluminum-body sidecar for the Scoiattolo was first offered, running on a 3.25x14in wheel.

The Scoiattolo continued to be offered even after the introduction of the Formichino, which was a vastly superior scooter. Production mercifully ended in 1957.

FORMICHINO NORMALE AND LUSSO 1954–1959 ★★★★

The Formichino, or Little Ant, was designed by Donnino Rumi and is without doubt a motorscooter masterpiece. Whereas the Vespa was designed for simplicity—of construction, operation, and repair—the Formichino was simply unique.

The chassis and bodywork were of an innovative unit design akin to Corradino d'Ascanio's Vespa. But instead of the stamped steel of the Wasp, the Rumi body was cast from aluminum alloy in three structural sections that were assembled with Phillip's-head studs.

A rear section formed a fender, seat, and engine mount (modified in 1956 into two sections); and two vertically split center section halves held the front of the engine, gas tank, and steering head. Two further, nonstructural cast-aluminum pieces were a headlamp shell and a front fender. The foundry work was done by a Rumi subsidiary, Metalpress, also of Bergamo. The scooter was connected in the center by the engine, taking to an extreme the engineering concept of an engine as a stressed member of a design.

The engine of the first series Formichino breathed through a single Dell'Orto UA 15S carburetor with a split intake manifold. With a compression ratio of 6.5:1, the 125cc created 6.5hp at 6000rpm via its four-speed, foot-change gearbox and a multiple-disk oil-bath clutch. For comparison, the Lambretta LD 125

MOTO RUMI

The Scooter for the Connoisseur

The World's Finest Scooter

of 1954 made only 4.8hp, a dramatic difference.

Early Formichinos rode solely on 4.00x8in tires but by 1958, 10in wheels and 3.50x10in tires were optional. Drum brakes of 125mm diameter were fitted front and rear.

The second series Formichino appeared without fanfare in 1956 bearing only subtle modifications. The rear body section was now cast in two pieces with the fender hinged to fold up, easing rear tire changes. A Veglia speedometer unit with odometer was also added.

With the introduction of the Formichino Sport in 1957, the standard model was called the Normale.

In 1958, the Formichino Lusso bowed with luxury accessories but specs similar to the Normale. Accessories included a long, two-person saddle, cast-aluminum passenger footpegs, chrome hubcaps, and assorted chrome trim. A wide range of paint colors was now available: standard Rumi gray, ivory, silver, sky blue, racing blue, gold, yellow, and, of course, rosso corsa, or Italian racing red.

Other options were offered through the Little Ant's life, including an extra pillion saddle, full legshields, several types of spare tire racks and luggage racks, as well as an assortment of swank chrome trim pieces, ideal for cruising around the duomo and essential in the land that made chrome exhaust tips what they are today.

Rumi exported its two-wheelers throughout the world. The US importer was Berti Corporation in New Hyde Park, New York. The Formichino was for sale in the United States as the Little Ant scooter with ads promising a full 65mph.

Also in 1958, Rumi advertised a 150cc Formichino based on a bored 125cc engine, according to Riccardo Crippa's Rumi: La moto dell'artista. Bore and stroke was 46x45mm, producing 9hp at 6500rpm. Other sources also claim a 175cc model, but Rumi had a unique way of advertising models that never actually went into production; whether the 150cc or 175cc Formichino went into production or remained a prototype is not known.

FORMICHINO SPORT 1957–1960 ★ ★ ★ ★ ★

In 1957, Rumi showed its Formichino Sport at the Fiera Milanese. The Sport featured new cylinder barrels cast in aluminum alloy with steel liners and fed initially by a single 22mm Dell'Orto; later versions came with twin 18mm Dell'Ortos on separate intake manifolds. Power was now up to 8hp at 7200rpm with a compression ratio of 7.0:1 and top speed of 105km/h or 69mph.

While the Normale featured a simple Rumi decal on the side of the headlamp, the Sport had an elaborate insignia with the Rumi emblem of a maritime anchor, reflecting the midget submarine heritage, patriotically backed by the Italian tricolore.

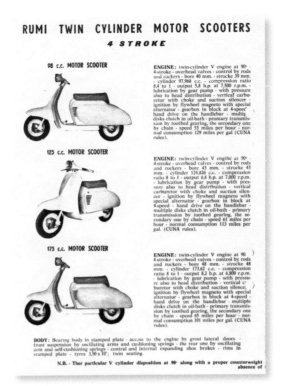

Standard tires were 3.50x10in and many race parts were optional by 1959: a range of dual Dell'Ortos and special alloy barrels with chrome bores.

FORMICHINO ECONOMICO 1958 ★ ★ ★ ★

In 1958, an odd economy model made its debut, the Formichino ST-EC or Tipo Economico. The chassis reverted to standard steel tubing covered by stamped-steel bodywork in the classic Lambretta style. The E was available solely in British Racing Green with a white flash over the gas tank.

The E used the Normale engine with 6hp at 6000rpm, but top speed was 50mph and gas consumption was 113mpg. According to Crippa, a 175cc ST-EC model was also advertised.

All in all, it was an odd scooter for Rumi, known for its sporting models. In the end, less than 1,000 were believed to have been constructed, all destined for export from Italy, although none are believed to have come to the United States.

FORMICHINO BOL D'OR 1959 ★ ★ ★ ★

In 1955, motorscooters first appeared at the premier endurance racing event, the Bol d'Or or Trophy of Gold held at the French Montlhéry circuit. Scooters had been racing all over the continent in back-road duels and small-time road races, but here was international competition and the potential for worldwide glory.

Classes for standard, sport, and racing scooters were initially set up, and the scooters ran for twenty-four hours with two riders allowed per scooter. At the end, the scooter completing the most laps won, and from 1955 through the last Bol d'Or scooter race in 1960, Rumis ruled. Their finest year was 1958, running against both scooters and motorcycles when the Foidelli/Bois team ran a Rumi Sport 2,095km or 1,302 miles at an average speed of 87.327km/h or 54.258mph to win.

The year 1958 also saw the debut of the ultimate Formichino model, the 125cc Bol d'Or. Based on the Sport, the production racer's engine had a compression ratio of 7.0:1 in alloy barrels with chrome bores pumping out 8.5hp at 7200rpm through two 18mm Dell'Orto carbs; dual 22mm Dell'Ortos were optional. Top speed in production trim was up to a staggering 75mph.

The Bol d'Or ran on 3.5x10in tires, tuned suspension, and was fitted with a long, slim dual seat; a supplementary gas tank was also available, styled like a first series Rumi Junior Gentleman motorcycle. The Bol d'Or was finished in brilliant gold and white and emblazoned with the Rumi Sport decal and tricolore.

In tuned competition trim, Sport and Bol d'Or models were typically fitted with short megaphone exhausts, dual 22mm carbs, and polished ports. Top speed was often up to 150km/h or 93.2mph.

RUMI V-TWIN SCOOTER PROTOTYPES
1960–1962 ★ ★ ★ ★ ★

In 1960, Rumi announced a motorcycle and scooter line based on a new modular four-stroke engine in three displacements: 98cc (40x39mm for 5.8hp at 7500rpm), 125cc (43x43mm for 6.8hp at 7000rpm), and 175cc (48x48mm for 8.2hp at 6800rpm). The 90 degree V-twin engine featured overhead valves run by pushrods and rocker arms; the V of the engine was mounted in line with the wheels.

The design of the Rumi V-twin scooters mimicked the established look of the Vespa and Lambretta. The body was of stamped steel surrounding a tube frame. Sidecovers were hinged to open laterally. Controls were finally all on the handlebar, with the exception of the foot-operated rear drum brake. Tires were 3.50x10in.

All in all, it looked like the right scooter at the right time. But suddenly Rumi switched gears and quit motor vehicle production. An official account of this change of heart was never made, but Rumi had returned to military contract work, leaving behind the fickle world of motorscooters and abandoning the V-twin scooters to fate in prototype limbo.

At the Köln Motorcycle Show in October 1992, a new Rumi racing motorcycle was shown; is there a possibility of a new Formichino in the future?

Runbaken GERMANY ★ ★ ★

In the 1910s, the Runbaken took the design of the Autoped and created the first electric scooter. The battery was placed behind the steering column and assured at least twenty miles of scooting.

Ruwisch GERMANY ★

The 1948-1950 Brummer scooter came with a 38cc Victoria engine although few were made.

Sacie ITALY ★

Powered by a 48cc Ducati, the Cuccioletta (or "little puppy") wrapped a metal shell over a basic bicycle frame and called it a scooter. The front wheel was 24in and the covered rear one was 20in making for an unusual ride. So unusual, in fact, that the Cuccioletta wasn't produced past its debut in 1948.

Sachs (SFM) GERMANY ★

This historic German company began in 1886 in Schweinfurt and specialized in bicycles and motorcycles. The company acquired Hercules, DKW, and Victoria in the 1960s, which produced moped-like scooters.

In the late 1990s, Sachs began reassembling Chinese-made scooters for the European market.

Safeticycles, Inc. USA ★ ★

The Safeticycle Cruiser from La Crosse, Wisconsin, was half scooter, half Ner-A-Car, the odd low-seat American motorcycle of the 1920s. As the firm's debut ad, appearing in the Saturday Evening Post, stated, "Nationally Advertised, Nationally Accepted." The first half of the statement was obviously true; the second half was wishful thinking.

The Safeticycle was a step-through bicycle riding atop large bicycle wheels; the seat height was below that of the rear wheel. The large wheels and mile-long wheelbase provided "no jumping bumps . . . no death grip . . . no bobble . . . no bounce," according to a flyer. A sidecar was also available.

But not many people took the ad's advice of "Eye it, try it, buy it." The Safeticycle Cruiser was and remains rare and collectible.

Salsbury USA

In 1935, the United States was sunk in the midst of the Great Depression with no end in sight. It was the days of The Grapes of Wrath, people selling pencils and apples on the streets or willing to work for food; job layoffs were rampant and making ends meet for those with jobs was a tightrope walk.

Onto this stage stepped E. Foster Salsbury with the idea of building a motorscooter to be called the Motor Glide. Salsbury was inspired in 1935 when he saw the great feminist and aviator Amelia Earhart dashing around the Lockheed airport at Burbank, California, on an ancient Motoped, a motorized scooter leftover from the 1910s.

Salsbury said in a 1992 interview that at the time he had "No idea what the market for a scooter would be. It was pure invention—very far out for those days." Yet he had an inkling, as he wrote in a corporate newsletter commemorating the scooter's later success: he "conceived the idea that this country needed a good but inexpensive mode of transportation." The Motor Glide was to be economical transportation for those without a car and double as an inexpensive second car for others.

MOTOR GLIDE 1935–1936 ★ ★ ★ ★ ★

Salsbury hired inventor Austin Elmore to construct the first Motor Glide in late 1935 working at Salsbury's brother's heating and plumbing shop in Oakland, according to Salsbury. The scooter used an Evinrude Speedibyke single-cylinder two-cycle engine with a 2×1 5/8in bore and stroke for 5.1ci or 82.5cc. The crankcase was made of aluminum alloy with fuel fed through a single carburetor into a two-port internal rotary intake valve. At a maximum of 3500rpm, the engine created 0.75hp. For simplicity, drive from the Speedibyke engine was via direct roller friction running onto the rear tire.

The Motor Glide used a duplex frame that surrounded the steering head at the front and supported a tube-frame rear section mounting the engine. Pressed-steel floorboards covered the center section.

When the prototype was ready for action, Salsbury packed his wife, daughter, and scooter into his car and drove from Oakland to Palm Springs for a vacation, stopping off at the February 1936 Airplane and Boating Show in Los Angeles' Pan-Pacific Auditorium. Salsbury displayed his scooter to barnstorming aviator Colonel Roscoe Turner who was thrilled by the Motor Glide after taking a ride; he immediately pronounced the scooter "The greatest woman catcher I have ever seen," Salsbury recalled.

Turner placed the prototype on display at his show booth and it drew instant attention: for child movie star Freddy Bartholomew of Little Lord Fauntleroy, it was love at first sight and he ordered one. In fact the scooter was such a success, Salsbury cancelled the family vacation and got to work, contracting a Los Angeles machine shop to begin production.

The Motor Glide Company announced the debut of its scooter in a February 1936 magazine ad with Turner's hearty endorsement. Turner was an irrepressible and flamboyant aviator who was probably better known as an early master of promotion and showmanship. He did, however, win the 1933 Bendix Trophy and 1934, 1938, and 1939 Thompson Trophy Air Races. He flew accompanied by his parachute-equipped pet lion cub, and was himself nattily attired in gleaming jackboots and a colonel's uniform, which was vaguely legitimized by an honorary commission in a state National Guard. He once crashed his plane in 1936 only to be saved by his huge silver belt buckle, which absorbed the impact, receiving a dent but saving Roscoe's life. Never mind his background, Turner was famous, and his boost for the neophyte Motor Glide must have meant life or death.

Roscoe Turner's new two-wheeled mount weighed 65lb and came "fully equipped" with lights, horn, and collapsible handlebars so it could be stowed in planes, boats, or cars for economical travel. As the ads stated, "Glide along effortlessly mile after mile. Ride it to work; visit friends and interesting places." This was the market sector the company hoped to attract: commercial use, not sport.

But while the rest of the scooter was proving itself, the same could not be said for the roller drive. On the reverse side of a Salsbury archival photo of this first scooter, an unknown hand noted that the drive system "worked fine on dry pavement."

Foster Salsbury estimated that only 25-30 of the roller-drive Motor Glides were ever built.

LEFT:

Wisconsin's Whizzer
Safticycle's Cruiser model was a strange concoction—half bicycle, half scooter. The benefits were obvious (to the copywriter): the large wheels saved the rider from "'death grip' steering" as well as "bobble," the bane of all scooter riders although they didn't know it yet.

RIGHT:

Boyfriend on the Back
The Motor Glide was introduced to the world at the February 1936 Airplane and Boating Show in Los Angeles; at the same time, ads in magazines showed Col. Roscoe Turner endorsing the first Motor Glide built by Austin Elmore, with direct roller drive to the rear wheel. The Motor Glide Company was soon to be renamed the Salsbury Corporation. Already in the '30s, women took the driver's seat, and their beau was relegated to the pillion.

NEW 1937 MODEL DE LUXE HIGH SPEED MOTOR GLIDE 1936–1937 ★ ★ ★ ★ ★

By November 1936, the new 1937 Model De Luxe High Speed Motor Glide was offered in American Bicyclist and Motorcycle magazine, available now from the newly formed Salsbury Corporation. The 1937 Model still used the Evinrude motor but with the crankshaft rotation reversed to allow chain drive to the rear wheel.

"Widely acclaimed in the West in 1936—Motor Glide rides forward to national distribution in 1937," according to this first ad. Based from Salsbury's new plant at 1515 East 75th Street in Los Angeles, a production line was now assembling up to six scooters at a time. And Roscoe Turner was back, now astride his 1937 Model.

Salsbury also printed its first full brochure in November 1936 with pictures of Roscoe Turner, the assembly line, and full specifications for the 1937 Model. With the chain drive, the scooter now ran up to 35mph while delivering 125mpg. Beyond the reversed rotation, the engine was the same 0.75hp unit with a flywheel magneto providing ignition and lighting, a cast-aluminum muffler, and 0.5 gallon gas tank. Tires were General's Jumbo Junior 12x3.50in, and a drum brake was fitted to the rear wheel, operated by a hand lever.

Styling had also developed from the prototype with steel bodywork encasing the motor at the rear; as the brochure stated, it was "Smartly streamlined for style and beauty." Original colors were High Gloss Jade Green or Chinese Red, each finished with "attractive" cream trim and chrome plating; special colors were also available upon request. Accessories included an electric horn, headlight, and taillight.

All of this was aimed at a market looking for an economical vehicle that was easy to use. Ads showing women on the Motor Glide were not just cheesecake, and operating instruction had only two steps: "First—Give the Motor Glide a push and step on. (Automatic compression release makes starting easy.) Second—Give it gas by opening the throttle with your right hand and away you go." The seat was "extremely comfortable," made of coiled springs and "amply padded with felt and hair." The step-through construction was ideal for skirts as there was "nothing to straddle." As Roscoe Turner attested, "Here's the smartest, safest, handiest and most economical motor transportation." What more could you want?

And so many people followed Roscoe Turner's lead. Actress Olivia de Havilland took a Motor Glide for a spin around the Hollywood studio lots. Vacationing Bing Crosby terrorized Honolulu on one. Johnnie "Scat" Davis, heartthrob of "Sweepstakes Winner," went hill climbing with his. Freddy Bartholomew rode his around Hollywood "like a streak of greased lightning," according to the Los Angeles Times. Salsbury capitalized on its location nearby the movie studios in their heydays, terming its scooters "Hollywood's Motor Glides" and stating in ad copy that the scooters were handy everywhere—"and, of course, around movie studios." It was image-building at its best.

MODEL 1937 AERO MOTOR GLIDE 1936–1937 ★ ★ ★ ★ ★

Nevertheless, Salsbury was not resting on its laurels. By December, after introducing the 1937 Model in November 1936, Salsbury announced a new model, the 1937 Aero Motor Glide with full bodywork enclosing a new Johnson four-stroke engine. This engine had a 2 1/8x1¾in bore and stroke for 6.2ci creating 0.75hp at 2400rpm. A flywheel magneto continued to supply spark while no less than four giant 6 volt batteries provided lighting. The Aero glided to a lower 30mph top speed but returned—as proved by an official AMA test—153mpg for your investment of around a nickel per gallon of gas. The Aero was priced at $119.50 while the De Luxe was $155. By early 1937, the original 1937 Model De Luxe was gone as the company concentrated on the Aero.

In the following months, Salsbury also introduced the Parcel Carrier attachment, a large bin that mounted on the rear of the Motor Glide for delivery services. This was followed by three optional Motor Glide models designed for commercial use. The Passenger Side Car Model SC-11 was a bathtub-like sidecar available with a single padded seat and a color scheme matching the scooter. The Express Side Car Model SC-12 followed the SC-11 styling but was merely a commercial carrier bin. Both sidecars rode on the 12in tires of the scooter with "suspension" supplied by the natural flex of the metal frame.

Finally, the Cycletow Model 64 was an ingenious set of giant "training wheels" that mounted to the rear end in line with the rear tire; these could be elevated for solo riding or lowered in place for towing of the scooter. Photos showed vacationers trotting along

Airbrushed 1937 Salsbury

The 1937 Aero Model boasted restyled bodywork to enclose the new Johnson four-stroke engine. It was while shopping for the new powerplant that E. Foster Salsbury contacted Cushman for a bid on its Husky engine; Salsbury declined Cushman's offer, and Cushman decided to enter the scooter market for itself. Oddly enough, Johnson would later merge with Evinrude—Salsbury's first engine-supplier—and buy out Cushman.

with their Motor Glides in tow and car dealers using them for picking up and delivering new cars. The idea followed Harley-Davidson's 1932 Servi-Car and Indian's Dispatch Tow. The Cycletow became the Model CT-60 for 1938.

With these added accessories, the Motor Glide was finding myriad new customers. A 1937 brochure shows Motor Glides in the faithful service of telegraph riders and messenger deliverers, postal carriers, police patrols, the US Army and Navy, and more. Foster Salsbury estimated that 200-300 1937 Aero Motor Glide units were built and sold in all.

MODELS 50 AND 60 1937–1938 ★★★★★

In late 1937, Salsbury introduced on the new 1938 Motor Glide its most revolutionary feature: the Self-Shifting Transmission, as the firm termed its new automatic clutch and transmission torque converters. The primary drive was via a v-shaped rubber belt running between pulleys. The belts shifted between the different-size pulleys for ratios of 14:1 in low to 4:1 in high. The automatic clutch allowed the engine to idle until the throttle was twisted. This automatic transmission technology was startlingly innovative in 1937; the reason it is commonplace today is due to Salsbury's designs, which are still state of the art on industrial engines and vehicles of all sorts, including the latest generation of Honda four-wheelers.

Two models were offered in 1938, both with the torque converter: the Model 50 with 5/8hp engine and the Model 60 with the 1-1½hp engine. And again Colonel Roscoe Turner was at the controls for the new ad campaign, stating that the 1938 Motor Glide "is the last word in personal transportation and far exceeds my fondest expectation for performance."

The bodywork styling for the new 1938 scoots remained similar to the 1937 Aero although the horn was moved atop the steering head and the headlamp ascended to the handlebars. The 1938 models were now finished stock in cream only with green striping; special colors were available at nominal extra cost.

And it all worked. It worked so well in fact that it set the style for all scooters that were to follow, from the Cushman and Vespa onward. Taking inspiration from the early American Motoped, English ABC Skootamota, and others, Salsbury and Elmore created a modern scooter that was a success. And all scooters that followed would share at least three of five of the Motor Glide's attributes of a motor placed next to the rear wheel in some form, step-through construction, bodywork covering the motor, small wheels, and an automatic transmission/clutch.

One reason for the Motor Glide's influence was that in 1938, Salsbury sent a sales agent to Europe armed with blueprints and photos to discuss licensing production to potential scooter manufacturers.

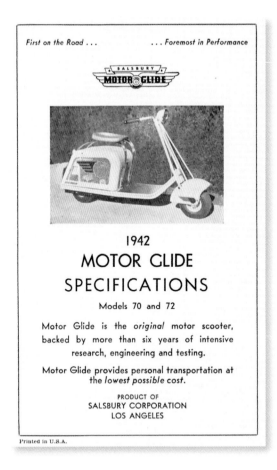

First on the Road . . .   . . . Foremost in Performance

SALSBURY
MOTOR GLIDE

1942
MOTOR GLIDE
SPECIFICATIONS
Models 70 and 72

Motor Glide is the *original* motor scooter, backed by more than six years of intensive research, engineering and testing.

Motor Glide provides personal transportation at the *lowest possible cost.*

PRODUCT OF
SALSBURY CORPORATION
LOS ANGELES

Printed in U.S.A.

1942 Salsbury Motor Glide
The Model 70 and 72, shown here, were available with four types of sidecars: a passenger sidecar with padded seat and hinged side door; a hinged-top merchandise sidecar; a huge closed commercial sidecar; and this utility sidecar, which was basically a box on wheels. The passenger and merchandise sidecars boasted streamlined fenders similar to the scooter. The DeLuxe Model 72 differed from the Model 70 in its "Floating Ride" seat that perched the cushion atop dual leaf springs for Gold Wing-like comfort circa 1939.

Foster Salsbury said in a 1992 interview that, while he was not on the trip, he believed that Piaggio was one of the firms met with. Piaggio—as well as the others that were approached—declined a Salsbury licensing agreement.

MODELS 70 AND 72 1939–1945 ★★★

For 1939, Salsbury completely revamped the Motor Glide, introducing the Model 70 with Standard Seat and Model 72 with DeLuxe Floating Ride Seat. The engine in both models was a new 2.3-2.7hp Lauson single-cylinder four-stroke measuring a square 2¼x2¼in for 8.94ci with a compression ratio of 6.0:1. Ignition was by flywheel magneto, lighting by a generator, cooling by air via "forced draft," and oiling by pump. The Self-Shifting Transmission was standard on the Model 72 and optional on the 70. Other developments included rubber engine mounts and a drive chain automatically oiled by crankcase oil vapor.

The suspension was also updated for unprecedented comfort. "Rubber snubbers" and tension coil springs "effectively cushion road shocks" at the front and rear, promised flyers. And the tires were now 3.50x12in but still with only a rear drum brake.

The most dramatic change was the new "aero-dynamic aircraft designing for style leadership," as Salsbury brochures waxed poetically. These

LEFT:

Dream Dealership

A Salsbury-Harley-Davidson dealership with a Model 85 DeLuxe on the Art Deco show stand and a Standard on the floor. Note the display engine on the stand as well as the Salsbury posters in the showroom.

LEFT:

Dream Dealership

A Salsbury-Harley-Davidson dealership with a Model 85 DeLuxe on the Art Deco show stand and a Standard on the floor. Note the display engine on the stand as well as the Salsbury posters in the showroom.

RIGHT:

Dual Salsburys

In 1946, Salsbury was acquired by Northrup, but the Model 85 had been designed by Salsbury engineer Lewis Thostenson during the end of World War II. Here at an outing along the California coast with a Model 85 DeLuxe, left, and Standard; note that only the DeLuxe has the added seat for the pillion riders. This wholesome gang looked like they're ready for some tennis then a milkshake— the perfect market that Northrup and new sales chief, E. Foster Salsbury, saw as their scooter's audience.

radical styling advances were most pronounced in the new Easy-Lift Streamlined Engine Hood, which truly looked as though it was "styled by the wind" with curves replacing the creases and folds of the older Motor Glides. The sides of the hood were now made of mesh, providing a tantalizing and seductive see-through view of the mechanicals. Motor Glide wing emblems were emblazoned over the fenders and hood mesh sides. The standard color was again Tacoma Cream with green striping and cadmium-plated parts.

The seats distinguished the two models. The Standard Seat of the 70 was a simple pad albeit covered in "durable quasi leather." The Floating Ride Seat of the 72 was actually a thinner pad, covered in Fabricoid, but mounted atop long leaf springs; the leaves doubled as bumpers at the tail. The Tandem Standard Seat was a lengthened version of the single; the Tandem DeLuxe added an extra Fabricoid pad to the leaf springs of the 72.

By 1939, you could order a Model 70 or 72 as fully optioned as your neighbor's Cadillac. The Special Equipment and Approved Accessories list from February 1, 1941, listed the following options: DeLuxe Floating Ride seat (optional for Model 70); Tandem DeLuxe seat; Tandem Standard seat; Tandem seat footrests; Salsbury Self-Shifting Transmission (optional for Model 70); Passenger Side Car; Express Side Car with open top; Express Side Car with hinged cover and latch; Parcel Carrier with hinged cover and latch; hand throttle control with cable; Flex Glass windshield; speedometer; Tow Glide; Vibra Disc horn with button, wiring, bracket, and 6 volt battery; and special paint colors.

The Models 70 and 72 continued their legacy through World War II during which they were built in small numbers. In the war years, as in the Depression years, scooters continued to be pressed into new services with gas rationing making the 100mpg attractive.

To counter Nazi aggressions in Europe, the US Army requested bids for military motorscooters in 1944. Salsbury was one of several makers alongside Cushman who provided scooters; Foster Salsbury estimated that as many as 200 Model 72s were sold to the US Navy for base transportation and communications during the war. For the Red Cross and armed services, Salsbury created a Mono-Ambulance Motor Glide with a covered stretcher on a sidecar chassis.

By 1945, Motor Glide production ended. Salsbury had something new up its sleeve for 1946.

SUPER-SCOOTER MODEL 85 STANDARD AND DELUXE 1946–1949 ★ ★ ★ ★ ★

It was outrageous. It was radical. It was the motorscooter of the future—and destined to be the most desirable motorscooter of all time.

Its styling was avant garde, years ahead of the Jet Age styling of the 1950s, more akin to a zeppelin on wheels. Yet the wheels were barely visible, hidden beneath flowing, streamlined fender skirts and so, along with the ease of the Self-Shifting Transmission, you felt as though you were not so much gliding— you were flying.

Salsbury spent the war years producing a small number of civilian scooters but had concentrated on materiel for the war effort. The firm also designed the Turret Truck, a motorized forklift with a revolving front end; it was licensed to Hyster Company in 1949.

Among its other work, Salsbury also developed an experimental wind tunnel for the aviation industry, which was used in early aerodynamic studies for fighters and bombers. Lessons learned in the new field of aviation aerodynamics would set the stage for the design of the new Salsbury scooter.

In 1944-1945, Salsbury sold his scooter business to the Los Angeles defense-contracting firm AVION, Inc., which in turn changed its name to Salsbury Motors, Inc., in 1946 and became a subsidiary of Northrop Aircraft Corporation.

Based from a new plant in Pomona, the new Model 85 scooter was introduced at a press preview in late 1946 on Fargo Street, the "steepest improved hill" in Los Angeles, according to Steve Hannagn Associates, Salsbury's new PR firm thanks to Northrop, which promoted the event. The 85 climbed the 32 degree slope with ease "although the grade is enough to stall many automobiles." The show was meant to impress the press with Salsbury's idea of a motorscooter "as a second car for moderate-income families."

Northrop called its new Model 85 Super-Scooter the Salsbury scooter; not the Motor Glide by Salsbury. Obviously, Northrop believed Salsbury was an established name—and it didn't want further confusion with Cushman's Auto Glide.

The Model 85 had been designed by engineer Lewis Thostenson during the end of World War II. Thostenson had been one of Salsbury's original engineers and continued on at Northrop; Foster Salsbury headed the scooter sales team for Northrop.

The Model 85 was available in Standard and DeLuxe versions, both using the same mechanicals but the latter with a Plexiglas windshield and fully developed front cockpit. The engine was a Salsbury-built 6hp four-stroke single-cylinder set at an angle toward the rear of the scooter. It featured the exclusive Straight-Shot carburetion system, a short, but admittedly angled intake manifold. Nevertheless, the 1946 brochure promised the power "will take you up steep hills at car speed."

The torque converter was standard on both models, and for further ease of operation, the 1946 brochure didn't even use the words throttle or brake when describing the two control pedals: they were simply the Stop and Go pedals. The 85 DeLuxe, however, could be ordered with an auxiliary hand throttle.

Perhaps the most interesting feature of the new 85 was the front and rear forks, which were one-sided with stub axles inspired by airplane strut design. But the suspension was provided by two, different-rate coil springs housed within an elongated steering head. At the rear, a single coil spring did the damping. The 85 had come a long way from the Motor Glide.

It was the bodywork of the 85 that caught your attention first and foremost. Both versions were bejeweled with a chrome bumper and a similar rear-end design. Within the tail bodywork was a spare tire and luggage compartment "ample for most shopping trips"; on top was a padded, leather-covered seat.

The Standard featured a large fender that enveloped the front wheel and lead up over the steering head in one smooth, bodacious expanse. The DeLuxe added a large cowling over the front fender surmounted by a Plexiglas windshield. Where the headlamp on the Standard was free standing, the DeLuxe headlamp was recessed into the cowling.

The design was pure Buck Rogers: at a time when Northrop was experimenting with its advanced XF-89 Scorpion jet fighter, the Salsbury scooter shared the Jet Age styling. And it was large. The size was unprecedented among scooters; it was certainly big enough to be a second car!

Northrop produced the Model 85 for two years during which time Foster Salsbury estimated 700-1,000 units were built and sold, including units exported to Germany. But as Salsbury remembered of the Model 85's demise, "Demand fell off when cars started becoming available again and Northrop halted production." It was a sad finale for a great scooter.

Salsbury's influence on all other scooters that followed cannot be overestimated. Austin Elmore and Foster Salsbury dictated the design of the modern motorscooter in their 1936 Motor Glide.

San Cristoforo ITALY ★★★

Having a company named for San Cristoforo, the protector of travelers (who was later impeached by the Vatican after having done centuries of good work), must have been good advertising for a scooter.

S. Cristoforo s.r.l. of Milan took over production of Gianca's Nibbio scooter in 1949. The Nibbio, Italian for "kite," had been one of the pioneering Italian scooters alongside the Vespa, and S. Cristoforo kept it in production until 1951.

When the Nibbio first rolled off the new assembly lines it was substantially updated from the Gianca model. The bodywork was all new, as was the 125cc two-stroke engine. With 5hp at 4700rpm and a three-speed gearbox, the Nibbio was now good for 75km/h.

In 1952, S. Cristoforo released its Simonetta 125cc scooter, which was in truth a Nibbio under a new name. The styling was slightly renewed but the motor was retained. The Simonetta was also built in France by Ravat.

Sanko Kogyo JAPAN ★★

Sanko Kogyo's Jet series of motorscooters was built primarily for the Japanese market in the 1950s. The line bowed in 1953 with the 175cc J5 producing 4.5hp at 4200rpm and riding on 4.00x8in tires. The styling was pure tractor.

By 1954, the Jet J5 had been dressed up with chrome trim, air ducts, and a jet ornament taking off from the front fender. The effect was still the same. In the same year, the Jet J7 was offered to combat the deluxe Rabbit and Pigeon models with an overhead-valve 250cc engine of 70×65mm for 6.7hp at 4500rpm and a top speed of 70km/h.

Santamaria ITALY ★

Powered by a Zündapp 70cc motor, the Santamaria scooter named Moncenisio debuted in 1958.

Essentially a covered scooter with the engine exposed, the Moncenisio was also available with a 50cc engine for Italian teenagers who didn't have their license.

Saroléa BELGIUM ★ ★ ★

Saroléa was one of the grand old motorcycle manufacturers that failed to find a market postwar. In 1956, Saroléa showed its Djinn scooter at the Salon de Bruxelles. Named for a desert spirit, the Djinn was a Rumi Formichino disguised by the Belgian maker's decal on the aluminum-alloy bodywork and Belgian Englebert whitewall tires. Saroléa built the Djinn in cooperation with Rumi in the late 1950s for the Belgian market.

Savas Sales USA ★

Savas of Owosso, Michigan, imported its Tourist scooter from Italy in the 1960s. The main advantage of the Tourist was that it could be pedaled for added acceleration from a stoplight or to make it down a hill.

Scomadi UK/THAILAND ★ ★ ★

Built by true Lambretta lovers, these limited-edition scooters were hand-built and essentially souped-up Slimline Innocenti-like scooters, with all the extras for ultimate performance (except for fiberglass side panels) for the TL (Turismo Leggera). The only trick was they used a Vespa GTS 250cc or GTS 300cc engine—was this sacrilege? Piaggio didn't keep the engine supply going, so Scomadi looked to China.

Scomadi took its prototype to Innocenti's hometown, Milano, for the 2013 Milan Motorcycle Show. The logo has a prowling panther ready to pounce, reminiscent of the Lamborghini toro, and the top has the tricolor Italian flag. Never mind that the name Scomadi got snickers that it sounded a bit too much like *scomodi*, or "uncomfortable" in Italian. Wisely, the Italian colors were replaced with the British Union Jack, and even the Who struck a deal to release a special-edition Scomadi. Oh wait, in *Quadrophenia*, Pete Townshend sings, "I drive a GS scooter with my hair cut neat," even though Jimmy drove a Lammie.

The much anticipated Scomadi scooters were slow in hitting the showroom amidst litigation between the Chinese manufacturer, Hanway (Changzhou Hanwei Vehicle Science & Technology Limited Company), and the Scomadi visionaries. Hanway "borrowed" the idea of a new Lambretta and released the Royal Alloy, much to the chagrin of Scomadi, who took its business elsewhere. A deal was struck with Thailand, and a new factory was built in 2020 to continue to produce the Turismo Tecnica. As of press time, Scomadi scooters were still unavailable in the US, but Royal Alloy had spearheaded the British, or rather Chinese/Italian, invasion.

Scootavia FRANCE ★ ★

M. A. Morin's heavy-looking scooter had the unusual advantage of principal parts made of magnesium and molded alpax. The engine originated as a 125cc Ydral, but from 1952 to 1954 (the last year of production), changed to a four-speed 175cc AMC engine. The lines of the rear of the scooter bore a strong resemblance to the DKW Hobby. The overgrown front fender, later copied by Peugeot, looked like a Parisian police hat with a bladelike visor where a bumper would usually lie. Although probably not sharpened, it would be exceptionally dangerous cruising down the Champs Elysées if an unaware tourist thought that stoplights were heeded in Paris.

Scooters India INDIA ★ ★ ★

In 1972, the Indian government-run Scooters India bought Innocenti's DL scooter tooling and continued manufacturing late-1960 Lambretta models. The firm retained the Lambretta DeLuxe Series tradition, making little change to the models besides adding turn signals and eventually making select body parts in plastic.

Scooters India offered three models: the 125 DL, 150 GP, and 200 GP. With a slightly higher compression ratio than the Innocenti-made SX 150 and SX 200, the Indian GP models were good for more horsepower and speed than their Italian counterparts. The 125 had 7.4hp for a 59mph top speed. The GP 150 (148cc at 57x58mm) ran to 7.8:1 and 9.3hp at 6300rpm for a 63mph top speed; by 1980, the GP 150 was breathing through a 22mm Dell'Orto SH with a compression ratio at 8.25:1 for a stupendous 9.4hp still at 6300rpm. Fuel consumption was a mere 90mpg, but who cared anymore?

The GP 200 was an over-bored 66x58mm version of the old Li Series engine fed via a 22mm Dell'Orto SH with an 8.2:1 cr fathering 12.4hp at 6300rpm. Top speed was a fleet-footed 71mph.

By 1997, Scooters India stopped production of all two-wheeled models but still claims it "possesses the world right of the trade name LAMBRETTA / LAMBRO." This is a hot topic and not necessarily accepted by those who want to bring back the Lambretta.

Scooterson USA ★

The Rolley scooter built by Romanian-born designer Mihnea de Vries in 2015 as a more stable version of the mini push scooter craze. The addition of a seat (even if uncomfortable) lands this electric mobile in this encyclopedia rather than on stand-up monopattino (single skate, in Italian) list of forgettable children's "scooters." The fat-tire design lends a degree of stability, which is necessary for the boasted top speeds of 30 mph and all sorts of cell phone apps keep you wired into your Scooterson.

Scootmule FRANCE ★

If the word jalopy could be applied to scooters, the quintessential would be the 1962 Scootmule. M. Gérard Beau's prototype had a 50cc Mosquito 38B engine with a design that differed little from a glorified scrap heap on wheels.

Scott UK ★★

While technically the Scott from 1908 may not qualify as a scooter, the step-through design with a an ample legshield and floorboards earns this hybrid a coveted place in the annals of scooter history. The Scott wasn't exactly overflowing in beauty, but the two-cylinder British bike deserves kudos for its revolutionary lines.

Scrooser GERMANY ★

While missing one of the essential elements of a classic motorscooter, the front legshield, the electric Scrooser has the step-through design, a seat, and small (yet wide) wheels. Scrooser boasts its German technology and was acquired by fellow compatriot Kumpan out of Remagen, Germany. Scrooser's cruiser has been copied ad nauseum in China. The result is that the self-balancing Scrooser may be the real deal, but the fat-tired low rider can still only reach 25 km/h (15 mph), and the battery gives up after 45 km (28 miles).

Segway USA ★

Segway built its name through the stand-up "scooter" that gaggles of tourists would hop on in scenic cities rather than using their feet, often bonking into other tourists and somehow suing the company for their bad driving. The company ceased production of the iconic stand-up mobile and incorporated its novel gyroscopic technology into an S-Pod lounge chair on two side-by-side wheels. Imagine the mechanized chairs in *WALL-E* or a Vespa without handlebars and a front wheel. More scooterlike, though, is the Ninebot eScooter E—that's two *E*s in case you missed that it's electric with a lithium-ion battery. Slated for release in 2021, this slick Segway can reach 62 mph (100 km/h) and go for 125 miles (200 km) on a charge before you're left by the side of the road.

Seith GERMANY ★

Victoria 38cc engines ran the Seith scooter designed for children from 1949-1950.

Serveta SPAIN ★★

In 1952, Lambretta Locomociones SA was founded in Eibar, outside of Bilbao in northern Spain, to import Italian-made scooters; the firm began licensed production in 1954. It later changed its name to Messrs Serveta Industrial SA, at which time the scooters were renamed Serveta scooters instead of Lambrettas.

The Servetas were rather crude with haphazard 6 volt electrics into the 1980s while competing scooters like the Vespa P200E boasted 12 volt, 100 watt electrics as well as electronic ignition. Serveta produced the Li 125 Slimline DL, 150 Special, and Jet 200. The 150 Special with Slimline styling had a bench seat above the side panels with a racing stripe interrupted by "150" numerals. Soon after, the Special had black trim and turn signals mounted with the new rectangular headlamps. This model was imported into the United States by Cosmopolitan Motors of Philadelphia.

The Jet 200, known as "la scooter que dura más" or the scooter that lasts longer, was equipped with a bench seat, racing stripes on the side panels (for added speed), and turn signals. The Jet 200 (a.k.a. the Lince 200 from 1975) was a hot scooter ideal for tuning and performance.

Servos GERMANY ★

Servos' lightweight scooter was called a "Volksmotorroller" in ads, the two-wheeled contender to the Volkswagen.

Built from 1953-1954, it was powered by a miniscule 36cc Victoria engine mounted atop the front fender and driving the front wheel via a chain. Dry weight was a mere 30kg.

The shape of the scooter bore relation to the Lambretta LC but without side panels and shrunk down to half size.

Shandong Zhongling CHINA ★

The Zhongqi are 125cc gas-powered scooters that match the other manufacturers' designs. The ZQ125T-13 at least comes in a matte orange with a fun design to its plastic bodywork.

Showa JAPAN ★★★

The Showa 125 Marine scooter was launched in the late 1950s with a scooter chassis and body riding atop large, 14in semi-disk wheels. Power came from a 125cc two-stroke.

Siambretta ARGENTINA ★★★

Siambretta built Lambrettas under license in Argentina in the 1950s and 1960s, also exporting its wares to neighboring South American countries Chile, Paraguay, and Uruguay.

Innocenti was also connected with industrial projects in Argentina, Brazil, Mexico, and the United States. In Venezuela in 1957, Ferdinando Innocenti beat out Fiat in a contract to produce an Italian version of the German Goggomobil, a four-wheeled midget car, which was called the Lambretta Goggo. With the help of the Venezuelan government, the rain forest at the head of the Orinoco river was stripped to make way for the $342 million mining complex for the steel necessary to make the Lambretta cars.

1952 Moretti
A small factory in the picturesque town of Reggio Emilia, put together a doozie of a scooter in the early fifties far before giants Piaggio and Innocenti had perfected their styling. SIM (Società Italiana Motorscooter) borrowed a Puch two-cylinder 125cc engine worthy of 85 km/h and tagged on swan wing chrome on the side panels and hood ornament. In spite of the attention to detail, such as the air intakes on the front fenders, SIM only produced a few of the Moretti scooters. Courtesy of the owner: Roberto Donati

Siamoto ITALY ★

Building from just 1996 to 1999, Siamoto produced a few scooters. The Siamoto Scross is an unusual hybrid of a scooter and motocross motorcycle. Powered by a 50cc Morini engine, the Scross was light enough that it could easily go off road.

Sillaro ITALY ★

Using wheels left over from its production of light motorcycles and mopeds, Sillaro of Bologna mounted them on its Scooter 48 in 1956. The slick covered moped with ample legshield and white-wall tires could top 55km/h in spite of the little 48cc engine.

SIM Moretti ITALY ★★★

The Società Italiana Motorscooters of Reggio Emilia introduced its first scooter in 1951 as a venture planned to mimic the sales success of Piaggio and Innocenti. The SIM Gran Lusso scooter was a joint venture with Giovanni Moretti, a small-scale producer of motorcycles and later, cars; engines came from the Austrian Puch firm.

The design followed the classic scooter tenets: a tube frame covered by steel bodywork, although on the Gran Lusso, the complete tail section hinged forward for engine access. The styling lacked any pretensions of elegance, going instead for practicality.

The Puch engine was a split-single design of 125cc with two bores of 38mm and a single stroke of 55mm and fed through a sole carburetor, providing 5.5hp at 4500rpm. The gearbox had three speeds with a left-foot selector pedal. The Gran Lusso was also built in France under license by Guiller.

In 1952, SIM added to its line with the Ariete, or Ram, scooter. Like the Lambrettas of the time, the Ariete lacked bodywork and had shaft drive via single-sided rear wheel support of light alloy. The engine was a two-stroke by SIM of 150cc from 57x58mm delivering 7.5hp at 5200rpm.

In 1953, an Ariete Sport version appeared with full bodywork inspired by the homely Gran Lusso styling.

SIM-Moretti flyers announced that its scooter was "The most elegant! The most perfect!" While that may be debatable, the SIM scooters never sold in the numbers projected and production was halted in the mid-1950s.

Simard FRANCE ★

Henry Lanoy dreamed of making a scooter all the way back in the 1920s, and finally assembled an electric prototype in 1938. Plans were laid for New-Map, a motorcycle manufacturer from Lyon, to begin building his design. Scooter plans took a backseat, however, when Hitler he needed more lebensraum and took over France.

Lanoy was not disheartened by the Vichy quislings and convinced another Lyon company, Simard, to make his electric scooter prototype in 1942 which earned a silver medal at the Grenoble and Lyon fairs. In 1946, the scooter received a two-stroke, 50cc Baby-Champion engine with a three-speed gearbox. Henry Lanoy tried again in 1949 with a more advanced scooter, but it was no match for the Italian competition.

Not one to give up, Les Etablissements Louis Simard, known more for its sidecars, decided to throw in a scooter at its stand at the Salon de Paris in 1952. The rear section was standard fare, but the front was a hybrid scrambler with plastic covers over the suspension giving the impression of a motocross scooter. In 1953, the evolved Simard was available either with a standard four-stroke 125cc AMC, an Ultima 125cc F12 with 5hp or a 200cc, 9hp F20 Ultima engine.

SIMAT ITALY ★★★★

Vittorio Belmondo pieced together an early monocoque Italian scooter in 1940 and later the 1941 Velta VB model. A scaled-down version was licensed to Volugrafo, which dropped scooters from the skies as Italian lightning-brigade paratrooper putt-putts. SIMAT goes down in history as the scooter that inspired Piaggio's Paperino in 1945.

Simplex USA ★★★

The Simplex Automatic scooter was a big scooter with an automatic transmission—items that the Simplex Manufacturing Corporation of New Orleans believed would help its scooter infiltrate the American motorcyclist's mindset when it was first offered in the late 1950s. As a 1957 ad stated, it was "a motorcycle man's motorscooter." Problem was, a motorcycle man wanted a motorcycle. The Simplex remained an anomaly from both markets: it was too large for putt-puttniks and too small for the Hells Angels.

Based on large, 4.00x20in wheels and a mile-long 48in wheelbase, the Simplex was a scooter with an identity crisis. The chassis was step-through and the 150cc engine was well hidden from prying hands beneath a simple fold of sheetmetal. The automatic transmission carried power to the rear wheel via a rubber V-belt.

The first Simplex motorscooter of 1957 carried its gas tank atop the rear fender behind the seat and was steered by low-profile handlebars. By 1960, the scooter had been refined with the gas tank hidden from view and protective legshields added. For the motorcycle man, Harley-Davidson-style high bars were added, topped by an optional windscreen for high-speed use.

Simplex also offered its Servicycle motorbike alongside the scooter based on the same engine but with styling that was half Whizzer, half Indian Chief, and sold only half of its builder's dreams.

By 1962, Simplex was offering its Sportsman T63 scooter mini-bike.

Success or failure, the Simplex motorscooter was a fascinating machine. And because it was never a marketing hit, there were not many of them built, so today they are quite rare and highly prized. All made more so by their eccentricity and obscurity.

Simson EAST GERMANY ★★

Under the brand of AWO, Simson presented in 1955 the Punktchen with a 49.5cc engine made by in Magdebourg at the Karl Marx factory.

The KR50 (Klein Roller or little scooter) of 1959 used 16in wheels as opposed to its predecessor's tiny wheel diameter. The 46.7cc engine gave 2.1hp at 5500rpm with a right kick start. Simson didn't have to worry about being late in the scooter market since it appeared that the other East Bloc makers often worked together with their state-owned business.

This didn't keep Simson from pushing its product on those who like "to be independent of the means of communication of the large city, save time and make distances become relatively little, SIMSON Moped or the SIMSON Small Size Scooter are the ideal vehicle for him."

Even the American handyman journal, Mechanix Illustrated, extolled their virtues in 1956, "With top speeds running up to 70mph-plus and powered by big two-stroke mills, the Jerry jobs are loaded for bear—and the buyer had better be loaded with dough, by scooter-buying standards."

In 1973, Simson returned to the scooter fold with its Schwalbe KR51-1, KR51-1S, and KR51-1K models. Although in typical scooter style, the Simson's design was just a mishmash of lines and easily forgettable. The big difference in the three KR models was the

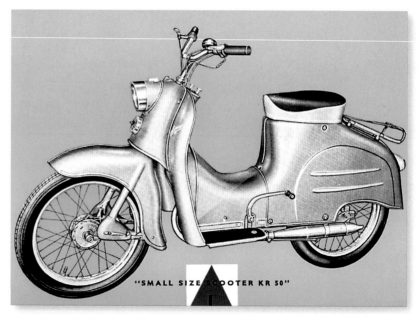

"SMALL SIZE SCOOTER KR 50"

color: blue, olive beige, and pastel white correspondingly. The 50cc Schwalbe had three gears and 3.6hp for 60km/h.

Long after the Berlin Wall fell, Simson produced scooters until 2002, with more than a million of the Schwalbe sold. Then in 2015, the Schwalbe (swallow) would fly again as the GOVECS Schwalbe with an electric motor but the same classic styling.

Sitta WEST GERMANY ★

In the early 1950s, Sitta made scooters with either a 119cc or 123cc two-stroke Jlo engines.

Société Industrielle de Troyes
FRANCE ★

In France in 1952, Société Industrielle de Troyes began production of the Innocenti's Lambretta LC model concurrent with ACMA's production of Vespas.

Socvel FRANCE ★

M. Henry Lanoy engineered the Stéfa scooter for the Société de construction de véhicules légers in 1951. The Stéfa I had a 98cc German Sachs engine and the Stéfa II contained a 125cc three-speed AMC. The Stéfa's body was unspectacular with an enclosed rear end and slit openings behind the drivers legs. In 1952, an 125cc Aubier-Dunne and four-speed 125cc Ydral engines were available.

Solifer FINLAND/CHINA ★

Solifer Oy made classic, covered mopeds beginning in the 1950s that are highly collectible. As ad copy mentions, in typical Finnish reticence to not brag: "Solifer-skoottereilla on ajanut jo monta suomalaista

Simson KR 50 Roller
Simson advertised its pokey KR 50 for those who like "to be independent of the means of communication of the large city, save time and make distances become relatively little, SIMSON Moped, or the SIMSON Small Size Scooter are the ideal vehicle for him."

"Motorcycle Man's Motorscooter"

This 1957 150cc Simplex tried to straddle the fence between the lucrative scooter market— in full boom by the late fifties— and the macho motorcycle world of The Wild One. With a 48-inch wheelbase, whopping 4.00 × 20-inch wheels, but a step-through frame, "the Simplex is the first scooter to combine all the advantages of a Motorcycle and Scooter without any of the disadvantages of either type of vehicle." By the early sixties, Simplex gave up the scooter trade and delved into Sportsman minibikes, and once again tried to appeal to two markets, "NOT TOO HEAVY—Not too LIGHT. The SPORTSMAN'S made JUST RIGHT for Man or Boy."Courtesy of the owner: Jim Kilau

sukupolvea," or "Many generations of Finns have already ridden Solifer scooters."

In the 2000s, Solifer rebranded Chinese-made sport scooters (F1 and R8) and the old-style Solifer Retro 4. The Retro Cruiser 4, on the other hand, is essentially a remake of the Honda Joker/Shadow, inspired by ape-hanger custom chopper motorcycles.

Sparta THE NETHERLANDS ★

Sparta began by offering a scooter with 50cc Jlo two-stroke and pedals for starting in 1953 . It soon launched its 3PK model with Villiers 98cc, but in 1953 the engines changed to Sachs.

Speed-Mors-Alcyon FRANCE ★★★

Already by 1943 Pierre Brissonet was hard at work on scooter designs. By mid-1949, Brissonet pieced together a prototype propelled by a two-speed, 50cc Motobécane Poney. By the end of the following year, the Speed scooter—based on the early prototype—debuted with a 98cc engine. The S1C Speed of 1951 used Brissonet's own engine of 115cc putting out 3.8hp.

The Speed ended up being produced by the Société Mors and the Etablissements Brissonet went back to making automobile accessories. The Mors-Speed carried a 125cc engine that now put out 6hp at 4600 to become a "grand routier" (big traveler).

The scooter to have, though, was the Paris-Nice S3 version. Although the wheels were mini 4x8in, the sleek design with the extensive front legshield hosting the headlamp made for a smooth, original scooter. "Conçu comme une Automobile" (Conceived as a car), bragged brochures for the Mors Speed.

What Speed began, Mors continued and then Alcyon finished. Etablissements Gentil à Courbevoie, or Alcyon for short, took over making scooters in 1955. By the next year, however, only a two-tone Paris-Nice was produced through 1958.

Speedway USA ★★

Speedway Motor Corporation of Kansas City, introduced its scooter and miniature motorcycle following World War II to compete with Cushman. By 1946, the firm had built some 300 scooters with production planned at forty-five scooters a day for 1947.

Both the Speedway scooter and motorcycle used the same one-cylinder air-cooled engine, which pumped out 6hp for a 60mph top speed.

Spencer & Cio CHILE ★

Under license from Piaggio, Spencer & Cio assembled Vespas for the South American market.

Sportcycle USA ★

The midget Sportcycle was available in the late 1930s through Popular Mechanics ads for a mere $39.

Stafford Mobile Pup UK

After the Ner-a-car, England produced the Stafford Mobile Pup in 1919 adding a comfortable seat and wider floorboard. The four-stroke engine measured 142cc and was placed on the left side of the front wheel. Special features included an optional seat for lazy scooterists and a little sidecar for junior to ride along.

Stella FRANCE ★★

The Stella prototype had finned side panels in the shape of a whale, giving the scooter the appearance of an amusement park water ride. Actually, though, the intended shape of the scooter was that of a cock, the symbol of Stella, as the marque's emblem had a white rooster atop a globe to wake up the world to the wonder of French scooters.

Stella was know for making great bicycles, one which won the Tour de France in 1953, so the jump into the scooter biz shouldn't have been such a leap. Although the lines of the Stella defied the imagination, with a fairly powerful 150cc Riedel engine producing 6hp, the 1951 Stella never went into full scale production. Three years later, however, Stella sold a scooter called the Sterva built by Sterling of Saint-Etienne.

Sterling Sterva FRANCE ★★

Sterling's Sterva took after the Moto Rumi Scoiattolo scooter, saddle bags and all. The Ydral engine was offered either as a 125cc on the Sterling JV125 model or as a 175cc on the Sterling JV175, the larger with a 6 volt battery. If the rider bored of the Ydral, Stervas also came with a 125cc SAAB engine (made by Etablissements René Briban), a 125cc Nervor and a 175cc Sachs. The Belgian company Van Hauwaert also made Stervas under license with a Minerva label on the scoot.

Sterzi ITALY ★

Brescia is known for producing pistols during the war, so perhaps the utilitarian Sterzi scooter couldn't shake the gun barrel design when it debuted at the Salone di Milano in 1958. The exposed engine of the Scooter 160 along with the lack of a legshield and no floorboards made this peppy scooter seem naked in spite of its 80km/h.

Stewart NEW ZEALAND ★

This boxy scooter was designed by Jack Stewart in New Zealand since he needed a bike that he could step on easily after he lost a leg in a motorcycle accident. Even though only 100 of these scooters were made from 1959 to 1963, BSA bought out the Stewart perhaps to stifle any competing brands to its beautiful BSA Sunbeam.

Stüdemann GERMANY ★

The Stüdemann Fibs scooter was armed with a 38cc Victoria engine in 1953.

Sun UK ★

Sun Cycle and Fittings Co. Ltd of Birmingham traced its lineage back to bicycle production at the turn of the century. In 1957, Sun entered the scooter fold with its Geni based on a 99cc Villiers 6F two-stroke engine delivering 2.8hp at 4000rpm with a two-speed gearbox shifted by foot lever and 15in wire-spoked wheels.

In 1959, the Geni was joined by the Sunwasp scooter, obviously trading on the Vespa's renown. The Sunwasp was a svelte scooter dressed by bodywork shared with Dayton and Panther's Princess. Mounted in the tube frame was a Villiers 173cc 2L two-stroke providing 7hp at 5000rpm with a three-speed gearbox and Siba electric leg.

Leading-link forks suspended the front 10in wheel and a swing-arm was at the rear. Drum 6in brakes were used at both ends.

The Geni and Sunwasp lasted into 1960, longer than Sun's motorcycle line. But the firm was soon sold to Raleigh and retired from business.

Sunlight Japan ★

From 1954 to 1961, Sunlight made a number of little two-strokes for the Japanese market, some of them under the name "Queen Sunlight."

Suzuki Japan ★

Suzuki eschewed scooters in its early years but offered its 50cc Address model in Japan and Europe in the 1990s after its mini plastic Suzuki Love in the '80s. In 2004, the enormous Burgman scooters were offered with either a 645cc or 385cc four-stroke engines. The space-age plastic scooters weighed in

Lounge Chair on Wheels
Comfort and speed is what the Suzuki Burgman is all about, as if it" everyone's dream to zip down the highway while relaxing on the couch.

at 524lb and 405lb respectively, so they needed the disc brakes and adjustable shocks to keep the beast in line. The Burgman 650 offered a feature to let the driver choose between normal and power automatic modes with the touch of a finger, definitely a far cry from foot-shifters or breaking cables.

Svalan Sweden ★

Maskin AB John Ericsson produced the Svalan scooter in the mid-1950s, which was nearly a spitting image of another Svensk make, the Apollo. Just as its godly cousin, the Svalan used a JB engine made in nearby Malmø.

Swallow Japan ★ ★

Swallow's Pop scooter first appeared on the Japanese market in 1955 with the 165cc 30C T-165, a long name for a little scooter. The Pop rode on 3.50x10in tires and created 6.15hp at 4400rpm. Its styling was sleek and bejeweled by chrome trim with turn signals mounted on the legshield and tail.

In 1956, Pop was back with two new models: the unclothed 80cc CP and the full-bodywork 125cc CM, both riding atop 2.50x18in tires. While the CM followed typical Japanese scooter styling, the CP was a radically ugly hybrid of scooter and motorcycle styling, which set a design point for the future Pops with abstract swallow-shaped air ducts on the sides. The most interesting feature of the Pops was the swing-arm rear end with dual shocks mounted underneath the seat in the style of the Vincent Rapide.

The 125cc Pop was restyled for 1957 with two-tone paint and 3.50x10in tires. By 1958, the Pop 125cc was up to 5.8hp at 5000rpm from its 52x58mm 125cc engine.

A 175cc Pop appeared in 1958 as well with styling identical to the 125cc. Riding on 3.50x10in tires, the 175cc of 62x58mm created 8.82hp at 5600rpm.

By the early 1960s, Swallow was gone, never having been able to build its nest in the Japanese market controlled by the large scooter makers Fuji and Mitsubishi.

Swallow UK ★★★

Swallow was a famous sidecar builder that ventured into the scooter market with its Gadabout appearing in late 1946 at the same time as the Vespa made its debut in Italy, and the Corgi was first promised for the UK market.

The Gadabout was a basic bare-bones scooter blending the front-end styling of a Lambretta Model A with the rear end of a Cushman 30 Series. A rigid duplex frame held unsprung front forks and a square cushion above the engine, which was covered by a folded sheet of steel that served as the tail section. Tires were 4.00x8in with 5in brakes at both ends.

The engine was a two-stroke 122cc Villiers 9D of prewar design backed by a three-speed gearbox. Weighing in on the heavy end, the scooter moved at a snail's pace compared with the Vespa of the time. A commercial sidecar was optional.

In 1950, the Mk II was offered with a Villiers 10D engine. Leading-link forks with bonded rubber suspension gave a better ride. In 1951, the 197cc Major joined the line with a 6E Villiers designed as a workhorse to pull the sidecar.

But by the end of 1951, the style, speed, and reliability of the Italian scooters had left the Gadabout and Major in the dust, and so Swallow returned to sidecar building, offering a small passenger sidecar for the Italian scooters.

Swiss Switzerland ★

The Swiss "Swiss" firm launched its Swiss-Boy RE1 scooter in 1951 with a Jlo 118cc engine with two speeds. The 4.6hp engine managed to push the Swiss to 65-70km/h, perhaps down the mountain.

SYM (Sanyang Motor Co.)

TAIWAN ★

This powerhouse production facility proved that Taiwan was indeed the new capital of the scooter world. Starting in 1954 as a manufacturer of electric lights for bikes, Sanyang soon moved into motorcycles and automobiles. Honda hired SYM to build its motorcycles in 1962 and assemble the Civic and Accord in 1969. SYM was so successful in Taiwan that

Honda took over sales in 2002, and SYM switched over to working with Hyundai.

The technology was there, so by 2021, the company made more than 35,000 cars a year and more than a million motorcycles and scooters annually. Distribution into the US was by fits and starts (an arsonist torched SYM's distributor's warehouse in Alabama), but they were finally readily available by 2015.

Perhaps most classic is the Fiddle series in 50, 125, and 200cc versions with classic lines and two-tone color schemes. Scooter purists should know that the new Lambretta V-Special is based on the four-stroke Fiddle III.

Apart from the attractive Mio and the Symphony (looking very much like the Aprilia Scarabeo), most of the other SYM scooters, such as the Citycom, veer toward the "underbones" crotch-rocket wannabes.

Taizhou Jiaojiang Zhiwei

CHINA ★

The Zhiwei scooter line from Taizhou Jiaojiang Zhiwei Motorcycle Manufacturing Company adds more of the gas-powered 125cc go-fast scooters to the streets.

Taizhou Senlong CHINA ★

The Yiben scooter comes in the smaller 50cc up to the 150cc version. It's built by Taizhou Senlong Motorcycle Manufacturing Company in Zhejiang province on the East China Sea.

Taizhou Wangye CHINA ★

Made by the Zhejiang Taizhou Wangye Power Group Motorcycle Company, the Hauzi, Wangye, and sometimes Xianfeng 125cc gasoline-powered scooters sought to conform to the competition with the plastic sport scooter look that was so "dangerous" in the '90s, but now seems so tediously ubiquitous. Even so, this company appealed to the German market (the German Rivero was essentially a rebranded Taizhou).

Taizhou Zhongneng CHINA ★

Not to be confused with the other Taizhou scooter manufacturer, Zhongneng built 125cc scooters with that very name and Qianxifeng two- and three-wheelers.

Taotao CHINA ★

Another small vehicle manufacturer in eastern China's Zhejiang province, Taotao Vehicles Company produces several lines of four-stroke sport scooters.

Tappella ITALY ★ ★

With a mess of tubes making up the frame, Tappella of Milan released its Moto-Scooter Fuchs Gran Sport in 1952. The powerplant was a Jlo 125cc two-stroke giving the speedster 5.5hp for a top speed of 100km/h. Nevertheless, this vehicle could barely be considered a scooter and only fits in the category because of the following models.

The Fuchs Gazzella had none of the power (only 3hp) or speed (no more than 60km/h) of its predecessor, but the bodywork fit it in the prestigious scooter club. The Gazzella was followed by the Fuchs Mod. 14 Carenato and the Fuchs Campagnola mod. 18.

Tell SWITZERLAND/CHINA ★

The Landi chain of Swiss supermarkets rebranded Chinese-made scooters as Tell for the Swiss hero William Tell, who rid the country of the Hapsburg scourge.

Tempo NORWAY/GERMANY ★ ★ ★

Jonas Øglænd produced bicycles in the southwestern Norwegian town of Sandnes using mostly German gears. In 1931, he mounted 75cc (and later 98cc) engines on his bicycles to make mopeds. Soon the frame was beefed up, and the beautiful Tempo mopeds became ubiquitous in Norway.

For a few years in the late 1950s, Tempo assembled its own version of the fantastic Progress scooter from the West German company Progress-Werke for the Scandinavian market. Although the Tempo Progress had a large 191cc engine and relatively stable 18in (45cm) wheels, it weighed in at 160kg (350lb), making the scooter not so speedy.

La vie est belle with a Terrot VMS2 125! Life is indeed beautiful with a Terrot motorscooter. The beautiful Miss Monde 1953, Denise Perrier, certainly enjoyed "her" Terrot, no doubt given to her by Terrot in exchange for this publicity photo. The Terrot was one of the most unique-looking scooters of all time, resembling a primped and coiffed French poodle on wheels—beautiful, in other words. It was, indubitably, "Une Splendide Réalisation 100% Française." Bien sûr, it goes without saying: Who else could build such a motorscooter?

Terrot FRANCE ★ ★ ★ ★

M. Samuel Renaud presented the first Terrot scooter, the VMS, at the Salon de Paris in October 1951, a rounded pontoon-shaped scooter in the style of 1950s American cars. The two-speed 98cc engine produced 2.6hp with the right foot control being first gear and the left for second.

Terrot's VMS2 of 1953 had seats for two with an enlarged motor of 125cc for 3.5hp; the VMS3 of 1954 had the same engine with left side kick and three-speeds. The Scooterrot of 1955-1957 was marketed in Britain by P & M Panther with its elaborate system of gear selection as an added luxury.

Magnat-Debon, a subsidiary of Terrot, produced the Terrot as well with the S1 of 1952 as the 98cc VMS, the S2 and S25 as the 98 and 125cc VMS2, and the S3 in two versions as the 125cc VMS3 classic and the VMS3 "présélective," aka the Scooterrot.

Testi ITALY ★

With Lamborghini making its Miura and Espada nearby, Testi made covered little scooters on 19in spoked wheels to navigate the streets of Bologna. From 1961 to 1966, this two-stroke putt-putts were produced with an FB Minarelli 48cc engine.

TGB TAIWAN ★

Taiwan Golden Bee, or TGB, originally produced Vespas for Piaggio in Taiwan beginning in 1978. Afterwards, TGB used this technology to make its own scooters.

TNT FRANCE/CHINA ★

The French company TNT assures us that "nos équipes ont mis tout leur savoir-faire" (our teams used all their knowledge) to make the TNT scooters, but they are still produced by Ningbo Longjia Motorcycle Company in China and sold there under the Longjia name. Several good-looking scooters make up their line, especially the Estate.

Tomos SLOVENIA/YUGOSLAVIA ★★

Yugoslavia President Josip Broz Tito and Emperor of Ethiopia Haile Selassie were present to open the Tomos factory in 1959. Soon Tomos-branded Puch scooters churned out of the factory. The Slovenian company survived the breakup of Yugoslavia and kept making vehicles but finally went bankrupt in 2019.

Toscane ITALY ★★★

The Toscane (Tuscan) dates back to 1947 and had a hovercraft design so far ahead of its time that the company only made it one year. The two-seater had a headlamp mounted on its fixed front fender, just as the early Vespas did. The small 98cc engine was the same as that mounted in the Nibbio scooter.

Tote Gote USA ★

In all of the hallowed motorscooter hall of fame, the Tote Gote was the sole scooter conceived as a motorized packhorse with travois to haul dead deer out of woods after a hunting expedition.

Thirty-year-old Ralph Bonham of Provo, Utah, built Tote Gotes in the early 1960s, which sold to hunters like himself who were almost cured of hunting by having to drag 200lb deer carcasses out of the mountains. The muscular Tote Gote could yank a 400lb load up a 45 degree slope, perhaps in anticipation of Bonham's dreams to bag an elk.

Catch a Tigress by the Tail

As one of the coolest scooters ever to hit pavement, the Tigress was a latecomer to the putt-putt arena as motorcycle giants Triumph and BSA finally bowed to the scooter mania and teamed up to produce a 250cc gem. Alas, this luxury scoot with a whooping dual cylinder, four-stroke engine was too late on the scene—not appearing in showrooms until 1960. The other nail in the BSA Sunbeam/Triumph Tigress' coffin was its distribution primarily through motorcycle dealers, an inferno any self-respecting Mod would avoid like the plague.

Townsend Engineering UK ★★★

The English Autoglider De Luxe appeared in 1919 created by Charles Ralph Townsend at Townsend Engineering Co. of Birmingham with a 269cc Villiers or 300cc Union engine mounted on the front 16in wheel. The Model A was seatless like the Autoped, but the Model D added a cushioned seat which doubled as suspension. Even though ads claimed top speed was 50km/h, bold scooterists claimed to have reached 80km/h on the sport version, although probably on a steep incline.

Toxozer CHINA ★

Don't let the name turn you off . . . well, maybe it should give you pause, at least. Or as the company says, "Electric vehicles are designed for not use on public roads." Also, kneepads are recommended. These fat-wheeled low riders are inexpensive and could generously be called "utilitarian."

Tramnitz GERMANY ★

In 1951, Kurt Tramnitz GmbH added a tachometer to its 98cc Jlo-powered Tram 100 for increased luxury. With the appearance of a two-humped camel, the scooter boasted 3.3hp for a 65km/h top speed.

Triumph TEC UK

Triumph was one of the most prolific and beloved motorcycles in the world. Its great vertical Speed Twin engine was designed by Edward Turner and remained in production for some four decades. And then it created a scooter.

TIGRESS TW2 AND TW2S 1959–1965 AND TSI 1960–1965 ★★★★

In 1957, Triumph, then owned by BSA, announced a prototype scooter, also designed by Turner. By October 1958, near-identical Triumph Tigress and BSA Sunbeams models were offered, each in two versions, a 175cc two-stroke single and a 250cc four-stroke twin.

The TW2 250cc shared engine parts with the 175cc from the clutch back, but the block and heads were cast in aluminum and were special to the four-stroke twin. The TW2s added electric start.

Performance of the overhead-valve vertical twin 250cc engine was all the Meridan factory could have wished for. In fact, the 250cc prototype was so fast it had to be detuned for production.

The frame of both models was a basic tube affair with an odd bolt-on headstock. The suspension was hydraulic front and rear. And the bodywork made it the "Sleekest smoothest scooter ever," according to Triumph at least.

The Tigress TS1 did not reach the public until 1960. Its 175cc engine was a creative amalgamation, a tool-room special based on the BSA Bantam with the Triumph Cub gearbox. A four-speed gearbox drove the rear wheel via an enclosed duplex chain, much like the Lambretta Li. Top speed was 55mph.

But the Tigress was not a success, arriving in the market with too much too late. The scooter boom had been in the early 1950s; by the 1960s, commuters were riding motorcycles or cars and scooters were forgotten by most.

Everyone within Triumph seemed to understand this except the top management. Don J. Brown, sales manager for the US West Coast importer, Johnson Motors, wrote a confidential three-page letter in 1958 prophesizing the scooter's failure. Brown stated that "My own view has been from the beginning that we are facing a 'market drift' from what . . . this country needs in the way of scooters. . . ." In fact it was a market drift from what any country needed.

But the Tigress did find one ready market: circuses loved the scooter. The heavy-duty body and hydraulic suspension made the Tigress ideal for trained bears to circumnavigate the circus ring to the crowd's never-ending awe.

TRIUMPH TINA 1962–1965 ★

Triumph released its Tina as an automatic 100cc scooter for first-time riders. The V-belt transmission drove the rear hub with automatic ratio changes; the only controls were throttle and brakes. Another boon to Learners was the start/drive control that wouldn't allow the scooter to move unless it was in the "on" position.

The Tina's engine was a two-stroke single with the horizontal cylinder directly in front of the 8in rear wheel.

TRIUMPH T10 1965–1970 ★

The T10 was a slightly redesigned Tina with the safety start/drive switch moved under the seat so the scooter would only go when the driver was seated. Other cosmetic changes were made as well, such as the front brake control moved to the left handlebar.

The T10 stayed on for five years but was never a success next to the ever-improving Italian designs.

Triumph TWN GERMANY ★★

Triumph was founded by two Germans, Siegfried Bettman and Maurice Schultz in Coventry, England, in 1897. When Triumph started making motorcycles in 1903, they opened a factory in Nürnberg, both making Triumph motorcycles. In 1929, the British half split with the German company taking the name of TEC Triumph (Triumph Engineering Co. Ltd. or simply TEC in Germany), and the German side was named TWN Triumph (Triumph Werke Nürnberg or simply TWN to the British).

TWN Triumph
The Triumph story began in Coventry, England when a pair of Germans formed a company in 1897 and moved into motorcycles by 1903. They opened a factory in Nürnberg which split from the English Triumph in 1929 becoming TWN, as opposed to the British TEC Triumph. While TEC dragged its feet in making the Tigress scooter with BSA, TWN built the Tessy, and the beautiful Contessa pictured.

TESSY STANDARD, LUXUS, AND SUPER (SUPERLATIVE) 1956–1957 ★ ★ ★

The Tessy had a "floorboard tunnel" or bridge between the rider's legs to facilitate airflow and two luggage carriers, one mounted on the stationary front fender. The Super was the luxury model with a 6 volt battery and electric starter instead of the Luxus' magneto. The Super also was more powerful with 8.5hp reaching 80km/h as opposed to Luxus' 7hp and the Standard's 6hp.

The Triumph factory in Nürnberg offered the Tessy in two color schemes, two-tone in beige and brown or light and dark blue, both with only the teardrop side panel in the darker color.

This flashy two-tone Tessy required adequate ad copy, as in the 1956 brochure: "The young lady isn't actually using her fingers to count the number of her admirers, but the advantages of the TESSY. An adding-machine would perhaps be more appropriate because her pretty little fingers will not be enough for the many advantages."

CONTESSA 1955–1957 ★ ★ ★

The Contessa's engine was based on the TWN Cornet—"the whispering motorcycle," according to TWN publicity. At the 38th Brussels Salon, the 200cc Contessa debuted in January 1955 with four speeds and a special selector that allowed the rider to get to neutral from any position. The Contessa was the true deluxe model with twin pistons moving in unison making for 9.5hp for 95km/h, 10in tires instead of the Tessy's 8in, a long, 52in wheelbase, and a 12 volt electric starter.

In 1957, when TWN had seriously over-produced the amount of two-wheelers that the market could bear, it concentrated on typewriters and office equipment, perhaps envisioning the impending Information Age. Gründig took control of TWN in

1958, however the Contessa design was acquired by its rival Hercules who renamed it the Viscount and replaced the engine with a 200cc Sachs.

Trobike UK ★★

The Trojan firm of Croydon was an English Lambretta importer that decided to build its own scooter in 1960. The Trobike was the result, based on an open duplex frame with a 94cc Clinton two-stroke and 5in tires. Predating the mini-bike craze of the mid-1960s, the Trobike lasted only a few years on the market.

Troll East GERMANY ★★★

The boxy Troll 60E, 100E, 120E, and 120D scooters were "the ideal vehicle for women," as well as for, "country doctors, country vicars, midwives, nurses, merchants, shoppers and messengers." In other words, the East German government thought these unimaginative scooters were the cure-all for just about anybody's transportation problem.

The small 60E used an engine from the VMO factory near Lamspringe, others all used Jlo engines, so had considerably more power. The Troll 100E produced 3.6hp for a top speed of 60km/h for the cardboard box-styled scooter. The 120D and 120E had 4hp for a top speed of 65km/h and 70km/h and still had the design of a World War I combat vehicle, less cannon.

Trotwood USA ★★

The Trotwood was an anomaly even in the world of scooter oddities. Built by Trotwood Trailers Inc. of Trotwood, Ohio, in the late 1930s, early 1940s, it was a "brand new design," according to ads, which was an understatement that would follow the scooter out of production.

The engine rode on the front forks and drove the front wheel; the whole front end was covered in a curved sheetmetal "trunk"—the catchword of the era for this kind of weird design was "streamlined."

From there things got even stranger. The driver sat atop a rear package compartment with feet in a step-in bathtub-like affair. Two rear wheels followed the front end around, both with drum brakes.

As the ads assured the dubious, the Trotwood was "Needed by merchants everywhere."

Tubauto FRANCE ★

The 1950 Le Scoto appeared with a 38cc Mosquito engine built by les Etablissements Chapuis de Neuilly under license from Garelli. Pedals were added to get a little exercise and the motor could be disengaged with a little lever. Le Scoto had many modifications from Tubauto's prototype the year before, but was still a commercial failure.

Tula RUSSIA ★★★

The year 1957 must have been the date when Soviet planners decided that motorscooters were the vehicles to transport the comrades. In the USSR, both the Tula and Vyatka made their debuts; in Poland and Romania, scooters were also introduced. Perhaps perestroika will someday bring the secret planning papers to light.

The Tula 200 scooter was announced in the August 1957 issue of the Russian motoring magazine Svet Motoru but what was not announced was that the scooter was a copy, replica, or rip-off—call it what you will—of the Goggo-Isaria scooter.

The T200 was powered by a Goggo-derived 197cc air-cooled two-stroke of 61x66mm, which was equipped with an electric starter, and rode atop 4.00x10in tires. With 8hp, it could hit 86km/h.

The T200 had a long career—or sentence, depending on your point of view. Introduced in 1957, it continued in production through the 1960s and was relieved in 1973 by the Tula Tourist.

The Tourist ran on the same mechanicals with the electric starter but updated the styling to 1959 with a look more than vaguely similar to the Lambretta TV 175 Series II. The Tula Tourist even went capitalist, being exported to various European countries in the 1970s.

TVS INDIA ★

Originally set up in 1911 as a bus company, T.V. Sundaram Iyengar moved into mopeds and motorcycles in 1962 and eventually a partnership with Suzuki in the 1980s. The company made three-wheeled vehicles, similar to Piaggio's Ape, and jumped into the scooter market with sporty bikes. In 2020, TVS bought out Norton Motorcycles, but there's still no word on whether this classic company of rocker bikes will make a lowly Mod scooter.

Twist 'N Go (TN'G)
USA-ITALY-CHINA ★

This modern upstart scooter make from Classic Motorcycles & Sidecars rides the craze by straddling the two kinds of buyers: speedsters and modsters. The Del Rey, paint in mother-of-barstool gray, has the downward tilt of crotch rockets but its oversized nose looks like it got popped one at the local watering hole. In spite of the Cezeta-inspired schnoz, the Del Rey sports a 125cc four-stroke engine with front disc brake to stop the speed. The 49cc LS is a mini version of the Del Rey with menacing black-and-red two-tone.

Those opting more for fashion over function choose their Touch 'N Go Italian city: Venice, Milano or Verona. The most popular Venice comes with a 49cc engine; the Milano offers the choice of a 50cc, 125cc or 150cc powerplant; and the 150cc Verona has a larger wheels for a smooth ride on the lengthier wheelbase.

TN'G scooters had parts from Taiwan and China but were assembled outside of Seattle, Washington.

Ujet LUXEMBOURG ★★

This ultramodern foldable scooter (or is it a moped?) is a space-age piece of cubist design that will awe anyone who sees it. Did Dalí design this? The orbital wheels have no center hub, and single-wall carbon nanotubes make up the tires. The 3,600-watt motor, brakes, and suspension are attached to the wheels to provide super quick acceleration, even if the top speed is a little over 30 mph (48 km/h). The silent scooter has speakers to produce optional noise for safety. All this advanced design, however, comes at a price.

Unu GERMANY/CHINA ★

This fully electric scooter even recharges when braking. It's made in China and distributed online to be delivered. The first version allowed customers to buy any color they wanted, as long as it was black. The second generation at least allowed seven color schemes. These high-tech scooters have digital keys through a phone app, so friends can hop on in the peer-to-peer scooter sharing scheme. The striking design seems like the next generation of scooters, but the limited power and speed of these electric vehicles puts them in the "moped" category. How humiliating! However, the promotion for the Unu is best in the original German: "Günstiger als öffentliche Verkehrsmittel," or "cheaper than public transport." Really?

URMW ROMANIA ★★

The Romanian URMW 150 scooter was introduced in 1957 with an engine based on the Polish Osa scooter. The 150cc engine featured a horizontal single cylinder and three-speed gearbox mounted in front of the rear wheel. Top speed was 80km/h, according to official propaganda.

Varel GERMANY ★

The Small Varel factory in Oldenburg bowed in 1951 featuring a 43cc engine pumping out an impressive 0.8-1hp on their FF scooter. The engine sat atop the front wheel in the style of the great French Velosolex moped, making it one of the few front-drive motorscooters. The FF's paneling consisted of a large rectangular piece of sheet metal curved as the front legshield in classic dustbin fashion and a floorboard mounted with Varel's Bauhaus-style logo. Varel also marketed the Varelli in 1951 with a 99cc Mota engine for 4.5hp and 70km/h, up from the FF's 40km/h. Varel's scooter production ceased in 1953.

Vectrix USA/POLAND ★

Founded in 2006 in New England, Vectrix was a large electric scooter that could supposedly reach 60 mph (96 km/h) in just seven seconds. Manufactured in Poland with American technology, the Vectrix seemed like the answer to scooter enthusiasts who wanted the pep of a two-stroke motor. The battery was partially recharged through regenerative braking, but the battery also cost thousands of dollars to replace and could be recharged approximately 1,500 times.

The Great Recession hit the company hard, even after the NYPD considered using Vectrix scooters—a long tradition of the "Fuzz with a Buzz" dating back to Salsbury Motor Glide scooters. Alas, the company liquidated all assets in 2014, and much of the assets went to Poland and gave rise to the GOVECS scooter.

Velocette Viceroy
As an offshoot of England's speedy Café Racers, Velocette armed its scooter with a powerful 248cc flat twin that was also used in the DMW Deemster scooter. Along with the BSA/Triumph scooter, the British market demanded fast and sporty scooters to compete with the Vespa GS and the Lambretta TV 175. Courtesy of François-Marie Dumas

Velocette UK ★ ★ ★

Veloce Ltd. of Birmingham built the Velocette, a long line of well-engineered motorcycles famous for their powerful single-cylinder engines and black and gold livery. In the late 1950s, Veloce developed its LE and Vogue models for the utility market. In 1961, the firm created a motorcycle that was later covered in body-work, becoming the Viceroy scooter.

The Viceroy's engine was an interesting two-stroke flat twin of 248cc based on a square 54x54mm bore and stroke. Reed valves fed the oil-fuel mix into the crankcase and an electric starter turned it over. The Viceroy engine was also used in a version of the DMW Deemster scooter.

The engine was mounted in the Viceroy just behind the front wheel for optimum balance and coupled with the flat twin engine design, which produced little vibration, the Viceroy was a smooth-running scooter.

A four-speed gearbox was driven by a duplex chain, feeding power through a clutch via a shaft drive to bevel gears at the rear wheel. The gearbox also doubled as a rear suspension pivot arm. The wheels were 12in diameter with 6in brakes on both ends.

The frame was a hefty tube affair, belying its motorcycle heritage. With the flowing bodywork in place, the Viceroy was a massive—and heavy—scooter.

But the scooter arrived on the scene too late. Veloce made the same wrong decision that Triumph-BSA-Sunbeam made in developing a scooter. The Viceroy last until 1964, and Velocette last only another seven years.

Veleco POLAND ★

Founded in 2017, this Polish company makes three- and four-wheeled vehicles that look like a scooter in the front and bridge the gap between handicapped "scooters" and the real two-wheel deal.

Velosolex FRANCE ★

Known for its moped with the motor mounted on the front wheel that has become a symbol of French mobility, Velosolex also made a scooter with an engine in front. The Micron from 1967 could only manage 30km/h. Since it lacked bike pedals—like its cousin the Velosolex, a permit was required by French law and the Micron failed to get a French audience.

Vento USA ★

This Laredo, Texas-based company produced scooter-sized sport bikes including the menacing-sounding: Zip r31 Turbocam, Triton r4, and the Phantom r4i. Added features were an anti-theft security system, remote-control ignition and a fancy digital clock.

Venus WEST GERMANY ★ ★

The Venus factory in Donauwörth focused solely on scooters during its three-year existence with three models having the same simple but attractive design. Venus offered three models: the Venus MS 150 and MS 175 of 1953-1955; and Venus DS 100 of 1954-1955.

Each model used Sachs engines, the larger MS models with two seats for passengers and an optional electric start (called the MSA). A notable design feature on the MS model was the "second fender" that extended the line on the side of the floorboard up to the front wheel's moving fender. The DS 100 with 97cc engine pumped out 2.7hp for a maximum speed of 55km/h; the MS 150 had a 147cc 6.5hp engine; and the MS 175 had a 174cc engine with 9.5hp. Both MS models boasted a top speed of 90km/h.

Vespa SA SPAIN ★ ★

Beginning in 1962, Vespa SA of Spain produced Vespa scooters under license from Piaggio conforming to the standard 125cc and 150cc models. In the 1980s and on into the 1990s, the firm continued to build Vespas, now from parts supplied by the Pontedara factory.

Viberti ITALY ★

Drawing from the initials of the designers Viberti and Victoria, the Vi Vi Scooter debuted in 1956 propelled by a German 48cc Victoria engine.

Victoria GERMANY ★ ★

Technically a moped, but considered a scooter, the Vicky of 1954 finished first place in an international scooter rally in the Tyrolean Alps at Merano, Italy. The two-stroke, two-speed Vicky had a small 48cc engine with a hand starter. The 20in wheels were larger than the true Victoria scooters. The Vicky was available in several different models including Luxus and Super Luxus, as well as a similar scooterette called the Preciosa.

The Nicky of 1954-1957 was another one of Victoria's scooterettes with a small 2.45hp 48cc engine. The lines were essentially two waves on large wheels with what appeared like a speaker cabinet on each side panel for the ultimate rock'n'roll scooter. Victoria ads boasted an added feature to appeal to even the most powerful executive: a clip to hold a briefcase on the inside of the legshield. In spite of these decadent luxuries and the gauge on the handlebars displaying the amount of gas in the tank, the Nicky's engine directly behind the front wheel gave away the moped-like design.

First introduced at the Frankfurt International Motorcycle show, the Peggy of 1955-1957 was a hit with its powerful 198cc horizontal engine. The design was similar to the Zündapp Bella, which in turn was based on the Parilla scooter. Perhaps Victoria borrowed the Parilla design directly considering that in 1956, Victoria had an agreement to use Parilla engines in some Victoria-Parilla motorcycles displayed at the Frankfurt Show.

The 10hp Peggy's push-button gearchange allowed it to reach a top speed of 95 km/h. Due to financial problems, Victoria decided to keep producing the Peggy scooter in 1956, after discontinuing it for a few months.

Vitacci USA/CHINA ★

This Texas-based company imports Chinese-made scooters and rebrands them for the US market. The wide range of modern scooters has 50cc to 250cc engines in a variety of bright colors.

Vittoria ITALY ★★★

Known for its beautiful bikes, Vittoria took an unusual turn into the world of scooters with a strangely beautiful Scooter 65. The stamped metal covering of everything but the engine and the headlamp protruding from the front wheel cover certainly turned heads at its 1950 debut. On the production model, the headlight was moved up the apron.

In 1952, another model was added to the line. The Vittoria Scooter 125 was somewhat more traditional, but still unusual. The semi-hydraulic rear suspension were complemented by front telescopic forks. The 125 Tipo 53 L (L for lusso, or "luxury") had a much more complete covering with interesting air ducts cut into the sidepanels.

Vivani ITALY ★

The Cicala (cicada) scooter was made in 1952 and powered with a small 50cc engine atop large wheels.

Vyatka USSR ★★

Vyatskiye Polyany Machine-Building Plant had proudly made submachine guns and shotguns since

1940. In the August 1957 issue of *Svet Motoru*, the Soviet Union announced a new miracle to the comrades: It had created not only a scooter, but a great scooter. Named the Vyatka, to Western eyes, it was but a Russian copy of the Vespa.

The Vyatka used a Russian-built Vespa motor of 150cc from 57x58mm bore and stroke, giving 5.5hp at 5000rpm with a three-speed gearbox and riding atop 4.00x10in tires. In the 1960s, a 175cc version appeared.

The Soviet Vyatka continued in production until the early 1970s, when a redesigned version was released. The new Vyatka had a 148cc engine of 57 × 58mm bore and stroke for 6 hp with a three-speed gearbox; although the specifications were the same as the Vespa copy, the new mechanicals were Russian designed.

Vostok SPAIN ★

Formed in 2016 in Bilbao to fill a market void of quality electric scooters, the Vostok 7 "llega lejos," or "goes far." Well, at most 130 km (80 miles) on one charge, which is nothing to scoff at. The slick scooter with a portable battery might just hit its mark. "Es tan limpia que la podrías aparcar en el salon de tu casa" ("it is so clean that you could park it in the living room of your house)". It's "totally silent," so you could drive it around your house as well.

Wabo THE NETHERLANDS ★

The Dutch Wabo scooter was powered by a choice of British Villiers two-stroke engines: the 99cc 4F with two-speed gearbox or the 147cc 30C with three speeds. Riding atop 16in wire-spoke wheels, the Wabo's tube frame was covered by industrial-styled bodywork. Two saddle seats were trailed by a luggage rack; a speedometer was mounted on the open handlebars. The Wabo scooter came and went in 1957.

Walba GERMANY ★★

The 2.8hp Walba 100 of 1949-1950 hardly had an impressive style, but as one of the first scooters produced in Germany, it offered an important mode of transport for the volk. In spite of its heavy 63kg weight for its small size, the 98cc Jlo engine pushed it to a fast top speed of 75km/h on its 8in wheels.

From 1950-1952, Walba offered its Kurier, Tourist, de Luxe, and Commodore models. Although the engines weren't updated much more than enlargements from the Walba 100, the design of the body was much improved. With a fake turbine engine and Martian-like front section, the Walba turned into a futuristic design that was right out of Fritz Lang's Metropolis. The phony turbine air intake makes the scooter into a small personal transport unit. Remember, this was the same era as when citizens believed they would soon be able to wear jet packs on their back to fly anywhere. Although the Walba was decidedly safer than bouncing around skyscrapers, the 8in wheels and near vertical front fork offered the same safety problems as the Vespa that many other German scooter manufacturers chose to avoid.

The Walba was armed with Jlo motors: the Kurier with a 118cc for 4hp and 75km/h, the Tourist and the de Luxe with a 122cc for 4.5hp and 70km/h, and the Commodore with a 173cc for 7.65hp and 85km/h. In 1952, the Walba was redesigned but kept its decorative turbine under the wing of Faka.

Wall Auto Wheel UK ★★

A very early British scooter similar to the French Monet-Goyon.

Warivo INDIA ★

These slick electric scooters use lithium-ion batteries and tubeless tires but only reach 40 km/h (25 mph). Warivo was just formed in 2018, but has its goal "to change each and every gasoline bike existing on the roads by battery operated e-bike and scooters."

Wasp AUSTRALIA/TAIWAN ★★

The Wasp somehow manages to capture the classic retro look of a Lambretta but with enough style to be able to have a modern look. Oh wait, that's because it essentially is the Lambretta LN. Chrome and other doodads to make it seem classic are jettisoned in favor of just sleek lines. This nice look also comes at a cost, however.

WFM POLAND ★★★

The Warszawska Fabryk Motocycli built the Osa M50 scooter at its Warsaw factory beginning in 1957. The engine was a 149cc two-stroke giving 6.5hp at 5000rpm via a three-speed gearbox. Tires were 3.25x14in, although they were all but hidden beneath the bulbous front fender and rear bodywork.

The Osa was imported into Great Britain in the late 1950s by CDS Trading Co. Ltd. in Surrey.

Wilkinson UK ★★★

This English firm produced early putt-putts based on the American Autoped in the 1910s.

Wolf USA/CHINA ★

Wolf is an American company that imports rebadged Chinese scooters from Znen (see page 313). The scooters are made for the US market, however, and serviced by Wolf.

Yamaha JAPAN ★

Perhaps the oddest expansion sideline was Yamaha's foray into the world of motorcycles and scooters. Torakusu Yamaha founded the Nippon Gakki firm in 1955 to produce musical instruments. With an education in clock making and a fascination with motorcycles, Yamaha's original plans had gone the way of all good intentions by 1960 and while musical instrument building continued, Yamaha created its first cycle and its SC-1 motorscooter.

The SC-1 was powered by a 175cc of 62x58mm bore and stroke producing 10.3hp at 5500rpm and riding atop 3.50x10in tires. The front forks were an odd triangulated , one-sided affair both front and rear. A speedometer, choke knob, and ignition key fit in the dashboard on the inside of the legshield with the headlamp mounted on the apron.

The styling of the SC-1 was designed as only the Japanese know how to do, mixing modern and old elements into a rolling sculpture of chrome and sheet metal.

The SC-1's companion was the moped-scooter MF-1, which also arrived in 1960 with a 50cc two-stroke engine and 2.25x25in tires.

In the 1980s, Yamaha created a wide-ranging series of modern small-displacement scooters designed largely for the youth market worldwide. Models in 50, 80, and 125cc included the Razz, Riva, and in Europe the Beluga. At the 1992 Bologna show, Yamaha displayed its Fly One scooterone—a larger scooter—with a 150cc four-stroke engine.

In 1993, Yamaha showed its Frog scooter with retro chic styling. Powered by a 250cc four-stroke engine, its was dressed in snappy two-tone with dual headlamp like frog eyes.

In 1996, one of Yamaha's first "maxi-scooters" hit the showroom. The 250cc Majesty had more boxy lines than its competitors but boasted a four-stroke, liquid cooled engine.

By 2004, Yamaha offered the classic-looking Vino scooter in the four-stroke 125cc, two-stroke 50cc Vino and Vino Classic. The Vino "makes you look like you just rolled out of a Fellini movie, and actually makes getting around town fun instead of frustrating," read the brochure copy with an obvious reference to Paparazzo in La Dolce Vita, and all the breakdowns of loyal Vespa riders everywhere. For riders more concerned with performance than looking

like a Cine Città extra, Yamaha built the twao-stroke Zuma with dual headlights, a design borrowed from Ducati. The high-performance Zuma for the relatively economical price has made this reliable scooter a favorite for the speedster crowd looking for a starter motorcycle.

Yard Marvel Manufacturing
USA ★

The Mountaineer scooter came from Spokane, Washington, in the 1960s. With its four-stroke 3hp engine, it was geared to climb most any mountain placed before it.

Yardman USA ★

Yardman's Motorette was based on a 3hp engine and sold for $269.50 in 1960.

Zanella ARGENTINA ★

The fratelli Zanella were born in Belluno, Italy, moving to Argentina in 1948 to start metallurgy company, Zanella HNOS y CIA. In 1957, they built their first mo-

*LEFT: **Zuma II**
While most scooter aficionados grudgingly accepted Yamaha's Vino because of its classic, yet plastic, design, the Zuma surprised as one of the bestsellers with its speed and flashy dual headlights like a starter Ducati.*

*BELOW: **Yamaha SC-1**
As one of the most diverse companies in the world—selling everything from clocks to drums to pianos, Yamaha took its turn in the scooter world with a peppy 175cc affair. Sometimes called the YC-1, the 1960 Yamaha SC-1 boasted a torque converter and produced a whopping 10.3hp to zip around Tokyo in style. Courtesy of the François-Marie Dumas Archives*

torcycles, with most of the parts imported from Italy. By the late 1950s, Zanella was producing its own scooters, which were also exported to neighboring South American countries.

Zeta ITALY ★

Zeta built a primitive scooter from 1948-1954 based on two-stroke Ducati Cucciolo 48cc and 60cc engines.

ZEV USA/CHINA ★

In a bid to revolutionize electric motors, Z Electric Vehicle (ZEV) Corporation was started by mechanical and aerospace engineers as a side project in 2006 to make more cost-effective scooters with a longer range. The engine is based in the rear hub for more efficiency, and the company claims it is the fastest, most powerful, most fuel efficient, and longest-range electric scooter on the market. Unfortunately, the company's founder Darus Zehrbach was convicted of defrauding buyers of his aircraft engines and sent to prison.

Zhejiang Hongyun CHINA ★

Several motorcycle/scooter manufacturers make their home in the eastern province of Zhejiang and make what are seemingly identical lines of plastic, sporty scooters. The Sanben and Mingya scooters are mostly gasoline-powered 125cc and 150cc bikes made by Zhejiang Hongyun Motorcycle Company.

Zhejiang Leike CHINA ★

The Fenghuolun models from Zhejiang Leike Machinery Industry Company are mostly gasoline-powered 125cc medium-size scooters, but some come in the lengthy BarcaLounger design with an oversized nose.

Zhejiang Mountain CHINA ★

When the millions of bicycles in China slowly were overrun by ubiquitous scooters, the lengthily named Zhejiang Mountain Qitianying Automobile Industry Company Limited was there to fill the gap with its 125cc Tianying scooters that matched all the other scooters on the road.

Zhejiang Riya CHINA ★

The Riya model is sporty scooter available in various sizes from 100cc to 300cc.

Zhejiang Shunqui CHINA ★

The Zhejiang Shunqi Vehicle Industry Company produced these gas-running Huatian scooters with mostly 125cc engines. One notable exception from the ho-hum sport scooters is the bizarre HT150T-10C with exposed chassis, looking like a scooter-cum-mini-bike. The Jiaji line of scooters seem nearly identical to the Huatian. Oh yes, Zhejiang also produced the Feiling, which apparently is different somehow. At least the deluxe Feiling FL 150T and the more moped-like FL70T have different size engines.

Zhejiang Tianben CHINA ★

Following the modern scooter lines, Zhejiang Tianben Vehicle Industry Company built the Tianben and Lingben line of gasoline-powered 125cc scooters. Oh, don't forget the Binqi line of scooters, which look suspiciously like all the others.

Zhejiang Xingyue CHINA ★

The Xingyue scooter has larger wheels for better stability and typically comes with a 150cc engine. The company also makes three-wheeled scooters with a covering over the top and smaller two wheels in the back.

Zhongyu CHINA ★

Specializing in motorcycles, the Guangdong Tayo Motorcycle Technology Co. in Jiangmen put out the Zhongyu ZY50QT-7 scooter, mostly available in China.

Znen CHINA ★

Znen is shorthand for Zhongneng Vehicle Group Company and a large producer of scooters in Taizhou in Zhejiang province along with so many other manufacturers. The scooters are often rebranded elsewhere, perhaps to make them seem more homegrown. You'll see them as Lexmoto, Mondial, Paparazzi, Tamoretti, and more.

Most notably, Znen purchased the classic Italian motorcycle brand Moto Morini in 2018 after fits and starts in which the brother of ex–prime minister (and alleged Mafioso) Silvio Berlusconi almost bought out the brand.

Zongshen CHINA ★

Formed in 1992, Chongqing Zongshen Power Machinery Co. grew quickly to produce hundreds of thousands of vehicles, including a four-stroke called Zongshen/Kangda Pexma. In 2004, Piaggio formed a joint venture with Zongshen to produce parts and scooters. Approximately 30 percent of Zongshen's scooters are exported from China.

Zipscoot USA ★

The Zipscoot arrived on the scene following World War II as a kit scooter from the Zipscoot Company of Toledo, Ohio, available for a mere $49.75—or just 25 cents for the plans if you wanted to build your own from a spare washing machine motor and odd bits of steel beams you had lying behind the barn.

Zoom USA ★

These modern electric mobiles disparagingly call themselves "moped scooters" and boast about a "cup holder" and "USB charger" rather than its speed, perhaps because it tops out at 30 mph (48 km/h). Riding on the scooter boom of the 2020s, Zoom offers this relatively inexpensive scoot to tool around town.

Zoppoli ITALY ★

The Motopiccola Z 48 was indeed small. Filippo Zoppoli had already experimented on the mini scooters parachuted in with the Allies during the war. This miniature scooter came either with a 48cc Ducati Cucciolo or Siata engine or the Ducati 60cc motor mounted on the diminutive putt-putt from 1947 to 1951.

Zündapp GERMANY

"Der Roller für den Motorradfahrer," the scooter for the motorcyclist claim usually failed for most scooter manufacturers, but Zündapp was the exception. In 1917, Zünderund Apparatebau GmbH (aka Zündapp) was formed as a conglomerate of three other German companies to assist in World War I by making fuses for artillery. Two years later, Ing. Fritz Neumeyer acquired Zündapp, which was making peacetime goods, and in two more years had Zündapp in the cycle business. It produced its first five motorcycles with British engines, and by 1924 had already produced 10,000 motorcycles with their own German Zündapp engines. Dr. Neumeyer went on to new projects, in particular he dreamed of making a people's car, or volkswagen, which Ferdinand Porsche made a prototype in 1934.

In 1937, with war looming around the corner and already rationed raw material, Zündapp Werke GmbH (their new name) had to limit motorcycle production and begin plane manufacturing. These four-cylinder ohv engines set many records, and after the war a French pilot broke two more world records with a confiscated Zündapp aero engine. The Zündapp factory was more than a third destroyed by allied bombing and postwar was occupied by American units. They were forced to cease production of transport and stick to making potato mashers, axles, and grain cleaning machines. Dr. Eitel-Friedrich Neumeyer got Zündapp back on the course of making motorcycles a couple of years later.

In 1951, Zündapp wanted to jump on the scooter bandwagon and developed a scooter prototype which was never to be developed. Instead, they looked to the reigning champion, Italy, for their first scooter design, building 150cc and 200cc versions instead of the original less than 125cc prototype. Seeing that Vespa and Lambretta were already being sufficiently copied, they turned instead to Moto Parilla scooters and brainstormed ideas from its attractive design. The first Bella is almost indistinguishable from the 1952 125cc Parilla scooter.

BELLA R150 1953–1955, BELLA R150 SUBURBANETTE 1953, AND BELLA R200 1954–1955 ★★★

The Bella was a hit when it first came out and was supposedly the most talked about scooter at the international Frankfurt show of 1953. The 147cc model with Bing carburetor had 7.3hp at 4700rpm for a maximum speed of 50mph. The frame of the Bella was a large diameter tube arching over the rear engine and had pressed steel body work attached to it as well as a 8.5 liter gas tank. The 12in wheels, the foot shifter for the four gears and partial "bridge" between the rider's legs give the Bella a near motorcycle image.

"It would be difficult to speak too highly of the Zündapp's navigational properties. Though a slight roll would manifest itself at low speeds, once the model was on the open road and motoring at anything over 30mph the steering would become rock steady." (Motor Cycling, Dec. 1953) This British magazine attributes the smooth ride to the large wheels as well as the long wheel base of 51.5in and top speed of 75mph make for an all around great touring scooter. The maker of Ambassador motorcycles, UK Concessionaires Ltd of Ascot, Berkshire, arranged with Zündapp in 1953 to begin selling the R150 into Britain.

When Zündapp began production of the 200cc Bella, they increased the flywheel generator from 60watts to 90watts and the battery from 7amp to an 8amp battery for more reliable current to the ignition and the lights. The headlamp was moved higher up on the front apron with the horn below it. The R200 was offered with a delivery van trailer or as the "Bella de luxe" model with a Steib LS-200 sidecar. Zündapp produced more than 18,000 R150s, almost 27,000 of the R200, and only 370 Suburbanettes.

Zündapp designed the Suburbanette for the American suburbs and sold them only in the United States. Its main difference was that it had higher handlebars, a dual seat, a front mudguard (to show off the telescopic forks), but did not have the all the paneling that the other Bellas had.

BELLA R151 AND R201 1955–1956 ★★★

Following the huge success of the first line of Bellas, Zündapp attempted to expand their line of scooters by producing a 125cc scooter which never hit the production line. Instead, the Bella was just updated with some considerable changes since it was the scooter "you are proud to be seen on" according to Zündapp's publicity. Electric start from 12 volt electrics were added along with restyled bodywork and dual seats as well as an improved air duct system to keep the two-stroke engine cool. The front legshield design was smoothed out as well as the metal reinforced. A new Bing carb was added resembling more an automobile's system than the previous motorcycle style set up. Another new feature included two attachment points for a Steib sidecar with an interchangeable wheel with the Bella that could be added after buying the scooter.

Zündapp produced only 2,500 of the 150cc model, realizing that the market demanded power so they manufactured 27,000 of the 200cc R201, the most of any of model Bella.

BELLA R153 AND R203 1956 ★ ★

After seeing the success of Harley-Davidsons and Indians in the American market, Zündapp made a special version of this model sold only in the United States with a kickstart and huge chopper handlebars. Exclaiming in an ad in Motorcyclist that "the World's outstanding motorscooters [were made] for shopping, work, school, fishing (will fit your boat) [sic]."

Although swing forks had been available on the domestic German models, these improved forks weren't available abroad until 1956 when Zündapp updated from the telefork which was to remain the standard for future Bellas. "Horsepower is up on some other German scooters, such as the Bella (10.7hp)." (Popular Science, July 1957, p.71) The 8hp Bella 150 came with a 6 volt battery and generator as opposed to the 10hp Bella 200 with 12 volt battery and electric starter which cost a quarter more than the 150. The German models had smaller handlebars and standard electric start. By now Zündapp realized the market for scooters was becoming saturated with other makes, so they made only 24,900 of the third series and produced fewer and fewer Bellas every year.

BELLA R154 1956–1958 AND R204 1957–1959 ★ ★

This 198cc Bella's cylinder inclined at 30 degrees like the Zündapp S Series motorcycles giving it 12.4hp at 5400rpm for a maximum speed of 65mph. In 1958, the more powerful R204 was considered "amongst the best scooters on the market" (Motor Cycling, Jan. 1, 1959). With the waning interest in scooters, fewer Zündapps roamed the streets of Germany, from 18,665 in 1955 to 6,228 in 1958. Consumers were looking to automobiles for transportation, and teenagers preferred cheaper mopeds instead of big 200cc scooters to get around. To make up for the dwindling revenue of the Bella, Zündapp continued to produce sewing machines as a major source of cash, as did the Swedish company Husqvarna,

BELLA R175S 1961–1964 ★ ★ ★

Only 2,000 of this model were produced with the 174cc, 60x62mm bore and stroke, producing 11hp at 5400rpm.

200 TYPE 551-026 AND 200 TYPE 560-025 1959-1962 ★ ★ ★

The fastest Bella that existed with 13.4hp, unfortunately, sales had plummeted and only about 2,000 of each of these models were made.

ROLLER 50 AND RS50 1964–1984 ★

These two scooters took the place of the Bella, but could not replace it as the best-selling machine for Zündapp during the '50s. These two new scooters were based on the Lambretta Slimline with the easily removable side panels, headlamp on the handlebars, 10in wheels (from the safer 12in wheels of the Bella) and handlebar gear change. One of the only differences from the Lambretta, besides the much smaller engine, was the fancy two-tone seat on some of these Zündapps. The two scooters had a 49cc engine based on the Zündapp Falconette moped with the smaller three-speed Roller 50 at 2.9hp at 4900rpm, and the four-speed RS50 Super at 4.6hp at 7000rpm. The RS50 was later updated slightly and renamed the RS50 Super Sport.

Unfortunately, the company fell on hard economic times in 1985 after producing 130,680 scooters and the entire Zündapp stock and machinery were sold to China. Approximately 1,500 Chinese went overland to Munich by train to pack up all the equipment to ship to the People's Republic. During the two weeks of loading, the Chinese workers slept in the packing crates to save money. Zündapp motorcycles were also being manufactured in Madra, India, by Enfield India, usually under a different name.

Bella Zündapp Bella
This 1957 Bella Model 203 was originally purchased from a Harley-Davidson dealership in Maine before the Milwaukee Miracle took a bizarre turn into scooters themselves. Perhaps if Harley had learned from Zündapp how solid and speedy a scooter could be, America would be crawling with Harley Toppers. Courtesy of the owner: Will Niskanen

Acknowledgments

Being the scribes putting down on paper with quill and ink the history and mythology of the motorscooter is a difficult and often thankless task. Difficult not so much because the threads in the web of history are lost in the mists of golden time, but more often because no one gives a hoot. Thankless, because most people simply smirk when you so much as mention scooters.

Still we toil late into the night by the light of a lone candle, striving to uncover the correct compression ratio of the first Cushman Auto-Glide or find out which Vespa model was Gina Lollobrigida's favorite. The task is made worthwhile because you, dear readers, are crazy for scooters just as we are.

No book writes itself, however, and no single authors are solely responsible for the book that bears their names alone. We owe thanks to the following scooteristi and accessories to the crime, listed here in alphabetical order: Kris Adams, the mod-est Mod; Robert H. Ammon; Ansgar; Bruno Baccari for allowing a scooter amid his motorcycles; Dan Baker and his mint Cushmans; Speed Racer John Britton; Fred Case for not selling me that basket-case Lambretta; Chank's scooter fonts; Casey Cole and the coolest scooter magazine ever printed; John Curnutt and his cool patches; Livio De Marchi and his all-wood scooters; Matt DeVries and his scooter connections; Roberto Donati & Paperino; Sesostikis Temple Motor Patrol Captain Jack Douglass; Francois-Marie Dumas and the whirlwind tour of Parisian scooterdom; Giovanni and Anna Erba for tours and photos of Lambrate; Shepard Fairey's command to Obey Scooter; Christophe Fresneau for keeping Bernardet scooters on the road; Walt Fulton; Ray Gabbard; Didier Ganneau; Tim Gartman R.I.P.; David Gaylin and *Motor Cycle Days*; Randolph Garner; Mustang maven Michael Gerald; Curt Giese; Paolo Giuri for sneaking us into la Piaggio in spite of impending strikes; Ole Birger Gjevre; Ruthann Godollei and her insight into Art Scooters; Noble Robert Gourlie; Bob Hedstrom and Scooterville amidst Hooverville; Gösta Karlsson; Jim Kilau, the man with the secret basement full of amazing scooters; Jim Kolbe and Scooterworks, Chicago; Hans Kruger and his scooter Xanadu; Herb and Linda Letourneau; Jeff Lewis and the Vespa Club of America for deeming Minneapolis/St. Paul worthy; W. Conway Link and his *Deutsches Motorrad Registry*; Noble Mark MacGillivray; Jessika Madison— Moddest of Mods; the Minneapolis Police Department—you can insult *me* but *not* my Lambretta; Philip McCaleb; Katy McCarthy for taking that ride on my Lambretta, even if Chris the Girl was there too; Roger McLaren; Joe Metzler; Vince Mross and West Coast Lambretta Works; Sam Niskanen; Will Niskanen; Lauró Orestano for lending me a Sfera and teaching me to drive like a fearless Italian; Robert Pirsig and the zen of motorscooter maintenance; Sam Pitmon and the Pacesetters Scooter Society; Mark Preston; Glenn Reid and his modern vintage posters; Imperial Shriner Photographer Tom Rousseau; Dott. Pietro Rozza & Christa Solbach of the Vespa Club Rome; E. Foster Salsbury; Halwart & Mila Schrader for believing in scooters auf Deutschesland; Herb Singe for loan of fantastic material from his collection of advertisements, brochures, and memorabilia from the early years of American scootering; Wallace Skyrman; Katy Smith and her Dylan reference; Vittorio Tessera, keeper of the Lambretta flame and the golden-fleeced Lambretta; Pete "I Don't Know Anything About Scooters" Townshend (he really said that); Mark Ulves; Becky Wallace and her mod archives; Jürgen Wangermann; Noble Rick Watt; Keith & Kim Weeks for their incredible collection of American scooters; Jeremy Wilker and the Regulars; Noble Frank Workman; and Steven Zasueta.

About the Author

Eric Dregni is professor of English, journalism, and Italian at Concordia University in St. Paul, Minnesota. The author of several books, he has written extensively about scooter culture in *Life Vespa* and other titles. He's also tackled everything from ice resurfacers (*Zamboni: Coolest Machines on Ice*) to roadside attractions, about which he's authored several books, including *The Impossible Road Trip*. He lives in Minneapolis.

Index

A

Abbottsford 176
ABC Skootamota 14, 20, 21, 107, 176
Achilles 176
Accumolli 176
ACMA 49, 98, 176–177
Adler 67, 177, 178
Adly 165, 177
Aeon 177
Aermoto 47, 52, 178
Aeromere 178
AGF 178
Agrati-Garelli 148, 178–179
AJS 179, 243
Aldimi 179
Alemanno 179
Allstate 120, 133, 134, 179–182
Allwyn 182
Alma 182
Alpino 182
Alzina, Hap 224
Amanda Water Scooter 124
Ambassador 182–183
Ambrosini 183
Amerivespa 174, 175
Ami 183, 262
Ammon, Charles 7, 26, 199
Ammon, Robert H. 7, 23, 26–27, 47, 82, 123, 144, 198, 199, 200, 202, 203, 207, 209
AMO 183
API 183
Apollo 183
Aprilia 183–184
aqua-scoot 124–125
Ardent 184
Ardito 184
Ariel 142, 184
Arosio 184
Arqin 184
d'Ascanio, Corradino 52, 53, 57, 163, 168, 172, 231, 232, 238, 270, 271
Askoll 184
Atala-Rizzato 184
Auto-Fauteuil 15, 64, 184–185
Auto-Glide 7, 23, 26–27, 32, 33, 43, 47, 198, 199–200, 201–202, 203

Autoglider 21, 185, 305
Automoto 185
Autoped 12, 16–17, 23, 91, 172, 176, 184, 185–186, 286
Autoscoot 186

B

Baccio 186
Bajaj 151, 152, 165, 186
Bangor Manufacturing Company 186
Baotian 186, 219
Bashan 186
Bastert 67, 103, 186–187
Beam 121, 187
Beckmann ASB 187
Beeline 187
Bella 70, 71, 314–315
bella figura 138, 139
Belmondo 187
Ben Hunt Manufacturing 188
Benelli 62, 187, 253
Benzhou 188
Bernardet 47, 64, 76, 115, 188–189
Beta 189
BFC 99, 189
Bianchi 189, 285
Binz 189, 226
Bird Engineering 189
Bitri 189
Bloom 190
B. M. Bonvicini 191
BM 190
BMW 170, 190, 222, 237, 264
Bond 74, 190–191
Boom 191
Boudier 191
Breton 191
Briggs & Stratton 18, 121, 187, 191, 192, 210, 244, 254, 259, 284
Brissonnet/Mors 192
Britax 192
Brockhouse Engineering 48, 192, 216
Brumana Pugliese 192–193
BSA 11, 74, 131, 142, 193, 305
B. S. Villa 194
Bug Engineering 194

C

C & E Manufacturing 194
Cagiva 194, 230
Camille Foucaud 194
Caproni Vizzola 194
Carabela 194
Carnielli 194
Carniti 194–195
CAS 185, 195
Casal 195
Casalini 195
Cazenave 195
Centaur 140, 141, 195
CF Moto 195
Changguang 195
Chicago Scooter Company 195
Chuangxin 195, 217
Cimatti 195
CityCoco 196
CL 196
Claeys-Flandria 196
Clark Engineering 196, 283
clubs 93, 95, 100, 129, 147, 156, 158, 159, 174, 275
Clymer, Floyd 33, 39
CM 196
Columbus Cycle Company 196
Comet Manufacturing Company 189, 196, 242, 248
Condor 196
Continental Motors 197, 211, 223
Cooper 45, 46, 197, 202, 283
Corgi 48, 52, 192, 193, 216
Cosmopolitan Motors 109, 197, 261, 267, 298
CPI 197
Crescent 197, 251
Crocker 23, 38, 39, 198
Crocker, Albert G. 38
Csepel 198
Cushman 7, 23, 26–27, 32, 33, 41, 43, 45–47, 51, 79, 80, 82–83, 90, 91, 96, 97, 98, 104, 120, 122–123, 144–145, 147, 161, 180, 182, 198–210, 259, 283, 293
Cushman, Clinton 27, 90
Cushman, Everett 27, 90

Custer 30, 210
Cycle-Scoot 210
ČZ 98, 153, 210

D

Daelim 210
Dafra 210
Danmotor 210
Dayang 210
Dayton 210–211
Delaplace 211
Delius 211
DEMM 195, 211, 248
Derbi 211
Derveaux 211
Diddley, Bo 11, 133, 134
Dilecta 211
DK 212
DKR 212
DKW 77, 185, 193, 212, 213, 225, 247, 291
DMW 183, 213, 309
La Dolce Vita (film) 136, 278, 312
Doodle Bug 91, 120, 121, 187
Douglas 74, 213–214
Ducati 108, 110, 161, 179, 191, 192, 214–215, 216, 233, 234, 235, 244, 291, 313, 314
Dürkopp 89, 107, 215
Duryea, Frank 13

E

Eagle 7, 82, 122–123, 144, 145, 204, 206–209
Earhart, Amelia 23, 24, 134, 291
Elleham 215–216
Elmore, Austin 23, 24, 30, 292, 294, 296
Elvish 216
engineering 90–91
Erla 216
Etablissements François 216
Etergo 216
Excelsior 74, 75, 192, 193, 216

F

Fairbanks-Morse 214

Faizant 216
Faka 216–217
Faroppa 217
Fat Bear 217
FB Mondial 62, 217
Feiying 217
Fenwick 217
FF 217, 308
FIAMC 217
Fiame 218
FIAT 52, 218, 270
Fimer 218
Fiorelli 218
The 500 Industries 218
Flyscooters 218
FM 218
Fochj 218
Foldmobile 218, 227, 247
Forall 219
Ford, Henry 13, 169
Forrest, Howard 79, 142,
    255, 256, 259
Forza 219
Franco, Generalissimo Fran-
    cisco 99, 252
Fratelli Molteni (FM) 218,
    250
Frera 219
Frisoni 219
Fuji Heavy Industries 72,
    219
Fulgur 220
Fulton, Walt 84, 86, 256,
    257, 258, 259

G

Gambles Stores 78, 91, 120,
    121, 179, 187, 219
GAOMA 220
Garelli 220, 307
Garrison Manufacturing 220
Gasuden 220
Genuine Scooter Company
    150, 195, 220, 221
GenZe by Mahindra
    220–221
Georgiana, Princess (The
    White Rose of Hunga-
    ry) 176
Gianca 221–222
Gianca Nibbio 53, 56
Giesse 222
Gilera 87, 164, 222, 278
Gitan 222
Glas Isaria 222
Glenco Products 222

Globe 223
Gloucestershire Aircraft
    Company 19, 223
Gogoro 223
Göricke 223
GOVECS 223, 300, 308
Gran Sport 84, 110, 111,
    213, 214, 248, 274,
    275, 304
Grasshopper 223
Griffon/FMC 223, 268
Gritzner-Kayser 223, 224
Guiller 224, 299
Guzzi 62, 87, 157, 224, 231
G. W. Davis Corporation
    210

H

Haojin 224
Haojue 224
Hap Alzina 224
Harley-Davidson 39, 79, 86,
    122, 127, 134, 178, 198,
    206, 207, 225, 257, 259,
    295, 315
Harper 225
Hartford 225
Hawk Tool & Engineering
    225
HDR 189, 226
Hebdige, Dick 106, 173
H. E. Bremer Company 191
Hedstrom, Bob 161, 172
Hedstrom, Oscar 13
Heinkel 105, 119, 126,
    226, 284
Helix 168, 170, 228
Hepburn, Audrey 11, 96,
    136, 139, 162, 269
Hercules 116, 226, 284, 285,
    291, 307
Hero 226
Hildebrand-Wolfmuller
    226
Hirano 140, 227
Hirundo 227
HMW 227
Hoffmann 66, 97, 227
Honda 73, 150, 152, 161,
    164, 168, 170, 182, 197,
    209, 226, 227–228, 229,
    230, 240, 259, 303
Horex 229
Humblot 229
Hummel-Sitta 229
Hunter 229

Husqvarna 63, 197, 229–
    230, 251, 266, 315

I

IFA 230, 252
IGM 230
Il Motore 230
IMN 230
Imperial Motor Industries
    185, 230
Indian 14, 39, 165, 198, 230,
    244, 256
Innocenti 49, 55, 58–59, 60,
    61, 69, 76, 84, 86, 87, 91,
    94, 100, 102, 106, 107,
    110, 112, 113, 125, 129,
    132, 134, 147, 149, 152,
    155, 165, 166, 182, 183,
    217, 231–236, 263, 264,
    267, 269, 272, 274, 275,
    277, 297, 298, 299
Innocenti, Ferdinando 10,
    52, 58, 59, 166, 231, 298
Isle of Man Scooter Rally
    86, 235
Iso 62, 153, 237
Italemmezeta 237
Italjet 151, 165, 184,
    237–238

J

James 238
J. B. Volkscooter 238
Jet 85, 238, 296
Jialing 238
Jiangsu Chuangxin Motor-
    cycle Manufacturing
    195
Jiangsu Dalong Jianhao 238
Jianshe 238
Jinan Dalong 238
Jinan Qingqi 238–239
Jincheng 239
Jinyi 239
JoeBe 127, 239
Jonghi 178, 216, 239
Jonway 239
Joker/Shadow 150, 228, 301
Junak 239
Juneng 239

K

Kawasaki 186, 239
Keen Power Cycle 23,
    239–240
Keeway 240

Kenilworth 240
Kieft 226, 240
Kinetic 240
Kingsbury 240
KR 240, 300
Kreidler 240
Kroboth 240–241
Krupp 16, 185, 241
KTM 223, 226, 241, 285
Kumpan, 241, 298
Kymco 173, 239, 241–242

L

Lacombe 242
Lambretta 9, 10, 49, 55, 57,
    58–61, 65, 68, 69, 70,
    71, 72, 80, 84, 85, 86, 87,
    89, 90, 91, 94, 97, 98,
    102, 103, 106, 107, 110,
    112, 113, 115, 117, 121,
    124, 125, 129, 130, 131,
    132, 134, 136, 137, 138,
    143, 147, 148, 149, 150,
    152, 153, 154, 155, 156,
    157–158, 162, 165–167,
    168, 169, 173, 174, 175,
    177, 178, 179, 181, 182,
    183, 184, 189, 190, 191,
    192, 193, 194, 195, 209,
    217, 225, 227, 229, 230,
    231–236, 237, 246, 250,
    251, 253, 255, 260, 261,
    263–264, 266, 267, 269,
    272, 274, 275, 277, 286,
    288, 289–290, 297, 298,
    303, 307, 311
Lance 242
LaRay 242
Laverda 98, 242
Lefol 242
LeJay 42, 242
Lenoble 242
Lexmoto, 243, 313
Liberia 243
Lifan 243
Lilac 243
Linhai 239, 243
Linlong 243
Lohner 243
Lollobrigida, Gina 88,
    137
Lohia (LML) 243
Loncin 243
Longjia 244, 305
Lowther Manufacturing
    Company 78, 230, 244

L. Ronney & Sons 283, 287–288
Lucciola 244
Lumen 244
Lutz 211, 244

M

Magnani, Anna 106
Mahindra 220–221
Maico 66, 109, 245
Maiolina 246
Mako 246
Malaguti 246
Malanca 246
Mammut 246
Mansfield, Jayne 89, 234
Manurhin 213, 247
Marinavia Farina 247
Marinetti, Filippo Tommaso 13, 164, 271
Mar-Max Products 247
Mars 247
Martin-Moulet 218, 227, 247
MAS 247
MBK (Italy) 247
MKB (France) 252–253
MBM 247
McLuhan, Marshall 150
MDS 247
Mead Cycle Company 23, 28, 29, 32, 78, 247–248, 254, 255
Meijer 248
Meister Fahradwerke 248
Mercier 248
Mercury 248
Messerschmitt 154, 248, 249
Meteora 248
MFB-Telaimotor 249
military motorscooters 45–49
Mi Val 250
Micro Manufacturing 249
Midget Motors Corporation 31, 235, 249
Militaire 19, 249
Minerva-Van Hauwaert 249
Minneapolis 249
Mitsubishi 72, 73, 249–250, 286, 287
Mochet 250
Modenas 253
Mods 10, 11, 129, 130, 131, 133, 136, 151, 155, 158, 162, 172, 221, 307
Molteni 218, 250

Monark 197, 251
Mondiale 251
Monet-Goyon 64, 251–252
Montesa 98, 99, 252
Montgomery "Monkey" Ward 73, 78, 120, 181, 187, 250, 286, 287
Mota 252, 308
Moto Ducati 108, 214
Motobécane/Motoconfort (MBK) 65, 252–253
Motobi 253
Motobic 253
Motoflash 253
Motom 165, 253
Motoped 11, 16–17, 23, 24, 134, 184, 185, 291
Motor Glide 7, 10, 23, 24, 27, 28, 29, 30, 32, 36, 37, 38, 39, 72, 81, 91, 150, 198, 199, 240, 242, 249, 254, 256, 282, 287, 291–296, 308
Motor Industry SA 253
Moto-Scoot 23, 28, 29, 32, 36, 40, 41, 42, 43, 49, 78, 79, 91, 200, 247–248, 254–255, 304
MotoTec 255
Motovespa 255
Mowag 255
Mussolini, Benito 52, 163, 214, 218, 269
Mustad 140, 255
Mustang 78, 79, 84, 86, 87, 142, 158, 207, 255–260
MV Agusta 55, 62, 260–261
MZ 193, 212, 237, 252, 261, 289

N

Nassetti 261
Neco 261
Negrini 261
Nera 262
Ner-A-Car 18, 262
Neue Amag 262
New Map 262, 299
Newman, Paul 134
Niu 171, 173, 262
Norlow 262
NSU (Neckarsulm Knitting Machine Union) 60, 66, 68, 69, 70, 77, 109, 116, 154, 194, 219, 248, 262–264, 285

NV Progress 264
N-Zeta 265

O

Ola Scooters 216, 265
OLD 265
Olmo 265
Orix A. Prina 265
ORLA 265
Oscar 265, 267

P

Paglianti 265
Pak-Jak 265
Palmieri & Gulinelli 265–266
Pandra 267
Pannonia 198, 266
Panther 211, 266, 302, 304
Parilla 62–63, 66, 87, 142, 266–267, 289, 310, 314
Patimo 267
Paul Vallée 65, 267
Pawa 267, 268
Peck, Gregory 11, 96, 136, 139, 162, 269
Peirspeed 268
Peripoli 268
Peugeot 15, 64, 185, 223, 238–239, 268
PGO 152, 253, 268–269
Phoenix 269
Piaggio 11, 52, 53, 54–57, 61, 74, 84, 86, 88, 89, 90, 95, 101, 102, 110–111, 112, 118, 147, 151, 155, 161, 162, 163, 164, 165, 166, 168, 170, 171, 174, 176, 177, 179, 180, 182, 184, 186, 189, 190, 195, 210, 211, 213–214, 218, 222, 227, 232, 242, 243, 248, 249, 260, 268–269, 269–281, 294, 297, 301, 304, 313
Piaggio, Enrico 10, 51, 52, 55, 77, 93, 255, 260
Piatti 74, 75, 179, 281
Picot 281
Pigeon 72, 73, 121, 220, 227, 238, 249–250, 267, 286, 287
Pirol 281
Pointer 282
Polaris 282
The Pope 11, 57, 87, 93, 136, 214

Pop Nanlee 282
Postlaufer 282
Powell 23, 31, 43, 46, 84, 87, 91, 135, 196, 206, 218, 282–284, 287
Power Cycle 23, 239–240
P. P. Roussey 242, 288
Prima 68, 69, 77, 109, 116, 263–264
Prior 226, 284
Progress 284–285, 304
Puch 109, 182, 196, 197, 198, 237, 285, 299
Puddlejumper 23, 30, 31

Q

Qianjiang (QJ) 187, 240, 285
Quadrophenia 131, 132, 133, 136, 158, 269, 297

R

Rabbit 72, 73, 219–220, 227, 250, 267, 296
Rabeneick 285, 286
Radior 285
Raleigh 189, 285, 302
Ranger 23, 28, 29, 247–248, 254, 255
Rapier 285
Ravat 222, 286, 296
Redding, Otis 129
Renmor 35, 286
REX 286
Reynolds 286
Rico 286
Riedel 286, 301
Rieju 286
Rivero 286
Riverside 73, 120, 121, 147, 173, 180, 250, 286, 287
Rizzato-Atala 286
Roadless 21
Rockers 11, 129, 130, 131, 136, 156, 161, 168, 275
Rockford Scooter Company 73, 250, 286, 287
Rock-Ola 23, 30, 33, 43, 91, 254, 287
Röhr 286, 287
Roman Holiday (film) 11, 96, 118, 136, 139, 150, 158, 162, 269
Royal Alloy 288
RSI 288
Rullier 288

Rumi 55, 63, 86, 96, 153, 195, 223, 267, 288–291, 297, 301
Runbaken 291
Ruwisch 291

S

Sachs (SFM) 291
Sacie 291
Safeticycles 291, 292
Salsbury 7, 10, 11, 23, 24, 25, 26, 28, 30, 32, 36, 37, 38, 43, 55, 72, 78, 79, 80, 81, 91, 102, 105, 126, 200, 201, 203, 206, 254, 256, 283, 291–296
Salsbury, E. Foster 7, 10, 23, 24, 26, 27, 28, 32, 33, 36, 55, 102, 105, 150, 198, 199, 254, 291
San Cristoforo 53, 221, 296
Sanko Kogyo 296
Santamaria 296–297
Saroléa 179, 297
Savas Sales 297
Scarabeo 139, 150, 151, 184
Scomadi 165, 297
Scootabout 23, 38, 39, 198
Scootavia 65, 297
Scooters India 152, 165, 166, 231, 234, 236, 265, 297
Scootmule 298
Scott 298
Scrooser 196, 298
Sears, Roebuck & Co. 91, 120, 179–182, 209
Segway 298
Seith 298
Serveta 60, 94, 298
Servos 298
Shadow/Joker 150, 228, 301
Showa 268
Shriners 7, 11, 144–145
Siamoto 299
Siambretta 153, 298
Siegal, Norman 28, 29, 33, 49, 247, 254
Sillaro 299
Silver Pigeon 72, 73, 121, 220, 227, 238, 249–250, 267, 286, 287
SIM Moretti 196, 299
Simard 299
SIMAT 52, 53, 260, 299

Simplex 18, 299–300, 301
Simson 223, 300
Sitta 300
Skootamota 14, 20–21, 107, 176
sno-scoots 124–125
Société Industrielle de Troyes 177, 300
Socvel 300
Sparta 230, 301
Speed-Mors-Alcyon 301
Speedway 301
Spencer & Cio 301
Sportcycle 301
Stafford Mobile Pup 301
Stella 150, 151, 171, 220, 221, 243, 247, 301
Sterling Sterva 301
Sterzi 302
Stüdemann 302
Sun 211, 216, 302
Sunlight 302
Super-Scooter 11, 79, 80, 81, 102, 295–296
Suzuki 161, 173, 238, 240, 302, 307
Svalan 302
Swallow (Japan) 302–303
Swallow (UK) 303
Swiss 276, 303
SYM (Sanyang Motor Co.) 303

T

Taizhou Jiaojiang Zhiwei 303
Taizhou Senlong 303
Taizhou Wangye 304
Taizhou Zhongneng 304
Taotao 304
Tappella 304
Teds (Teddy Boys) 129
Tell 304
Tempo 304
Terrot 11, 65, 304
Testi 304
TGB 304
TNT 244, 305
Tomos 305
Toscane 305
Tote Gote 305
Townsend Engineering 21, 185, 305
Townshend, Pete 11, 132,

136, 297
Toxozer 305
Tramnitz 305
Triumph 74, 75, 129, 131, 136, 163, 193, 309
Triumph TEC 212, 305–306
Triumph TWN 67, 306
Trobike 307
Troll 261, 307
Trotwood 307
Tubauto 307
Turismo Veloce 91, 110, 112, 234, 235
Turner, Edward 193, 305
Turner, Colonel Roscoe 7, 23–25, 37, 198, 199, 292, 293, 294
Turtleback 9, 79, 80, 82, 83, 97, 144
TVS 307
Twist 'N Go 307–308

U

Ujet 308
Unibus 19, 223
Unu 308
URMW 308

V

Varel 308
Vectrix 308
Vélauto 14, 251
Velocette 74, 309
Velocifero 139, 150, 151, 238
Velosolex 217, 253, 308, 309
Vento 309
Venus 309
Vespa 7, 10–11, 26, 49, 51, 52, 53, 54, 55, 56, 57, 58, 59, 60, 61, 62, 64, 72, 74, 76, 84, 85, 88, 89, 90, 93, 94, 95, 96, 97, 98, 99, 104, 106, 107, 110, 111, 112, 115, 117, 118, 124, 127, 129, 132, 133, 135, 136, 137, 138, 139, 147, 148, 149, 150, 151, 155, 157, 158, 159, 161, 162, 163, 165, 166, 168, 169, 171, 172, 174, 175, 176, 178, 179, 181, 182, 206, 209, 211, 213, 214, 222, 227, 230, 231, 242, 248, 249, 260, 269–281, 311

Vespa SA 309
Viberti 309
Victoria 63, 266, 291, 298, 302, 309–310
Vincent 9, 74, 124, 281
Vino 150, 312
Vitacci 310
Vittoria 194, 310
Vivani 310
Vostok 311
Vyatka (Vjatka) 239, 307, 308, 312

W

Warivo 311
Wasp 311
The Who 11, 129, 132, 133, 136, 269, 297
Wabo 311
Walba 217, 311
Wall Auto Wheel 311
WFM 311
Wilkinson 312
Wolf 312

Y

Yamaha 150, 161, 164, 177, 193, 194, 212, 243, 253, 312
Yard Marvel Manufacturing 312
Yardman 312

Z

Zanella 243, 312–313
Zeta 313
ZEV 313
Zhejiang Hongyun 313
Zhejiang Leike 313
Zhejiang Mountain 313
Zhejiang Riya 313
Zhejiang Shunqui 313
Zhejiang Tianben 313
Zhejiang Xingyue 313
Zipscoot 34, 254, 313
Zhongyu 313
Znen 179, 218, 228, 243, 313
Zog, King 52, 176
Zongshen 313
Zoom 314
Zoppoli 314
Zündapp 66, 70, 71, 91, 187, 217, 245, 296, 314–315